UN9
RISD
86406.

58

THE AGRARIAN QUESTION AND THE PEASANT MOVEMENT IN COLOMBIA

For a list of books in this series please turn to page 287.

The United Nations Research Institute for Social Development is an autonomous United Nations activity, established for the purpose of conducting research into "problems and policies of social development and relationships between various types of social development and economic development during different phases of economic growth." The studies of the Institute are intended to contribute to (a) the work of the United Nations Secretariat in the field of social policy, social development planning, and balanced economic and social development; (b) regional planning institutes set up under the auspices of the United Nations; (c) national institutes in the field of economic and/or social development and planning.

The views expressed in this publication are the author's and do not necessarily reflect those of UNRISD or the United Nations. The names and the written documents of graphical material used do not entail any judgment on the part of UNRISD or the United Nations concerning the legal status of any country, territory, city or zone, or their authorities, or their frontiers or borders.

THE AGRARIAN QUESTION AND THE PEASANT MOVEMENT IN COLOMBIA

Struggles of the National Peasant Association 1967–1981

LEON ZAMOSC

Department of Sociology
University of California, San Diego

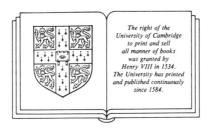

*The right of the
University of Cambridge
to print and sell
all manner of books
was granted by
Henry VIII in 1534.
The University has printed
and published continuously
since 1584.*

Cambridge University Press

Cambridge
London   New York   New Rochelle
Melbourne   Sydney

United Nations Research Institute for Social Development

Palais des Nations
1211 Geneva 10, Switzerland

Published by the Press Syndicate of the University of Cambridge
The Pitt Building, Trumpington Street, Cambridge CB2 1RP
32 East 57th Street, New York, NY 10022, USA
10 Stamford Road, Oakleigh, Melbourne 3166, Australia

First published 1986

Printed in the United States of America

Library of Congress Cataloging-in-Publication Data
Zamosc, Leon.
The agrarian question and the peasant movement in
Colombia.
(Cambridge Latin American studies; 58)
Bibliography: p.
1. Peasant uprisings – Colombia.   2. Peasantry –
Colombia – Political activity.   3. Asociación Nacional
de Usuarios Campesinos (Colombia)   4. Land tenure –
Colombia.   I. Title.   II. Series.
HD516.Z36   1986   322.4'4'09861   85–19479

British Library Cataloguing in Publication Data
Zamosc, Leon
The agrarian question and the peasant movement in
Colombia : struggles of the National Peasant
Association 1967–1981. – (Cambridge Latin American
studies; 58)
1. Peasantry – Colombia – Political activity –
History – 20th century   2. Revolutionists –
Colombia – History – 20th century
I. Title
322.4'2'09861   HD1339.C6

ISBN 0 521 32010 0

To Ximena, with love

Contents

Tables, figures, and maps

Tables

Figures

Maps

Foreword

There have been few good histories of peasant movements. The nature of the evidence is partly to blame for this. Peasants were mostly illiterate, and the few literates who stood by them or led them too often died a martyr's death. With the participants' own tale seldom recorded, what has been left is silence, or else the chronicles of the victors over the peasants, whose evidence is as twisted and indecent as a snapshot of victims by their executioners.

This silence and the biases of evidence are still with us as far as the history of the present – a sociology of the contemporary peasants – is concerned. In our own communication-saturated society, peasants still seldom tell their own tale, and their leaders still die violently the world over. And not for the plebeian rebels and activists are the cushioned émigré life or the foreign universities where most of the opposition's memoirs and tracts are nowadays written.

But it is not simply a matter of evidence. If beauty lies in the eyes of the beholder, so do the mystification and the lie. Those who write about peasants are as a rule outsiders to them. It is not only that they usually meet peasants for a moment and a glimpse, or not at all; more important is that they fail to acknowledge the peasants' way of life as different, yet reasonable on its own terms, and as changing but with different alternatives. What usually occurs instead of observation, immersion, "understanding from the inside," is a version of Theory of Progress, into which facts are drawn to adorn a presupposed model, rather than to test it. The model is invariably a repetition of the observer's own history, followed by a paradise of riches and of liberty to all, in the light of a pet theory taken from elsewhere. Peasants are the bottleneck to its realization, a bother to be bulldozed out ("for their own sake" can be added). They are never treated as the subject of history, the makers of their own future. Also, to this mode of thought peasants are necessarily backward in the face of the writer's own "forwardness." They are just as necessarily those that will be defeated – and few like to identify with losers. That is how and why peasants come to be treated as fodder, by politicians for their schemes and by scholars for their intellectual construct. The bitterly divided reactionary juntas, the liberal politicians, and the revolutionary challengers often agree in this single sphere.

Against such blinds, the honorable exceptions of writings and deeds shine the brighter. Books like those by F. Znaniecki, R. Hilton, E. Le Roy Ladurie, J. Womack, or J. Scott show how an alternative approach, the one of "taking the peasant side," is not only more ethical but also adds to perception. Such illuminations often come not from social scientists but from novelists such as Carlo Levi of Italy, Traven of Mexico, or Vasilii Shuknin of contemporary Russia. In consequence, there has been a slowly growing core of good books by those who have elevated peasants from a footnote to the text, not replacing progressivist mythology by a peasant one of pastoral bliss, but taking account of what Marx expressed so well, namely, that "It is not history as if she was a person apart who uses men as means to work out her purposes, but history itself is nothing but the activity of men pursuing their purposes." One should add "also women," and say that the "pursuing of ends" can be done in different ways, sometimes as subjects and otherwise as objects of history. Which is, of course, the crux of the matter in analyzing the struggles for freedom.

This book belongs to the tradition I call more honorable and more perceptive — that is, one of treating peasants as a topic in itself, as a subject of and within the social reality. Good luck and perseverance gave its author invaluable access to vital information about one of the most significant peasant political efforts of the 1970s in Latin America — the rise and fall of the ANUC of Colombia. Zamosc watched it throughout the full cycle of rise, climax, defeat, retreat, and disintegration. For the most relevant five years, he was immersed in the peasant communities taking part in ANUC.

The book presents an analysis of a major peasant movement, its internal dynamics, and its interdependence with forces external to itself, written by a sympathetic observer/participant who was in it to tell its truthful tale, rather than to grind his own axe. The resulting realism is the book's main strength. It does not glorify peasants or their leaders; they are corruptible and defeatable, but this does not make them putty in everybody's hands. Their ability to act effectively was subject to various conditions, of which political democracy and external catalysts were the most important. But once established, the movement rapidly gained its own momentum. Contrary to what the landlords and government ministers said these were not barbarians on the rampage; their ability to think and act politically was impressive. Contrary to the super-left would-be manipulators, their fight was not just with the bourgeoisie, rural or urban, and with the landlords, but mostly with the repressive and ambivalent state. Equally ambivalent, and having an important impact on the movement, was the new factor of the intervention of international and national development agencies. This produced an equation very different from those so often assumed. More expectedly, the peasant movement was multidirectional in the aims of its subdivisions, social and regional. It was also exposed to a multiplicity of external forces and propaganda efforts. The politicized peasants were therefore subject to many ambivalences, not unlike other movements powered by plebeian spontaneity in the contemporary developing societies. Finally, they were essentially weaker than the state apparatus, for as long as it stood firm. It is the opening of the confrontation of forces external to itself and/or the moments when the state apparatus is shaken or rendered ambivalent through defeat, political crisis, or vacillitating reforms that makes the peasant mass assert its significance the world over.

Of particular significance is Zamosc's analysis of ANUC as an authentic peasant organization, showing how its leadership grew from below and was transformed, and how problems of diversity within unity were handled in it, revealing the specific dynamics of mass organization. Land invasion as a political tool and tactic (rather than as a pauper's "grab") offers an important lesson of revolt and counterrevolution. The issue of regional peasantries, which we know mostly from theoretical debate, in this book is given an important direct expression via the study of political phenomena in its social and economic context. The triangle of fundamentally different yet intertwined forces – the state, the revolutionary opposition, and a peasant mass movement – is analyzed in the specific context of a Latin American society.

To recapitulate, contrary to much philosophizing about peasants, development, and revolution, Zamosc's book provides a massive testimony and analysis of a contemporary peasantry as a class in a major struggle. The result is complex and rich, with both unity and diversity, the internal and the external, being drawn and considered. Readers cannot help but learn from it, whether they agree or disagree with the author.

But does it all matter? After all, ANUC was defeated, was it not? Also, although one might pity the poor wretches, the future of mankind is peasant-free, is it not? So, why bother? Better to leave it to the archivists of curios. Not so, because there is no society, present or future, without its past, and the history of the victors, for the victors, and by the victors is not only indecent, but also bad history and bad sociology, for it makes us understand less the ways in which human societies operate and change. In particular, it hides systematically the effect of alternative futures that are selected or foreclosed by political struggle. Plebeian struggles or their absence influenced and continue to influence in a major way societies' future shapes (compare nineteenth-century France and Germany, early-twentieth-century Mexico and Egypt, Russia and India, or today's Czechoslovakia and Hungary). Also, the nature of post-peasant society is defined by the way in which the peasants eventually transform and, of course, the peasants' frequent trick of nondisappearance and reappearance, contrary to planners' plans, is also something to be kept in mind.

This book reveals the Colombia that tourists, politicians, and bourgeois seldom see, and also helps comparatively to perceive the more general issue of plebeian as well as peasant movements and the actual fabric of their political action. Nonetheless, a good book should also be paid the higher tribute of pointing to the issues it raises that will need further study. What happened must be considered more fully in the broader context of Colombia outside the main axis of state versus peasant confrontation – the lack of political response by the major parties, workers' unions, and others to the peasants' challenge must be looked at in order to make the picture clearer. Furthermore, the structure of the participants' consciousness underlying the action must be considered more fully; it should not remain in footnotes alone. Still to be seen are the long-term effects, manifest and tacit, of ANUC's struggle on the country's long-term development. Zamosc has opened up, one may say stirred up, all these issues with an intensity that stands in direct relation to the book's virtues. Only trivia does not need a follow-up of argument, extension, and reconsideration. This book is anything but trivial. It will teach many things about real peasants, and more.

Teodor Shanin

Foreword by UNRISD

This volume presents the findings of one of the case studies carried out in Colombia under the Popular Participation Project of UNRISD, the United Nations Research Institute for Social Development. The Project focused on the organized activities of the "excluded" – peasants, workers, ethnic groups, poor urban dwellers – to increase their control over resources, decision-making processes, and regulative institutions of the larger society. It also analyzed in a historical perspective the encounter between such social movements and those social forces, structures, and ideologies that maintain an unequal distribution of power and wealth; and it looked more particularly at the role of the state in these encounter sequences. While the emphasis on the study of social movements reflected a rejection of a technocratic approach to the issues involved, the broader aim of the Project was to help clarify the idea of people's participation in order to make it operationally more useful. The Project included a number of research, action-research, and sub-debate activities that were complementary and linked together through a general debate carried out by the Institute on the theory and practice of participation.

In 1980 a series of studies were initiated in Colombia with the aim of exploring the characteristics and results of the major peasant struggles and movements that took place between 1950 and 1980. The studies, carried out by researchers from the *Centro de Investigación y Educación Popular* (CINEP) in Bogotá focused principally on the rise and decline of the *Asociación Nacional de Usuarios Campesinos* (ANUC), the most important organized peasant movement in Colombia. The investigations were undertaken both because it was felt that the Colombian example could yield important insights into the dynamics of peasant movements and their dialectical relationship with the state, and also because of the interest of the present ANUC leadership in obtaining an objective history of the organization as a basis for future policy.

The present volume presents the results of one of these studies. It traces the history of ANUC on the basis of documentary evidence and extensive interviews and fieldwork; deals with a range of questions that are important to rural participatory movements elsewhere; and shows the vulnerability of officially sponsored peasant movements to sudden changes in government policy, particularly in cases where the state calls the movements into being in order to mobilize support for policies that are unwelcome to other elite sectors and dominant forces. Problems of leadership of participatory movements, and particularly of the difficulty and often inability of the members to control the leadership, are also discussed and confirm results from studies within the Project in Bolivia and Mexico. The study equally shows that as peasant movements grow, they have difficulties in dealing with the increasing socioeconomic differentiation and consequent fragmentation of their membership, a result also found in the study in Thailand within the Project.

Leon Zamosc has taught sociology at universities in Colombia and the United States and has directed two research projects on peasant movements in Colombia at CINEP. He is currently a member of the Sociology Department at the University of California, San Diego.

The study benefitted from a contribution of the Inter-American Foundation (IAF) and the final preparation of the text for publication was partly financed by the International Development Research Center (IDRC) of Canada.

Matthias Stiefel
Project Leader
Participation Project

Acknowledgments

My greatest debt of gratitude is to Teodor Shanin, not only for his continuous support, able supervision, and friendship, but also for his example of dedicated scholarship, which has inspired me since I was an undergraduate student at the University of Haifa. Peter Worsley, Eric Wolf, William Roseberry, Edward Hansen, and Orlando Fals Borda offered valuable advice and excellent comments on the preliminary Spanish and English versions of the work.

In Colombia, I enjoyed the encouragement and trust of Alejandro Angulo; the help of Cristina Escobar, Silvia Rivera, and Diana Medrano in the fieldwork; and the comradeship of Ibán de Rementería, Juan Gaviria, and Ricardo Dávila. I would also like to express my thanks to the many peasants, activists, and officials who spared time to talk about their experiences in the formal and informal interviews conducted as part of this research.

Financial support for my study came from a research fellowship of the University of Manchester, a grant from the Foreign Area Fellowship Program of Oxford, and funds from the UNRISD/CINEP research project on popular participation in Colombia. I am also grateful to the secretarial staff of CINEP in Bogotá and of the Sociology Department in Manchester, who were most helpful and patient with me.

Finally, I am indebted to Jennifer Clegg and Pauline Brooks for their help in making my original English manuscript readable; to Helen Greenberg for her skillful editorial work on the final text; and to Susan Allen-Mills for her interest in my study and her assistance in the production of the book.

Leon Zamosc

Abbreviations

ACC	Peasant Colombian Action
ADAGRI	Association for Integral Agricultural Development
ANAPO	Popular National Alliance
ANIF	National Association of Financial Institutions
ANUC	National Association of Peasant Users
CERA	Executive Committees of Agrarian Reform
CINEP	Research and Popular Education Center
CIRA	Interamerican Center for Agrarian Reform
CRIC	Regional Indian Council of Cauca
CSTC	Confederation of Syndicates of Colombian Workers
CTC	Confederation of Colombian Workers
CUC	Council for Peasant Unity
DANE	Department of National Statistics
DOC	Division of Peasant Organization
DRI	Integrated Rural Development
ELN	National Liberation Army
EPL	Popular Liberation Army
FANAL	National Agrarian Federation
FARC	Revolutionary Armed Forces of Colombia
FEDEGAN	Federation of Cattle Breeders
FENSA	National Federation of Agrarian Syndicates
FUP	Front for the Unity of the People
IICA	Interamerican Institute for Agricultural Sciences
INCORA	Colombian Institute of Agrarian Reform
Liga ML	Marxist Leninist League
M-19	April 19 Movement
MNDP	National Democratic Popular Movement
MOIR	Independent Revolutionary Workers' Movement
MRL	Revolutionary Liberal Movement
OCIDEC	Independent Peasant Organization of Casanare
ORP	People's Revolutionary Organization
PAN	Plan for Food and Nutrition
PCML	Marxist Leninist New Communist Party
SAC	Society of Colombian Agriculturalists

SENALDE	National Employment Service
UNO	Union of National Opposition
URS	Socialist Revolutionary Union
UTC	Union of Colombian Workers

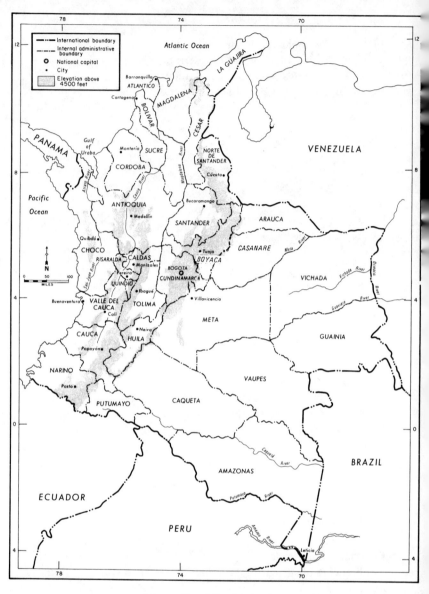

Map 1. Republic of Colombia.

Introduction

By inducing structural changes, redefining old social cleavages, and giving rise to new class contradictions in the countryside, the transformations related to the development of capitalism also create favorable conditions for the emergence of agrarian movements. As social and political agents that strive to shape reality according to the aspirations of a class or a class alliance, these organized forms of collective action may themselves become factors of socioeconomic change in the countryside. Rural social movements are particularly relevant when their outcome focuses on the crucial alternative between an evolution based upon a peasant pattern of farming, with widespread ownership of land, or one dominated by landlords and entrepreneurs who monopolize the means of production and exclude the peasants. Since most countries come to the threshold of capitalism with traditional rural structures in which peasants are the main sector of the population, it is the peasants who seem to have most to win or lose. This fact, however, has not always created social movements representing the interests of the peasantry. On the one hand, in only a few cases has the agrarian question been settled by dramatic struggles leading to sudden shifts in one direction or the other. Instead, there has usually been a protracted process of socioeconomic change that permitted gradual transformations without major social and political upheavals. On the other hand, there have been few cases in which the alternative between peasant and landlord paths appeared to be a clear-cut issue. Most frequently, both patterns of agrarian evolution have coexisted within the same country as part of special circumstances that limited their opposition to particular regions or branches of agricultural production. Moreover, it is well known that the peasants have special difficulties regarding the organization and representation of their interests. Heterogeneous class composition and other factors have typically combined to confine their collective mobilization to particular local or regional issues. On the rare occasions when the peasants have been able to flex their political muscles at the societal level, their influence has usually been transient and heavily conditioned by their dependence upon more powerful or influential allies.

Still, and despite all these restrictions, during the last hundred years peasants and farmers have not only taken part in the main national and social revolutions, but have also produced social movements and political parties that were both massive and independent, such as Mexican and Bolivian agrarianism, American populism, agrarian socialism in Canada, and the parties of the Green International in Eastern Europe and the Balkans. In all these large-scale mobilizations, the pressure for a non-monopolistic development of agriculture played a major or at least a predominant role. Thus, there have been many cases in which the resolution of the agrarian question has shifted from the natural spontaneity of purely socioeconomic change to more deliberate political conflict. Furthermore, the historical evidence of these cases definitely questions the heuristic value of some taken-for-granted arguments concerning the presumed impossibility of an independent peasant movement. Peasant movements and national peasant parties have not only existed, but have also left deep marks on the history of their countries. Even though they were usually defeated, in many cases they disappeared only after attaining partial goals of resistance and consolidation or after achieving radical agrarian reforms that implied significant socioeconomic and political transformations of the entire society.

In the history of social movements and agrarian struggles in Colombia, the Asociación Nacional de Usuarios Campesinos (ANUC, the National Association of Peasant Users) is the only organization that was able, at least during part of its existence, to articulate autonomously the demands of the peasants on a national scale. By resisting the landlord path of agrarian evolution and by trying to force a resolution of the agrarian question that would favor the peasants throughout the country, ANUC's struggles in the first half of the 1970s were one of the great peasant challenges described in the preceding paragraph. In terms of the Colombian experience, the basic character of ANUC clearly distinguishes it from earlier peasant mobilizations of the twentieth century. The rural struggles of the late 1920s and early 1930s were the first major battles on the agrarian question in Colombia, but although those struggles caused a national political debate and led to some reforms, they failed to develop into a unified peasant movement and were confined mainly to some coffee-growing areas in which the peasant and landlord economies had become acutely antagonistic. The much more widespread clashes of the Violencia during the 1950s aligned the peasants with the conflicting factions of the dominant classes, and even though that civil war had regional effects upon the evolution of the agrarian question, it led only to marginal struggles in defense of the interests of the peasantry as a class.

Given this general introductory appraisal of ANUC's historical importance, let us consider three central issues that will further clarify the nature of the peasant movement and give some additional clues to its importance. The first issue is the already mentioned definition of ANUC as agent and interpreter of the aspirations of the peasantry as a class. In the 1960s, the agrarian question was not posed as a uniform issue in Colombia. Instead, it was defined by a set of contradictions that involved the varying attitudes of different class sectors toward the possibility of a free peasant economy. For some groups, the main problem was to gain access to land of their own. Others needed to improve their conditions of reproduction in order to preserve and strengthen the existing peasant economy. Still others had more specific socioeconomic and ethnic-cultural demands. Despite this great diversity, ANUC emerged as an unifying force during the early 1970s, coordinating the demands of these sectors and expressing their grievances on three main battlefronts: the struggle for land, the defense of the colonists, and the protection of the small-holders. In general, then, the main issues raised by ANUC have to do with its effectiveness as a unified peasant movement and its social and economic impact. In terms of the agrarian conflicts related to the capitalist process in Colombia, the central concerns involve not only questions of class but also the way in which the struggles developed on the different fronts, the results of these struggles, and their combined effect upon the resolution of the agrarian question. In terms of the current upsurge of research and debate on peasantry and capitalism, ANUC's case offers a contemporary opportunity to study both the specifics of peasant political action and the potential of the peasants to influence, by their class struggle, the patterns of agrarian development under capitalism.

A further relevant aspect of ANUC's experience is the changing nature of the relationship between the peasant movement and the Colombian state. On the one hand, it was the reformist policies of the state that led to the creation of ANUC as a semiofficial peasant association in 1967. Taking into account both the special organizational difficulties of the peasants and the conditions that prevailed in Colombia in the wake of the Violencia, it can be speculated that perhaps a national peasant move-ment would have never emerged without this initiative from above. On the other hand, the counterreformist government policy after 1970 became one of the main factors behind ANUC's radicalization and led to open confrontation between the peasant movement and the state – a confron-tation that became one of the main axes of conflict in the subsequent struggles. What therefore comes to the fore is the state's involvement in the resolution of the agrarian question. Given the nature of the Colombian state under the National Front, this issue suggests a second line of inquiry that encompasses three different levels: the ways in which the agrarian question appeared, as a problem, at each juncture in the process of cap-italist development, the projects that the dominant classes attempted to impose at each juncture, and the effects of such projects in terms of class realignments and shifts in state policy. In the last instance, the changing relationships between ANUC and the state dramatized the crucial importance of the class alliances and oppositions in which the peasants were involved.

Finally, this question of the peasants' allies leads to a third significant issue: the political and ideological orientations of ANUC during its confrontation cycle. After the collapse of the reformist alliance that had created the conditions for its development, ANUC adopted the typical attitudes of a revolutionary movement. At the beginning, its revolutionary orientations were directly related to the links that the peasant leaders had established with the political left, especially the new Maoist organizations. Later, with the successive breaks between the peasant movement and these groups, ANUC redefined its revolutionary attitudes as part of an attempt to create an independent political force of its own within the leftist camp. Given the weaknesses of the socialist opposition and the working-class movement in Colombia, these political definitions of the peasant movement arc crucial for any analytical approach to the question of peasant political participation. It is necessary to examine the factors that account for the peasants' receptivity to leftist influences. It is also important to study the effects of radical politicization upon the peasant struggles and the general evolution of the peasant movement. For once in Colombia's history, ANUC's rise provided a real chance for the left to exert considerable ideological and political influence upon large sections of the population nationwide. The outcome of this unique historical opportunity deserves special attention and careful assessment.

These considerations define the three central problems focused on in this book: the agrarian contradictions that provided the framework for the peasant struggles, the changing relationships between the peasant movement and the state, and the politics and ideology of the peasant challenge. The exploration of the issues encompassed by these problems provides the basis for a tentative answer, advanced in Chapter 10, to the paramount question of the historical significance of ANUC in the capitalist development of Colombia. In dealing with these issues, this study approaches the peasant movement as a protagonist in the drama of the class struggles that marked Colombia's recent socioeconomic and political history. This emphasis on class analysis is, of course, only one possible approach to the understanding of political conflicts and social movements. Meaningful insights can undoubtedly be derived from models of conflict resolution; from theories that stress the institutions of the political system; and from more conventional approaches that focus upon features of a social movement such as leadership, following, organization, goals, and means of action. It was mainly because of the structural nature of the central questions and concerns that class analysis was considered to be most suitable for this research. However, considerable efforts were made to overcome the reductionist limitations usually inherent in any analytical approach. Thus, although the political and ideological developments are explained by reference to the underlying class contradictions, special attention has been given to the ways in which ideology and politics, in turn, influenced the structural processes with their own capacity for objective determination. Similarly, the characteristics of ANUC as an organization are referred to at appropriate points, even though they have not been employed as basic categories of analysis.

A further note concerns the scope of this book. As originally conceived, it was to deal in depth with the different battlefronts of the peasant movement in Colombia and was to include a comparative analysis leading to broader conclusions on theoretical issues posed by peasant mobilization and political participation. Unfortunately, these goals proved too ambitious. Only the most central theoretical issues have been raised and briefly discussed in the last chapter, in the hope that it will be possible to carry out the much needed comparative elaboration in a future study. With regard to the treatment of the subject itself, it would have been ideal to provide an equally exhaustive analysis of each battlefront of the peasant movement. But priorities had to be defined and, as a result, most of the analytical effort was devoted to the regions of land struggle. Although it is true that this introduces an element of unbalance, this limitation is largely compensated for by the nature of the subject itself. In fact, it was in the regions of land struggle that the peasant movement reached its height and achieved its most tangible results. The main factors involved in the other battlefronts were also present in these areas: The issues posed by the demands of peasants with land and agricultural workers, for example, were as relevant in these regions as in the others. Furthermore, other elements, such as the politicization of the peasant movement, were particularly influential in the areas of land struggle. Still, throughout the work a consistent effort was made to maintain an overall perspective, both by recurrent reflections on the differences between the areas of land struggle and the other battlefronts of the peasant movement and by a selective analysis of the main processes that affected ANUC's performance on these other battlefronts.

This research started with two years of background bibliographical work, which was carried out in Manchester and focused upon general aspects of Colombian society and relevant issues in the field of peasant studies. The actual fieldwork began in 1977 and lasted until early 1982. The first year in Colombia was spent largely in libraries and archives, using secondary sources in order to sketch the historical evolution of the agrarian question and the peasant struggles. The collection of more specific data on ANUC, including documents of the organization and interviews with government officials, political activists, peasant leaders, and rank-

and-file members of the movement, was started in 1979. By mid-1981 this research had become an integral part of a broader project on popular participation in Colombia, a project sponsored by the United Nations Research Institute for Social Development (UNRISD) and conducted in the country by the Research and Popular Education Center (CINEP). With better resources, access was gained to the more remote Colombian regions that had not been visited in the previous stage of fieldwork. The collection of data led to the formation of a special archive that includes 148 interviews, 435 documents of the national and regional associations of ANUC, collections of ANUC's journals and bulletins, 84 documents of other organizations related to the *usuarios*, and 742 entries regarding articles on the peasant movement in Colombian newspapers and magazines. This archive on ANUC, which has been organized by subject and includes a thematic index, is open to the public and can be consulted at CINEP's library in Bogotá.

To summarize, this work outlines the overall direction of ANUC and emphasizes the movement's action in the areas of land struggle. The analytical perspective is largely concerned with the class contradictions involved in the historical developments spurred by the peasant *usuarios*. This book uses a chronological format in analyzing the main structural factors that shaped the rise and fall of the peasant movement and the land struggles during the 1970s. In Chapter 1, the historical evolution of the agrarian question in Colombia is traced in order to explore the structural agrarian contradictions after the Violencia. Chapter 2 examines the political prospects for the emergence of a peasant movement in the 1960s, considering the immediate precedents of the struggle for land and inquiring into the motives that eventually led to the creation of ANUC. Chapter 3 provides a detailed account of the 1971 waves of land invasions, considering the role played by direct action in ANUC's radicalization and studying the development of the peasant movement on its different battlefronts. Chapters 4, 5, and 6 follow the subsequent evolution of the battle for land, taking into account the effects of repression and other changing elements of state policy and paying special attention to the leftist politicization of the peasant struggles. Chapters 7 and 8 deal with the consequences of broader socioeconomic changes in the areas of land struggle, studying ANUC's attempts to develop new forms of agitation among the agricultural laborers and in the peasant settlements that emerged after the land struggles. Chapter 9 examines the factors of decline leading to the final crisis of the peasant radicalism of the 1970s, considering the dimensions of that crisis and observing its final outcome at the beginning of the 1980s. Chapter 10 summarizes the main aspects of this study, advancing conclusions and raising problems and questions for further research.

1

The agrarian question in Colombia

The agrarian question can be posed as follows: what is the pattern of agrarian evolution that prevails in capitalist society?[1] The development of capitalism in different countries has shown that there are two basic alternatives. One of them, the "landlord path" of evolution, features the concentration of land ownership, which creates favorable conditions for a capitalist agriculture based upon wage labor and large-scale production. The second alternative, the "peasant path," is characterized by the distribution of land among large numbers of smallholders, which leads to peasant farming based upon family labor. These alternatives are opposite poles that define a whole range of possible mixed outcomes in which both patterns of production appear side by side.[2] The importance of the agrarian question can be measured by the consequences of its resolution: The socioeconomic structure of the countryside shapes the conditions for economic performance, defines the relative strength of the rural social classes, and sets the stage for their participation in the political processes linked to the development of capitalism.[3] The way in which the agrarian question is resolved depends, in turn, upon a complex mix of historical, socio-economic, and political factors unique to each country.[4] As a first step in the study of these unique dimensions in Colombia, the first section of this chapter will briefly trace the history of the agrarian question in light of the changes that marked the emergence and development of capitalism. The second section will deal with the socioeconomic factors of the agrarian question during the 1960s, emphasizing the way in which these factors defined the antagonistic landlord and peasant paths and shaped the structural conditions for a peasant movement in Colombia.

The historical background

Part of the specificity of Colombia's historical development is due to the ways in which geography has conditioned the socioeconomic processes. Located between the Atlantic and Pacific oceans at the northernmost tip of the South American subcontinent, the country is dominated by three Andean mountain ranges separated by two broad valleys running south to north. Beyond the mountains, extensive plains with savannas and forests

7

mark the landscape of the Atlantic Coast, the Eastern Llanos, and the southeastern Amazon Basin. Although the country's latitude is tropical, the climate is determined mainly by topography. The Andean ranges produce changes of temperature according to altitude, thus defining three main thermal levels of cold highlands, temperate slopes, and hot valleys and plains. Climate clearly influenced the original spatial distribution of population. The indigenous peoples developed sedentary cultures mainly in the healthier cooler areas, so that their gold and agricultural surpluses attracted the *conquistadores* and the early Spanish settlers to the highlands.[5] Only later, under the double pressure of land concentration and population growth, did the downward movement to settle the slopes and plains begin in earnest. Furthermore, the size and abrupt relief of the country posed great obstacles to transportation and communications. Coupled with the diversity of ecological conditions, these difficulties led to the early differentiation of distinct regions and hindered the development of the national market. In addition, since high shipping costs raised the prices of exported commodities to noncompetitive levels, the transportation problem was also the main cause of the country's comparatively late integration into the international market.[6]

A second factor was the demographic situation found by the Spanish at the time of their conquest. From the point of view of its Indian population, Colombia was midway between densely populated regions like México or Perú and sparsely populated areas like the River Plate.[7] There were, therefore, sufficient grounds for the consolidation of a local aristocracy of landlords who received rights to the surpluses and labor of the Indian communities. But since these opportunities were limited, their early monopolization led to the formation of significant groups of poor Spanish *vecinos* (neighbors) who had no option but to settle as peasants and artisans in different parts of the country and in the emerging towns.[8] At the same time, imported diseases and harsh exploitation caused a drastic reduction of the Indian population during the early colonial period.[9] As a result, African slaves were introduced into mines and *haciendas* of Antioquia, the Cauca Valley, and some points on the Atlantic Coast. However, given the diminishing importance of gold mining, it proved very difficult for the Spanish to stem the flow of runaway slaves.[10] Combined with the decimation of the Indian communities in the highlands and the downward colonization movements, the decline of slavery contributed to a very rapid mixture of racial stocks. Consequently, a highly miscegenated population, with a predominance of Spanish and Indian elements in the highlands and Negroid shades in the lowlands, has been the hallmark of Colombia since colonial times.[11]

For the Spanish, the establishment of an export economy appeared to be the shortest route to personal fortune and the general prosperity of the colony. Since gold is an exceptionally valuable commodity in relation to its volume and weight, bullion exports had been less affected by transportation costs and provided the basis for the country's vital commercial link with Europe until the eighteenth century.[12] However, when gold mining declined, neither the Bourbon reforms of the late colonial period nor the free-trade republican policies after 1820 were successful in promoting other exports. Topography, the development of chemical substitutes, and the presence of cheaper competitors in the international market easily defeated the short-lived export "booms" of Colombian quinine, indigo, rubber, and tobacco during the nineteenth century.[13] In the absence of the economic stimulation usually associated with the development of the export sector, and given the ecological fragmentation, the socioeconomic processes of the nineteenth century led to the formation of regions that were relatively isolated economically.[14] As centers of administration, political life, commercial activities, and artisan production, the cities and provincial towns played a pivotal role in these regions. But the real bases of economic and social life were located in the countryside, where *haciendas* and peasants produced surpluses for the limited regional markets as part of their traditional pattern of cattle raising and agricultural production.

In Colombia, as in most Latin American countries, the formation of the *haciendas* and the peasantry was a long process that can be traced back to the evolution of the colonial agrarian regime. In the New Kingdom of Granada (1564–1718), the original systems of Indian exploitation were *encomienda* and *concierto*. The *encomenderos* extracted tribute in kind from the Indian communities in exchange for protection and religious instruction. *Concierto* was a form of draft labor by which crown officials allocated workers from the Indian communities to neighboring settlers who had received land leases, or *mercedes de tierras*. Later, under the policy of *composiciones*, the Indian communities were granted collective land ownership as *resguardos*, while the land leases became the private property of the Spanish settlers. With the rapid decline of the Indian population, the periodic *reducciones* carried out by the crown led to a continuous transfer of *resguardo* lands to the landowners. By the eighteenth century, the *resguardos* could no longer provide significant agricultural surpluses and had ceased to be a dependable source of draft labor. Consequently, during the Viceroyalty of Nueva Granada (1718–1810) the remaining *encomiendas* were abrogated and the *concierto* system was abolished. In the meantime, miscegenation had given rise to a growing population of *mestizos* who, given their mixed ethnic definition, did not qualify for land in the Indian *resguardos*. These *mestizos* were incorporated into the *haciendas* as *agregados*, a vague category that included different types of tenants, sharecroppers, and peons tied by bondage debts. All in all, then, the continuous monopolization of land and the gradual dissolution of the Indian communities enabled the *haciendas* to gain direct control over the available labor. This process involved, at the same time, the racial redefinition, dispossession, and subjection of the exploited population. The liquidation of the *resguardos* was accelerated by the 1780 Bourbon reforms, which authorized their privatization in certain circumstances, and was almost completed in 1820 with a republican decree that ordered repartition of communal property among individual members and paved the way for an intensive landlord assault based upon forcible sales. Nevertheless, there were some cases in which the Indians refused parcelization and kept their *resguardos* intact, notably in Cauca, Caldas, and Tolima. In many other places, and especially throughout the eastern Andean range, where there was much *mestizo* influence, many communities accepted privatization but managed to resist the landlord pressure and maintained their control over a substantial part of the land.[15]

Most authors agree that the development of the Colombian *hacienda* reflected the local aristocracy's use of its power to adapt to the prevailing conditions of restricted trade, abundance of land, and scarcity of labor.[16] Basically self-sufficient economically, the *hacienda* provided cattle and foods to supply the provincial towns and responded easily to occasional opportunities for commercial expansion beyond the regional limits. On the other hand, land monopolization and the establishment of servile relations of production prevented free access to the land and ensured the subjection and control of the labor force on the estates. During the nineteenth century, racial miscegenation, dissolution of Indian *resguardos*, and consolidation of *haciendas* gradually led to the formation of extensive estates, a subordinated peasantry on these estates, and a free peasantry that managed to resist landlord encroachments. A parallel process was taking place in the colonization of new areas on the slopes and plains. In these areas, poor Spanish settlers, *mestizos*, and runaway slaves were trying to gain access to the land in order to establish the basis of their freedom as peasants. They invariably met with the opposition of landowners who held title to enormous tracts of virgin forest. Some of these titles had originally been granted by the crown; others were republican concessions to generals and patricians who had been involved in the Wars of Independence. But most of them had been obtained through the speculative practices of landowners who used their influence to get the lion's share from the legal processes of public land allocation. In this situation, the colonization movements involved continuous conflict between those who were taking actual possession by working the land and those who held ownership claims to it. Throughout the nineteenth century, the de facto and legal outcomes of these struggles between axes and titles led either to the establishment of sectors of free peasants, as in most areas of Antioqueño colonization in the west, or to *haciendas* that subjected the colonists to rent and sharecropping, as was usually the case on the eastern slopes and the Atlantic Coast.[17]

The end of the old agrarian regime and the colonization movements thus provided the framework for the regional formation of extensive landed property and peasant sectors in Colombia. This basic nineteenth-century structure would later evolve into the *minifundia* in the highlands, mixed patterns on the slopes, and extreme *latifundia* in the plains that will be studied in the following section. In terms of social conflict, it has already been indicated that the establishment of this structure involved a continuous struggle over the land. However, this struggle was mainly local and was usually fought in the courts. In the existing studies of Colombia's social history, there are many references to legal disputes over land, but little mention is made of actual uprisings or rebellions during the nineteenth century.[18] Since the evidence clearly shows the complacent bias of the judges in favor of the landowners, the absence of any significant armed or political challenge by the Indians and colonists is an eloquent sign of the power of the landowning class. The Liberal and Conservative parties, the two main political forces in the republic, were both controlled by the landowners.[19] Not surprisingly, land was not a political issue; legislation and most of the allocation of titles to public lands were clearly aimed at promoting land monopolization.[20] Of course, there were other sources of cleavage. The Liberal Party included stronger commercial interests, and there were sharp ideological differences on such issues as federalism versus centralism, free trade versus protectionism, and the relationship between church and state.[21] Bipartisan politics were a mixture of electoral maneuvers and showdowns of force, and in both activities the peasants were mobilized as captive clients who furnished votes and militiamen for the regional bosses, or *gamonales*.[22] The Liberals prevailed between 1849 and 1886, but their free-trade policies proved insufficient to consolidate an export economy and their extreme federalism pushed the country to the brink of political disintegration. The reaction to this was the so-called Conservative Republic, a long period of rule by the Conservative Party that lasted until 1930 and was marked by strong centralism and a certain degree of economic protectionism.[23]

It was during the Conservative Republic that the stable link with the international market was finally established through the development of coffee production and export. The temperate climate of the Andean slopes was particularly suitable for the crop, and cultivation was encouraged both by the favorable prices abroad and by the marked reduction of transportation costs that followed the introduction of steam navigation along the Magdalena River.[24] The main growing areas were located in the west, where coffee became an integral part of the Antioqueño colonization movements and the major peasant crop in Antioquia, Caldas, and the northern portions of the departments of Tolima and Valle. In the east, coffee was also introduced by the landowners in temperate-climate *haciendas* of Santander, Cundinamarca, and eastern Tolima.[25] Total production expanded from 150,000 sacks in 1894 to more than 2 million sacks by the mid-1920s.[26] This remarkable growth of the external sector made the fortunes of many landowners and merchants, who began to import machinery for new industries.[27] An infrastructure of railways and roads was developed to facilitate coffee exports, and this helped to improve the commercial links between the regions and enlarge the market for imported consumer goods.[28] In less than thirty years, coffee exports had completely transformed the economy of the country, leading to a massive incorporation of peasants, creating conditions for capital accumulation, encouraging the formation of a national market, and providing the basis for a national industry. Coffee was spurring the development of capitalism in Colombia.[29]

The social and political consequences of rapid economic change soon became apparent. By 1930, 26 percent of the 7.4 million Colombians were living in the cities, and many trade unions had been created by the incipient working class under the influence of young radical Liberals and the Socialists who would later form the Communist Party.[30] In the countryside, the agrarian question was arising for the first time as a relevant and contested political issue. The main foci of discontent were the coffee *haciendas* of the east, which were worked by subordinated peasants. The peasants wanted their share of the benefits of the export prosperity and demanded the right to cultivate coffee on their own plots. With the help of Liberals and Communists, numerous peasant leagues were formed and conflicts over land escalated, especially on the slopes of Cundinamarca and Tolima.[31] In other parts of the country, the increasing demand for food for the towns refueled the land disputes in colonization areas and led to growing protests regarding terms of tenancy and sharecropping on many *haciendas*. The remaining Indian communities were also affected by the waves of rural agitation, raising their own claims for the restitution of *resguardo* lands that had been lost to landowners in Cauca and southern Tolima.[32] Nevertheless, these battles of the late 1920s and early 1930s remained largely isolated. There were significant peasant organizations in the areas of coffee *haciendas*, but even there no unified peasant movement developed.[33] At the political level, the peasants' cause was outspokenly supported by some progressives in the Liberal Party. Some party ideologists, expressing the concerns of the commercial and industrial bourgeoisie, believed that the traditional *hacienda* system was an obstacle to the development of a dynamic agriculture, hindered the free movement of labor power, and prevented adequate growth of the internal market.[34] In the meantime, the Conservative government was repressing rural unrest with a heavy hand and was also coercing the urban trade unions in the strikes that followed the Depression beginning in 1928.[35] Against this background of discontent and protest, and promising substantial changes to the popular classes, the Liberal Party won the elections and returned to power in 1930.

Under the Liberal Republic, the social pressures generated by the export economy and incipient industrialization were eased by reforms. Trade unions were allowed to organize, and laws were passed to regulate workers' rights and settle industrial conflicts.[36] Agrarian Law 200 of 1936, which recognized the primacy of social considerations in land disputes, had little effect upon the patterns of land property because it granted the landlords a ten-year period of grace to "clean" their titles and put their lands to productive use. However, the main source of rural trouble was eliminated when the state bought most of the affected coffee *haciendas* and sold them back to the peasants.[37] To a large extent, the reforms of the 1930s reflected the way in which change and continuity in the class interests of the traditional parties helped to maintain the bipartisan political pattern in the twentieth century. The landowning, commercial, and industrial interests had not become divided along clear-cut party lines; each party represented segments of every dominant class and group in Colombian society.[38] The strength of the landowners in the Liberal Party prevented radical agrarian transformations, leading to compromises that checked the peasant challenge and, at the same time, kept intact the networks of patronage that maintained clientelist bipartisan control in the countryside.[39] On the other hand, since the exporting and industrial economy had begun under Conservative rule, the Liberal Party was able to accommodate, as the opposition, the demands of the new urban groups that had emerged.[40] In the cities, the traditional bases of "hereditary" party identification were more easily dissolved, so that the "welfarist" approach of the Liberals secured their relative urban hegemony from the beginning. Thus, the radical middle-class party that developed as a third alternative in other Latin American countries never emerged in Colombia. Reformist approaches and even radical oppositions would instead arise from factions within the Liberal Party. Since the Communists managed to attain only limited influence in the trade union movement and in some peasant areas, the bipartisan pattern of political domination survived the "great transformation" and remained characteristic of Colombian politics in the new phase of capitalist development.

Neither the appeasing effects of the Liberal reforms nor the new political balance achieved by the Liberal Republic lasted for long. The industrialization process, based upon the substitution of imported manufactured goods, gained momentum during the 1930s and 1940s. As urbanization grew, the emerging middle classes began to make demands and the working class coalesced around the Confederation of Colombian Workers (CTC), a unified trade union central controlled by radical Liberals and Communists.[41] Deeply divided between an elitist faction of traditional politicians and a new generation of radical middle-class militants, the Liberal Party had increasing problems in balancing the interests of the dominant groups with the demands of the subordinated classes.[42] At the same time, the Conservative reaction to its minority political status was particularly violent. To erode the legitimacy of the Liberal governments, the Conservative Party used tactics of abstention and political harassment. As a result, especially in the countryside, electoral campaigns and election days after 1930 were marked by continuous riots led by gangs and mobs whose activities were carefully orchestrated by local Conservative *gamonales*.[43] Finally, internal opposition within the Liberal Party took the form of a radical populist movement under the charismatic leadership of Jorge Eliecer Gaitán. Commanding massive urban support and gaining a foothold among many peasants in Liberal areas, Gaitán launched his candidacy for the presidency in 1946.[44] The moderate Liberals, who at that stage still controlled the party machinery and wanted to check the populist tide, decided to nominate Gabriel Turbay as their official candidate. Taking advantage of the Liberal division, the Conservative leader and candidate, Mariano Ospina Pérez, won the 1946 election. Gaitán became the official leader of the Liberal Party in 1947, and given the Liberal majority in the country, his victory in the following election was almost certain.[45] Colombia seemed to have arrived, through its own distinct path of bipartisan politics, at the verge of the same type of populist regime that prevailed in most industrializing Latin American countries in the post–World War II period.[46]

The Conservative government was fully aware that Gaitán's triumph was only a matter of time. Thus, it gave some cabinet posts to moderate Liberals and systematically repressed the opposition. Trying to counteract labor's support for Gaitán, the Conservatives banned the CTC and, with the help of the Catholic Church, created the Union of Colombian Workers (UTC) as a parallel trade union central. Numerous strikes and demonstrations were fiercely repressed in the cities, violence started to spread to the countryside, and the Liberal ministers left the cabinet, blaming the government for instigating most of the disturbances and killings.[47] Against this background of widespread unrest, the situation finally exploded with Gaitán's assassination on April 9, 1948. Bogotá and other cities were shattered by spontaneous rioting, but the government regained urban control by resorting to military occupation. After the failure of the Liberal attempt to find a negotiated and peaceful solution, the de facto dictatorship of the Conservative Party began and the country plunged into the long civil war known as the Violencia.[48]

Since the army controlled the cities, the Violencia took root in the rural areas, where both parties were well entrenched by the traditional patterns of political clientelism. When the regional and local *gamonales* mobilized their peasant clients, bipartisan strife unfolded as a series of increasingly bloody clashes and *vendettas* between neighboring communities. The army took part in punitive expeditions against Liberal villages, although its main thrust was directed against the Liberal guerrillas who had started to operate in some parts of the country, especially in the Eastern Llanos. By 1951 and 1952, however, significant changes were occurring amid the uproar of the factional struggle. In the coffee areas and throughout the highlands, landlords and peasants were beginning to use the Violencia to settle by force old and new land disputes. In the central departments of Cundinamarca, Tolima, and Huila, the Communist Party was organizing strongholds of self-defense among uprooted peasants who tried to resettle in marginal mountainous areas. In the Eastern Llanos, some Liberal armed groups were slipping away from the control of the political bosses, so that many Liberal landowners became targets for compulsory "contributions" to support the guerrilla activities. In addition, widespread banditry was developing behind the partisan banners, as more and more of the originally political gangs were now bent on private revenge and economic profit.[49]

The dominant classes perceived that the struggle was beginning to go beyond bipartisan conflict, threatening to spread into far more dangerous class antagonisms. To prevent this, it was necessary to end the fighting, and a military coup seemed to be the only realistic option when the authority of the state was collapsing. Thus, in 1953 the army took power with the open support of both traditional parties, opening a new phase in the Violencia that would last until 1957. During this period, the military government, headed by Gustavo Rojas Pinilla, granted a general amnesty and achieved an almost complete demobilization of the armed peasants. The indiscriminate assaults and retaliations gradually ended, and the Violencia was reduced to counterinsurgent campaigns by the army against bandits, Communist strongholds, and recalcitrant Liberal guerrillas who refused to lay down their arms. As these nuclei of resistance were being subdued, the equilibrium between the Liberal and Conservative parties was partially restored and the pacification of the country proceeded. In the process, however, Rojas Pinilla launched a political project of his own, asserting his charismatic personality and borrowing the style and themes of Argentina's General Juan Perón under the slogan of "Colombia above the parties."[50]

For the second time the traditional parties faced the common threat of populism, this time in the shape of a prospective caesarist regime that could block their return to power. Negotiations between Liberals and Conservatives were quickly conducted until a final agreement, the National Front, was reached.[51] The Front was an institutional compromise by which both sides were to share power for sixteen years in a bipartisan coalition based upon the principles of alternation, parity, and exclusiveness. The presidency would alternate between the two parties, all legislative bodies and high administrative positions would be equally divided, and only Liberals and Conservatives would be allowed to stand as candidates in the elections.[52] In 1957 Rojas Pinilla was overthrown by officers who were loyal to the traditional parties, the provisions of the pact were overwhelmingly approved as constitutional amendments in a national plebiscite, and the agreement began to be carried out the following year with the election of the Liberal Alberto Lleras Camargo as the first president of the National Front.[53] Much of the rhetoric of national reconstruction focused upon the need to destroy the "enemies of peace," that is, the gangs of bandits and the "subversive" Communists who had created "independent republics" of their own.[54] With the full backing of the army, this goal was largely achieved: In 1964 and 1965 only a few bandit gangs were still on the loose and, by that time, the last Communist strongholds of peasant self-defense had been occupied by the army in Marquetalia, El Pato, and Riochiquito.[55] Another favorite topic in the discussions on national reconstruction was that of how to heal the social wounds of the civil war. Much of this talk centered on the need for agrarian reform, which will be considered in the first section of the following chapter.

The Violencia, which took about 200,000 lives, was an extraordinarily complex historical phenomenon. Its causes were rooted in the previous processes of social formation in Colombia and in the socioeconomic and political changes associated with industrialization. What began as a populist challenge of the subordinate classes developed into factional struggle based on vertical class alignments along traditional bipartisan lines. In the process, the conflict moved from the cities to the countryside, where it assumed different forms and expressed many underlying contradictions that, in some regions, slowly began to turn back the axis of confrontation toward a horizontal class definition. Given the many aspects of the Violencia, and taking into account its changing nature, it is hardly surprising that it has been interpreted in many different ways. Emphasizing the political dimension, some authors have seen the civil war as a logical consequence of acute bipartisan competition within a traditional regime that had failed to develop sufficient institutional bases for competitive democracy.[56] Stressing the more general class contradictions in Colombian society, other scholars have considered the Violencia as an aborted social revolution, a popular struggle for change distorted into banditry and irrational strife due to the absence of leadership, organization, and ideology.[57] A third group of researchers have focused upon the agrarian setting of the Violencia, arguing that the conflicts can be partially seen as the landowners' revenge for the peasant gains of the 1930s and suggesting a link between these conflicts and the subsequent development of capitalist production in the countryside.[58] Finally, the more recent approaches have been integrative, seeing in the Violencia a partial collapse of the state that, being itself the result of political and social cleavages, caused different types of social and political contradictions to be transformed into intense intraclass and interclass conflicts.[59]

A thorough discussion on the historical interpretation of the Violencia is beyond the scope of this book. Still, the insights and evidence of existing research can provide a basis for a final comment on some basic points that are particularly relevant here. One of these points has to do with the political consequences of the Violencia. In retrospect, and taking into account the experience of other Latin American countries, one of the most significant results of the civil war was the fact that it blocked the populist alternative in Colombia. When the violence was over, the same dominant classes emerged in control of the battered but still very much alive bipartisan system of clientelist domination. The way in which the populist challenge of the subordinate classes was checked led to the strict definition of the state as a tool of the ruling classes. Rather than an arena of class conflict, an institutional representation of the balance of class forces, or even an autonomous force that played a social role of its own,[60] the state created by the National Front agreement froze any expression of social conflict, excluded the subordinate classes from politics, and gave all institutional power to the two political parties of the dominant classes.

A second relevant point concerns the effects of the civil war upon the patterns of agrarian evolution. Here it should be remembered that although the Violencia was marked by political determination, class contradictions and land struggles became increasingly important in its last stages. According to the available data, at least 200,000 agricultural parcels changed hands and 1 million people emigrated – including 150,000 to Venezuela – as a result of violence.[61] Since capitalist agriculture started to develop in the inner valleys during the 1950s, these massive numbers created the impression of a causal relationship between the Violencia, land concentration, and the development of agrarian capitalism. However, recent regional studies have shown a far more complex picture that includes not only landlord encroachments against peasants but also gains by peasants at the expense of landlords, dispossession of peasants by peasants in factional strife between neighboring rival villages, and recurrent processes of repeasantization in lands that had been sold cheaply or abandoned by other peasants or landlords.[62] Moreover, the evidence indicates that much of the land concentration and emigration in the coffee areas was due to the effects of the great depression in international coffee prices after 1954, not to the Violencia itself.[63] Finally, regional research has also shown that the plain areas of the inner valleys, that is, the main centers of subsequent development of capitalist agriculture, had been only marginally affected by the Violencia.[64] All in all, then, the civil war took a heavy toll in terms of peasant displacement and dissolution, but evidence contradicts both the argument that the peasant losses strongly favored the landlord path of evolution and the notion that the Violencia was necessary for the development of capitalist agriculture. Much more regional research is needed to lay the foundations for a final assessment, but a preliminary conclusion strongly suggests that although the Violencia caused significant changes in the affected areas, the multidirectional nature of these changes makes it impossible to discern a clear or overall pattern in the evolution of the agrarian question in the country as a whole.

Much of this multidirectionality in the effects of the Violencia was due to its complex socioeconomic setting. As will be seen in the following section, the opposition between the peasant and landlord paths of evolution assumed different forms across the regions, and the perspectives did not always depend on direct confrontations. In fact, most of the peasant losses during the Violencia occurred in *minifundia* areas in the highlands and slopes, where the future of peasant agriculture depended mainly upon the dynamics of the peasant economy and not upon a struggle for land against the landlords. Coupled with the overriding importance of political determinations in the Violencia, this leads to a third and final general point, namely, that although the Violencia was largely a peasant war, the peasants did not fight to win the agrarian issue. They fought for their interests only in the course and as a derivation of fighting for the interests of others, and this usually involved direct conflict with each other. In this sense, the class struggle in the conflicts in some areas should not obscure the fact that the Violencia was the last, and the most important, of the clientelist wars in Colombia. Whether or not this war created conditions for other types of subsequent class struggles by the peasantry is a different issue; as such, it will be raised in the first section of the following chapter.

Agriculture, regional agrarian structures, and peasant sectors in the 1960s

As shown in the previous section, the incidents related to the Violencia extended well into the 1960s. However, given the way in which the conflicts developed, only the first phase of the Violencia can be considered as an actual civil war, with total disruption of the economy and the society. After 1953, the disturbances rapidly receded to clearly circumscribed or peripheral areas, taking the form of banditry and defensive guerrilla warfare that affected only slightly the main centers of economic activity. Conditions thus favored a relatively swift normalization of the economy, so much so that the 1950s and the first half of the 1960s would emerge, paradoxically, as a period of substantial economic growth. This growth was especially visible in the cities, where, as in other Latin American countries, industry was taking advantage of the postwar situation to take a huge leap forward in substituting imported manufactures for direct and intermediate consumption.[65] Table 1.1 provides clear evidence of this process of industrial consolidation. Between 1951 and 1964, a period in which Colombia's population increased from 11.2 to 17.4 million, the four main cities alone – Bogotá, Medellín, Cali, and Barranquilla – came to include a fifth of the country's total population. Personnel employed in industry increased by 69.7 percent, the value of manufactured goods by 130.9 percent, and the participation of manufacture in the Gross Domestic Product (GDP) by 3.7 percent. The changing composition of manufactured imports clearly indicated that industrial expansion was rapidly leading to self-sufficiency in consumption goods and that the substitution of intermediate goods was proceeding rapidly.

The acceleration of industrial growth created serious challenges for Colombia's agriculture. On the one hand, the hard currency provided by agricultural exports, basically coffee, became more essential than ever because of the need to buy industrial machinery and equipment abroad. On the other hand, only rapid expansion and diversification would enable the agricultural sector to supply the raw materials for industry and foodstuffs needed for the urban population. During the early 1950s, it seemed clear that agriculture was lagging. Coffee production remained at the same annual level of 6.0 million sacks.[66] Furthermore, traditional peasant farming was responding slowly to the increasing demand, and the rapid development of mechanized agriculture in some regions was still insufficient to fill the gap. As a result, the country had to supplement its foreign reserves with international loans and to import not only some agricultural raw materials like cotton, oil seeds, and barley but also occasionally maize and beans for direct consumption.[67] However, the situation improved significantly during the second half of the 1950s and the early 1960s. By 1967, coffee production was increasing again, the country had recovered agricultural self-sufficiency and was exporting some of the previously imported products, and the annual growth rate of agricultural output for the period 1950–1967 was estimated at 3.3 percent, that is, slightly over the 3.2 percent annual rate of population growth registered between the 1951 and 1964 censuses.[68] At the beginning of

Table 1.1. *Some indicators of industrial expansion in Colombia, 1951–1964*

	Urbanization		Industry		Manufactured imports (Percentage distribution by type of goods)		
Year	Urban population as percentage of total population	Population in four main cities as percentage of total population	Manpower employed in manufacture (000's)	Value of manufactured commodities (Col. $ millions)[a]	Manufacture as percentage of GDP	Consumer goods	Intermediate goods	Capital goods
1951	38.9	12.8	274.0	2246.8	14.8	21.7	34.7	43.6
1964	52.8	20.6	465.0	5188.2	18.5	6.2	29.7	64.1

[a] Col. $ at constant 1958 prices.

Sources: DANE, *Censo Nacional de Población*, 1951. DANE, *Censo Nacional de Población*, 1964. J.A. Bejarano, "La economía colombiana desde 1950," 1978, p. 17. S. Kalmanovitz, *La Agricultura en Colombia*, Part 1, 1978, p. 135.

the 1970s, then, agriculture was responding successfully to the challenges of industrial consolidation in Colombia. Comparing the annual averages of the early 1950s and late 1960s, Table 1.2 shows that although the growth of manufacturing had reduced the agricultural share of the GDP, total agricultural production had almost doubled, coffee exports had expanded by almost a third, and the increases in new lines of agricultural exports were partially compensating for the downturn in international coffee prices.

One of the most conspicuous elements in the agricultural recovery of the late 1950s and 1960s was the spectacular expansion of large-scale mechanized agriculture. At a time when most discussions and hopes related to the problems of underdevelopment focused on notions of "socioeconomic dualism," "modernization," and the "green revolution," the Colombian experience attracted international attention and was frequently presented as a showcase of success for the developing countries.[69] In general terms, this process seemed to support the theses of the renowned American economist Lauchin Currie, who, after visiting the country as head of a mission of the International Bank for Reconstruction and Development in 1948, had proposed a controversial program for accelerated development under the name "Operation Colombia."[70] In Currie's opinion, the irrational use of labor power and land in agriculture was the main obstacle to economic growth in Colombia. The plains and more fertile areas were used for extensive cattle raising, while most of the labor was being wasted in the inefficient *minifundista* agriculture on the worst soils of the mountains and slopes. The development of a more productive modern agriculture in the plains would create conditions for a massive transfer of population to the cities and, therefore, for an accelerated expansion of industry. Consequently, Operation Colombia included recommendations on policies to stimulate both large-scale mechanized agriculture and some strategic sectors of the urban economy that, like the building industry, offered better prospects for a rapid absorption of masses of new workers.[71]

Many American analysts and Colombian politicians, however, believed that the Violencia had drastically changed the socioeconomic and political conditions in the country. In their opinion, the fact that the trends seemed to confirm Currie's predictions, even without a systematic implementation of an Operation Colombia, was not a blessing but a matter of deep concern. Behind the economic success of agriculture, they saw the specter of a great social and political crisis in the making. Under the influence of President John F. Kennedy's Alliance for Progress policy, which itself was a result of the fears caused by the Cuban Revolution, it was argued that the development of entrepreneurial agriculture was only aggravating the problems of unemployment and low peasant incomes, that industry would not be able to absorb the massive rural emigration, that in the

Table 1.2. The performance of Colombia's agricultural sector, 1950–1969

Annual average	Agriculture as percentage of GDP	Volume of agricultural production (million tons)	Agricultural exports as percentage of total exports	Coffee exports (millions of 60-kg bags)	Value of coffee exports (U.S. $ millions)	Value of agricultural exports other than coffee (U.S. $ millions)	Agricultural foreign trade balance excluding coffee (U.S. $ millions)
1950–1954	36.5	14.3	85.3ᵃ	6.0	417.1	16.8	−12.8
1965–1969	29.9	21.2	75.7	7.9	350.6	61.0	37.9

ᵃAnnual average, 1952–1954.

Source: S. Kalmanovitz, *La Agricultura en Colombia*, Part 1, 1978, pp. 135 and 138–140. R. Junguito et al., *Economia Cafetera Colombiana*, 1980, p. 34. Sociedad de Agricultores de Colombia, *Bases Para una Política Agropecuaria*, 1978, pp. 70–71. Federación de Cafeteros de Colombia, *Boletín Estadístico*, 1950–1965. DANE, *Anuario de Comercio Exterior*, 1965–1969. FAO, *Yearbook of Food and Agricultural Statistics*, 1952–1970.

long run peasant poverty would strangle the expansion of the internal market for industrial goods, and that, given the recent Violencia, all these factors were creating a dangerous social and political situation.[72] As will be seen later, during the late 1950s and early 1960s it was the social and political dangers that particularly worried the Colombian politicians and fueled the controversial debates on agrarian reform. In any case, the crucial point was that the full relevance of the agrarian question was coming to the forefront. Indeed, most of the apprehensions flowed from the perception that an entrepreneurial-landlord path of agrarian evolution, with its consequences and problems, was coming to prevail. To a large extent, this perception was based upon the belief that agrarian capitalism had expanded at the expense of peasant agriculture, a view that was fully shared by some Marxist analysts, who saw in these developments the validation of the "iron laws" of capitalist penetration in agriculture.[73]

The arguments about the destruction of the peasant economy and the overwhelming triumph of agrarian capitalism seemed to be supported by evidence of three major factors or processes: the massive migration from the countryside, the concentration of landed property, and the contrast between the rapid growth of the so-called commercial crops and the poor performance of the traditional ones. With regard to rural migration, the 1964 census indicated that the net population shift to the cities between 1951 and 1964 was about 2.3 million.[74] According to that figure, the 800,000 people displaced by the Violencia accounted for only a third of the total migration. Since the 1964 census also showed that, at a 3.2 percent rate of annual increase, Colombia's population had been the third fastest growing one in Latin America during the 1950s and early 1960s,[75] it seemed reasonable to assume that the scale of migration was an expression of a massive dissolution of peasant society resulting from strong demographic pressure. This assumption was reinforced by the high concentration of landed property in the country: It was because the peasants lacked sufficient land that the demographic pressures forced them to leave the countryside and come to the towns.

The first agricultural census of 1960 clearly showed the extent of land concentration. Taking into account the accepted convention that, in Colombia, considers units smaller than 20 hectares to be peasant units,[76] the census data presented in Table 1.3 indicate that more than 1 million peasant families occupied only 15 percent of the agricultural land, while fewer than 7,000 landowners controlled approximately 40 percent of the total area in estates larger than 500 hectares. Furthermore, the census showed that 36.5 percent of the units smaller than 20 hectares were worked by tenants and sharecroppers on behalf of bigger landowners. In the absence of a similar previous census, it was impossible to evaluate the process of land concentration. Still, and despite the fact that the data

Table 1.3. *Distribution of land in Colombia, by number and size of farms, 1960*

Size of farms (hectares)	Agricultural Census, 1960			
	Number of farms (000's)	Percentage	Area in hectares (000's)	Percentage
Under 4.9	756.6	62.6	1,238.9	4.5
5.0–9.9	169.1	14.0	1,164.7	4.3
10.0–19.9	114.2	9.4	1,572.1	5.7
20.0–49.9	86.8	7.2	2,638.6	9.7
50.0–99.9	39.9	3.3	2,680.4	9.8
100.0–499.9	36.0	3.0	6,990.4	25.6
500.0–999.9	4.1	0.3	2,730.7	10.0
Over 1,000.0	2.7	0.2	8,321.6	30.4
Total	1,209.6	100.0	27,337.8	100.0

Source: DANE, *Censo Nacional Agropecuario*, 1960.

were not strictly comparable, some researchers used the results of a 1954 national agricultural sample of the Department of National Statistics (DANE) as a basis for impressionist appraisals suggesting that land concentration and peasant dissolution had been proceeding rapidly between 1954 and 1960.[77]

Another vital factor was the rapid development of capitalist agriculture and the apparent stagnation of peasant production. The "take-off" of agrarian capitalism had caused impressive changes in some areas of traditional *latifundia*, especially in the fertile plains of the Magdalena and Cauca valleys. Livestock was rapidly removed, paving the way for the cultivation of sugar cane, cotton, rice, soybeans, and other oleaginous crops either by the landowners themselves or by a new breed of entrepreneurs who rented the land and took advantage of special credit schemes provided by the government after the mid-1950s. This change ended the servile relations of production typical of the traditional *haciendas*. Moreover, it increased the need for permanent and seasonal wage laborers and led to increasing capital investments in machinery, new techniques, and their related inputs. The performance of this modern entrepreneurial sector was contrasted to the meager results of the peasant economy by means of a rough classification of the main lines of agricultural production. This classification showed that the big entrepreneurs were getting more than 70 percent of the agricultural credit and that the output of the commercial crops of capitalist agriculture had increased at an average annual rate of

8.2 percent during the 1950s and 1960s, compared with only 1.0 percent for the traditional crops of peasant agriculture.[78]

Still, and despite its undeniable significance, this evidence alone was insufficient to sustain a one-sided argument that the peasants were being crushed by the expansion of agrarian capitalism. Taken together, the 1960 agricultural census and the 1964 population census showed that in the early 1960s the peasantry accounted for more than 80 percent of all agricultural units in the country and for approximately a third of the total Colombian population. Although it was obviously true that the migration reflected substantial ongoing peasant dissolution, this must have occurred mainly at the weakest level, that is, among those peasants with the smallest resources and the least access to land. On the other hand, the concentration of landed property that resulted from peasant extinction and migration was favorable not only to the big landowners but also, as with the effects of the Violencia, to other peasants who could consolidate or improve their position by buying the lands of those who were leaving. In other words, it could be argued that the extinction of some peasants made possible the reconstitution and strengthening of others. This argument was indirectly supported by the fact that the population census of 1964, in contrast to that of 1954, showed not a decrease but even a slight increase in the proportion of the rural population engaged in independent farming and domestic labor.[79] Finally, it was at the level of agricultural production itself that the importance of the peasantry could be best appreciated. Table 1.4 shows that the rough classification of traditional and commercial crops distorted the picture of agricultural specialization in Colombia. The distribution of production according to farm-size categories in the 1960s could be better described not in terms of clear-cut peasant and entrepreneurial types of crops but in terms of a continuum with different degrees of peasant and entrepreneurial predominance in each line of production. Capitalist agriculture seemed to be dominating those crops grown on the plains, where land concentration was higher and topographic conditions were favorable for mechanization. The peasants prevailed on the temperate slopes and cold highlands, where the abrupt relief ruled out the use of machinery and intensive labor was required. Cutting across the varying degrees of specialization by products, and despite the greater increases in predominantly entrepreneurial crops, two crucial figures stood out in the statistics of 1960: The peasantry still accounted for 61.3 percent of the total volume of agricultural production, including 50 percent of coffee, the main export crop of Colombia.

To obtain an unbiased picture of Colombia's countryside during the 1960s, it is necessary to put the pieces of data in their right perspective, analyzing carefully the processes that were taking place both among the peasants and among the owners of extensive landed property. First, the

Table 1.4. *The pattern of agricultural specialization in Colombia, 1960*

16 main crops	Production, 1960 (000 tons)	Distribution of total production according to size of farm[a] Smaller than 20 hectares (%)	Larger than 20 hectares (%)	Ecological setting of crops	Increase (decrease) in production vis-à-vis 1950[b] (%)
Brown traditional sugar	7,125	100.0	—	Temperate slopes	(11.9)
Tobacco	25	81.3	18.7	Temperate slopes	25.0
Potatoes	973	66.4	33.6	Cold highlands	81.5
Wheat	142	59.7	40.3	Cold highlands	39.2
Plantain	1,484	55.9	44.1	All areas	28.6
Yuca	652	52.3	47.7	All areas	(18.6)
Beans	50	50.0	50.0	Cold highlands	72.4
Coffee	480	50.0	50.0	Temperate slopes	42.0
Cacao	14	48.9	51.1	Hot plains	75.0
Maize	932	47.1	52.9	All areas	86.4
Sesame	20	41.8	58.2	Hot plains	81.8
Bananas	557	37.5	62.5	Hot plains	48.9
Barley	106	33.9	66.1	Cold highlands	112.0
Rice	450	17.3	88.7	Hot plains	86.7
Cotton fiber and seed	182	13.0	87.0	Hot plains	766.6
White centrifugal sugar	3,298	—	100.0	Hot plains	117.7
Total	16,490				
Percentage of total	100.0	61.3	38.7		

[a] As estimated by V.M. Moncayo and F. Rojas (see below).

[b] Percentage increase (decrease) = $\dfrac{\text{Production 1960} - \text{Production 1950}}{\text{Production 1950}}$

Sources: S. Kalmanovitz, *La Agricultura en Colombia*, Part I, 1978, pp. 138–140. V.M. Moncayo and F. Rojas, *Producción Campesina y Capitalismo*, 1979, pp. 150–155.

evidence does not seem to support either the argument of a general liquidation of the peasantry or the understanding of the peasant dissolution as an absolute differentiation leading to a clear dichotomy of rural workers and entrepreneurs. In terms of the viability of small-scale agriculture in Colombia's capitalist system, the dissolution of the poorer peasants could be said to be a weeding out of the weaker elements, leaving those who were fit to become the basis of a more stable peasant economy. This tendency was strengthened mainly in the domain of labor-intensive crops grown in the cold and temperate mountain areas, where peasant farming had a number of advantages.

Second, even though agrarian capitalism was leaping forward, its expansion did not totally transform all the previous structures in the plains. Rather, it was a selective process based upon regional enclaves that developed where conditions were particularly suitable for capital investment in mechanized lines of production. Side by side with such enclaves, there were vast areas where the old *haciendas* still prevailed during the 1960s, with their traditional systems of cattle raising and servile subjection of various peasant groups.

It would therefore be equally wrong to conclude that the peasant economy was being completely destroyed, that the development of agrarian capitalism was massive, or that the latter was taking place at the expense of the former. Given the types of access to the means of production, agriculture was evolving along both paths, encouraging a double specialization in space and in type of crops, and causing changes in both the peasantry and the traditional *latifundia*. However, and precisely because everything depended upon a given distribution of land as the means of production, the process as a whole was turning against the peasants, since both the feasibility of small-scale agriculture and the expansion of agrarian capitalism implied the dissolution of much of the peasantry.

This picture shows that the agrarian question in Colombia was at the crossroads during the sixties. The consolidation of industrial capitalism had created an environment in which, for the first time in the history of the nation, the crucial alternative between the peasant and landlord paths of evolution was a pertinent national issue. Still, the recognition of this root of the structural conflict is only a first step, because far from being homogeneous, the opposition of the peasant and landlord roads was expressed in many different ways. In other words, it was a general contradiction that manifested itself in different kinds of antagonism, according to the structures prevailing in different regions. This diversity presupposed a plurality of peasant class sectors, whose circumstances and demands were very different in spite of their shared aspiration for a favorable resolution of the agrarian question. In outlining the scenario of the contradiction between the two paths of agrarian evolution, a more detailed analysis is necessary to clarify the various antagonisms and to identify the class sectors involved. In terms of such structural regionalization, four patterns were dominant in the Colombian countryside.[80]

First, there were the already mentioned areas of peasant economy in the Andean departments: Nariño and Cauca in the south; Antioquia and Caldas in the west; and Cundinamarca, Boyacá, Santander, and North Santander in the east. In these regions, the dominant tendencies were the stabilization of some peasant groups and the dissolution of others who had been reduced to extremely small *minifundia*. In terms of the viability of small-scale agriculture, two sectors could be singled out. One group, the stable peasants, wanted to improve the conditions of reproduction that would strengthen and further improve their situation. The second group were the landless, who required land for their reconstitution as peasants. Since the local structures made it impossible for the landless to obtain land, the demands of the stable peasants were more relevant for the regional processes. Consequently, the most representative claims in these areas had to do with the improvement of prices, marketing systems, access to credit, and adequate provision of other general services.[81]

The colonization areas were a second type of regional structure, located beyond the economic frontier in such places as Caquetá, Putumayo, Ariari (southern Meta), Sarare (Arauca), Urabá (Antioquia), and Middle Magdalena. Here the migration movements that began during the Violencia and persisted as a result of peasant dissolution in the Andes represented an attempt to create new bases for a restoration of the peasant economy. However, the absence of the basic conditions of reproduction defeated most of the colonists. A transient peasant economy was formed, continuously moving and extending the agricultural frontier, leaving behind a concentration process in which new cattle *latifundia* expanded on the freshly cleared lands that the landowners bought from the colonists. In such circumstances, the defense of a peasant path of evolution required not the improvement but the establishment of basic services that could have enabled peasant families to settle permanently on the new lands, thus making their possession truly effective. Therefore, although there were clusters of stable peasants who had managed to establish roots, the majority of colonists in precarious conditions were the ones who embodied the main contradiction on the colonization frontier, because their destiny would determine the future peasant or landlord character of the regional economy. In this sense, the most important demands were those connected with roads, communications, and all the infrastructure that was needed to bring the products to the market, the prices of the pioneering crops, the basic credits, the procedures of land titling, and the introduction of services to support the peasant economy and to make the extremely difficult conditions of life more bearable.[82]

A third type of agrarian framework was the areas of traditional *latifundia*, situated mainly in the plains of the Atlantic Coast (including the departments of Córdoba, Sucre, Bolívar, Atlántico, Cesar, and Magdalena) and in the extensive Eastern Llanos (Casanare and the northern part of Meta). Here a number of processes occurred that, to a certain extent, have to be seen as different stages in the formation of large-scale landed property. In some regions, the *haciendas* were still opening up their own lands. This was achieved through pasture rent, a form of production by which the peasants cleared the forests, used the land for a couple of years in subsistence crops for themselves, and then returned it with artificial pasture for the landlord to introduce his cattle. In other places where all forests had already been cleared, the subordination of peasant sectors continued, either with pasture rent in fallow lands or by means of new types of rent in kind and money. In the more marginal areas, the whole process was just beginning. Landed property was not clearly defined and the landlords were involved in disputes over public lands, forests, draining swamps, river islands, and beaches against both peasant colonists and local people who still maintained forms of natural economy based upon fishing and mobile subsistence agriculture. As will be seen later, there were many different types of situations, but the important point is that, underlying all of them was a basic contradiction focused upon the control of land as the means of production. This antagonism became more acute during the 1960s because the threat of agrarian reform and the development of capitalist agriculture were increasingly throwing into crisis the old patterns of the *haciendas*. In fact, the massive eviction of peasants and the acceleration of landlord enclosures wherever the definition of property was unclear would become clear expressions of the primacy of the conflict over land in the areas of *latifundia*. The landless emerged, therefore, as the main sector of the peasantry, and the possibility of an independent peasant economy clearly depended upon the result of their impending struggle to break the power of the landowners, destroy large-scale property, and establish themselves as free peasants.[83]

The fourth and last type of regional structure was agrarian capitalism. This structure prevailed in the fertile plains of the departments of Valle, Tolima, and Huila and was also beginning to develop in some places on the Atlantic Coast. As already stated, the expansion of these enclaves involved the displacement of the traditional forms of production of the *haciendas*, the investment of capital, the introduction of machinery, and the use of wage labor. To the extent that this process had proletarianized the labor force, the dominant contradiction focused on the new form of capitalist exploitation, making the agricultural workers the most relevant sector in the class conflict. The main demands concerned job security, wages, and working conditions. However, in addition to the relatively recent proletarianization process, there was another problem: the inability of agrarian capitalism to provide permanent and full employment for the labor force. There were therefore disjunctions that, in certain cases, motivated agricultural laborers to try to reconstitute themselves as peasants by gaining direct access to land. This aspiration, which was later clearly manifested in some regional struggles, could be considered regressive from the point of view of capitalist development, but it was seen as progressive in terms of the battle for a peasant path of evolution, because agrarian capitalism was challenged precisely where it had already taken root.[84]

On the basis of these brief outlines, it is possible to delineate a basic scheme of the main regional agrarian structures in Colombia during the 1960s. This scheme is presented in Figure 1.1, including the orientations of the main class sectors from the point of view of an independent peasant economy, the corresponding demands, and the direction taken by these demands. Supplementing this schematic summary, Table 1.5 classifies the Colombian departments according to their predominant types of agrarian structures.

What conclusions can be drawn from this discussion about the potential development of a national peasant movement in Colombia? The first obvious inference is that since the agrarian question had reached a critical point, there was a deep cleavage that provided sufficient grounds for a major challenge by the peasantry. However, the situation was more complex, because the root of the conflict created many different kinds of contradictions involving different types of peasant sectors. Any eventual national peasant movement would therefore have to develop on several fronts simultaneously. This meant that such a movement would have to integrate the grievances and demands of the various peasant sectors, articulating them into a unified and general attempt to force a change in favor of a peasant path of agrarian development.

In the second place, the ramifications of the agrarian conflict make it possible to separate the domains where an eventual national peasant movement would have to take the offensive from those where its actions would have to be essentially defensive. It must be remembered that, since access to land and to favorable conditions of reproduction are the cornerstones of any free peasant economy, there were two different levels of priority from the point of view of peasant demands. In the areas of peasant economy and colonization, where access to land did exist, the main problems had to do with the conditions of reproduction that would make possible the defense of such access, stabilizing the colonists and consolidating the already stable peasants. On the other hand, the landless peasants, and in some cases the rural wage laborers as well, had to gain access to the land itself if they were to establish themselves as free peasants. This could

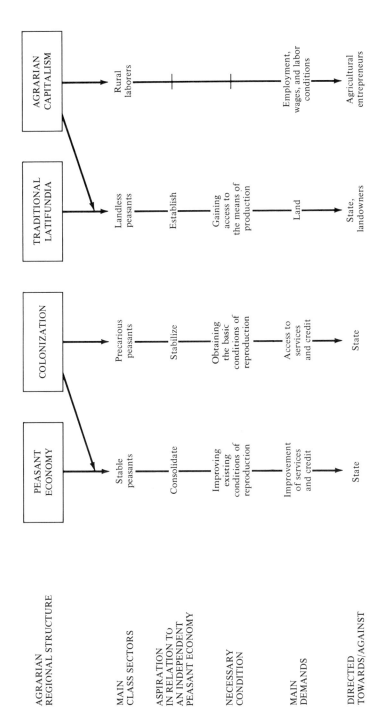

Figure 1.1. Agrarian regional structures, main class sectors and their demands.

AGRARIAN REGIONAL STRUCTURE	PEASANT ECONOMY	COLONIZATION	TRADITIONAL LATIFUNDIA	AGRARIAN CAPITALISM
MAIN CLASS SECTORS	Stable peasants	Precarious peasants	Landless peasants	Rural laborers
ASPIRATION IN RELATION TO AN INDEPENDENT PEASANT ECONOMY	Consolidate	Stabilize	Establish	
NECESSARY CONDITION	Improving existing conditions of reproduction	Obtaining the basic conditions of reproduction	Gaining access to the means of production	Employment, wages, and labor conditions
MAIN DEMANDS	Improvement of services and credit	Access to services and credit	Land	
DIRECTED TOWARDS/AGAINST	State	State	State, landowners	Agricultural entrepreneurs

Table 1.5. *Classification of the Colombian departments according to their prevailing agrarian structures in the 1960s*

Peasant economy	Colonization	Traditional latifundia	Agrarian capitalism
Antioquia	Arauca	Atlántico	Huila
Boyacá	Caquetá	Bolívar	Tolima
Caldas	Chocó	Casanare	Valle del Cauca
Cauca	Meta (south)	Cesar	
Cundinamarca	Putumayo	Córdoba	
Nariño	Territories of	Guajira	
North Santander	Amazonas	Magdalena	
Quindío		Meta (north)	
Risaralda		Sucre	
Santander			

Source: See note 80 to Chapter 1.

happen only by posing a direct challenge to the existing distribution of landed property in the areas of *latifundia* and agrarian capitalism.

Third, knowing the distinct types of antagonism in the countryside makes it possible to anticipate the relative intensity of future conflicts in each case. Here, it has to be remembered that while the defensive line of large-scale property was designed to preserve the monopoly over land in areas of *latifundia* and agrarian capitalism, there were also processes of land concentration that, especially in the colonization areas, were developing into full-blown bridgeheads of the landlord path in peasant territory. There were situations, then, in which the defensive and offensive spaces of both peasants and landowners overlapped. This created a greater potential for conflict in the areas of *latifundia* and colonization, since these were precisely the places where the peasant–landlord polarization was still undefined. Finally, all these elements lead to the identification of the three main battlefronts of any prospective national peasant movement: the struggle for land, the defense of the colonists, and the protection of the already established peasant economy. Since such a broad peasant movement could not remain indifferent to the problems of other related class sectors and groups such as the wage laborers and the Indian communities, there were a number of other more specific dimensions of action that could also become relevant during a general mobilization in the countryside.

At this point, a different issue begins to take shape. No doubt, structural analysis and the consideration of broad socioeconomic changes have been useful in clarifying the contradictions that created potential unrest and space for an eventual peasant movement in Colombia. But structural contradictions alone cannot wholly explain their actual expression in collective action and social conflict. The historical experience of Latin America, where centuries of blatant exploitation produced only a handful of significant peasant rebellions or agrarian movements,[85] clearly shows that, however necessary, objective sources of conflict alone are not sufficient to create such a conflict at the sociopolitical level. Other factors, including political and ideological ones, must exist for a peasant movement to arise. Moreover, special conditions are required for a peasant mobilization to transcend local or regional levels and to develop a nationwide appeal with large-scale repercussions. Consequently, to assess the real potential for a peasant movement in Colombia during the 1960s, it is necessary to examine these further aspects of the problem, relating them to the concrete expressions of peasant unrest and organization that were developing at the time.

2

Reformism and the beginnings of the peasant movement

The political dimension of the agrarian question in Colombia during the 1960s was dominated by the reformist policies of the National Front. In terms of both purported goals and ideological justification, the political, social, and economic components of the reformist approach usually appear to be tightly integrated.[1] However, when the question is considered in concrete terms, it is always possible to distinguish shades of emphasis in a particular reformist policy. From this point of view, and focusing upon the underlying motivations, two different phases of agrarian reformism under the National Front can be discerned. During the administrations of Alberto Lleras Camargo (1958–1962) and Guillermo León Valencia (1962–1966), the emphasis was clearly upon political imperatives: the movement toward limited agrarian reform was seen as necessary to reestablish peace and rebuild the power of the dominant classes after the civil war. Later, under the government of Carlos Lleras Restrepo (1966–1970), the emphasis was shifted toward the social and economic aspects of reform. As will be seen in the second and third sections of this chapter, peasant support was sought as part of an attempt to carry out a more substantial agrarian reform that would help to overcome the limitations of the existing model of capitalist accumulation.

Agrarian reform and the political outlook for a peasant movement

To understand why political motives predominated during the first phase of agrarian reform, it is necessary to remember the consequences of the civil war in the countryside. The ones most worrying for the architects of the National Front were the erosion of the power of the traditional parties and the class conflict inherent in the peasant struggles in some places toward the end of the Violencia. The fear of a possible expansion of the strongholds of peasant self-defense commanded by the Communists and the need to restore political control over the rural population both indicated that concessions to the peasantry were crucial. The commitment to agrarian reform was, therefore, one of the key components of the proposed programs designed to restore harmony among the social classes

34

under the hegemony of the same classes that had been responsible for the civil war.[2] Added to these internal factors was the great external pressure caused by the new hemispheric policy that the United States was trying to impose under the banner of the Alliance for Progress. The U.S. government was pressing the dominant classes of the Latin American countries to adopt agrarian reforms similar to those carried out in Eastern Europe and the Balkans as a *cordon sanitaire* against the Russian Revolution. Such reforms, it was argued, would prevent more revolutionary developments along Cuban lines.[3] Thus, political pressures from different sources largely overshadowed the social and economic ingredients of reformism. It is true that, as shown in the second section of Chapter 1, the arguments for reform stressed the fact that strengthening the peasantry would enlarge the internal market and curb any possible excesses of the migratory process. However, even this speculation was subordinated to the need for "class harmony," because those who argued in this direction were eager to point out that a more egalitarian rural structure would stabilize the political system.[4] On the other hand, the question of increasing agricultural output was only a secondary justification for agrarian reform. This was so not only because agriculture seemed to be responding successfully to the needs of industrial development, but also because agrarian capitalism enjoyed the full support of a state that, in spite of its reformist rhetoric, assisted the big landowners and rural entrepreneurs with fiscal incentives and special programs of credit and technological development.[5]

The approval of Law 135 of 1961, the Agrarian Social Reform Law, came as proof that a broad political consensus had been reached among the dominant classes. When the law was submitted to a Congress completely controlled by Liberals and Conservatives, only the most doctrinaire Conservatives opposed it. The law was the result of a long bargaining process during which the reluctant landowning class succeeded in softening the criteria for expropriation and securing indemnification procedures with acceptable terms of payment for the land. In addition to land redistribution, the agrarian reform law had several other interrelated objectives: reconstruction of the peasantry in *minifundia* areas, support of colonization movements, improvement of productivity by means of technical assistance, increasing incomes through the promotion of peasant cooperatives and marketing programs, raising standards of living by providing better services, and so on.[6] However, these ambitious goals could not hide the fact that agrarian reform was conceived as a social palliative rather than as a transformation of the rural economy.

Throughout its initial period under the administration of President Guillermo León Valencia, the Colombian Institute of Agrarian Reform (INCORA) worked almost exclusively to treat the problems caused by the Violencia. A number of regional projects of land acquisition and redistribution were started in areas that had been affected by the war and had a high potential for conflict over land in the departments of Tolima, Huila, Cundinamarca, Antioquia, Santander, and North Santander. INCORA also took over from the official rural bank, the Caja Agraria, the job of assisting a few thousand displaced families who were now trying to resettle in colonization fronts of Caquetá, Ariari in Meta, and Sarare in Arauca.

By contrast, very little was done in the areas of *latifundia*, where the major redistribution effort should theoretically have taken place. With the exception of the Eastern Llanos, these areas had been largely spared by the Violencia. As a result, INCORA's action was restricted to certain regions where serious land conflicts had actually developed. As will be shown, these regions included the Lower Sinú area in Córdoba, the dried-up swamps of Atlántico, the banana zone in Magdalena, the Llanos of Casanare, and the oil fields area of Middle Magdalena. INCORA's intervention in these cases, coupled with its inactivity in the other places where there were still no signs of open conflict, confirmed the fact that INCORA was acting more as a "fire fighter" than as an active agent in the general abolition of *latifundia*.[7] What is more, it created an important precedent for the future, because the peasantry learned from the very beginning that direct action was the only way to begin the institutional process of agrarian reform.

By the mid-1960s, then, it seemed clear that agrarian reform would not involve serious structural change without a major challenge by the peasants themselves. It is therefore pertinent to ask, what were the prospects for such a challenge from below, that is, for the development of a social movement that would articulate the demands of the peasantry as a class? In considering this question, the social and political conditions after the Violencia should be examined with reference to four main factors that, according to the literature on the subject, are usually associated with the emergence of a peasant movement: increased class conflicts in the countryside, the development of organizational links that unite the peasants, a strong legitimation for contentious attitudes, and the existence of allies who support and promote peasant mobilization.[8]

With regard to the intensity of class antagonisms in the countryside, the earlier discussion on the Violencia has highlighted its political determination. The rural population had been divided along party lines and, on the bases of their traditional loyalties, the peasants had fought against each other in support of the contending factions of the dominant classes. In the Violencia, class conflict was marked by its late development, heterogeneity, and marginality. The Communists and some radical Liberals had attempted to turn the war into a class confrontation, but these attempts were thwarted by the Liberal–Conservative political agreement that ended the conflict. It would be wrong to assume that after the war class contradictions had been uniformly aggravated throughout the country. Although in some areas the Violencia created a strong potential for confrontation between peasants and landowners, in other places the underlying conflicts had been resolved in favor of either side. Furthermore, there were regions in which the antagonisms simply withered away as a result of massive migration, which, in turn, led to the development of new contradictions in colonization areas where the refugees occupied unused land which was claimed by absentee landowners. Here again one encounters the multidirectional nature of the effects of the Violencia, not only because the civil war had mixed consequences in terms of establishing the conditions for further interclass conflict but also because intraclass confrontations had played such an important role in the immediate past. Indeed, the years of factional killing, retaliation, and revenge had left deep resentments among the peasants themselves, so that even though class contradictions had been aggravated in some cases, these effects were largely overshadowed by the erosion of the bases for peasant class solidarity.

As for the organizational factor, one of the most conspicuous signs of the weakness of the peasantry as a class was the disappearance of most of the peasant associations that had been forming at the grass-roots level since the 1920s and 1930s. The Ministry of Labor estimated that, out of 567 registered peasant leagues and syndicates, only 89 were still active in 1965.[9] Since more than half of these active groups belonged to the Atlantic Coast, an area that had been only marginally touched by the Violencia, it seemed clear that the civil war had had a devastating effect upon the existing elements of peasant organization. The Communist Party had managed to retain control over some of the old peasant leagues of Cundinamarca, and in the more marginal parts of the central area of the country, its mobile guerrillas were still resisting the army after the destruction of their "independent republics." Although this activity hardly represented a serious challenge, the church and the Conservatives launched a crusade to counteract the Communist influence by means of the National Agrarian Federation (FANAL), a rural branch of the already mentioned trade-union central UTC. FANAL proclaimed its adherence to the social doctrines of the church and defined its goals in terms of reformist principles. In the villages, it collected funds for mutual help and trained local militias for civil defense against bandits and guerrillas. Raising petitions for agrarian reform but being careful to moderate the expression of class demands at the grass-roots level, FANAL claimed that it had organized more than 200 peasant syndicates in different parts of the country during the 1960s.[10] However, the extent of FANAL's influence was clearly restricted to a few scattered areas, and given its partisan identification, it seemed highly unlikely that the organization would develop a broad national appeal as a peasant movement.

In fact, the only massive organizational drive at the grass-roots level after the Violencia was undertaken by the government itself. One of the first laws passed under the National Front (Law 14 of 1958) included provisions for the creation of committees of Acción Comunal, neighborhood associations that would contribute to "pacification" by trying to enroll all members of the rural and urban communities in local activities such as construction and repair of schools and roads, mutual help, recreation, and so on. By vertically integrating all sectors of the population around "shared communal concerns," Acción Comunal was opposed in principle to horizontal class associations. Consequently, the committees functioned from the start as paternalist tools of Liberal and Conservative *gamonales* who supplied or obtained the funds for their activities.[11] The fact that almost 9,000 committees had been formed by 1966[12] confirmed the centrality of Acción Comunal as a mechanism for the renewed hegemony of the dominant classes after the civil war.

As for ideological legitimation, it should be noted that in the 1960s some authors speculated that the Violencia had created conditions for widespread popular distrust of the government and the traditional parties.[13] This argument was, again, only partially true. Rejection of the traditional politics predominated in places where the violence had become a class struggle and in colonization areas where the refugees of the Violencia were trying to resettle. But little change occurred in the regions that had been spared by the war and, in retrospect, in the areas of more intense bipartisan conflict; the traditional loyalties seemed, if anything, to have been further strengthened by the Violencia. On the other hand, the readiness to lay down arms indicated that there was a deep popular desire for the reestablishment of peace, which must have enabled the Liberal and Conservative parties to recover at least part of their lost ideological ground when they presented themselves as peacemakers with the National Front agreement. Moreover, the agrarian reform and Acción Comunal initiatives showed that the National Front was trying to strengthen the bases for the "relegitimation" of the ruling classes by anticipating the demands of the subordinate classes and providing safe channels that would guarantee their continued control over the expression of these demands. Since ideological legitimation was being monopolized from above, popular grievances could hardly be expressed by the opposition. In the name of peace, it proved all too easy for the National Front to label all attempts of horizontal class association "antisocial banditry" or "Communist subversion" that were only prolonging the agony of a useless war.

Finally, after the Violencia, there were no serious potential allies for an eventual challenge by the peasantry as a class. In the early 1960s, all the fractions of the dominant classes solidly supported the National Front. The trade-union movement had split into the pro-Liberal CTC, the pro-Conservative UTC, and the pro-Communist Confederation of Syndicates of Colombian Workers (CSTC). Thus, being itself fragmented and generally subjected to the political control of the traditional parties, the working class was unable to provide alternatives for a concerted opposition.[14] Furthermore, none of the political forces opposing the National Front during the early 1960s managed to develop strong bases of support among the peasants. The National Liberation Army (ELN), a guerrilla movement created in 1964 by students who tried to emulate the Cuban revolutionary experience, was never able to expand its activities beyond its original *foco* in the Middle Magdalena area.[15] The old Communist guerrilla groups, which in 1966 were reorganized as the Revolutionary Armed Forces of Colombia (FARC), also kept a very low profile of defensive activity limited to their original region of influence.[16] The failure of the leftist guerrillas clearly indicated that the peasants were in no mood to respond to revolutionary calls for what they regarded as a continuation of violence. As for other nonviolent appeals from the opposition, the main one was that of the Revolutionary Liberal Movement (MRL), a faction of the Liberal Party that had originally rejected the National Front and proposed a more radical agrarian reform. Although the peasant electoral response seemed to be positive in areas of traditional Liberal influence, the MRL collapsed when its main leader, Alfonso López Michelsen, reentered the mainstream of the Liberal Party in the mid-1960s.[17]

To sum up, then, it can be argued that although the Violencia had created some favorable conditions for an eventual peasant challenge, it had also erected formidable barriers that precluded that such a challenge would follow as a direct continuation of the civil war. In addition to the preventive measures of the dominant classes, the main obstacles were the erosion of solidarity at the grass-roots level, the organizational weakness and isolation of the peasantry as a class, and the absence of legitimation to sustain contentious attitudes after the bloodshed. Yet, as the period of the Violencia was beginning to fade, both the socioeconomic structural changes described in the previous section and the political realities of the National Front started to shape a completely new situation during the 1960s. For one thing, the obvious deterioration of the situation of large sections of the peasantry and the government's policy of agrarian reform provided a strong legitimation for the peasants' case. This legitimation created more favorable conditions for the articulation of peasant demands through organizations at the grass-roots level, which, in turn, led to the development of many local and regional conflicts over land. All these conflicts expressed the centrality of agrarian reform in the redefinition of the cleavages in the countryside, and most of them developed in areas that had been spared or only slightly affected by the civil war. Since these peasant battles of the 1960s underlined the changing agrarian conditions and were the precedent for the full-blown land struggles of the 1970s, it is worthwhile to take a closer look at their development.

The best-known conflict of the 1960s was the one that affected the southern half of the department of Atlántico and the adjacent municipalities of Bolívar and Magdalena. Originally, the area had been covered by forests and by the lakes and swamps formed by the lower course of the River Magdalena, but since the turn of the century the dry lands had been gradually occupied by cattle *haciendas*. After obtaining their titles, the landowners had subjected the local population to the pasture-rent system, in which the peasant tenants slashed and burnt the forests, used the land for subsistence crops, and returned it with already sown artificial pasture. The landowners introduced their cattle and assigned new portions of the forests to the tenants, so that the process was continuously repeated in a two-year cycle. Throughout the first half of the twentieth century, pasture-rent was the dominant form of production all over the Atlantic Coast, making possible the opening up of lands and the establishment of cattle *latifundia*. Although in southern Atlántico most of the virgin forests had already been cleared by the 1930s and 1940s, the pasture-rent system was maintained in the secondary forest that grew in the fallow lands within the *haciendas*. The subordinated peasants used to grow transient summer crops when the water receded and the alluvial soils of the banks and swamps could be cultivated. But because of the lack of water in the dry lands, the landowners also moved their cattle toward the lakes during the summer. Thus, disputes over the use of alluvial terrain became a source of continuous friction between peasants, who regarded these terrains as public lands, and landowners, who claimed them as their property. Local skirmishes developed into generalized unrest after the construction of the ditches and canals of Calamar in the mid-1950s, when marshes and lakes began to drain and the landowners proceeded to extend their fences. Spontaneous land invasions were followed by the formation of peasant leagues organized to defend their possession of the new public lands. With the involvement of FANAL and the help of workers' unions from Barranquilla, the peasant leagues multiplied rapidly in Manatí, Sabanalarga, Suán, Campo de la Cruz, Repelón, Candelaria, Calamar, and other municipalities. The land struggles continued into the 1960s amid recurrent invasions, evictions, demonstrations, and imprisonments. The turning point came in 1964, when the Valencia administration declared all the dried-up areas to be public lands. INCORA rushed in and the peasant leagues increased their pressure to obtain the titles that would legalize their de facto occupation of the land. By the late 1960s, this battle had been largely won by the peasants. INCORA had issued most of the titles and a new structure of small and middle peasants had emerged, which distinguished the municipalities of southern Atlántico and the neighboring areas from the prevailing landscape of *latifundia* in the rest of the Atlantic Coast. There were still some pending cases of disputed terrain, but the main concerns of the peasants now had to do with new issues such as the regulation of the use of water in the irrigation districts and the problems related to the inadequacy of INCORA's programs of credit and agricultural extension.[18]

A second well-known struggle developed in the region of the Lower Sinú in the department of Córdoba. This was also an area of relatively recent formation of *haciendas*, but there was a concentration of free peasantry occupying a neck of land that the River Sinú had been forming over the years in the Cispatá Bay. In the mid-1950s the river suddenly changed its course, gaining a straight outlet to the sea through Tinajones. The peasants' land began to be washed away by the sea and had to be abandoned. Many families emigrated to the Upper Sinú area, to Urabá, and even to Venezuela, but a few hundred peasants decided to squat in neighboring estates of the municipalities of San Bernardo del Viento and Lorica. The main struggles developed in Tinajones and Cicará, *haciendas* that belonged to the regionally powerful landowners Cabrera and Martínez. Although the landowners tried to expel the squatters with the assistance of the local authorities, the peasants managed to resist. With the organization of some syndicates by FANAL in 1960, the conflict intensified, attracting the attention of the national press and, eventually, the intervention of INCORA. In 1963, the Institute bought 17,000 hectares and began a program of settlements and irrigation works in La Doctrina. However, only 200 families gained access to land under the program. As a result, the problem remained largely unsolved and the pattern of continuing evictions and new invasions was still going on toward the end of the 1960s.[19]

Another unsolved conflict, also on the Atlantic coastline, was that of the possessions of the Frutera de Sevilla Company (a subsidiary of the United Fruit Company) in the banana zone of the department of Magdalena. The company occupied an area of 50,000 hectares between the Fundación and Córdoba rivers. There was an irrigation district and a railway network for internal transportation. Seeking greater productivity and lower wages, the Frutera Company had decided to move to Urabá, abandoning the plantation but trying to keep control over the banana marketing process. Part of the land was sold to big entrepreneurs who had already been exploiting the plantations under tenancy contracts. Another part was donated to INCORA for redistribution among hundreds of peasants who had also been working for the company as small share-

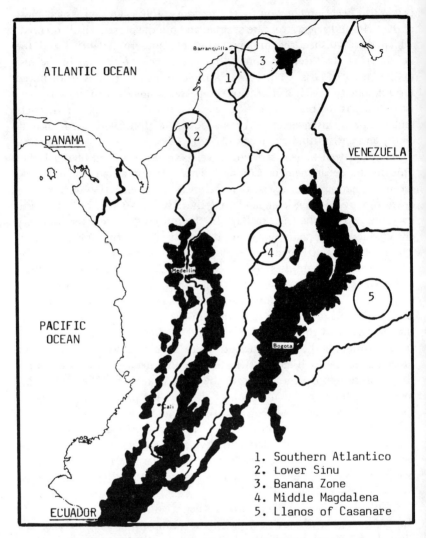

ATLANTIC OCEAN

PANAMA

VENEZUELA

PACIFIC
OCEAN

ECUADOR

1. Southern Atlantico
2. Lower Sinu
3. Banana Zone
4. Middle Magdalena
5. Llanos of Casanare

Map 2. Main areas of land struggle during the 1960s.

croppers. However, when the company finally left in 1964, the situation
was almost chaotic. The original titles were unclear, and there was great
confusion about the demarcation lines between the tracts of land that had
been sold and those that had been donated. A dispute developed, including
not only the entrepreneurs and the peasant sharecroppers but also the
former wage laborers of the Frutera Company who now wished to settle
on the land and obtain a share of the plantations. In spite of INCORA's
intervention in the arbitration and adjudication processes, the conflict es-

calated and led to invasions, evictions, and repression. As a result, the banana zone remained one of the main focal points of rural unrest in the countryside.[20]

A little-known but highly significant fourth regional battle was waged by the colonists of the Middle Magdalena against the Shell Condor Oil Company. In the 1930s, all the area that surrounds what is today the thriving oil center of Barrancabermeja was covered by primeval forests. The sole economic activity was the provision of kindling wood for the steamships that carried commercial traffic along the river, an activity undertaken by small colonists who supplemented their livelihood with occasional fishing and transient crops. In 1937 the Shell Company received a huge land concession from the government and began to drill for oil, ousting the woodcutters and establishing a kind of sovereign state of its own. In the early 1950s the company expanded the oil fields, buying additional land from absentee landowners and pushing out a large number of colonists who were trying to resettle after fleeing from the Violencia in the highlands. By the end of the 1950s and the early 1960s, conflict over these lands had increased because, in spite of its rapid development, the oil industry could not absorb the continuous inflow of migrants. With the support of the oil workers' unions, many of those who failed to become workers in Barrancabermeja began to invade the possessions of the company in order to survive by tilling the land. Shell Condor organized a force of private guards to destroy the crops and evict the squatters, but the peasants gradually managed to take part of the land. The climax came in 1967, when a massive invasion took place following the refusal of the Lleras Restrepo administration to renew the concession to the company. The State Oil Enterprise ECOPETROL took over the exploitation of the wells, and special arrangements were made by INCORA to distribute the land among the colonists. As a result of this success, the peasants obtained some 160,000 hectares in the municipalities of Yondó, Campo Casabe, El Tigre, San Luis Beltrán, and Barrancabermeja.[21]

Perhaps the least known of the great conflicts for land in the 1960s was that of the Eastern Llanos of Casanare. With more than 4 million hectares of natural pasture, this area was until the late 1950s an almost perfect feudal stronghold. There were no fences, and 200 landowners controlled the region with enormous herds of cattle. The "herd economy" had defined a particular pattern of settlement, absorbing a gradual immigration from the Boyacá highlands and creating the *llanero* as a distinct social type. Only a few had permanent work in herding, and the typical *llaneros* were more peasants than cowboys. They worked for the landlords doing seasonal herding jobs – rounding up the cattle, marking the calves, counting and selecting, and so on. The rest of the time they took part with their families in subsistence agriculture, fishing, and hunting. With the permission of the herd owners, all these activities were undertaken along the river banks, which were the only places where forests grew amid the monotonous grasslands. In this situation of total peasant dependency, the landlords enjoyed absolute political power. During the Violencia, the Eastern Llanos had been the main area of operations for the Liberal guerrillas that, with the support of both peasants and landowners, resisted the Conservative government and the army. This factional solidarity began to crack only toward the end of the civil war, when the landowners started to refuse to supply the cattle that were needed to maintain the guerrillas. There were many squabbles about this issue, and the landlords' prestige was further damaged when they recommended laying down arms and accepting the amnesty offer of the military government. The fact that the peasants lost much of their respect for the landlords would have an important ideological influence in the land struggles of the 1960s. However, the main cause of these struggles was a differentiation process by which some peasants had established themselves as owners of small herds. These peasants rarely had more than ten animals, and they were dependent upon the permission and help of the landlords. After the passage of the Agrarian Reform Law of 1961, the established peasants learned that most of the Eastern Llanos was public land, and immediately began to apply for titles. The landlords reacted by trying to expel them but, in the meantime, most of the dependent peasants were following suit in the rush for titles, so that landlord evictions and peasant resistance became widespread. The conflict developed across the central areas of Yopal, Nunchía, and Aguazul, and later extended to the more remote municipalities of Pore, Mane, and Trinidad. Camilo Torres, who was later to become a Latin American symbol as a revolutionary priest, spent a few months in the area. With the assistance of some militants of the student movement, he organized a regional peasant organization, the Association for Integral Agricultural Development (ADAGRI). From its headquarters in Yopal, ADAGRI played a key role in the struggles, making the peasants aware of their rights, providing legal advice, and supplying inspiration and ideas for direct actions related to occupation of the land. After 1965 the peasants achieved great successes in spite of increasing landlord repression. Hamlets and small villages were sprouting up in the previously uninhabited prairies and, by 1970, most of the peasants had gained access to land of their own in Casanare.[22]

In addition to the struggles that affected entire regions, there were many other more local land disputes and demands. Their causes were often similar to those already reviewed. Disputes over alluvial banks and swamps, for example, were endemic in many places of Córdoba during the 1960s.[23] Between 1963 and 1968 there were numerous invasions, evictions, and claims for INCORA intervention in marginal areas of

Sumapaz in Cundinamarca, Puerto Berrío in Antioquia, Cumaral and Puerto López in Meta, and the municipalities of Codazzi, Tamalameque, Gloria, and Pailitas in Cesar.[24] In most of these cases, the problems were related to the status of property on public or idle land that was claimed by both colonists and absentee landowners. In other cases, they were the result of more direct pressure for land redistribution. This pressure came from two groups. One group consisted of tenants and sharecroppers, who began to resist landlord enclosures and demanded the breakup of *haciendas* in temperate and cold areas. The most conspicuous examples were the local disturbances of Quinchía in Risaralda, Bomboná and Buesaco in Nariño, Belalcázar in Caldas, Córdoba in Quindío, Girón and San Vicente in Santander, Fusagasugá and Arbeláez in Cundinamarca, and Fredonia in Antioquia.[25] The second group was the agricultural laborers, who also started to claim access to land in places where capitalist agriculture was expanding. After the Agrarian Reform Law of 1961 and until 1968, rural workers took part in a number of land invasions and incidents in such places as Roldanillo in Valle, Aipe in Huila, Armero in Tolima, and the municipalities of Corinto, Tejada, Miranda, and Santander de Quilichao in the sugar estates of northern Cauca.[26]

Having considered the conflicts of the 1960s, we can draw several conclusions about the developing struggle over land. First, the increasing number of conflicts and the regional scope of some of them were indicative not only of the breadth and depth of the existing contradictions, but also of the disposition of the landless peasants to translate their demands into direct action against the landowners and the authorities. Second, except for the eviction of tenants and sharecroppers in the areas of cattle *latifundia* – a process that began in earnest only after 1968 – all the dimensions of the conflict over land had been clear since the mid-1960s. Disputes over public or idle lands were common in marginal regions, land concentration was challenged in many areas of cattle *latifundia*, the subordinated peasants of the highlands demanded the splitting up of traditional *haciendas*, and even some groups of agricultural workers were pressing for land in the more developed inner valleys. Third, the struggles of the 1960s revealed that significant elements of organization were being developed at the local and regional levels. Peasant groups, leagues, and syndicates were multiplying, either spontaneously out of the conflicts themselves or because of the involvement of external factors like FANAL, urban workers' trade unions, and friendly groups of students and intellectuals. Finally, it should be stressed that some of the battles led to remarkable peasant victories and that, all in all, the land struggles of the 1960s helped the peasants to learn their own strength and the possibilities of autonomous action.

Less contentious but also increasingly visible was the activity of numerous groups that were sprouting up in the areas of peasant economy and colonization. Encouraged by the promises of agrarian reform regarding the improvement of the situation of the *minifundistas*, many new spontaneous associations, Acción Comunal committees, and FANAL syndicates started to raise local demands in different areas of Santander, Cundinamarca, Antioquia, Caldas, and Nariño. Most of these demands were for credit, irrigation systems, marketing programs, and other services.[27] Similar organizational processes at the grass-roots level were noticeable in the colonization areas, especially in Caquetá, Ariari, Sarare, and Putumayo, where INCORA had pledged to support the colonists by increasing services, constructing roads and schools, and so on.[28] In all these regions, where the memories of the Violencia were very much alive, the demands were made peacefully, mainly in the form of respectful petitions signed by neighbors and submitted to the proper authorities or state agencies. However, the open expression of demands and the organizational beginnings implied, by themselves, a significant departure from the tense quietness that had followed the civil war. To a large extent, this change showed that during the second half of the 1960s peasant discontent was not restricted to the areas of *latifundia*, but was also extending to the other potential battlefronts involved in the resolution of the agrarian question.

Taken together, the factors discussed in this section and in the second part of the previous chapter seem to support the argument that by the end of the 1960s a favorable situation was being created for the development of a peasant movement in Colombia. At the structural level, industrial consolidation and the Violencia itself had helped to create a broad national arena for the expression of the different underlying agrarian contradictions. Politically and ideologically, the fact that agrarian reform emerged at the center of this arena was rapidly changing the adverse legacy of the civil war and encouraging organizational initiatives and belligerent attitudes among the peasants, especially in the struggle for land. Nevertheless, much more was needed to create a movement that would articulate the peasants' grievances on a national scale: Class solidarity among the peasants had to be strengthened, organizational bridges were necessary to unite the various peasant groups, a source of legitimation was required to sustain a strong challenge after the Violencia and, above all, the peasantry needed allies. Indeed, taking into account the special difficulties of the peasants in developing their own national organizations, and following the consensus of researchers on peasant political participation, the main clues to the formation of national movements lie in the alliances between the peasantry and other classes or groups that define their own social projects and, in doing so, may find common interests with the peasants and help their mobilization.[29] In the Colombian case, perhaps a national peasant movement would never have emerged without the politics of alliances of some sectors of the bourgeoisie that, during the Lleras Restrepo administration, supported a more resolute approach to agrarian reformism and endorsed an initiative aimed at organizing the peasantry by the state itself.

The reformist thrust of Lleras Restrepo

While no serious agrarian reform was being implemented, the Colombian economy as a whole had entered a deep recession by the mid-1960s. Import substitution, which had been the backbone of industrial development, was clearly reaching its limit. The market for consumer goods had been saturated during the 1950s, and industry was now completing the substitution of imported intermediate and capital goods up to the limit of what was possible within the national economy.[30] Moreover, the international prices of coffee had been permanently depressed since the previous decade, so that the problems of insufficient internal demand were aggravated by the lack of foreign reserves that were needed to buy industrial equipment abroad.[31] As a consequence of this double strangulation, the industrial sector began to stagnate. With continuous migration that agrarian reform was not really trying to contain, urban unemployment emerged as the most conspicuous and crucial problem. During the intercensal period of 1951–1964 the urban population had grown at an annual rate of 5.4 percent, but the absorption of new workers by industry went down from a yearly average of 4.3 percent between 1953 and 1963 to less than 2.0 percent in the following years.[32] Unemployment, which had been slowly increasing from 1.2 percent in 1951 to 4.9 percent in 1964, soared to 13.0 percent in the four major cities during 1967.[33] Now the specter of class struggle seemed to be rising over the urban centers, where a mass of unemployed and marginal migrants had become a source of social tension that threatened the precarious equilibrium achieved by the National Front. Capitalizing on the growing discontent and unrest in the cities, General Rojas Pinilla was making an impressive political comeback. In just a few years, his populist movement, the Popular National Alliance (ANAPO), had grown from a faction of the Conservative Party to a significant force that included opposition sectors of the Liberal Party as well.[34] Putting forward a candidate of its own for the 1966 election of a Liberal president, ANAPO gained a remarkable 28.1 percent of the ballot.[35] Most of the votes came from the cities, where popular support for ANAPO was continuously growing. Since he would be able to stand as a conservative candidate, Rojas Pinilla had a good chance to win the next presidential election in 1970.

Again the dominant classes were being challenged by the rise of populism. Resisting Gaitán in the 1940s, they had thrown the country into civil war. To prevent the transformation of the Rojas Pinilla dictatorship into a populist regime during the 1950s, they had agreed to freeze politics within a constitutional coalition between the two traditional parties. Now, in the late 1960s, Rojas Pinilla's populism was returning, this time through the back door of the National Front itself. The progressive Liberal leader Lleras Restrepo, who had become the president after the 1966 election, was the strongest spokesman of the reformists in the Colombian industrial, financial, and commercial circles.[36] For him and his followers, it seemed clear that populism could not be curbed by sheer force or political manipulation. It was necessary to try to overcome the social and economic crisis that, apart from impairing capitalist accumulation, was refueling populism at the political level. Keeping an eye on the rising star of ANAPO, President Lleras Restrepo set his administration to the tune of an aggressive economic policy under the slogan of "National Transformation." Many measures were adopted to tackle the most crucial problems: the structural limitations of the capitalist accumulation process and their main consequence, unemployment. The Constitutional Reform increased state intervention in the economy, giving the executive branch great autonomy in handling taxation, foreign exchange, finances, and credit.[37] The promotion of manufactured exports was considered to be the key to expand the market for national industrial production while at the same time bringing in much needed foreign currency. A Statute of Foreign Exchange was therefore enacted, combining a policy of slow devaluation with favorable credit schemes and fiscal incentives for industrial exporters. New exports were also encouraged by the creation of the Institute for the Promotion of Exports and by the pioneering role of the Colombian government in the formation of the subcontinental economic community, the Andean Pact.[38] Since low wages would be a decisive influence on the competitiveness of Colombian manufactures in the international market, a Labor Reform Act established the foundations for the future coercive exploitation of the labor force, restricting strikes and other activities of the workers' unions.[39] Still, initiatives designed to reactivate industrial expansion were not sufficient, by themselves, to solve the unemployment problem. In the judgment of Lleras Restrepo, "during the coming years urban demand of labour for industries and services will not surpass supply but, on the contrary, the latter will have an excess that will be extremely difficult to absorb . . . in such conditions, whatever contributes to bind the peasant population to the land can be considered as socially and economically useful, even though in some cases it may imply the prolongation of an economy of simple subsistence."[40] Clearly, the new president thought that it was necessary to attack the second root of the problem of urban unemployment: the massive dissolution of the peasantry. Thus, as the urban situation began to be perceived as intolerable, the urgent need to check the migratory tide spurred reform in the countryside.

This time, agrarian reformism could not remain at the level of cosmetic readjustments and blatant demagogic manipulation. It had to achieve social and economic effects that would revitalize the peasantry. Obviously, this redefinition of the reformist approach had political elements. First, it has already been indicated that a paramount political goal was to reinforce the dominant classes' National Front coalition against the populist urban upsurge. Second, Lleras Restrepo saw some cause for concern in the "revolutionary infiltrators" who were trying "to reap the benefits of peasant poverty and ignorance."[41] The ELN and FARC were still operating and a new guerrilla movement, the Maoist Popular Liberation Army (EPL), had appeared in 1967 in the Upper Sinú.[42] Finally, there were many indications that Lleras Restrepo was also interested in "providing himself with a strong electoral base among the peasantry for a second presidential bid" after the end of the National Front in 1974.[43] However, all these political motives appeared to be conditioned by, and therefore subordinated to, the central aims of renewing the expansion of the national economy and keeping the peasants in the countryside. It was only by making substantial socioeconomic improvements that these political objectives could be realized. Lleras Restrepo, who represented an agrarian tradition within the Liberal Party, had himself been the chief protagonist in the process of formulating and passing the Agrarian Reform Law of 1961.[44] Speeding up this reform to meet what he perceived as the most urgent priorities of national capitalism and the dominant classes, therefore, suited his well-known commitment to Latin American reformism and his reputation as a friend of the peasants. Consequently, INCORA's pace of activity was quickened as soon as the new administration began. In the areas of *latifundia*, the existing regional projects were expanded and new ones were started in the coastal departments of Sucre, Magdalena, and Cesar.[45] Moreover, legislation was prepared to introduce compulsory redistribution of land in all the *haciendas* where rent and sharecropping were the pattern of peasant tenancy.

Precisely because it was seriously meant, the renewed thrust for agrarian reformism was resisted by the landowning class. The landowners had coexisted peacefully with a rhetorical reformism that, so far, had not particularly harmed their interests. A pattern had been established over the years, and they were not now in the mood to accept an agrarian reform at their expense, especially when the situation in the countryside did not seem to justify the apprehensions caused by the Cuban Revolution and the national guerrillas. The proposed law on peasant tenants and sharecroppers was strongly objected to in Congress, both by the Conservative

Party and by a sector of the Liberal Party that also represented the land-owners' interests. A number of modifications were introduced until the bill was narrowly passed as Law 1 of 1968, recognizing the rights of tenants and sharecroppers to the land but imposing so many restrictions that its effective application was, at best, dubious.[46] This was in line with the framework provided by Law 135 of 1961. In fact, the legal procedures of land expropriation and acquisition involved embarrassing transactions with the landowners, never-ending bureaucratic dealings, and prohibitive financial costs for the government. Without adequate legal instruments, it was clear that the Lleras Restrepo administration had few chances of accelerating agrarian reform if its efforts were limited to institutional action by the state.

Behind the state stood the National Front, a political agreement that expressed the common interests of the country's dominant classes and groups. Since land redistribution clearly exceeded the limits of these common interests, the reformists had to create external pressures to undermine the position of the landowning class, thus changing the balance of forces within the National Front and creating a more favorable climate for the implementation of their agrarian policy. There was only one social sector from whom such external pressure could come: the peasants themselves. As the agrarian question moved toward the center of the political arena, the peasantry appeared as the natural ally of bourgeois reformism because, as a class, it had a crucial stake in the resolution of that issue. If the peasants could be organized and mobilized on a national scale, it would be possible to force the landowners to compromise on land redistribution in the *latifundia* areas. Further, an organized peasantry would strengthen the resistance of the peasant economy in the regions of *minifundia* and colonization, presenting demands in an orderly manner and increasing the effectiveness of state support. To provide a channel for the expression of peasant grievances and to instigate, to some degree, an open struggle against the landlords seemed to be a sensible alternative for a reformist approach that was blocked by the coalition of the ruling classes.

With these considerations in mind, Lleras Restrepo decided to appeal to the peasantry by a massive participatory project conducted by the state. He had given some hints about his intentions during the electoral campaign, and as soon as he was elected, he set up a special Operational Committee to devise a plan for the association of the *usuarios* (users) of the state agricultural services.[47] The main purposes of the *usuarios* associations would be to promote direct peasant participation in the provision of services and to help implement agrarian reform. The committee had to develop the idea of peasant participation, studying ways in which existing experiences could be used, suggesting the educational steps that had to be undertaken to prepare state officials and future peasant leaders, and indicating what kinds of communication techniques should be tried during the first phase of promotion and organization. The committee included senior executives of official institutions, political figures of both parties, and representatives of the church hierarchy and FANAL.[48] As a result of internal discrepancies, the Operational Committee produced two different proposals, submitting both reports to the president a few days after he took office in August 1966.[49] On the basis of these recommendations, Lleras Restrepo drew up a final version of the policy and issued the Presidential Decree 755 of May 2, 1967. Stressing the need for popular participation in social change and in national affairs generally, the decree ordained the registration of the users of state agricultural services, defining as *usuarios* both the actual and the potential beneficiaries. After the registration process began, the Ministry of Agriculture would conduct a national campaign to establish the local, regional, and national frameworks of the Asociación Nacional de Usuarios Campesinos (ANUC). The functions of ANUC were specified in a long list, in which representation in the official institutions and "collaboration in the massive application of agrarian reform" were the most important items. Finally, the document specified all the services in which the *usuarios* would participate and enumerated the duties that had to be fulfilled by officials to ensure the involvement of the organized peasants.[50] With the enactment of Decree 755, Lleras Restrepo had set the stage for peasant mobilization, using ANUC to spearhead the agrarian project of bourgeois reformism.

Having clarified the main factors that prompted Lleras Restrepo to appeal to the peasantry, other relevant issues should be discussed. The more specific issues have to do with the nature of the reformist initiative: Why did peasant mobilization take the form of a new organization created by the state, and why was it focused on participation in the management of agricultural services? In answering these questions, the alternatives faced by the Lleras Restrepo administration have to be taken into account. If the peasants were to advance their claims and exert effective pressure, they needed an organization that would represent their interest as a class. However, this had to be done without endangering the basic premises of the National Front; that is, in such a way as to minimize the opposition of the ruling coalition and, at the same time, to ensure maximum control over the mobilized peasantry. This could not be done by using the organizations that already existed in the countryside. Strengthening FANAL was out of the question, since it was controlled by the church and the Conservative Party, and any effort in that direction would only play into the hands of the regressive forces that might block reform at a critical moment.[51] The committees of Acción Comunal were based upon the principle of vertical integration of the different rural sectors, and since they reproduced local patterns of clientelist domination, they could not be used to promote the demands of the peasantry as a class.[52] A new organization had to be created, an organization that could bring together the peasants in a trade unionist manner and detach them from the traditional structures of power.[53] But such an organization could not be based upon total peasant autonomy, because an autonomous peasant movement would be difficult for the dominant classes to control. Nor could it respond to an initiative of progressive Liberal Party members, since such a partisan move by the government would be seen as a severe violation of the National Front. Lleras Restrepo squared the circle by establishing a direct corporatist bridge between the peasantry and the state, one that enabled the government to organize the peasants in the name of general national goals that transcended narrow party interests.

The proposal for peasant participation in the administration of services and agrarian reform was tailored to Lleras Restrepo's design. On the one hand, it could be presented as a reformulation of an old idea, one that would not arouse fear and opposition. Since 1946 the Liberal politician had repeatedly advocated the direct involvement of users of agricultural services as a means of curbing the "vices engendered by bureaucracy" and ensuring proper delivery according to the real needs of every region.[54] During the enactment of Law 135 in 1961, Lleras Restrepo had managed to introduce a vague provision about the desirability of peasant participation in agrarian reform.[55] In fact, during the electoral campaign, he and his collaborators had been outspoken in their criticism of the meager results of land redistribution until 1966, considering them as unequivocal proof that "without the peasants themselves as subjects and agents, agrarian reform would remain unfulfilled."[56] On the other hand, popular participation was an unquestionably democratic idea that provided a powerful legitimation for the project. Since the Punta del Este Conference in 1961, and as part of its Alliance for Progress policy, the United States had been encouraging "popular participation in national programs of social and economic development" in Latin America.[57] This fact strengthened the case for peasant participation, a case that enjoyed such overwhelming support by the social sciences and the philosophy of democracy that it was almost impossible to raise any ideological objection to it.

Nonetheless, the real problem was political, not ideological. Ideological legitimation could make the opposition of the landowners more difficult and embarrassing, but it would not remove it. That was the reason why Lleras Restrepo created ANUC by presidential decree rather than through a regular legislative process whose outcome would have been uncertain given the landowners' influence in Congress.[58] In the same way, the offer of direct peasant involvement in the management of agricultural services should not be considered merely as an attempt to achieve an ideal form of popular participation; it was primarily a way to crystallize the political presence of the peasants that was needed for a more ambitious agrarian reform in the future. As Mario Suárez Melo, the coordinator of ANUC's promotion campaign, admitted in retrospect, "our challenge was the creation of a massive organization and we had to find a factor that would make possible the association of the peasantry . . . that stimulus was the participation of the peasant movement in the administration of the rural services, and everything was built around that mechanism of participation."[59]

A more general issue raised by Lleras Restrepo's appeal to the peasantry was its significance as an expression of the underlying class antagonisms in Colombian society. Here the question can be formulated as follows: What did the creation of ANUC mean in terms of the class conflicts and realignments in the second half of the 1960s? It has been said that ANUC was launched as an element of pressure that would help implement a more radical policy of agrarian reform against the opposition of the landowning class. However, in order to understand the significance of this crucial move, one must also take into account its objective implications for the interests of the different groups within the peasant class. In this sense, with the emergence of ANUC the terms were being dramatically changed. Reformism, previously confined to the mitigation of class conflicts in the countryside, was now mobilizing the peasantry in order to exacerbate them. The peasants, who had been reduced to passive social objects during the demagogic phase of agrarian reform, were now being urged to participate directly through a channel that made possible the convergence and expression of grievances and demands linked to the different types of agrarian contradictions. It is true that, in terms of the structures existing in the countryside, bourgeois reformism did not envisage an absolutely peasant definition of the agrarian question. On this point, Lleras Restrepo argued that although "we aim at the promotion of a family type property combined with medium sized property for reasons that are both social and economic . . . large scale property is not proscribed because it is fairly evident that much of the land is not suitable for a peasant type of exploitation."[60] In other words, the rural entrepreneurs were reassured that large-scale property was not going to be touched if it was put to productive use; in fact, both capitalist agriculture and cattle raising were supported and even stimulated during the Lleras Restrepo administration.[61]

Nevertheless, from the point of view of the peasantry, the general outlook was highly favorable. On the one hand, the peasant economy would be reinforced in the regions of *minifundia* and colonization, which would be helped by the direct intervention of ANUC in the provision of the state services. On the other hand, the landless peasants were offered help in areas of *latifundia*, where ANUC's pressure upon the landowners was bound to be crucial. Altogether, then, ANUC appeared to go well beyond the definition of a mere political counterweight. Insofar as the reformist project responded to the basic interests of the peasants, it was a move toward an effective alliance between the peasantry and the bourgeoisie. Thus, it can be said that ANUC was emerging as a class organization as well as the instrument of a prospective class alliance in which both the initiative and the control of the process rested with the reformist sectors of the Colombian bourgeoisie.

ANUC: Organization from above

A huge organizational effort was necessary to translate the idea of peasant mobilization into reality during the Lleras Restrepo administration. Consequently, the promotion campaign was conceived from the beginning as a "large scale operation" that would employ all available means to achieve maximum coverage.[62] As soon as Decree 755 was issued, a special committee took charge of the task at the Ministry of Agriculture. The team included lawyers, sociologists, and communication experts whose first step was to prepare registration forms and design a membership card for the future peasant *usuarios*.[63] Hundreds of thousands of forms were printed and sent to the agencies of the agricultural institutes throughout the country. Decree 755 had stipulated that both actual and potential beneficiaries of services could be considered *usuarios*. Registration was a simple process: The peasants had to apply at the local agencies, their completed forms were sent to the Ministry of Agriculture in Bogotá, and the ministry sent back the laminated membership cards for distribution among the *usuarios* after entering their names in a central registry.[64] From the outset, this process was accompanied by a huge publicity campaign, including radio networks, newspapers, posters, and leaflets that disseminated information about the project and extended a invitation to all peasants.[65] However, much more attention was paid to the qualification of strategic persons who would act as "multipliers" at the grass-roots level.[66] More than fifty regional seminars were conducted to instruct some 4,500 functionaries of the official institutions on the new participation policy.[67] Furthermore, ten regional courses were organized to inform and involve some 500 peasant leaders of the existing syndicates, leagues, cooperatives, and Acción Comunal committees.[68] But the most important qualification effort was the preparation of the promoters who would be in charge of the actual organizational work in the field. Because the Lleras Restrepo administration wanted the future peasant association to appear to be politically neutral, the promoters were selected on the basis of their professional skill and not by the usual method of partisan quotas. Notices were placed in the newspapers, 75 candidates were chosen from among 300 applicants, and a six-month period of intensive training was initiated, covering such topics as communication techniques, group dynamics, rural development, and community organization.[69]

As the number of registered *usuarios* increased and the promoters started to build the first municipal associations, the peasant organization campaign gained momentum. Figure 2.1, which summarizes the promotion process of ANUC on the basis of available information, shows that the main event in the first half of 1968 was the Peasant March in the first week of June.[70] The local authorities, the church, and the army helped to coordinate the march, and it was estimated that more than a million peasants converged on the 153 assembly points arranged by the Ministry of Agriculture. President Lleras Restrepo visited four of these rallies, announcing that the advent of ANUC heralded the beginning of "peasant co-government" and that the massive turnout of the people, "unprecedented in the political history of the country, has to be interpreted as the emergence of an organized peasant class that gains in self-consciousness and is ready to support the programs that will benefit it."[71] However, the gathering of crowds during the Peasant March was more the expression of collective behavior than the disciplined act of a "self-conscious" and organized peasant class. It is true that, as indicated by Table 2.1, more than 600,000 *usuarios* had already been registered, but the event had been promoted by radios and pulpits, not by a still nonexistent peasant union. All the same, the march clearly demonstrated that there was an enthusiastic peasant response to the idea of popular participation. Furthermore, the rallies provided a platform from which emerging peasant leaders could address the crowds on the same footing as the politicians. More important still, the fact that the peasants were meeting together for the first time in such numbers helped to enhance a feeling of common identity and nourished the expectation that their grievances and problems would be finally acknowledged by society.

During the second half of 1968, the promoters worked steadily to form the local associations. They had been deployed according to the distribution of the rural population in the different regions, so that there were usually two or three of them in most of the departments. The Ministry of Agriculture's Resolution 061 of February 1968, which set the rules for the organization of ANUC, had stipulated that the first step was the establishment of municipal associations. Representatives of these local units would then create the departmental associations and, later, the national framework.[72] Upon arrival at a municipality, the promoter visited the different *veredas* (rural neighborhoods) to identify potential leaders. This was done by gathering the opinions of a reasonable proportion of the families regarding trustworthy people whom they believed would represent the peasants and defend their rights. The promoter invited those who had been most frequently nominated to a special meeting, where,

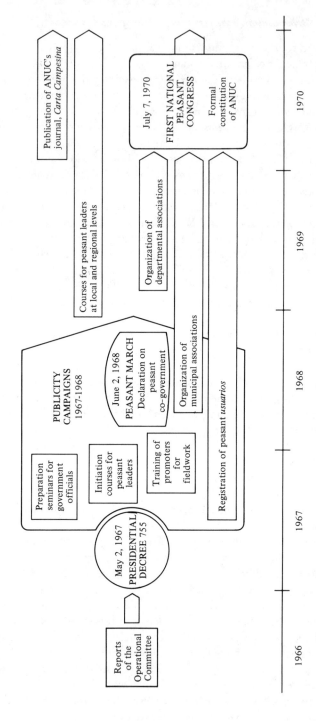

Figure 2.1. The promotion of ANUC, 1966–1970.

Table 2.1. *ANUC's organizational campaign in numbers, 1968–1971*

	Registered members	Departmental Associations	Municipal Associations	Leadership courses	Trained leaders
March 1968	600,000	—	—	10	500
June 1969	700,000	2	210	92	3,428
Feb. 1970	765,000	5	307	185	4,700
Nov. 1970	908,358	24	529	298	7,197
Oct. 1971	989,306	28	634	506	13,983

Sources: Ministerio de Agricultura, *Campaña Nacional de Organización Campesina: Informe 1968*, 1968, p. 15. M. Suárez Melo, "Campaña nacional de organización campesina," 1969, pp. 70–71. *Carta Campesina*, Nos. 1 and 3, February and March 1970. Ministerio de Agricultura, "Memorando sobre el estado de organización campesina," 1970. Ministerio de Agricultura, "Resumen de trabajos realizados en organización campesina," 1971.

after introducing the aims of the organization campaign, he discussed local problems and the possibilities of peasant action. After recruiting the help of these potential leaders, he organized a general assembly of the *usuarios* of the municipality. In this forum, the discussion of peasant needs and organization was expanded, the municipal association was formally created, and the *usuarios* voted to choose the committee that would be in charge of their affairs.[73] This process was repeated again and again until most of the municipalities had been organized and the establishment of the departmental associations had become possible.

In the meantime, a "massive plan for training rural leaders" was launched toward the end of 1968.[74] The committee members of neighboring municipalities gathered for special weekend courses that provided basic instruction on leadership roles and group techniques, information about state services, and an orientation on the rights of the *usuarios*. As Table 2.1 shows, some 3,000 local leaders had already been trained in these courses by mid-1969. By then, more than 200 municipal associations had been formed and two departmental associations inaugurated in Sucre and Valle.[75]

ANUC's organizational structure, defined by Resolution 061, was a rigid hierarchy. Figure 2.2 shows that the Municipal Associations were the cornerstone of the organization.[76] The local assembly, composed of at least 10 percent of the municipality's registered *usuarios*, elected a Junta Directiva whose five members rotated among themselves the roles of president, secretary, and treasurer. Presentation of lists was forbidden; individuals were nominated, and those who were mentioned the greatest number of times were selected. The Municipal Associations coordinated the Veredal Committees in different parts of the municipality and could also designate special committees for particular tasks. Above the Municipal

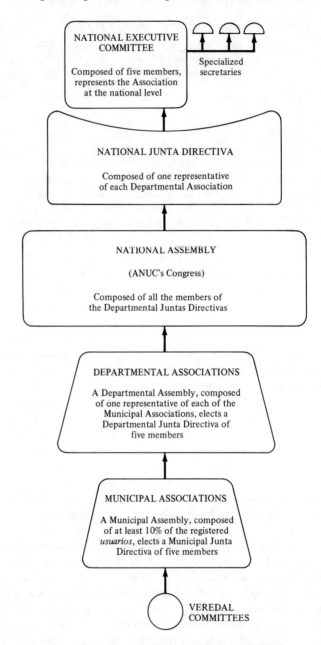

Figure 2.2. The organizational structure of ANUC.

Associations were the regional frameworks of ANUC, the Departmental Associations. Here the assembly was made up of one representative of each of the Municipal Juntas Directivas, so that the number of delegates varied according to the number of municipalities in the department. A Departmental Junta Directiva of five members was elected, following the already described procedure of individual ballot. Next in the hierarchy, the National Assembly was the most important authority within ANUC. It was composed of all the members of the Departmental Juntas Directivas, who met every two years in a National Congress where the overall problems of the peasantry were discussed and general policy guidelines were established. Again using the individual ballot, the Congress elected the National Junta Directiva, which had to include one representative of each Departmental Association. This National Junta operated as a consultative body; it was convened twice a year to define concrete policies and supervise the National Executive Committee. The latter, made up of five men individually elected by the National Junta Directiva among its members, concentrated the delegated power of the organization and was responsible for carrying out the ordinary work in representing the *usuarios*. In doing so, the Executive Committee could establish secretaries to handle special functions like finances and propaganda.

Presidential Decree 2420 of September 1968 restructured the state institutions in the agricultural sector. Among other provisions, it established criteria for peasant representation in the main decentralized institutes and created the Division of Peasant Organization (DOC) within the Ministry of Agriculture. The chairman of ANUC's promotion committee, Mario Suárez Melo, was appointed director of the DOC, his collaborators occupied the managerial posts along with secretarial staff in Bogotá, and the promoters also became an integral part of the DOC as field organizers. There was a clear parallel between the hierarchical structure of ANUC and the institutional arrangement of the DOC at the Ministry of Agriculture. The field promoters assisted the municipal associations; their work was supervised by senior regional promoters, who, in turn, were responsible for advising the departmental associations of the *usuarios*. At the national level, the director and staff of the DOC coordinated the central events of ANUC and permanently assisted the leaders of its Executive Committee.

At the beginning of the promotion campaign, President Lleras Restrepo had stressed that "the creation of the *usuarios'* associations does not represent an attempt to grant official status to the peasant organization, much less an attempt to exert governmental control upon such organization."[77] However, ANUC's early pattern clearly contradicted this statement. First, the Ministry of Agriculture officially registered the peasant *usuarios* and granted legal recognition to the associations. Second, the presence of a ministerial officer was required for the constitution of an association to be considered valid, and the Ministry of Agriculture was empowered by law to apply sanctions and even "to abrogate the registration of associations engaged in activities contrary to the spirit of Decree 755 of 1967."[78] Third, the field promoters and the central DOC personnel played a major role in preparing and carrying out most of ANUC's activities at the local, regional, and national levels. Fourth, the headquarters of the peasant organization were located in the Ministry of Agriculture building, along with the offices of the DOC. Fifth, the ministerial budget provided funds for the transportation and salaries of national and regional leaders, for peasant meetings and courses, for the publication of ANUC's materials, and for all the current expenses of the national and regional associations. Altogether, then, ANUC's relationship with the state was one of complete dependence on both the formal and informal levels. It is true that, in the strict sense, ANUC was not part of the state structure. Nevertheless, it had an undeniable semiofficial status. Coupled with the pattern of unilateral control, this semiofficial status defined ANUC as an extension of the state.

The institutionalization of the campaign was matched by its substantial accomplishments: By early 1970, the year in which Lleras Restrepo would step down from the presidency, almost 5,000 *usuarios* belonging to some 300 municipal associations had taken part in leadership courses. Five departmental associations were in operation, regional representatives of ANUC were meeting frequently, and an embryonic national leadership was beginning to appear. Under the guidance of the DOC, these national leaders prepared documents on peasant situation and demands. Delegations of *usuarios* submitted the peasants' views on the agrarian issues not only to high-level functionaries but also to politicians and candidates for the 1970 elections.[79] In the field, the emerging peasant leaders were now directly involved in the work alongside the promoters, and the move to organize was accelerated so that the constitution of the national association would be secured before Lleras Restrepo left office. *Carta Campesina*, a special journal written and edited by peasants and DOC advisers, began to be published every two weeks for massive distribution.[80] Another joint team of peasant leaders and functionaries coordinated the tasks in preparation for the first national assembly of the *usuarios*.[81] As a result of this feverish activity, all the departmental associations were organized on time and their representatives converged on Bogotá on July 7, exactly one month before the presidential takeover. To crown this remarkable feat of organization, Lleras Restrepo personally inaugurated the First National Congress of ANUC. His successor, the Conservative Misael Pastrana, was to inherit an organized peasant class when he took over as the last president of the National Front.

Table 2.2. *Registration of peasant usuarios, according to the prevailing agrarian structures in the regions, 1968–1971*

Regions[a]	Registered *usuarios* 1968–1971	Percentage of total *usuarios*	Registered *usuarios* as a percentage of the economically active population
Predominance of the peasant economy	531,177	53.7	36.8
Predominance of agrarian capitalism	171,481	17.3	42.9
Predominance of traditional latifundia	215,226	21.6	48.9
Predominance of colonization	71,442	7.2	61.3
Total	989,306	100.0	

[a]Regional data based upon the aggregation of departmental data according to the classification presented in Table 1.5.

Sources: Ministerio de Agricultura, "Resumen de trabajos realizados en organización campesina," 1971. DANE, *Censo Nacional de Poblacion*, 1964.

What were the implications of ANUC's organizational patterns? First, the very success of the promotion campaign guaranteed a massive emerging peasant movement. Regardless of the variable local conditions and agrarian situations, the sweeping efforts of the government had reached the most remote corners of the country, uniting all the different types of peasants in a single, all-embracing organization. Second, "organization from above" had paradoxically created a structure "built from below." ANUC's construction had not followed the typical clientelist pattern of downward links and intermediate brokers. The organization had started at the grass-roots levels and the successive stages had been based on the principle of representation. Despite the hierarchical rigidity and all the possible biases, construction from below created favorable conditions for true peasant representation. Third, and as a consequence of this true representation and the national scope of the campaign, the structural diversity of the peasantry clearly influenced the results of the organizational drive. Table 2.2, where the number of registered *usuarios* is presented according to the prevailing agrarian structures in the departments, shows that more than half of ANUC's members belonged to the *minifundia* areas. However, if the figures are considered in relation to the economically active population, it can be seen that ANUC's following was relatively larger in the regions of *latifundia* and colonization. The fact that the landless peasants and the colonists had been more responsive to the organization campaign can be interpreted as a further sign of ANUC's representative nature, because it indicates that the movement was more powerful precisely where, as has been shown in the previous chapter, the peasant sectors were affected by sharper contradictions. A fourth factor was the solid legitimation of the peasant movement. ANUC was fully backed by the authority of the state, and its organization was an invitation to exercise rights that had been always postponed. The government itself encouraged the peasants to demand their due, and this fact was a powerful motivation for the peasants.

Four main elements thus defined the character of ANUC: national scope, heterogeneous class composition, authentic representation, and institutional legitimation. These factors had a significant influence on the formation of the movement's leadership. ANUC's nationwide scope and complex class composition were reflected, from the very beginning, by the varied social extraction of its national leaders. Following the rules established by the Ministry of Agriculture, the National Junta Directiva elected by ANUC's first congress in 1970 was composed of 24 delegates on behalf of the 24 regional associations. The whole spectrum of the "plebeian" rural classes was represented, including different types of independent peasants, subordinated tenants and sharecroppers, colonists, and agricultural workers.[82] Although most of the delegates came from traditional Conservative or Liberal backgrounds, only a few were strongly committed to either party. For some of them, participation in ANUC was their first experience of active involvement in public affairs. Many others were veteran activists from spontaneous local leagues and other organizations such as Acción Comunal and FANAL. The five leaders elected to the first Executive Committee of the *usuarios* represented a cross section of these different groups in terms of both their social extraction and their previous experience of organizational activity.[83]

True representation, which resulted from the fact that ANUC had been built from below, created favorable conditions for the emergence of genuine peasant leadership. According to the rules, peasant *usuarios* were the actual and potential beneficiaries of the agricultural state services. Since the definition was vague, anyone could, at least formally, become a peasant *usuario*. Many of the early lists included rural merchants, professionals, landowners, and *gamonales*, who registered as *usuarios* in order to become "insiders" in new developments that could affect their local spheres of interest.[84] In most cases, however, this infiltration was blocked from the outset by the DOC promoters. As already explained, the idea of organizing the peasantry was an attempt to bypass the politics of clientelism in the countryside. Accordingly, the DOC handbooks emphasized that the beneficiaries were to be the "authentic" and "traditionally marginalized" peasants.[85] These instructions were faithfully followed, especially at the meetings in which the associations were established and the local Juntas elected. Among the peasant testimonies, there are many references to the way in which the organizers confiscated the membership cards of infiltrators, warned the *usuarios* against external influences, and encouraged them to choose representatives from their own ranks.[86] Thus, the DOC promoters played a crucial role not only in consolidating ANUC's genuine peasant identity but also in ensuring the rise of leaders who truly represented the composition of the movement at the grass-roots levels.

Finally, the type of leadership that developed among the *usuarios* was conditioned by the institutional legitimation of ANUC. Following a classic distinction, leadership can be classified into charismatic, legal, and traditional types, according to the sources of legitimation.[87] Taking into account specific leadership functions in social movements, another classification involves charismatic leaders who actually lead and inspire collective action, administrators who specialize in organizational affairs, and intellectuals who develop the ideological values.[88] The conditions surrounding the creation of ANUC determined the formation of a peasant leadership that was legal by the first classification and administrative by the second. Indeed, it was the state, through the process of peasant organization, that promoted and legitimized the leaders. On the other hand, most of the charismatic and ideological tasks were done by the promoters and the DOC personnel, leaving to the emerging peasant leaders the organizational function of mediating between the rank-and-file peasants and the inspiration and ideology that came from the outside. This, of course, does not mean that ANUC's leaders were lacking in charisma. After all, it is because of their personal qualities that individuals are accepted or promoted as group leaders. But the type of leadership that they assume depends upon structural factors affecting the group, and in ANUC's case these factors emphasized a bureaucratic (i.e., legal/administrative) type of leadership. Reinforced by organizational norms that deemphasized personalities in favor of the rotation of roles and collective decision making, this bureaucratic leadership characterized not only the early phase of ANUC but also its subsequent evolution. In fact, the *usuarios* never had outstanding charismatic leaders, that is, celebrities who embodied the movement. For this reason, no attempt is made here to follow the developments in terms of the individual actors involved. Instead, emphasis will be placed upon factions, rather than personalities whenever the analysis deals with processes related to ANUC's leadership.[89]

No social movement can continue to act on any significant scale without an adequate organization. In this sense, the *usuarios* were, from the outset, in a privileged position. Providing transmission channels, frameworks for encounter and deliberation, and mechanisms for the promotion of leaders, ANUC made it possible to gather, elaborate, and express peasant demands.

Table 2.3. *The pattern of peasant institutional representation, 1968*

Institutes	Peasant representation at the national level	Peasant representation at regional and local levels
Instituto Colombiano de Reforma Agraria (INCORA) (agrarian reform)	Participation on INCORA's national board: 2 peasant representatives out of a total of 15 members	Committees of 5 peasant representatives with advisory and liaison functions on each regional project of INCORA. Committees of 7 peasant representatives with liaison functions in each of the local irrigation districts of INCORA
Caja Agraria (agricultural credits)	Participation on the national board of the Caja Agraria: 1 peasant representative out of a total of 5 members	Participation on the consultive boards of the local branches of the Caja Agraria, advisory functions: 2 peasant representatives out of 6 members
Instituto Colombiano Agropecuario (ICA) (agricultural extension and technical assistance)	Participation on ICA's national board: 1 peasant representative out of a total of 8 members	Advisory committees of 3 peasant representatives with consultive and liaison functions in each regional station and agency of ICA
Instituto de Mercadeo Agropecuario (IDEMA) (agricultural marketing)	Participation on IDEMA's national board: 1 peasant representative out of a total of 9 members	Advisory committees of 2 peasant representatives with consultive and liaison functions in regional agencies of IDEMA. Possibility of direct contracts between IDEMA and Municipal Associations of ANUC in cooperative marketing transactions
Instituto de Recursos Naturales (INDERENA) (natural resources)	Participation on the national board of IN-DERENA: 1 peasant representative out of a total of 7 members	Provisions for peasant representation with advisory functions on regional projects (unspecified)

Source: Law 1st 1968; Presidential Decrees 182/Feb. 1968, 955/June 1968, 2420/Sept. 1968

However, the movement's actions were restricted by the framework of institutional representation imposed by the state. The potential consequences of this constraint will be briefly discussed. In general terms, the formal power granted by the forms of peasant representation failed to match the expectations that had been generated by the organization of the *usuarios*. Table 2.3, which presents the patterns of representation mandated by government decrees and regulations, clearly shows the low level of peasant participation. Although the peasant delegates could vote on the national boards of the official institutes, their real weight was minimal. At the regional level, the representatives of the *usuarios* were used only for consultation and liaison; they did not help make the actual decisions.[90] This introduces a crucial issue, namely, the fragile nature of the dependency of the peasant movement on the state. With the state under the control of the bourgeois reformist politicians, peasant allies had been mobilized by a corporatist institutional arrangement. But the formal power given to the *usuarios* was not sufficient, by itself, to define the action of the state. On the national board of INCORA, for example, peasant participation would only result in frustration if the two *usuarios* were always to be outvoted by the thirteen opposite votes cast by the bureaucrats and the politicians. In other words, the corporatist arrangement could work only if the class alliance persisted and a favorable policy toward the peasants was maintained by the state. Against this background, there were two special dangers: a reformist failure to deliver the goods within a reasonable period of time and a shift in class alignments leading to the abandonment of agrarian reform as state policy. Either of these developments might destroy ANUC's dependence on the state. The specter of a mobilized peasantry on the loose had haunted the more reluctant members of the 1966 Operational Committee when they warned President Lleras Restrepo that "grave consequences may follow if the State creates needs without the means to give satisfaction to them . . . rising aspirations are transformed into dangerous growing frustrations when the balance between hope and fulfillment is broken."[91]

3

The radicalization of ANUC and the great waves of land invasions

ANUC had emerged with a national scope and great organizational sophistication. The movement was also highly representative, not only because it was composed of real peasants but also because it expressed various types of contradictions that affected the peasantry throughout the country. Favorable conditions had been created for the exertion of effective pressure, and the actual form and content of such pressure depended upon the future course of state policies. With the end of the Lleras Restrepo administration, the vacillations of the new Conservative government would come as a sign that reformism and the underlying class alignments were being undermined. After reviewing the events involved in the downfall of the reformist alliance and ANUC's radicalization, this chapter will examine the subsequent development of the agrarian struggles and their effects upon the evolution of the peasant movement.

The land question as the focus of peasant confrontation

Because of the precedents set in the 1960s, and also because of the direction that the Lleras Restrepo administration wanted the peasant movement to take, land redistribution was firmly established, from the outset, as the central concern of the *usuarios*. During the promotion campaign, special attention was paid to the regions of high land concentration, and priority was given to those places where peasant unrest was more conspicuous. It was precisely in these areas that the message of the DOC field promoters proved to be more influential. The promoters had been trained in special courses organized by the Interamerican Institutes for Agricultural Sciences and Agrarian Reform (IICA and CIRA). They had been instructed by Brazilian, Argentinian, Chilean, and Colombian tutors who belonged to the first generation of radical Latin American social scientists of the 1960s.[1] Now, within the framework of a massive organizational effort legitimized by the state, these promoters taught the peasants their notions of radical reformism. In countless seminars and discussions, they analyzed the local problems with the *usuarios*, instructing them on their rights to the land, encouraging an attitude of independence toward the traditional *gamonales*, and fostering rebellion against the unjustices of the rural situation.[2] Reaffirming the seriousness of the government's intentions, Lleras Restrepo had personally inaugurated the first departmental association of ANUC in Sucre. In that assembly, convened in February 1969, the president told an audience of 2,000 mainly landless peasants that the government had gone half way and that it was now up to the *usuarios* to bridge the gap: "I do not believe that violence solves everything, but we need a rapid change equivalent to a revolution."[3] This open incitement, backed by the state's legitimation, stimulated radical forms of expression among the hundreds of organized groups that were sprouting up throughout the country and demanding the much talked-about agrarian reform.[4]

The organizational rise of the peasantry, the increasing activity of INCORA, and the approval of Law 1 of 1968 hardened the attitudes of the landowners. Entrenched in their positions of power, they launched a massive eviction campaign in the *haciendas* and stepped up their offensive in disputes against colonists, resorting to the local authorities in order to suppress the growing peasant resistance. In Sucre, there had been strong protests since 1969 against landlord encroachments in San Onofre and other municipalities. In February 1970 the increasing agitation led to a number of peasant land invasions in San Pedro, Betulia, and Toluviejo. There was a sense of general social disturbance, and the governor had to initiate "peace talks" with ANUC in the departmental capital, Sincelejo.[5] In Córdoba, there were new land seizures in the Lower Sinú area and in Lorica, where the peasants urged "more effectiveness in agrarian reform."[6] In Atlántico, earlier conflicts about dried-up swamps were reactivated in Campo de la Cruz.[7] In Quindío and Risaralda, the *usuarios* demanded "freedom of organization," urging land redistribution in favor of tenants and occupying *haciendas* in Montenegro and La Tebaida.[8] In Huila, the press reported land invasions in Campoalegre and Villavieja, organized "in support of agrarian reform."[9] In Cundinamarca, the occupiers responded with force to police repression in Silvania and Valle de Ubaté.[10] As the departmental associations of ANUC were being created, demands for land and for modifications of the Agrarian Reform Law proliferated in the form of public statements and petitions addressed to the official institutes.[11] The Society of Colombian Agriculturalists (SAC) and the Federation of Cattle Breeders (FEDEGAN) began to express their "serious concern" about the disturbances, but the first national meetings of ANUC's leaders further increased the pressure. The *usuarios* announced that only more rapid land redistribution would ease the growing rural unrest, that the peasants would vote in the next elections according to the candidates' commitment to agrarian reform, and that they would resort to their own means if the expected changes failed to take place.[12] Government officials acknowledged the aggravation of the land problems, stressing the need to speed the reform process and appealing to the peasants for patience.[13] Thus, toward the end of 1969 and the beginning of 1970, the struggle for land was ceasing to be a fragmentary and regional question. It was becoming a national issue, and ANUC was becoming its agent.

ANUC's Declaration of Principles, issued by the First National Congress of July 1970, clearly showed that access to land was the main concern of the new peasant movement. Its central point was a call for a "swift, drastic and massive agrarian reform including land redistribution and complementary programs of credit, technical assistance and marketing."[14] One of the national leaders of the *usuarios* forcefully delivered the message in his opening address to the congress, saying that "the great social problems of the peasants, which stem from lack of understanding and the unequal distribution of the land, need urgent peaceful solutions because, it they are not solved, the people will resort to their own means in order to put an end to their misery and-dispair."[15] Although the tone was radical, the demands remained within the limits of reformism. The *usuarios* still identified their goals with the declared aims of government policy, and despite the signs of unrest in the rural areas, the peasantry had backed the National Front in the crucial 1970 presidential election. The official candidate, the Conservative Misael Pastrana, had pledged to continue Lleras Restrepo's policies of agrarian reform and peasant participation. On the April 1970 ballot, Pastrana defeated ANAPO's Rojas Pinilla by a very slight margin, and the regional returns showed that the peasant votes had tipped the balance in his favor.[16] During the stormy aftermath of the election, when the Anapistas claimed that the results had been fraudulently manipulated by the Lleras Restrepo administration, many *usuarios'* associations sent telegrams supporting the government and the legitimacy of the election.[17] In a special paragraph, the Declaration of Principles issued by ANUC's First Congress stressed that "the recent election has demonstrated the decision power of the peasantry," adding that the movement would be independent and that the peasants would always vote "taking into account the political conduct of those who hope to be backed by the peasantry."[18] The Declaration stated that the solution to the peasants' problems was "not a question of class struggle" but "a question of struggling against backwardness and marginality."[19] The emphasis on peaceful means was candidly expressed by the compromising attitude toward the landowners, who were urged "stop avoiding the problems and accept the dialogue with the peasants and the State."[20]

In general, the *usuarios* remained true to reformism and loyal to the National Front. Demanding land redistribution but insisting upon peaceful solutions and helping to check the challenge of populism, the emerging peasant movement was openly showing its willingness to maintain the class alignments established during the Lleras Restrepo administration.

Influenced by a growing spirit of autonomy that reflected the perceived support at the grass-roots level, the peasants expressed this willingness from a position of self-conscious strength. In addition to the leaders' veiled allusions regarding the possible use of noninstitutional means, the Declaration of Principles stated that the *usuarios* would support the new Conservative government "only if the programs of peasant organization and agrarian reform are maintained and expanded."[21]

Despite his preelection promises and the fact that he had come to power on the crest of the peasant votes that had overshadowed ANAPO's urban victory, President Pastrana hardly shared Lleras Restrepo's enthusiasm for the peasant organization.[22] The landowners had a decisive voice in the Conservative Party, and in addition, the economic situation was beginning to change as a result of Lleras Restrepo's measures, so that agrarian reform no longer appeared as necessary as it had before to the bourgeoisie. These factors, which resulted in the breakdown of the reformist project, will be considered in the following chapter. For the time being, it is sufficient to state that, in addition to the ambiguity of its future agrarian policies, the Pastrana administration approached ANUC as a Liberal clientelist stronghold whose popular ascendancy had to be strictly controlled.[23] The new director of the DOC, Víctor Calle, indicated this attitude in his first press conference, stating that "the house of the peasant associations had to be put in order" and that ANUC was to a large extent "a phantom organization created through a bureaucratic and fictitious promotion."[24] The landowners' federations, SAC and FEDEGAN, which had been using the newspapers to express their distaste for ANUC's participation in the official institutes, took advantage of the early signs of government vacillation to redouble their propaganda campaign against the *usuarios* and INCORA.[25] Only a few weeks had passed since the new administration had taken over, and the situation was changing rapidly. A suspicious government with an indecisive agrarian reform policy was keeping ANUC at a distance and, at the same time, the opposition to the peasant movement was emerging in full strength.

With an organization that could coordinate activities at the grass-roots levels, ANUC was already in a position to bring pressure to bear upon the state. In contrast to the previous spontaneous land struggles, which consisted of isolated cases of land invasions and resistance to eviction, the expressions of unrest during the last months of 1970 were well organized and included public demonstrations, massive rallies at official institutes, and direct confrontations with the authorities. Thus, in addition to the numerous land seizures that took place in Meta, Urabá, the banana zone in Magdalena, southern Atlántico, and the Indian area of the department of Cauca, there were other incidents that had even greater impact as a result of their organizational significance and their effect upon national public opinion.[26] In Cundinamarca, 200 peasants from nine municipalities of the Bogotá Plain and Valle de Ubaté took part in a powerful demonstration at the central offices of INCORA in Bogotá.[27] In Valle, many *usuarios* from Tuluá and San Pedro took over INCORA's regional headquarters, demanding "land to alleviate the situation of unemployment."[28] In Tolima, the *usuarios* occupied nine estates in Guamo, Flandes, and Purificación, putting up large posters calling for INCORA's intervention and a "just land redistribution"; Guamo's municipal hall was under siege for several days as the peasants tried to force negotiations about the invaded land.[29] In Huila, 500 peasants from Campoalegre, Aipe, Villavieja, Palermo, and other municipalities converged on the departmental capital, Neiva, seizing the governor's palace and submitting a list of the estates that should be taken over by INCORA to solve the problem of the landless peasants. A few days later, *usuarios* who had been evicted from neighboring lands occupied the village of Palermo, claiming land, lighting fires, and stoning the police and the municipal hall.[30] But it was in Sucre, the department where ANUC had more strength and organizational development, that the greatest mobilization took place: In late November, a huge march of 5,000 peasants ended in the central square of Sincelejo, where, for a whole day, the *usuarios* voiced their demands for an effective process of land expropriation and redistribution.[31]

The upsurge of peasant militancy caused an immediate reaction. Politicians, representatives of the landowners' federations, and even some government officials were indignant, demanding a heavy hand to control the peasant movement and accusing INCORA's personnel of instigating the land invasions.[32] The government declared that although it had no plans to shelve agrarian reform, it would not permit illegal acts and the subversion of public order in the countryside.[33] The security and intelligence services of the state leaked to the press some reports about presumed "Communist conspiracies related to the rural invasions."[34] Among the national leaders of ANUC, who had been discussing since October a possible plan for a massive and coordinated movement of land occupation throughout the country, positions began to polarize on the future direction of the land struggle. One group, composed of loyal Liberals and Conservatives, thought that a direct assault would cause a total break with the state, something that had to be avoided at any cost. Another group, including both Liberals and Conservatives who were beginning to be influenced by Trotskyite militants and advisers from the Communist Party, argued that agrarian reform was a farce, that confrontation with the state had already begun, and that the only possible course was de facto occupation of the land by direct peasant action.[35] At the second meeting of ANUC's National Junta (Bogotá, January 1971), the radical faction obtained the support of the majority. They agreed on the need to draw up a new platform emphasizing the political, ideological, and organizational autonomy of the movement vis-à-vis the state and the traditional political parties. In addition, the *usuarios'* delegates decided to carry out a massive campaign of land occupations during the second half of the following month, nominating a "secret committee" for the tasks of preparation and coordination.[36] Thus occurred the radicalization of the peasant movement, and the struggle for land became the main issue. No doubt, important ideological factors were involved: Unfulfilled expectations inflamed discontent, which was fanned by the leftist political groups. However, the main cause was rooted in the class alignments and contradictions. From this perspective, three crucial elements can be singled out. The first was the isolation of the peasantry, an isolation caused by the defeat of reformism and the consolidation of strong opposition by the dominant classes. The second element was the aggravation of conflicts over land, marked by the increasing pace of landowner encroachments and the growing resolve of the peasants to intensify their resistance and offensive. The third element was the rise of the more combative groups within the peasant movement. All these factors will be considered in greater detail later in this chapter and in Chapter 4.

The wave of land invasions that took place on February 21 and the following days opened the most intense period of land struggles in the history of Colombia, confirming the appeal, dominant position, and ability to mobilize that ANUC had achieved as a mass organization. It was estimated that more than 15,000 families participated in these actions, occupying some 350 estates in thirteen departments, especially in the Atlantic Coast and the plains of Huila and Tolima.[37] Warning the peasants that they should avoid being dragged into violence by the landowners and the authorities,[38] ANUC's Executive Committee attributed the events to the intolerable social situation of the landless and the insensitivity of a government that was failing to achieve agrarian reform and was turning against the peasant organization.[39] It was announced that the *usuarios* would not give up their hope for social change, and the popular sectors and workers' trade unions were called on to support the peasants' battle.[40] Responding to the Minister of Government, who had declared that the land invasions were part of a deliberate plan to subvert public order, ANUC's Executive Committee demanded the expropriation of the invaded lands and gave a six-month ultimatum to the government for the extension of legal titles to those "who had rightfully taken them."[41] To emphasize its political independence at a time of deepening confrontation, ANUC demanded budgetary and administrative autonomy from the state, refused to acknowledge the negotiations that some former officials of the Lleras Restrepo administration had begun with the government, and rejected an invitation to the next national convention of the Liberal Party.[42]

With the massive mobilization of the peasantry, the ambiguities of the Pastrana administration came clearly to the fore, creating serious contradictions within the government itself. While the Minister of Government, Abelardo Forero Benavídez, called the land seizures "a subversion of public order," the Minister of Agriculture, J. Emilio Valderrama, considered them "social conflicts that demanded economic and social solutions."[43] The police and the army were ordered to evict the peasant invaders, but INCORA's instructions called for the Institute to mediate and begin negotiations with peasants and landowners on the occupied lands. This situation quickly became untenable for the government. Enormous pressures were being exerted by both Conservative and Liberal congressmen, by the chairmen of the federations of the big landowners, industrialists, financiers, and merchants, and by hundreds of telegrams that poured in from frightened landlords who urged action "to save the motherland."[44] Finally, President Pastrana gave clear indications of its more definite position. The DOC field promoters, whose purge had begun even before the land invasions, were fired and replaced during the following months.[45] Carlos Villamil Chaux, who had been kept as INCORA's director as a gesture of continuity with the Lleras Restrepo administration, was dismissed in March.[46] In April the government withdrew the budget for *Carta Campesina*, the newsletter that ANUC had been publishing since early 1970.[47] By mid-1971, the hostility toward ANUC and the reversal of the agrarian reform policy were so evident that the Minister of Agriculture, J. Emilio Valderrama, a progressive Conservative who had been advocating discussions with the peasants, resigned, declaring that he could no longer participate in the government.[48] Víctor Calle, who supported Valderrama's views, was quickly fired and replaced by a hard-liner as director of the DOC.[49]

In the meantime, ANUC's radicalization was becoming manifest in a series of documents that justified the actions of the *usuarios* and marked the independent course of the peasant movement. In the *Plataforma Ideológica* approved at the third meeting of the National Junta (Villa del Rosario, June 1971), ANUC defined itself as "an organization of the middle, poor and salaried peasants, independent of the government and the political parties, that strives to form an alliance with the working class and other popular sectors in order to fight for a more just society in Colombia."[50] Though the *Plataforma* outlined other claims of the peasantry, the focus was on access to land; the main demands were immediate and free redistribution, expropriation without indemnification of all *latifundia*, limitation of the size of land property, promotion of communal settlements, collectivization of capitalist agricultural enterprises, elimination of backward relations of production, and recognition of the de facto possession of lands seized by the peasants. The *Plataforma Ideológica* was followed a few months later by the *Mandato Campesino*, a document on the land struggles, issued at the fourth meeting of the National Junta (Fúquene, August 1971).[51] Under the slogan *"tierra sin patronos"* ("land without masters"), the points of the *Plataforma* were here reformulated not as demands or aspirations of the organization but as a concrete program for struggle. Instead of begging the dominant classes for agrarian reform, the peasants should accomplish it themselves, expropriating the landowners directly and ignoring the legal mechanisms of the state. For that purpose, ANUC would create local and regional Executive Committees of Agrarian Reform (CERA) special groups that would carry out operational and juridical functions according to guidelines specified in the *Mandato*. The document was clearly revolutionary, trying to create nuclei of popular power in the countryside and stressing collectivization as the future form of agriculture in Colombia.

The *Mandato Campesino* was accompanied by another declaration in which the fourth meeting of ANUC's National Junta defined the agrarian problem as a political question, arguing that the traditional parties were committed to the interests of the dominant classes and that the peasant movement should ally with the working class to change the existing structures by revolution.[52] Both documents caused much controversy among the peasant leaders. They had been drawn up under the guidance of influential advisers who belonged to the Communist Party and the Socialist Bloc, a group recently formed by Trotskyites. There were many expressions of dissent, coming not only from Liberals and Conservatives who opposed the left-wing orientations, but also from others who were beginning to be influenced by Maoist radicals.[53] Still, the documents were approved by a substantial majority and no open breaks occurred at this stage. In the meantime, the *Mandato* legitimized the continuation of the peasant offensive in the land struggles. During October and November 1971, ANUC launched a second wave of land invasions that proved to be as intense as the previous one. In just three days, 120 estates were occupied in seven departments, and after two months of action it was estimated that 300 *haciendas*, totalling about 150,000 hectares, had been affected.[54] Openly challenging the establishment, the *usuarios* carried out three land seizures in Córdoba during a visit of INCORA's director to the departmental capital, Montería; they occupied an estate of the archbishop of the Pereira Diocese in western Caldas; and they even invaded, on two occasions, a property of the new Minister of Agriculture, Hernán Jaramillo Ocampo, in Chimichagua, Cesar.[55] Amid the social ferment produced by the aggravation of the agrarian crisis, ANUC sent the government a special memorandum indicating that the land invasions reflected the "popular will to put a remedy to the passivity of the State through direct action."[56] In addition, the document demanded recognition of the peasants' rights over the occupied lands, respect for ANUC's autonomy and for the decisions of the CERA committees, abolition of the state-of-siege provisions, and immediate measures to improve the economic situation of the peasantry as a whole.

Regional outlines of the land conflicts

The land invasions of late 1971 pushed the contradictions to their climax at the national level, prompting a clear definition of the change that was already under way in the state's agrarian policy. But neither the official reaction nor its effects upon the peasants' land struggles can be fully discussed without first examining the nature of these struggles. Where did the conflicts occur, what were their roots, and how were they articulated by ANUC at the regional level? Furthermore, what were the characteristics of the land struggles, how did they develop, and what factors influenced their development? To answer these questions, it is necessary to move from the national to the regional scene and the main dimensions of the land struggles. This is the subject of the present and following sections. The starting point is information about the land invasions of 1971, presented in Table 3.1 as part of the general statistics on the land seizures during the 1970s.[57]

Taking as a reference point both the regional agrarian structures discussed in the second section of Chapter 1 and the predominance of these structures in the different departments, it is clear that most of the land struggles during 1971 and the decade as a whole occurred in the areas of cattle *latifundia* and in places where these estates were combined with the emergence of agrarian capitalism. This is confirmed by the regional aggregation of the data in Table 3.2, which shows that 76.9% of the land invasions in 1971 took place in the Atlantic Coast, in the two great inner valleys and in the Eastern Llanos. The remaining ones occurred almost entirely in the Andean departments, since land occupation in the areas of colonization were exceptions that amounted to just 1.5 percent of the total. In the first of these regional categories, the conflicts developed mainly in the departments of Córdoba, Sucre, Bolívar, Magdalena, and Huila, which alone accounted for more than half of the land invasions. These data generally support the statements made in the second section of Chapter 1 on the relationship between the types of agrarian structures and the degree of potential peasant pressure over the land. However, these observations are too general. In fact, up to now, the discussion has focused upon the predominance of certain agrarian patterns in the departments; this makes it possible to analyze the land struggles in regional terms but is insufficient to attain an adequate understanding of the conflicts them-

Table 3.1. *Peasant land invasions, by department, 1970–1978*

Departments	1970	1971	1972	1973	1974	1975	1976	1977	1978	Total
Sucre	4	60	11	24	63	27		10		199
Huila	6	69	17		4	7	8	1		112
Córdoba	1	80	5	7	8	4			2	107
Magdalena	1	90	9	1	1	1				103
Antioquia	1	31		6	24	5				67
Bolívar		54	1	3	3			3	2	66
Tolima	12	43		1		5	2			63
Cauca	1	32	1	4	11					49
Meta[a]	10	24	1		1	2	1	4	2	45
Cesar		30	4	1	4	2	3			44
Cundinamarca	3	26		2	1		1			33
Atlántico	2	17			1	5				25
Casanare		23								23
Santander		15		2	1	3		2		23
Caldas		13				1				14
Valle	3	11								14
North Santander		9	1							10
Quindío	3	4	2							9
Boyacá		6	1			1				8
Guajira		2			1	3				6
Nariño		2				2				4
Caquetá		1				2				3
Risaralda		1	1							2
Chocó		2								2
Total	47	645	54	51	123	70	15	20	6	1031

[a]Includes adjacent areas of Casanare and Guaviare.
Source: CINEP's Archive on ANUC, section on land invasions (see note 57 of Chapter 3).

selves. To grasp the nature of the different conflicts and draw more tangible and meaningful conclusions, one must analyze them at the regional level.

In the Atlantic Coast, where the land invasions in 1971 had greater intensity, the underlying contradictions were rooted in various regional processes. To clarify ANUC's struggles, it is therefore necessary to consider four areas of conflict: the banana zone, the littoral strip, the western savannas, and the southeastern lowlands. In the first of these areas, the origins and early development of the conflict on the abandoned possessions of the Frutera de Sevilla Company were reviewed in the first section of Chapter 2.[58] During the promotion period of ANUC in 1969 and 1970, disputes were aggravated because the entrepreneurs who had bought many of the company's plantations were now trying to set up an ambitious banana marketing consortium. A campaign of harassment was launched against the former small tenants in order to pave the way for a rapid

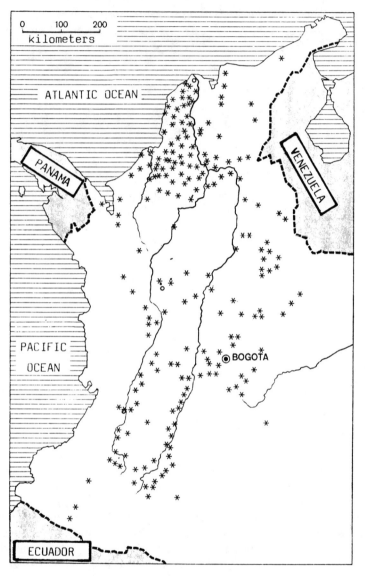

Map 3. Geographical location of the municipalities affected by land invasions, 1971.

process of land concentration. ANUC came just in time to integrate the spontaneous groups and syndicates into a unified front, so that the initial activities of resistance and defense were soon overtaken by a more general peasant offensive. During the national land invasions in 1971, more than

Table 3.2. *The 1971 peasant land invasions, by region*

Region	Number of land invasions, 1971	Percentage
Atlantic Coast	333	50.8
Inner valleys	123	18.8
Andean range	139	21.2
Eastern Llanos	40	6.1
Colonization fronts	10	1.5
Total	645	100.0

Source: CINEP's Archive on ANUC, section on land invasions (see note 57 of Chapter 3).

40 land seizures occurred in the municipalities of Ciénaga, Aracataca, Fundación, and Santa Marta.

Along the Caribbean coastline, the battles of 1971 were also a direct continuation of the struggles of the 1960s.[59] In southern Atlántico and in the area of the Canal del Dique in Bolívar, the question of the public lands created by drainage gave rise to a last movement of land occupations that settled most of the pending disputes in favor of the peasants and ended the local cycles of land struggles. In Córdoba, the conflict of the Lower Sinú area remained unsolved in spite of INCORA's intervention and, on the basis of previous experiences, the land invasions recurred in San Bernardo del Viento and expanded to the adjacent municipalities of San Antero and Puerto Escondido. In the neighboring Ciénaga Grande, there were numerous peasant occupations in Lorica, Purísima, and Chimá, where the landowners had extended their fences to the banks of the lake in order to get rid of the peasants and avoid INCORA's declaration of these banks as public land. In the part of the coastline that corresponded to Sucre, the Morrosquillo Gulf, the *haciendas* were smaller and the peasant population was scarce, so that only a few land invasions were registered in Toluviejo and San Onofre, where some sharecroppers had been demanding land redistribution since 1965. Throughout the coastal strip, ANUC's formation had been based upon the creation of new groups and the restructuring of the existing leagues and syndicates, many of which kept their affiliation to FANAL and their contact with the Liberal trade unions of Barranquilla. With the exception of the area corresponding to the department of Córdoba, it was clear that the main struggles were already over and that the new demands concerned problems other than that of access to land. This fact, coupled with the influence of the traditional parties through FANAL and the Liberal syndicates, made the peasant

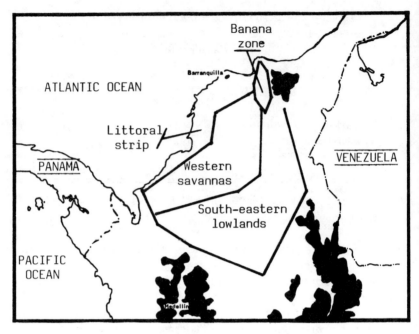

Map 4. Areas of land struggle on the Atlantic Coast.

movement in this area less radical than that of the rest of the Atlantic Coast.

In the western savannas of Córdoba, Sucre, and Bolívar, the consolidation of the cattle *latifundia* was an old process that had begun in centers of colonial *haciendas* in the vicinity of Monteria and Sincelejo. The struggles of 1971 had few precedents and, in fact, responded to new problems created by the sudden disruption of the relations of production toward the end of the 1960s.[60] After cutting down the forests and opening up the land for the landowners, the peasants had been subordinated by large-scale property owners in the usual pattern in areas of cattle *latifundia*. There was a small area where the peasants worked as tobacco sharecroppers, including the municipalities of Ovejas, Carmen de Bolívar, and San Juan Nepomuceno. But the dominant form of production throughout the region was pasture-rent, even in the more developed department of Córdoba, where an incipient proletarianization process was under way. The peasants lived in hamlets on the roadsides and between the boundaries of the *haciendas*. The pasture-rent system operated on the principles that have already been described for other regions. After clearing the bushes in parts of the estate that had been put to rest, the tenants cultivated rice, yuca, ñam, and maize for themselves. Later, they had to sow pastures and return the land to the landlord, who would bring in his cattle and give new fallow land to the peasants in a cycle that was repeated every couple of years. The first symptoms of change in this remarkably stable structure came with the emergence of agrarian capitalism, which, especially in Córdoba, began to take over pasture land for semimechanized crops like cotton. However, more than the expansion of a capitalist agriculture that was only beginning, the real cause of the crisis of the traditional pasture-rent system was the landlords' reaction to Law 1 of 1968. Because this law granted potential rights to tenants, the landowners began to get rid of them on a massive scale, abolishing the customary patterns of access to land within a couple of years.

Thus, the deep unrest generated by the abrupt collapse of the subordinated peasant economy was the main force behind the extraordinary agitation of the *usuarios* in the western savannas of the Atlantic Coast. At the organizational level, the special promotion efforts during 1968 and 1969 had helped to create agitation amongst the peasants, setting the stage for ANUC's great development in this area, particularly in the department of Sucre. The evictions created a potentially explosive situation during the second half of 1970, when ANUC's mobilizations had already shown broad coverage, good organizational consistency, and a great deal of coordination ability. All these qualities were manifested in the struggles of 1971, when the western savannas had more than 130 land occupations and became the central focus in the national waves of invasions. The most seriously affected municipalities were Montería, Cereté, Ciénaga de Oro, and Pueblo Nuevo in the department of Córdoba; Corozal, Betulia, Ovejas, and San Pedro in Sucre; and San Jacinto, Magangué, and El Carmen in Bolívar. The number of land invasions was greater in Córdoba, but their organization was much better in Sucre, where the preparations were more elaborate and the resistance to eviction later strengthened. The strength of the *usuarios* frightened the landowners and motivated them to compromise: In a defensive move without parallel in any other part of the country, the Sucre landowners offered, through their regional branch of FEDEGAN, to hand over 10 percent of their lands for agrarian reform purposes. ANUC's radicalism intensified even more during late 1971, when Córdoba, Sucre, and Bolívar became central targets for the work of the Maoist groups: the Marxist-Leninist New Communist Party (PCML) and the Marxist-Leninist League (Liga ML). As will be seen later, the influence of the ML groups would become a key factor in ANUC's development in the western savannas, leading to greater peasant politicization and, especially in Sucre, to the promotion of some peasant leaders with distinctly Maoist leanings.

The last region in the Atlantic Coast extends from the swamps and lake of Ayapel in Córdoba to the department of Cesar, spanning the southern parts of Sucre, Bolívar, and Magdalena.[61] This is an area of lowlands and frequent floods, criss-crossed by many streams and the major rivers San Jorge, Cauca, and Magdalena. Due to its marginality and remoteness, the region was covered with natural forest until the 1940s and 1950s. Population was scarce and livelihood depended upon fishing and a shifting slash-and-burn agriculture of subsistence crops like yuca and maize. The notion of property began to develop only when merchants from Antioquia started to show titles and introduced fences and cattle. During the early stages of the process, the landowners were forced to pay wages to open up the forests, because there was still plenty of public land and the peasant-fishermen could maintain their freedom. But as time went by, enclosures continued until the locals were cornered in the areas of flooding and forced to surrender to the pressure of the *haciendas*. The new forms of production were variations of the pasture-rent system, affecting the pasture tenants, and others who had bondage debts. Peasant resistance took the form of continuous invasions of the fenced forests in order to carry on with their subsistence crops, especially when the floods pushed them out from the river islands and banks. A second source of permanent friction was landlord encroachment upon communal lands, which had caused the sporadic appearance of peasant syndicates in southern Magdalena and Cesar since the 1940s.

These antagonisms intensified after the Violencia when refugee colonists entered from the highlands of Antioquia, Tolima, Huila, Santander, and North Santander. The colonists occupied many idle lands and forests belonging to the landowners, the local disputes began to escalate during the 1960s, and a regional struggle emerged in 1970 with the promotion of ANUC's committees. Facing the organization of the peasants and the threat of expropriation, the landowners mobilized the local authorities and hired armed men in an eviction campaign that, in many cases, affected families who had been on the land for more than ten years. Encouraged by the official legitimation, the *usuarios* increased their resistance as ANUC gained strength at the grass-roots level. With the land invasions of 1971, the conflict extended well beyond attempts to recover the lands that had been lost by the colonists; it also included the occupation of other *haciendas* by the local peasant-fishermen who had been cornered in the flooding areas. More than 100 land seizures occurred as part of a wave that was especially intense in the municipalities of Plato, Tenerife, Santana, and El Banco in Magdalena; Chimichagua, Curumaní, and Tamalameque in Cesar; and the area of Mompós and Loba in Bolívar. From the very start, these struggles were marked by the brutal repression of some landowners, who would attain national notoriety for their ferocious reaction against the peasants.

Outside the Atlantic Coast, most of ANUC's land invasions took place in the great inner valleys, especially in the departments of Huila and

Tolima. These inner valleys, settled early in the history of the country, were characterized by very old cattle *latifundia* in the plains and a peasant economy in the highlands. During the 1950s and 1960s, the big estates had undergone considerable transformations in the more fertile areas.[62] These areas became the centers of development of capitalist agriculture in Colombia, rapidly increasing the production of mechanized and semi-mechanized crops, particularly rice and cotton in the Valley of the River Magdalena and sugar cane in the Valley of the River Cauca. These changes destroyed the precapitalist forms of production, resulting in migration to the big cities and the formation of regional groups of rural workers who handled the new types of commercial crops. By the end of the 1960s, the centers of capitalist agriculture were still surrounded by cattle estates in the marginal plains; on the slopes, the free peasantry coexisted with some traditional *haciendas* that included small tenants and sharecroppers. Against this background, the land demands that had been expressed locally in previous years and were later integrated by ANUC in 1969 and 1970 came from two different groups: the agricultural laborers and the sub-ordinated peasants of the *haciendas*. In the department of Tolima, with the exception of a couple of invasions staged by tenants on the hills of Cajamarca and Planadas, the rural laborers were the protagonists of the struggles. Their movement of land occupations started in Guamo and extended to Espinal, Flandes, Coello, and Armero in the north and Purificación, Saldaña, and Natagaima in the south. These laborers, who had been tenants and sharecroppers until the 1950s and were now working on the rice and cotton estates, lived in the municipal towns and in small villages along the main roads. From there, the local associations of *usuarios* organized the invasion of properties that included extensive sown areas and had been recently improved with infrastructural works and irrigation districts.

A similar pattern was visible in Huila, where the number of land seizures was larger than in Tolima and where the main groups of invaders were also agricultural workers in the rice-producing municipalities. The main focus was Campoalegre, and the battle expanded across the northern plain of the department to Yaguará, Palermo, Aipe, and Villavieja. However, tenants and sharecroppers also fought over land in the marginal plains and slopes of the south, seizing parts of traditional and cattle *haciendas* in municipalities like Garzón, Gigante, Paicol, Pitalito, and Altamira.

In the department of Valle there was less pressure upon the land, perhaps because the proletarianization process was older and had been better absorbed by the industrial development of its capital, Cali. In any case, ANUC's invasions were organized by agricultural laborers who were either protesting against the displacement of workers by machinery in Tuluá,

San Pedro, and Zarzal, or seizing suburban lands to build their homes near the sugar estates and mills of Palmira, Candelaria, and Cali. All in all, the struggles of 1971 in Tolima, Huila, and Valle showed that the main contradictions in the inner valleys were related to the development of agrarian capitalism and that the more belligerent groups were the rural workers and the landless peasants. However, these departmental associations of ANUC involved other established peasant sectors as well, and the main leaders came from these sectors and not from the ranks of the landless and the workers. Moreover, perhaps as a result of the previous Violencia, loyalties to the traditional parties were deeply rooted and had been further strengthened by the activities of FANAL during the 1960s. All this was reflected in the attitudes of the regional leaders of the *usuarios*. In the initial phase these leaders were marked by radicalism, participation in ANUC's national processes, and active support of the land invasions. But later, when the land struggles became the focus of the increasing left-wing politicization of the peasant movement, they became an element of restraint and opposition.

In the Andean departments the land struggles of 1971 were limited to the local level.[63] In the mountain areas, the contradictions that led to actual land invasions had two basic roots. First, tenants and sharecroppers of old-fashioned *haciendas* were either resisting eviction or demanding the redistribution of the land. These conflicts were intense in the central area of the department of Santander, on the western slopes of Cundinamarca, in the basin of the River Mueche in Boyacá, in southwestern Antioquia, and on the banks of the River Cauca in Caldas and Risaralda. There were other isolated cases in Quindío, North Santander, Cauca, and Nariño. Altogether, the land seizures of tenants and sharecroppers came to approximately half of the 140 land invasions in the Andean departments. A second source of friction was the situation in the *resguardo* areas, where the land had been occupied by the remaining Indian communities in an attempt to recover lands that had been lost to neighboring landowners in the historical process of dispossession and reduction. There were two main areas of agitation: the department of Cauca, where Páez and Guambian communities invaded more than twenty *haciendas* in Toribío, Caloto, Silvia and Totoró; and the area of the Cañamomo and Lomaprieta group in the department of Caldas, where ten estates were occupied by Indians in the municipalities of Riosucio and Supía. There were also invasions by agricultural workers, but this was a minor action – mainly a few occupations encouraged by ANUC Cundinamarca in the Bogotá Plain. In addition to these situations in the highlands, some of the land invasions in the Andean departments took place in the lower and warmer areas. They were similar to those of other regions. More than twenty of the land seizures in Santander and Antioquia occurred in the Middle Magdalena, in the Lower Cauca, and in Urabá, areas of conflict between colonists and landowners on the possession of public lands. A particular case was that of the Zulia and Cúcuta valleys in North Santander, where migrant laborers who had been recently expelled from Venezuela occupied a number of properties in an area of irrigation works.

Finally, in the Eastern Llanos, the battles for land were less intense in 1971 than they had been during the second half of the 1960s. It has already been seen that the previous land struggles in Casanare had led to a broad-based independent peasant economy. Still, in 1969 and 1970, there were some places where disputes remained unsolved, and in most cases the peasants had not yet received their official titles.[64] It was against this background that ANUC was promoted in Casanare. As a result of student influence, the leaders of the already mentioned ADAGRI were now related to the Maoist legalist party, the Independent Revolutionary Worker's Movement (MOIR). They had taken part in elections with their own peasant lists, obtaining representation in the local councils. As an organization promoted by the government, ANUC was at first regarded with suspicion. However, ADAGRI dissolved itself and became part of the *usuarios'* movement. Since ANUC was taking over an existing organization, the DOC promoters concentrated upon providing legal advice to the peasants in their negotiations with INCORA on land titles. The seizures of 1971 took place mainly in Nunchía. Compared with the agitations of the 1960s, these struggles were much less intense and marked the end of peasant pressure in Casanare. In the department of Meta there had been few previous land struggles, and the invasions of 1971 were very limited. ANUC's promotion had been superficial in the grasslands, and the few land occupations that took place were related to the eviction of sharecroppers in some *haciendas* of Puerto López, San Carlos de Guaroa, and Castilla la Nueva. The development of ANUC in Meta had been mainly in the piedmont areas of established peasant economy and in the colonization zone of the River Ariari basin. In that region some land invasions took place in Granada, Fuente de Oro, and San Juan de Aramá, where the colonists took over some stretches of forest claimed by the landowners on the borders between the grasslands and the woodland colonization range. For the rest, there were no other conflicts over land in the colonization fronts. The only invasion in Caquetá in 1971 was purely symbolic: Occupying a private property of the regional director of INCORA, the *usuarios* expressed both their "solidarity with the struggles waged by our landless brothers in the rest of the country" and their protest over INCORA's inefficiency in solving the problems of the colonists in the region.[65]

Table 3.3. *The 1971 peasant land invasions, by types of sectors involved*

Sector	Number of land invasions, 1971	Percentage
Tenants and sharecroppers in traditional haciendas	265	41.1
Colonists on idle or public lands also claimed by landowners	232	35.9
Agricultural laborers in areas of agrarian capitalism	114	17.7
Indian communities	34	5.3
Total	645	100.0

Source: CINEP's Archive on ANUC, section on land invasions (see note 57 of Chapter 3).

Dimensions and factors in the land struggles

On the basis of the information in the preceding section, it is possible to consider the content and scope of the land struggles, their relationship to the previous historical processes, the ways in which the invasions were carried out, and the factors that influenced their effectiveness. On the first point, the meaning of the confrontations is clarified when the land invasions are grouped together not by region, but according to the underlying antagonism. From this perspective, Table 3.3 indicates that approximately 41 percent of the land seizures involved peasants who were, or had just ceased to be, tenants and sharecroppers on the cattle *latifundia* and the traditional *haciendas*. The second main category, disputes between colonists and landowners over unused and public lands, accounted for some 36 percent of the cases. Less numerous were the land invasions by agricultural laborers and Indians, which accounted for 18 and 5 percent of the total cases, respectively. It should be remembered that the landlord pattern of agrarian development in Colombia has followed three historical steps: first, the concentration of land and the subordination of the peasant economy; second, the dissolution of the precapitalist relations of production; and third, the eventual emergence of agrarian capitalism. Seen from this angle, it is clear that the peasant offensive had reached the scale of a general attack on the landlord path of development, because it struck simultaneously at all three stages of that process: The colonists were questioning the formation of extensive landed property, tenants and sharecroppers were attempting to impose a peasant solution on the problem of servile relations of production, and the rural workers and Indians were trying to live again as peasants. However, in spite of their character and ubiquity, the land struggles of 1971 cannot be considered a revolutionary onslaught on the entire rural structure. Only in some regions of the Atlantic Coast, Huila and Tolima, was the movement concentrated and strong. Also, the land invasions affected only 8.3 percent of the 7,800 properties larger than 500 hectares that had been registered in the agricultural census of the previous year.[66] For these reasons, it can be concluded that although ANUC's land struggles had great significance as a general assault on the landlord path, they were limited to areas where the contradictions were acute and the conditions favorable for peasant mobilization.

As to the relationship between the land battles and the previous history of agrarian conflict in Colombia, regional analysis makes it possible to illuminate the discussion on the connection between ANUC's struggles and the Violencia of the 1950s. Table 3.4 shows the incidence of both conflicts in terms of the affected municipalities in each department. These data, coupled with the information in Table 3.1 on the intensity of the land invasions by department, indicate almost an opposition between the areas of the Violencia and those of land struggles in the 1970s. The Atlantic Coast, where ANUC's land invasions were strong, was precisely the area where the effects of the Violencia had been less noticeable. The Andean departments, on the other hand, contained most of the municipalities ransacked by the Violencia but were only marginally affected by the land occupations of the *usuarios*. Even in those departments in which both the Violencia and the land invasions were strong, it is difficult to discern a clear connection between them. In spite of the extent of the Violencia in the inner valleys, the land struggles were equally distributed among municipalities that had and had not been affected in the 1950s. Furthermore, the regional studies on the Violencia in Tolima and Huila indicate that the plains where most land invasions occurred had been largely spared by the Violencia.[67] Table 3.4 does not include information on the Eastern Llanos, where there was a similar pattern of Violencia in the 1950s and land struggles in the late 1960s and early 1970s.[68] However, it has been already shown that although the civil war in the Llanos helped to create conditions for the subsequent land struggle, the main causes of that struggle did not lie in the Violencia itself but in the peasant transformation that took place within the *latifundia*. As noted in Chapter 1, some authors suggested that the Violencia was a landowner revenge for the peasant struggles of the 1930s, an argument that is only partially supported by the evidence of more recent studies of regional history. In any case, although that point is still not settled, the evidence presented in this book strongly implies that the land struggles of the 1970s were certainly not a "revenge for the revenge." Instead of concentrating in the mountainous areas that had been the setting for factional strife, both ANUC's struggles and the preceding ones of the 1960s developed mainly

Table 3.4. *Compared incidence of the Violencia and the land struggles of the 1970s, by region and department*

	Total number of municipalities	Municipalities ransacked by the Violencia in the 1950s	Municipalities affected by land invasions in the 1970s (A)	Municipalities ransacked by the Violencia and affected by invasions (B)	B/A ratio
Atlantic Coast					
Córdoba	22	2	16	2	0.12
Sucre	23	1	19	1	0.05
Bolívar	29	7	24	6	0.25
Atlántico	23		9		0.00
Magdalena	20		11		0.00
Cesar	13		7		0.00
Guajira	7		2		0.00
Total	137	10	88	9	0.10
Percentage of total	100.0	7.2	64.2	6.5	
Inner valleys					
Valle	42	24	7	2	0.28
Tolima	44	41	10	8	0.80
Huila	36	13	20	9	0.45
Total	122	78	37	19	0.51
Percentage of total	100.0	63.9	30.3	15.5	
Andean depts.					
Cundinamarca	111	15	15	3	0.20
Boyacá	113	18	4	3	0.75
Santander	77	14	5	2	0.40
North Santander	35	8	3		0.00

Antioquia	109	39	17	11	0.64
Caldas	49	28	9	9	1.00
Cauca	36	7	14	3	0.21
Nariño	51		3		0.00
Total	581	129	70	31	0.44
Percentage of total	100.0	22.2	12.0	5.3	
Grand total	840	217	195	59	0.30
	100.0	25.8	23.2	7.0	

Sources: G. Guzmán et al., *La Violencia en Colombia*, 1962. P. Oquist, *Violence, Conflict and Politics in Colombia*, 1980. CINEP's Archive on ANUC, section on land invasions (see note 57 of Chapter 3)

in the lowlands that were beginning to be fully integrated into the economic frontier. In this sense, these struggles marked the last extension of the conflict between landlords and peasants – a long historical conflict that, following the expansion of the economic frontier, had moved down from the highlands to the slopes, finally reaching the hot marginal lowlands.[69]

Turning now to the way the land invasions were carried out, there are many descriptions of two types: the interviews that were conducted as part of this research and the accounts of journalists and researchers who witnessed the events, especially on the Atlantic Coast.[70] The process usually began with the creation of a committee of *usuarios* that took the name of the place that was going to be occupied and began to prepare, with as much forethought as possible, the conditions for the actual seizure of the land. It has already been said that, in spite of their great intensity, the land struggles of 1971 failed to produce total upheaval in the countryside. The movement was not strong enough to encourage the peasants to claim all the land, as it might have been in a truly revolutionary situation. This meant that a land invasion never embraced a whole estate, but only part of it.[71] A number of exploratory visits were made in order to choose the area. It was necessary to consider how much land was needed by the families in the group, the availability of water, the distance from the houses of the administrators and landowners, the existence of nearby roads, and other factors. Inquiries were also made about the owner of the *hacienda*, his additional properties, his habits, the frequency of his visits to the estate, and so on. Once the place had been selected, the information was passed on to INCORA, along with a petition for the expropriation of the land.

In the meantime, the preparations for the land invasion were intensified. Money was gathered to buy seeds and food. The backyards of the present dwellings of the committee families were intensively cultivated in seed beds with yuca, maize, and other crops in order to have as many plants as possible to transplant to the invaded area. The peasants also prefabricated parts of the huts that would be later assembled at the new site, letting them weather in the open so that they would seem to be older constructions. Finally, the land was secretly occupied at night, the huts were hurriedly erected, the bush was cleared, and the peasants planted as many seeds as they could. The purpose of these activities was to give the impression that the place had been occupied for a long time, establishing de facto improvements that would be registered in the official minutes of the dispute and would later serve as favorable precedents in the negotiations with the landowner. When the latter heard about the invasion, he would bring in the police or an army patrol. An inspector would note all the details of the case, while the peasants reacted with peaceful resistance, accepting their eviction amid heated discussions on agrarian reform and their right to the land. In most cases, they were simply dispersed or jailed for a few hours. The landowner used men and bulldozers to destroy the plants and huts but, a few days later, the committee reorganized itself and reoccupied the place. A long sequence of evictions and reinvasions would usually follow until the confrontation became tougher and the dispute began to attract the attention of the authorities and INCORA. As the conflict stepped up, the peasants would start to disrupt the functioning of the *hacienda*, breaking up fences to let the cattle escape, mixing up the landowner's herds, and so on. All this was done with the idea that the landowner would eventually get tired of the permanent harassment and would agree to negotiate about the invaded portion of his estate with the peasants and INCORA.[72]

Thus, a land invasion could be prolonged for a long time until its final resolution. Success depended on the peasants' ability to show greater endurance than the landlords in this long war of attrition. In this, the relative cohesion of the invaders' committees played a crucial role. The land occupations of late 1971 and early 1972 included memorable invasions involving up to 400 families on the Atlantic Coast. But the committees were usually composed of thirty to forty families, which was the most suitable size to avoid both the weakness of an excessively small group and the possible fragmentation of a larger one.[73] In addition to size, two other factors influenced cohesiveness: the local character of the land invasions and the kinship ties among the committee members. In Sucre, for example, where the land invasions were characterized by tenacious peasant resistance and many successful outcomes, the groups were formed by families who were interrelated, lived in the same hamlet, and operated on neighboring *haciendas* where they had previously worked as tenants.[74] Under these conditions, it was easier to develop the cooperation, the mutual help, and the collective defense that were required to achieve the goal. This incidence of kinship and localism in the successful invasions was noticeable in all regions, especially in those places where the conflicts involved tenants and sharecroppers.[75] By contrast, when the invaders were rural laborers, the committees were generally composed of unrelated and little acquainted families who had been recruited in other *veredas* and, in some cases, even in different municipalities. In these situations, disagreements and rivalries came more readily to the surface and the struggle was more frequently abandoned. This obviously undermined the groups' capacity for resistance, something that was evident in many land invasions of Huila, Tolima, and the central area of Córdoba. Similar problems occurred in southern Bolívar, Magdalena, and Cesar, where the invasion committees included peasant colonists who came from different highland areas, had different cultural backgrounds, and found it very difficult to maintain their cohesion until the end.

Apart from these factors within the invasion committees, the effectiveness of the land struggles was also influenced by the more general context in which they were waged. The official legitimation of the Lleras Restrepo administration and the early vacillations of the Pastrana administration regarding the treatment of the land invasions were factors that operated at the national level and, as such, have already been considered. Therefore, attention should now be directed to the regions in which the land struggles were developing. At the regional level, the main ingredient for success was the *usuarios'* integration and coordination in managing the conflicts. From this point of view, the better performances were those of the departmental associations of ANUC in Sucre, Huila, and Córdoba and also, to some extent, in Bolívar and Tolima. In these cases, ANUC's better organization made possible coherent planning and increased the possibility of success. The censuses of *usuarios* conducted by ANUC in Sucre and Huila, for example, provided detailed information not only about the families who wanted to join the committees but also about all the estates that could be defined as targets for the land invasions.[76] Centralized organization made it possible to synchronize the seizures, so that the authorities would not be able to carry out evictions at all areas simultaneously. It was also possible to maintain permanent pressure upon the occupied areas, replacing the committees whose members had been jailed with other groups that immediately converged on the same place. Moreover, the committees that won became a source of support for others who were just beginning, providing small parcels of land for subsistence until their own land invasion occurred and helping them with food, tools, and seeds.[77] The relative ease of communication and transportation in the plains also helped the coordination of the struggles in the inner valleys and the western savannas of the Atlantic Coast.

The coordination of the struggle at the regional level also facilitated the development of links between ANUC and other groups. Many functionaries of INCORA who sympathized with the *usuarios* could leak valuable information about the estates that would be more likely to be expropriated as a result of peasant pressure.[78] It was also possible to maintain regular urban contacts with civil committees, unions of workers and employees, and even some merchants who supported the peasant struggles in a solidarity movement that was especially noticeable in regional capitals such as Montería, Sincelejo, Magangué, and Neiva.[79] But undoubtedly, the key element was the fact that the large-scale organization of the land struggles endowed ANUC with extraordinary strength and transformed the peasant movement into a powerful factor in certain regions. This was especially true in Sucre, Córdoba, and Huila, where both the authorities and the landowners' federations were forced to acknowledge the peasant leaders and conduct high-level negotiations with them. In the occupied estates, the landowners were frightened by the intensity of the peasant mobilization and the combativeness of the committees that had taken the land. As a result of all these factors, the battle of 1971 led to the negotiation of most of the affected lands and, therefore, to a great victory of ANUC in these departments. In Magdalena and Cesar, where an intense struggle was taking place under conditions that made it difficult for ANUC to organize at the regional level, the successes were less significant and the landlords found it easier to consolidate their own resistance.

The uneven development of the peasant movement

When considering the place of the battle for land in ANUC's radicalization process, a crucial issue is the way in which the different types of struggles interacted with other factors and resulted in an uneven development of the peasant movement at the regional level. This issue is especially relevant because it sets a comparative standard that allows one to draw additional conclusions on the significance of the land struggles and provides an opportunity to review, at least briefly, the main developments in the other battlefronts of ANUC. Furthermore, it also helps to establish some general points that are necessary to analyze the subsequent evolution of the peasant movement.

Starting with the regions of land struggle, the central issue is that the desire for land stood out from the other peasant demands because it brought politics to the fore. It is not difficult to understand this point when one considers that, given the politics of clientelism in Colombia, the landowners were always the most important factors of local power. In fact, it was the very ownership of the land that sustained their formidable political power. In the western savannas of the Atlantic Coast, for example, the servile relations of production had been the basis of clientelism. The typical Liberal or Conservative *gamonal* was a landowner who, by monopolizing the land in a given area, had turned the local population into tenants and sharecroppers. Since there was no other way to make a living for the landless peasants, the landowner was able to define this subordination as a "favor." The *gamonal* would also show concern for some community affairs and occasionally helped the families with their individual problems. He further strengthened his position by using traditional institutions such as *compadrazgo*, in which the godfather relationship reinforced the bond of personal dependency, and the *corralejas*, popular bullfight festivals that enhanced his prestige by marking the renewal of the tenancy agreements. In addition to the economic benefits derived from subordination, there was a crucial political bonus: At election time, the peasants had to reciprocate all the favors by voting for the *gamonal* or his political "lieutenants."[80] Thus, property and power were closely intertwined in the socioeconomic, political, and cultural clientelist milieu, which, with regional variations, also prevailed in the other areas of land struggle. In these circumstances, the peasants' demand for land of their own was much more than a claim to the means of subsistence. It was also a political demand, because land expropriation implied the destruction of the political power of the landowning class and the clientelist system.

In contrast to other demands such as credit and services, then, the aspiration for land was a challenge to the regime of landed property and involved a direct confrontation with another social class. This political dimension of the land struggle had a decisive effect upon ANUC. As the basic form of direct action, the land invasions were an illegal act, defying both the authorities and the landowners. This led to the consolidation of radical leadership, because those who were either loyal to the *gamonales* or simply afraid were replaced by others who were more committed to the peasant struggle.[81] In addition, since direct illegal action was taking place amid the crisis of the original reformist legitimation, the time was right for radical ideology. In fact, it could be said that a radical ideology of opposition became necessary to sustain the peasant movement in the areas of land struggle. This need was fulfilled by leftist movements like the Socialist Bloc and the PCML, which, given their concept of the revolutionary process in Colombia, were attracted to the situation that seemed to be developing in the countryside.[82]

Radical leadership, organizational strength, and leftist politicization would thus characterize ANUC in the areas of land struggle. The nature of the peasant confrontation in these areas created conditions for a more radical movement than that of other regions where the demands were more economic in character. However, due to the uneven influence of certain factors, this radicalization was not everywhere the same. Some conflicts had already been settled, and new peasant sectors with different types of interests had emerged in places like Atlántico and Casanare. In the departments of Bolívar, Magdalena, and Cesar, the conflicts had many roots, which caused some dispersion and hindered the organizational cohesiveness of ANUC at the regional level. In the inner valleys, the importance of the established peasants of the mountains and slopes was clearly felt in the departmental associations of Huila, Tolima, and Valle. Politically, the influence of the left-wing groups was also uneven: They concentrated most of their work in Sucre, Córdoba, Bolívar, and Antioquia; their presence was only marginal and sporadic in the other departments. Moreover, either because of the previous work of organizations like FANAL in the Caribbean littoral or the more marked partisan loyalties in the Andes and the inner valleys, there were regions in which the traditional parties blocked the ideological influence of the left. All these differences were pushed into the background in a situation in which the radicalization of the peasant movement was focused on the struggle for land, but they would later become important when ANUC was forced to assume clearer positions to resist the counteroffensive of the state and the dominant classes.

In the areas of colonization, the struggle for land was not the central issue. This is not surprising when one remembers that, as was indicated in the second section of Chapter 1, the main problems in these areas had to do with conditions of reproduction, not with access to land. The colonists battled against nature, opening up virgin forests in remote places where everything was public land that was not even disputed by the landowners and their titles. Nonetheless, even under these conditions, the struggle for survival acquired a social dimension because, as previously indicated, the absence of basic services hindered peasant agriculture. It is true that some groups managed to establish themselves as peasants. But in many other cases the landlords followed, buying the cleared lands, turning them into grasslands, and pushing the colonists farther into the forest in a never-ending cycle of property concentration at the expense of a transient peasant economy. This explains both the strong response of the colonists to ANUC and the fact that their demands for basic services were directed to the state and especially to INCORA, which was in charge of the programs supporting the colonization process.[83]

In contrast to the land struggle, where direct action took the form of land invasions, the struggle of the *usuarios* in the colonization areas was characterized by occupation of the compounds of the state institutes and, in two cases, by massive civil strikes. The first of these great strikes took place in the Sarare region in Arauca, where unrest had developed after INCORA's failure to construct roads and provide credit. Encouraged by the struggles of the landless in other parts of the country, the *usuarios* of the area staged a general strike in March 1971. In that strike, 2,000 colonists took over the main town of the region, Saravena, and presented petitions demanding the construction of roads and bridges, the establishment of a centralized marketing system to sell peasant produce in the main cities, the availability of credit, and the provision of electricity, water, and communications for Saravena. The strike continued for thirteen days, until a ministerial commission came from Bogotá and signed a government agreement to meet many of the colonists' demands.[84]

The second massive mobilization was that of Caquetá, the most important colonization front. By mid-1971 there were great floods throughout the area, and ANUC initiated negotiations to obtain relief programs, cancel debts, and obtain new credits for the affected families. The *usuarios* also asked for roads, services, and fixed prices for the two main commercial crops of the colonists, rice and maize. Nothing was obtained in spite of months of increasing pressure and, in the end, ANUC Caquetá decided to organize a regional civil strike in July 1972. More than 10,000 peasants converged on the regional capital, Florencia, and occupied it for eight days. The demands included better prices for peasant crops, suspension of debts for ruined colonists, construction of roads, control of transport prices, and establishment of schools and health centers. President Pastrana sent three army battalions to Florencia and invited a delegation of *usuarios* to negotiate in Bogotá. Finally, the strike was called off when the government increased the prices of maize and rice and promised to carry out studies with a view to extending the services and developing the roads in the region.[85]

There were other expressions of protest in more secondary colonization fronts like Ariari, Putumayo, and the Pacific Littoral, but they did not reach the massive dimensions and repercussions of the strikes of Sarare and Caquetá.[86]

Although less intense than in the areas of land struggle, then, the radicalization of ANUC was also quite marked in some of the colonization fronts.[87] But the bases of this process were different. While the central element in the land struggles was the political nature of the demand for land, in the colonization areas the main factor was the weakness of the traditional power structure. The "crisis of authority" had two sources: the remoteness of the colonization fronts from the centers of institutional power and the loss of prestige of the traditional parties, whose confrontation had originally displaced the colonists from the highlands during the Violencia.[88] Radical leaders emerged among the *usuarios* of Caquetá and Sarare, but not in the other colonization fronts. Perhaps the reason was that the influence of the left was far less than that in the areas of land struggle. None of the left-wing groups or parties developed a real presence in any of the colonization areas during the first half of the 1970s. In Caquetá and Sarare, leftist ideology was spread by independent intellectuals who were advising the peasant leaders personally and not as part of a coordinated penetration by a political group.[89] Another factor that raised doubts about the future of radicalism in the colonization areas was the heterogeneity of the peasantry, which included stable, well-to-do groups along with the majority of marginal colonists. This created the possibility that, by meeting some economic demands, like the construction of roads, the government could erode the more important bases of discontent without solving the problems of the majority and without making significant political concessions.

In the Andean departments, the land struggle was not the focus of the peasant movement. It is true that population pressures and peasant dissolution created an objective need for land. But because of the predominance of the *minifundia*, in most places there were simply no landlords to fight against. The existing large estates were usually fully exploited by their owners and, in contrast to other cases of traditional *haciendas* and absentee landowners, there was little legal or moral justification for their occupation. Whereas in the colonization fronts the absence of land struggles reflected the abundance of land, in the Andean areas land was scarce. Therefore, it was extremely difficult to mobilize the peasants for land occupations. The most important demands in the *minifundia* areas were made by the more stable peasants, whose strong loyalty to the traditional parties was alien to the spirit of revolutionary discourse. The radicalization of ANUC did not include the emergence of radical leaders and the influence of leftist ideologies. Usually the original leaders remained, many of whom were Liberal and Conservative affluent peasants who agreed that ANUC should be independent as a trade union, supported the demands of the landless peasants of other areas, but also insisted on maintaining the link with the state and keeping their own activity within legal limits.[90] This was in accord with the economic nature of the demands of the landed peasants, demands for improved state services that implied no political challenge.

Given the more conservative nature of their demands and the traditional political influence, radicalism was rarely dominant among the *usuarios* in the Andean departments.[91] Although the demands were duly expressed by the local and regional organizations of ANUC, they usually took the form of petitions by delegations and, at most, local demonstrations. In fact, the only regionally coordinated protest in 1971 occurred in Nariño, where *usuarios* from different municipalities demonstrated in front of the regional office of the Caja Agraria in Pasto, demanding improvements in the credit programs.[92] By contrast, the only case of peasant belligerency in the Andes was a local one: the civil strike of the municipality of Quinchía in Risaralda. This was a special situation of strong discontent caused by the sudden imposition of a high tax due to nonexisting services of rural social security, which outraged the peasants.[93] There was regional coordination and great radicalism in the Indian struggles of the department of Cauca; this was, again, a special case. What originally began as part of the *usuarios*' organization had developed into the Regional Indian Council of Cauca (CRIC), which maintained a special relationship with ANUC but conducted its own struggles for land, for the restoration of the *resguardos*, and for the revival of Indian culture.[94] Thus, it can be concluded that, in general, the *usuarios* had much more conservative attitudes in the areas of *minifundia*, attitudes characteristic of the Andean departmental associations of ANUC. It is true that exceptions existed and that because of the great diversity of situations, the picture was more complex and many special factors were operating. However, since this book focuses mainly upon ANUC's land struggles and the corresponding areas, this discussion cannot proceed beyond a general level. As with the colonization fronts, further elaboration on the processes and trends in the areas of established peasant economy would require a more detailed study of the regions involved.

4

Counterreform

The response of the dominant classes to the peasant land struggles would have drastic consequences for the evolution of the agrarian question in Colombia. Throughout the rest of the Pastrana administration, the counteroffensive would eradicate all traces of reform in state policy, transforming it into an instrument of defense of the landowners' interests, support for capitalist agriculture, and the curbing of peasant aspirations.

Reversion of agrarian policy under the Pastrana administration

Pastrana's counteroffensive had started with the restriction on ANUC after the invasions of February 1971 and the public declarations of the new Minister of Agriculture, Jaramillo Ocampo. The minister had denounced the *Mandato Campesino* as a call for subversion, and in September he attacked some of the activities of INCORA and the whole idea of agrarian reform in a congressional debate.[1] During the second wave of land invasions in October and November 1971, the clamor for counterreform reached hysterical proportions. The editorial pages of the Conservative newspapers urged action against the danger of "agrarian communism," brandishing such "proofs" as the use of agricultural tools made in Czechoslovakia in one case of land occupation and the showing of a Russian film in some INCORA seminars on cooperativism.[2] The federations of landowners (including SAC, FEDEGAN, and the associations of planters and growers of sugar, rice, cotton, cacao, and grains) submitted a joint memorandum to the government demanding "an immediate end to the impending threat to the institutions and the social peace of the Nation."[3] When the debate on the land invasions was about to open in the Senate, President Pastrana announced at a meeting of rice growers in late November that the government would not yield to peasant pressure, that the land invasions would be severely repressed, and that there would be no titles for those who sought to benefit by agrarian reform after taking the land by force.[4] Finally, the Conservative senator Hugo Escobar Sierra presented to Congress a detailed report about the land invasions in December 1971. With the support of representatives of all shades of Conservative and Liberal opinion, Escobar Sierra accompanied his report with an inflammatory speech, stressing the presumed connections between the land struggles and subversion and inviting "all the parties and sectors to reach a great national agreement on agrarian reform and save the country from the dreadful consequences of a red revolution in the countryside."[5] Promptly responding to the congressional call, the government summoned representatives of the two political parties and the private sector to a special meeting in the town of Chicoral in early January 1972.

The Pact of Chicoral was a formal declaration of agrarian counterreform. In exchange for the payment of taxes that would be determined by the census value of their estates, the landowners were assured of both restricted agrarian reform and unlimited support for large-scale agricultural production. The criteria used to define the estates as liable to expropriation and redistribution were tightened. In the cases of expropriation, Law 135 of 1961 was modified so that compensation would depend on the commercial value of the land and not its census value, a greater proportion would be paid in cash, and high interest would be paid on the remaining debt. INCORA's potential activity was therefore doubly curtailed, because it would have much less scope for intervention and budget cuts would bring its action to a standstill. Further, the government would provide financial incentives for the expansion of mechanized agriculture, capitalizing the Agricultural Financial Fund with a fixed compulsory proportion of the loans of all the private and public banks.[6] To translate the terms of the agreement into national laws, President Pastrana summoned the Congress to extra sessions.[7]

As expected, the Pact of Chicoral was strongly condemned by ANUC and unanimously praised by the landowners' federations.[8] All the factions of the Conservative and Liberal parties endorsed it, including many who had supported the reformist leanings of the previous administration.[9] There was, of course, criticism from ex-President Lleras Restrepo, his closest followers, and a few progressive Conservatives such as J. Emilio Valderrama, but these were ignored.[10] In fact, the participation of some well-known Lleristas in the meeting at Chicoral had been a clear indication that the reformist sector within the Liberal Party was rapidly disintegrating.[11] Lleras Restrepo lost most of his influence and, as proved by his 1978 failure to win the Liberal nomination for the presidency, he would not be able to reenter the mainstream of Colombian politics.[12] To some extent, the collapse of reformism can be explained by three political factors: the strength of the landowning interests in both traditional parties, the fears aroused by the leftist connotations of the peasants' radicalism, and the apparent easing of the urban pressures after ANAPO's 1970 electoral defeat. However, the main reasons were found in the deeper level of the socioeconomic processes that were changing the relationships among the social classes.

In terms of class alignments and oppositions, the Pact of Chicoral marked the final breakdown of the attempt to forge an alliance between the peasantry and the bourgeoisie. While the former was pushed into isolation, the latter became part of a new entente with the landowners. The interests of large-scale property and financial capital were focused on an agribusiness type of development, but the change of heart of the industrialists was due to the redefinition of their priorities according to the new orientations of Colombian capitalist accumulation. For Lleras Restrepo, promotion of industrial exports had been a necessary adjustment to reproduce the previous scheme by expanding the internal market. However, the success of these measures had created new conditions in which production for export was becoming the key element in a new phase of capitalism.[13] This was related to the changing international division of labor, the inclusion of peripheral countries as suppliers of certain manufactured goods, and the sale of these commodities to the developed countries. All these tendencies became manifest in the 1960s and were further stimulated during the expansion of the world economy that began in 1968 and 1969. In Colombia, the internal and external incentives induced a rapid growth of the manufactured exports, which grew to US $100 million in 1970 and increased by 500 percent in the four subsequent years.[14]

The acceleration of a new accumulation process spearheaded by the export industry caused both employment and internal consumption to increase, defining new imperatives for the industrial bourgeoisie and destroying its previous reformist sympathies. Reestablishment of the peasantry to expand the internal market became almost irrelevant in a world where the markets were being opened abroad and in the big industrial cities themselves as a result of the increases in workers' consumption. Checking the rural–urban migration could even be self-defeating, since lower wages were needed to compete successfully in the international market, especially when salaries had been rising until 1970 and the rate of increase in urban employment doubled the rate of growth of urban population in an unprecedented expansion that was creating more jobs in three years than during the entire 1960s.[15] The same imperatives of cheaper wages and external competitiveness aroused the interest of the industrialists in raw materials and foodstuffs that could be supplied more cheaply by the greater productivity of capitalist agriculture than by traditional peasant production. Politically, the populist challenge had been timely curbed, and the improvement of the urban situation was defusing much of the previous discontent. In short, agrarian reformism was no longer indispensable, and since it could even become an obstacle, the industrial bourgeoisie had been induced to close ranks with the other dominant sectors against the peasantry. After being defeated during the 1960s, the neo-Liberal strategies that Lauchin Currie had been proposing for Colombia's development became paradoxically relevant as a result of the application of the reformist policies.[16] The development plan adopted by the Pastrana administration in 1972 under the name of "the four strategies" clearly expressed the alignment of the interests of the bourgeois sectors and the landowners while, at the same time, it began to rationalize the new capitalist model at the level of state economic policy.[17]

The politics of division and repression

The Pact of Chicoral was the basis of counterreform and the platform for unlimited support of the landlord path of agrarian evolution in Colombia's countryside. Nonetheless, implementation of this policy required more than the modification of existing laws and the provision of money for capitalist agriculture. It was also necessary to curb the militant upsurge of the peasants, who, by means of ANUC, were using direct and autonomous action in an attempt to impose their own solution to the agrarian question. This policy of restraint took two forms: the splitting of ANUC and the repression of the land struggles. On the first of these, it must be recalled that there were precedents for dissent among the *usuarios* on basic issues such as the direction of the struggles, the relationship with the state, and the political positions of the peasant movement. The radicalization process and the leftist influences had aggravated these contradictions, causing reservations and separate meetings among the loyalist leaders both after the adoption of the *Mandato Campesino* and during the land invasions of late 1971.[18]

The final crisis between radicals and loyalists developed at the fifth meeting of ANUC's National Junta (Tolú, February 1972), where the *usuarios* approved two crucial resolutions. Denouncing the Pact of Chicoral as "a reactionary project in favour of the interests of the landowners and capitalists," the first of these resolutions rejected the government's counterreform, reaffirmed the guidelines of the *Mandato Campesino*, and announced the *usuarios'* intention "to continue the struggle until the final victory."[19] Minister Jaramillo Ocampo, who had come to the meeting to "explain" the changes proposed by the government, was strongly rebutted and practically expelled by the peasants.[20] The second key resolution of ANUC's fifth National Junta concerned peasant participation in future elections. Considering "the existing regime and the political parties as responsible for the exploitation and misery of the masses, the unjust distribution of the land, and the violence and repression against the people," the document called on the peasants to abstain in the elections and use other means "to defeat the reactionary policies of the dominant classes."[21] The nature of these resolutions and the hostile treatment of the minister amounted to a formal declaration of war against the government and the traditional parties. Throughout the three days of debate, the loyalist leaders within the National Junta had opposed these positions.[22] However, the majority of the delegates consistently voted against their motions and supported the radicals. Frustrated by their defeat and encouraged by confidential promises by government officials, the loyalists decided to abandon the Junta meeting.[23] After leaving Tolú, they issued a statement supporting Minister Jaramillo Ocampo's public condemnation of "the communist infiltration and the subversive attitudes that prevail in ANUC."[24]

Taking advantage of the cleavage among the *usuarios*, Jaramillo Ocampo negotiated with the dissidents and launched a divisive offensive within the peasant movement.[25] For this purpose he used the ministerial DOC, whose original staff and field promoters had been by then almost totally purged and replaced by faithful Conservatives.[26] With the help of the government, the loyalist leaders organized a special meeting at Neiva, where they again denounced ANUC's "communist" tendencies, declared the leadership of the movement vacant, and appointed a provisional Executive Committee.[27] After an intensive campaign to recruit the support of local and regional *usuario* leaders, ANUC was formally split at the Second National Congress organized by the government in Armenia during November 1972.[28] This assembly was totally manipulated by Jaramillo Ocampo's functionaries, who pushed aside the main peasant leaders and replaced them with others who would be less likely to emphasize aspirations for further autonomy.[29] The government extended its full recognition and financial support to the loyalists, who began to be known as the "Armenia Line" of ANUC, after the city where the congress had been staged. On the regional level, the Armenia Line gained control of a number of departmental associations. As shown in Table 4.1, most of these associations were located in the less radical *minifundia* departments. In the areas of land struggle, only Huila and Tolima supported the loyalists. Still, even in these cases, the more belligerent municipal associations rejected the leadership of the loyalists.[30] Lacking effective leaders, despised by the more conscientious groups at the grass-roots level, and totally subservient to a government that was determined to make no concessions to the peasantry, the new ANUC Armenia was reduced during its early years to a divisive tool that played no role in the representation of peasant demands.[31]

ANUC's majority, which no longer had legal government recognition, meanwhile held its own Second National Congress in July 1972. The

Table 4.1. *ANUC's split: radical and loyalist departmental associations in 1972*

Departmental associations of the radical Sincelejo Line	Departmental associations of the loyalist Armenia Line[a]	Other departmental associations[b]
Caldas	Antioquia	Cundinamarca
Cauca	Boyacá	Casanare
Nariño	North Santander	Valle del Cauca
Risaralda	Quindío	
Santander	Chocó	
Arauca	Atlántico	
Caquetá	Guajira	
Putumayo	Huila	
Bolívar	Tolima	
Cesar		
Córdoba		
Magdalena		
Meta		
Sucre		

[a] A substantial number of municipal associations from Antioquia, Huila, and Tolima rejected the regional leadership of the Armenia Line and continued to support ANUC Sincelejo.

[b] Controlled by activists of the Communist Party, ANUC's Departmental Association of Cundinamarca adhered to the Armenia Line because of the abstentionist stance adopted by the Fifth National Junta. The legalist Maoists of MOIR, who also opposed electoral abstentionism, reorganized the regional association of Casanare as the Independent Peasant Organization of Casanare (OCIDEC). Valle del Cauca, which had originally been influenced by Christian Democratic leaders, eventually abandoned the Armenia Line and practically disappeared as an organized group.

assembly, which took place in the city of Sincelejo, included delegates from most of the departmental associations of ANUC. A total of 10,000 peasants of Sucre and other regions participated in the demonstration that inaugurated the congress, giving ample proof of the support enjoyed by the radicals at the grass-roots level.[32] With the exception of Cundinamarca and Casanare, where the peasant leadership opposed abstentionism as a result of the influence of the Communist Party and MOIR, all the radical leaders had reaffirmed their adherence to the belligerent "Sincelejo Line."[33] Table 4.1 shows that ANUC Sincelejo controlled a majority of the regional associations, including a number of *minifundia* departments, all the relevant regions of colonization, and the key areas of land struggle. Maintaining the original organizational statute of the *usuarios*, ANUC Sincelejo started to rebuild the departmental organizations that had been lost to the loyalists. At the national level, the Second National Congress elected a new National Junta and a new Executive Committee, promoting radical leaders to replace those who had defected to the Armenia Line.[34] In general, ANUC Sincelejo had retained the support of most *usuarios* and survived the initial shock of the split. However, the government's relentless divisive campaign would have a corrosive effect upon the subsequent evolution of radical ANUC, a topic that will be considered in a moment and again later in this book.

The second component of Pastrana's policy of restraint of the peasant movement was increasing repression, which, since late 1971 and early 1972, was directed especially to the areas that had been most affected by the land invasions. Repression, of course, was nothing new. There had been many retaliations and violent evictions from the beginning of the land struggles. The landowners used their political power to mobilize the local authorities, and in some cases they used gangs to oust the peasant invaders. During the conflicts of early 1971 there were a number of bloody incidents in different parts of the country; the *usuarios* had denounced these incidents as attempts by the landowners to revive the mood of the Violencia.[35] However, these had been isolated cases which reflected defensive reactions of the landowners rather than deliberate state policy. The official treatment of invasions was quite moderate because INCORA's intervention gave some legitimation to the de facto occupations, and the evictions carried out by the authorities were usually peaceful and led only to short imprisonments or simple dispersion of the peasant groups. This situation would change radically as the hardening of the government's attitude developed into an open confrontation with the peasant movement. In the invasions of late 1971, repression had already become a clear official policy: INCORA's functionaries were instructed not to interfere, the police and the army were ordered to use harsher methods in the evictions, and military majors were put in charge of the more affected municipalities.[36] After the Pact of Chicoral, the assaults on the land invaders increased, including the mobilization of army battalions, the militarization of entire regions, and the imprisonment of whole groups of families who were kept for long periods in jail and subjected to ill-treatment and abuse. The so-called *pájaros*, thugs armed and paid by the landowners, began to retaliate against the peasants with impunity.[37] INCORA announced that it would no longer negotiate about invaded lands and that it would adopt sanctions against whoever took part in land occupations; this meant that there would be blacklists, including the names of all those who were losing their right to land reform by their involvement in illegal acts.[38] In fact, the official violence soon went beyond the land struggle to attack the organization itself. This became clear with the severe repression of the Peasant Marches of September 1972, organized by ANUC Sincelejo to

claim its legitimacy against the fabrication of the pro-governmental
ANUC.[39] The coercive treatment of the land invasions, the persecution
of the peasant leaders, the use of military justice under the state of siege,
and the continuous harassment of ANUC became, after 1972, the official
policy toward the peasant movement.

How did the government's counteroffensive affect the land struggle?
To begin with, the division was important in causing some regions to
withdraw from the battle for land. The leaders of the loyalist Armenia
Line stated that it was necessary to keep the movement within the limits
of law and order, restraining impulses toward direct action at the grass-
roots level. The most significant effects were felt in Huila and Tolima,
where the land invasions ceased almost completely after the fifth meeting
of the National Junta.[40] In many Andean areas, in the department of
Atlántico, and in the coastal municipalities of Córdoba, Sucre, Bolívar,
and Magdalena, the influence of ANUC Armenia also ended the land
seizures.[41] In addition to the role played by the regional leaders, there
were other reasons why the *usuarios* of these regions supported the less
radical sectors. As noted in the regional analysis, these factors were the
less serious contradictions in the Andean departments and Caribbean
Littoral, as well as the strong loyalty to the traditional parties in these
areas and in the inner valleys. Furthermore, even in the regions of most
intense land struggle, where the peasants had remained faithful to ANUC
Sincelejo, the split would affect the continuity of the battles. Throughout
the western savannas of the Atlantic Coast and in other places, the dispute
over legitimacy forced the radicals to devote most of their efforts to
activities that distracted the groups from the land struggle. The holding
of the Second National Congress in Sincelejo, the peasant marches, and
the educational regional seminars in which the question of legitimacy was
discussed demanded all the attention of ANUC Sincelejo throughout 1972
and part of 1973.[42] Personnel were diverted to these activities at the cost
of losing the momentum that had been gained with the land invasions.
The government took advantage of this situation to reorganize repressive
measures that had been previously dwarfed by the very magnitude of the
peasant offensive. The reinforcement of the military machinery and the
reduced intensity of the conflicts made it easier to repress the land invasions
during 1972 and 1973. Moreover, INCORA was now controlled by new
functionaries who were loyal to the counterreformist government, so that
the Institute ceased to mediate in the disputes and, in most cases, openly
boycotted the *usuarios*.[43] This showed the peasants that the official vacillations were over, that future invasions would be violent, and that the
results would hardly be as favorable as they had been before.

5

The contradictory influences of peasant politicization

The analysis of the land struggles and the review of developments within ANUC's National Junta have stressed the importance of leftist influences in the radicalization of the *usuarios*. After briefly considering the reorganizational tasks of ANUC Sincelejo due to the government's counteroffensive, the first section of this chapter will study the continued struggle for land during the remaining years of the Pastrana administration. The second section will examine the way in which leftist politicization, a central factor in the struggle, created internal contradictions that would have fateful consequences for the peasant movement.

Factors of continuity in the land struggles

The data on the land invasions of 1972 and 1973 clearly show their decline. Table 3.1 indicates that only 54 and 51 land occupations, respectively, occurred during these years, as against the 645 that had marked the extraordinary climax of 1971. Although the divisive and repressive measures of the Pastrana administration were key factors, they cannot completely account for this decline. Paradoxically, an equally important factor was the very success of the 1971 mobilizations. Most of the occupied lands had been taken over by INCORA and were now under negotiation, so that the de facto possession of the squatters was becoming seemingly irreversible as time went by and more and more improvements were made on the land. In Sucre, for example, where ANUC's departmental association had presented in 1970 a list of 5,500 families who wanted land, it is estimated that by 1973 and early 1974 at least 4,000 families had obtained holdings on estates that had been invaded and later negotiated by INCORA.[1] This indicates that the partial satisfaction of the "land hunger" that resulted from the peasants' initial victory reduced the intensity of the struggle, decreasing the contradictions in the most affected areas. This issue will be considered in detail in the first part of Chapter 8. For the time being, however, it is worthwhile to note that the relative calm following the land invasions was especially noticeable among the most radical peasant groups, who, precisely because of their radicalism, were more likely to have obtained land after the first battles. Furthermore, the consolidation of the squatters created new problems associated with the legalization of their tenure and the farming of the land. This involved a total change in the goals and priorities of the peasant committees, which now approached the struggle for land not as a question of their own immediate needs but as a matter of solidarity with other groups of still landless peasants.

The decreasing battle for land was influenced by another fact as well: The leadership of ANUC Sincelejo had to engage in other tasks to create a viable basis for the continuity of the peasant movement. The loss of the organizational channels previously supplied by the government made it necessary to develop new ones.[2] Many leaders from the more secure areas were shifted to other departments in order to counteract the Armenia Line and try to reestablish contacts with local and regional associations. The national leaders had to devote most of their time to strengthening the organizational structure, maintaining communications and doing all the coordination formerly handled by the promoters and other DOC personnel.

The lack of funds to sustain the movement's activities was a crucial problem at the beginning.[3] Looking for other financial sources, ANUC approached radical social scientists who were carrying out community projects funded by foreign institutions. One of those who came to the rescue was the international renowned sociologist Orlando Fals Borda, whose group of research and social action La Rosca, was coordinating a number of community projects at the grass-roots level in Córdoba and other areas.[4] Fals Borda unreservedly helped the *usuarios*, transferring funds from his own projects and offering his contacts with European sources.[5] Starting with these contacts, ANUC developed solid links with many charitable foundations, religious organizations, farmers' unions, and other foreign institutions.[6] These relationships would provide continuous funding during the subsequent development of the peasant movement. In Holland, the country where ANUC's cause raised more sympathies, a group of Colombian and Dutch intellectuals created a special organization to coordinate the solidarity campaign. The agency, Aktie Colombia, placed commercials in the Dutch media, collected private donations for ANUC, and encouraged the public to send letters of protest to the Colombian government.[7]

In the work at the grass-roots level, the most important task was to promote greater activism on the other battlefronts of ANUC. Although access to land had been the decisive element in the organization, the radicalization process had also shown that these other contradictions could propel the peasants to action, especially in the colonization areas. Direct confrontation with the state and the dominant classes demanded the concentration of all sources of strength and the simultaneous exertion of pressure at different points. In addition, the contest for legitimacy against

ANUC Armenia had more priority in the other regions than in the areas of land struggle. These imperatives, as well as the need to balance the activity of the movement by promoting the interests of the other peasant sectors, had already been evident at the Second National Congress of Sincelejo, where much attention was given to the ways in which ANUC could press the demands of the *minifundistas*, the colonists, the Indians, and agricultural laborers.[8] On the struggle for land, the Second Congress reconsidered the *Mandato Campesino* program. It was acknowledged that the invasion committees had not been able to operate as CERA because the *Mandato* had been tailored to a revolutionary upsurge that, in fact, did not exist. More important still, it was decided to replace the previous Trotskyite-inspired slogan *"Tierra sin patronos"* ("land without masters") with the new motto *"Tierra para quien la trabaja"* ("land for those who till it").[9] This change reflected the growing political influence of the Maoist groups within the peasant movement, which will be considered in detail in the next section.

At the tenth meeting of the National Junta (Popayán, January 1974), it was decided that the Third National Congress of ANUC Sincelejo would take place in Bogotá by the end of August, and that the movement should increase its activity on all fronts to promote the event, create a show of strength, and again stir up public opinion on the peasant question.[10] The situation appeared to be favorable. It was an election period that marked the end of both the hostile Pastrana administration and the National Front agreement. The first free election seemed likely to result in a landslide victory for the Liberal candidate, Alfonso López Michelsen, who had been the leader of the MRL radical Liberal opposition of the early 1960s and had supported Lleras Restrepo on the Agrarian Reform Law in 1961. Although the conflicts had declined, the land struggles had continued in some departments and, at the national level, the leadership of ANUC had missed no opportunity to keep the debate alive and denounce the counterreformist policies, especially when Laws 4 and 5 of 1973 were passed, sanctioning the provisions of the Pact of Chicoral.[11] Thus, in February and March 1974, the Executive Committee of the Sincelejo Line called on the *usuarios* for a renewed peasant assault on *latifundia* throughout the country. In spite of the factors that prevented a repetition of a wave of invasions similar to those of 1971, there was a significant response at the grass-roots level. More than 100 land occupations were carried out in what would be the last of the great peasant offensives of the 1970s. However, Table 3.1 shows that the 1974 mobilization was confined to only a few regions, primarily the departments of Sucre and Antioquia. It is therefore necessary to analyze the developments on the regional level in order to investigate the reasons for this selective continuation of the land struggles.

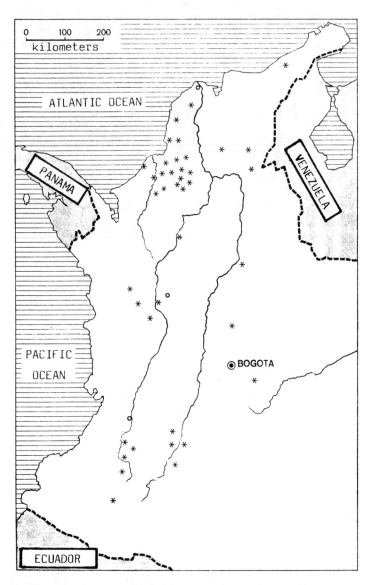

Map 5. Geographical location of the municipalities affected by land invasions, 1974.

For reasons that were considered in Chapter 3, the fighting spirit of the peasants was particularly strong in Sucre.[12] In spite of the victories of 1971, official repression had kept some invaders from the land, and many of those peasants now lived provisionally on holdings that had been won by other committees. This maintained a strong potential for conflict, which was aggravated by the refusal of Minister Jaramillo Ocampo to consider the proposal for negotiations advanced by the big landowners themselves through FEDEGAN. During the last months of 1972, repression had led to the imposition of a curfew during the Peasant March and to the first death among the *usuarios* during a violent eviction in Toluviejo. Still, ANUC's departmental association in Sucre was strongly influenced by the PCML and the Liga ML, and these groups kept urging the local committees to take direct action. Many of the land invasions began to be carried out by "peeling cows," that is, by taking the landowners' cattle to feed the occupants. Besides stealing cattle, some groups were accused of looting, robbing buses, and even conducting paramilitary training. The land invasions of February 1973 had been characterized by great violence and desperate resistance to the evictions by the police and the army. The land battles and the massive demonstrations involving many students caused the authorities to militarize the most affected municipalities, but repressive means alone were insufficient. INCORA received the green light to conduct negotiations with ANUC and FEDEGAN, a special multilateral committee was created, and an Emergency Plan was outlined, including a provision to redistribute 12,000 additional hectares within a two-year period. As a result of the agreement the mobilizations ceased, but, from September on, the *usuarios* had begun to protest against the delay in the implementation of the Emergency Plan.

Thus, the atmosphere was again highly charged in the department when the call for a renewed peasant offensive came in early 1974. A coordinated operation of land seizures began in Corozal, Los Palmitos, Ovejas, San Pedro, and nine other municipalities of the central savannas. This time, however, ANUC had to face a governor with a great deal of political tact. Gustavo Dáger Chadid, a close associate of López Michelsen, had gained some influence over the peasants, showing sympathy for their demands and interest in their organization. In Los Palmitos, for example, he had encouraged the reunification of the Armenia and Sincelejo lines at the level of the *usuarios'* municipal association. When the wave of land invasions took place, the governor reacted swiftly and skillfully, urging the landowners to make "small sacrifices" and asking the collaboration of the *usuarios* to avoid repression and violence. During the subsequent months and until the elections of mid-1974, Dáger Chadid continuously negotiated with the departmental leaders of ANUC. Successive outbreaks and truces developed, with frequent visits of the governor to Bogotá in order to speed up the Emergency Plan and many personal appearances conveying a message of peace to peasant invasion committees and demonstrating crowds. In the end, Dáger Chadid secured INCORA's intervention in the main invaded *haciendas*, proposed a new truce until the elections, and brought in army troops from Barranquilla in order to emphasize his resolve to use repression if peace was not reestablished. After a heated internal debate, ANUC Sucre accepted the truce and turned its attention to the impending Third National Congress, thus signaling the end of the battle for land in the central savannas of Sucre. Important victories had been achieved through a combination of outright pressure and high-level negotiations, a formula that distinguished the struggles of ANUC Sucre from those of all the other regional associations of ANUC and reflected the higher political and organizational level of the peasantry in that department.

In the department of Antioquia, the 1974 conflicts were centered in Urrao and some *veredas* of neighboring municipalities.[13] Throughout this area, known as the "Antioqueño southwest," the land struggles were related to the eviction of sharecroppers from traditional *haciendas* on the slopes of the River Cauca and in the smaller valleys of Pabón and Penderisco. Because of an unfulfilled INCORA program of land redistribution, Urrao had been in 1971 the main focus of land invasions in Antioquia. Since 1972, the dominant political influence in the Antioqueño southwest had been the Liga ML. In Urrao, the *usuarios* had been strongly radicalized and politicized by the continuous presence of many young student militants from the departmental capital, Medellín. The land invasions started in February 1974 and continued during the following months, in a succession of evictions and reinvasions marked by an increasing and fierce repression by the authorities. As a result, the peasants obtained only enough land to establish three new settlements, along with the other ten that had been developed after the battles of 1971. The main local leaders of ANUC spent the second half of the year in jail, being released only after a great regional demonstration involving *usuarios* from all the southwestern municipalities. Strong repression had been evident since 1971 in the traditionally Conservative department of Antioquia; there was continuous harassment of the *usuarios'* activities, ruthless persecution of the radical leaders, and extremely harsh sentences for those who had been convicted for the few land occupations of 1973.

Although there were fewer cases than in Sucre and the Antioqueño southwest, intense land struggles also occurred in other departments during 1974. Córdoba registered the largest land invasion in the history of ANUC, that of the Mundo Nuevo *hacienda*, occupied by some 600 families in the municipality of Montería.[14] In the adjoining locality of Cereté, a number of groups who had taken portions of the Chuchurubí estate in 1971 were forcibly evicted and subjected to military repression when they tried to recover the land. By late February the departmental association of ANUC had organized the March of the Bricks, which began as a campaign to build a Peasant House in the capital, Montería, and ended with widespread disturbances and the massive stoning of INCORA's regional headquarters. In April, 2,000 *usuarios* again converged on IN-CORA's offices, denouncing the evictions and pressing for the legal recognition of the de facto occupations. At the same time, 100 women occupied the Municipal Hall of Cereté demanding freedom for their husbands, who had been detained after yet another attempt to recover Chuchurubí. Amid the intense debate in the PCML and the other influential political groups in Córdoba, all this agitation led to a civil strike in Montería a few days before the inauguration of ANUC's Third National Congress in Bogotá.

Meanwhile, in the department of Cauca, there had been a number of land occupations in the municipalities of Caldono, Caloto, and Jambaló.[15] The seizures were part of a new initiative of *resguardo* reconstitution launched by the Indian movement CRIC since its own Third Congress in 1973. The Indians were strongly influenced by a group of independent leftist advisers, mainly anthropologists, who had played a crucial role in the creation of CRIC. Although the land occupations of 1974 were carefully prepared, the landowners of Cauca resorted to traditional methods for dealing with Indian rebelliousness: The authorities brutally evicted the groups, there were collective arrests, tortures, and a number of Indian leaders were assassinated by the gangs of *pájaros*. The land struggle was also reactivated in the department of Huila, where followers of the Sincelejo Line had been trying the undermine the hegemony of ANUC Armenia since 1973.[16] The municipality of Campoalegre became the center of reorganizational efforts by *usuario* activists who had been sent in from other regions. In March 1974 there were attempted land seizures with the help of agricultural laborers from Tello, Campoalegre, Villavieja, and Yaguará. The leaders of the Armenia Line organized counterdemonstrations and finally the authorities evicted the occupants, using "methods of abduction and coercion" that were strongly protested by the Human Rights Committee of the city of Neiva.

In the departments of Cesar and Magdalena there were few new conflicts, and most of the 1974 clashes took place in *haciendas* that had been occupied in previous years.[17] In Chimichagua, three peasants were killed during the forcible eviction of *usuarios* from the Barlovento estate, and five more deaths resulted from similar incidents in three other municipalities of Cesar. In June 1974, the departmental association of ANUC announced that the armed bands of the landowners were cooperating with the authorities and that a number of peasant leaders were being tortured at the base of the La Popa Battalion in Bosconia. A similar retaliation campaign was under way in Aracataca, Santana, Plato, and El Difícil, municipalities of the department of Magdalena, in which gangs of *pájaros* and the army were forcing the peasants to relinquish their claims and abandon their holdings. In the rest of the country, the land invasions of 1974 were only isolated affairs. The most relevant one was that of the "frontier refugees" who occupied 3,000 hectares in Mingueo, in the department of Guajira.[18] These included a few hundred families who had fled from the Violencia in the 1950s and had settled in a border area in the Motilones Hills claimed by Venezuela. In 1973 Venezuela renewed its claim, occupying the area with its army and ousting the peasants. The governments of Colombia and Venezuela had discussed indemnification payments, but the refugee problem remained unsolved. ANUC organized the peasants and, after a failed attempt to invade another estate in Cesar, the Aguas Dulces *hacienda* was finally seized in Mingueo. The conflict worsened when the frontier refugees took over the government building and tried to stage a civil strike in the regional capital, Riohacha. A departmental curfew was declared by the authorities, troops moved in, and a student was killed in the disturbances that followed.

This review of the conflicts that preceded ANUC's Third National Congress reveals the important changes that were taking place in the land struggles. The lessening of some contradictions, the reorganization of ANUC and, above all, the repressive attacks by the government had different impacts at the regional level but together progressively inhibited the *usuarios'* combativeness. In such unfavorable circumstances, the movement became selective: It defended its previous conquests in those places where landowners' revenge was beginning and went on the offensive only in areas where conditions were favorable. The regional analysis has shown that one important condition was that of persistent conflicts with high potential for peasant unrest.

Since the spontaneity and official legitimation of the first battles were now being destroyed by the counteroffensive of the landowners and the state, the existing contradictions were not enough to sustain the struggle. In this sense, the most significant factors of the 1974 struggles were the organizational cohesiveness and the radical politicization that ANUC had achieved in the affected regions. With regard to the first factor, it is clear that the struggle for land continued where the peasant movement had been able to develop vigorous organizations at local and regional levels, as in the cases of Sucre, the Antioqueño southwest, Córdoba, and the work of CRIC in the Indian *resguardos* of Cauca. However, there were attempts to maintain the offensive in other places that, for special reasons of propaganda or competition against the Armenia Line, were defined as crucial by ANUC's leadership (including Huila, Tolima, and the area of the frontier refugees in Mingueo, Guajira). The organizational strength, which partially compensated for the lost earlier spontaneity, was closely related to the second factor, politicization. Leftist politicization replaced the ideological support of the earlier state-fostered reformism. Further, from this point of view, it is clear that the regions where the battle continued stood out from the others. In all these areas, revolutionary radicalism had now become the dominant ideology due to the work of ANUC's Educational Committees and the influence of leftist intellectuals and militants who had converged on the main areas of conflict. However, since the politicization of the peasant movement would have contradictory effects upon the evolution of the land struggles, this process demands closer examination.

Dissent and political factionalism

In ANUC's early phase, the peasant leaders had simply reproduced the reformist ideology transmitted by the DOC promoters, incorporating in some cases populist and leftist ideas stemming from their previous experiences. The subsequent break with the government changed the bearings of the struggle for land, leading to a search for other ideas that would transcend reformism and place the struggle in a broader revolutionary perspective. The national leaders of ANUC had been influenced by intellectuals who belonged to the Communist Party but advised the *usuarios* in a personal, not partisan, capacity. In fact, the pro-Soviet Colombian Communist Party had attacked ANUC from the outset as a clientelist extension of Lleras Restrepo's reformist Liberalism, and its negative attitude persisted later when the radicalized *usuarios* adopted independent positions and refused to accept Communist control of popular opposition in Colombia. The final break came in the fifth meeting of ANUC's National Junta at Tolú, where the *usuarios* adopted an abstentionist line opposed to the Communist Party's policy of electoral participation. The Communists maintained their hold over many municipal associations in Cundinamarca, aligning them with the officialist ANUC Armenia and supporting the latter against the radical *usuarios*. This initiated what would prove to be a permanent conflict between the Communist Party and ANUC Sincelejo.[19] The electoral abstention decreed at Tolú also provoked a rift between ANUC and the legalist Maoists of MOIR. This resulted in the loss of the *usuarios'* departmental association of Casanare, which then reorganized itself under the name of the Independent Peasant Organization of Casanare (OCIDEC).[20]

Among the left wing sectors, the first group that fully realized the political potential of ANUC was the Socialist Bloc. The Bloc had been formed in 1971 as an amalgamation of various Trotskyite groups that had sprung up independently among intellectuals, university students, and teachers' unions of Bogotá and Cali. Since they saw the Colombian revolution as a proletarian revolt, the Trotskyites faced a problem when the question of agitating among the peasants was raised. If the revolution was socialist, how could it be compatible with the promotion of the bourgeois-democratic peasant demands? This dilemma was never really resolved by the militants of the Bloc, who decided to support the peasant movement in order to prevent the Liberal politicians from making political capital of the democratic struggles of the people. Originally, the Trotskyites exerted their influence as advisers of the national peasant leaders and as collaborators in the preparation of ANUC's basic documents. In 1972, their work expanded to the departmental associations as part of the program of seminars organized by ANUC to consolidate stable cadres among the spontaneous peasant leaders who had emerged in 1971.[21]

By that time, however, a more powerful political influence was beginning to be felt in the main areas of land struggles. In Sucre, Córdoba, Bolívar, and Antioquia, the Maoist militants of the PCML and the Liga ML were penetrating the peasant movement at the grass-roots level. Like MOIR, these groups had emerged as splinters of the Communist Party, drawing off the younger activists after the Sino–Soviet split of the mid 1960's. But while MOIR had adopted a legalist strategy based upon electoral participation and trade-union urban work, the PCML and the Liga ML believed that conditions were ripe in Colombia for an armed revolutionary takeover like that of Communist China. Although the approach of the Maoist radicals was similar to that of the Trotskyites on this point of "revolution now," their position on the nature of the revolution was totally different. For them, the democratic nature of the peasant struggle was not a problem, but rather an opportunity to develop a revolutionary praxis based upon an orthodox, rigid conception of the Maoist model. The PCML and Liga ML differed on strategic and tactical issues, but they shared the view that at that stage Colombia's revolution was democratic and not proletarian. The immediate step was a "popular democratic revolution on the road to socialism," whose success depended upon the working-class vanguards' ability to organize the spontaneous and amorphous revolt of the masses into a coherent armed struggle in the countryside. In other words, it was to be an agrarian revolution commanded by proletarian cadres, a process that the radical ML groups believed had favorable prospects because the "vague consciousness" of the peasant masses had already created the necessary conditions for insurrection.

The PCML, by far the more important of the two ML groups, had established the already mentioned EPL, an armed detachment that was trying to develop guerrilla warfare in the forests of the Upper Sinú, an area that could eventually be linked to the regions of more intense land struggle on the Atlantic Coast. The key to political praxis was the "Bolshevization Campaign" launched by PCML in 1971. In this campaign, all party cadres had to abandon everything else and "go to the masses," inspiring their daily behavior in the "three permanents" of the teachings of Mao Tse Tung: proletarian purity, absolute discipline, and love of the people. Most of the radical Maoist militants were teenagers who had been extremely active in the student agitations that took place in the universities and secondary schools of the main Colombian cities during early 1971. To some extent, the Bolshevization Campaign of the PCML was boosted by the strong repression of the student movement. When scores of teenagers were expelled from the schools, many ML militants moved to the areas of rural conflict, particularly from the main centers of Maoist activity in Medellín, Barranquilla, and Montería.[22]

The influence of the Socialist Bloc was external. Few militants were involved on a full-time basis, and their activity was limited to providing advice for ANUC's national leaders and developing regional courses for peasant delegates. By contrast, the ML activists came to the countryside in significant numbers and were concentrating their efforts at the grassroots level. No attempt was made by the Maoist groups to penetrate the national leadership of ANUC. The basic idea was to get directly involved in the land struggles, participate in the daily problems with the rank-and-file peasants, and assume leadership at local levels in preparation for the impending insurrection. In addition, there were doctrinary differences that made the ML's message more suitable for the peasants. The Trotskyites insisted on the proletariat as the main force of the revolution, downgrading the peasant struggle. Their motto, "Land without masters," confused the peasants, many of whom perceived a contradiction between its proletarian content and their own aspiration for an economy based upon individual ownership of the land. The Maoist slogan "Land for those who till it" avoided this problem, because although the ML groups also envisaged a collective agricultural future, the slogan was sufficiently ambiguous to avoid the issue and mobilize the peasantry. Since the ML concept also placed the peasantry at the center of the revolution, the Maoist ideology proved to be far more appealing than that of the Trotskyites. "Land for those who till it" was overwhelmingly approved as the official motto of the *usuarios* by the Second National Congress, and by 1973 the ML activists had completely undermined the influence of the Socialist Bloc within the peasant movement.[23]

However, the harmony between the ML groups and ANUC's leadership was short-lived. After the Second National Congress, the Maoists in the main areas of land struggle began to arouse objections regarding the direction they wanted the struggles to take and their agitation among the peasants. To understand these problems, it is necessary to keep in mind the strong conviction of the ML activists about a revolutionary situation in the countryside, a conviction feeding the belief that it was absolutely essential to instigate continuous clashes between the masses and the government in order to ignite the spark that would start a general insurrection. At the level of concrete action, this approach implied a dramatic change in the way the land invasions and mobilizations were carried out. In places under ML influence, resistance to eviction ceased to be peaceful, and the peasants were induced to respond to the authorities with force; this provoked an even harsher repression and led to deaths and months of imprisonment for the invaders. The attempts to escalate the land struggles into armed conflicts were matched by the aggressive mood thats the Maoists tried to inject into the public demonstrations, inflaming the peasants and opposing the prudent dispersal of the crowds facing police and army troops.

A second problem with the ML groups was their attitude toward the development of the peasant economy in the new settlements that emerged in the lands conquered by the invasion committees. This topic will be considered in detail in Chapter 8. For now, suffice to say that the Maoist militants thought that the "bourgeois tendencies" of the peasant had to be firmly curtailed in order to preserve the revolutionary potential in the countryside. Consequently, they not only tried to prevent the peasants from cultivating beyond the subsistence level, but they also prohibited contact with official agricultural institutions and even dictated consumption patterns and details of daily life such as what clothing to wear and what radio programs to hear. Arguing that such extremist attitudes could lead to widespread desertion among the rank-and-file peasants, many regional and national leaders of ANUC began to oppose the ML even though they themselves had originally sponsored their contact with the base groups.[24] The internal debate, which began after the disturbances of the Peasant Marches of September 1972 on the Atlantic Coast, later became more intense as a result of the violent clashes and the first deaths of *usuarios* in land invasions of Sucre and Córdoba. Finally, the controversy developed into a full-blown affair during 1973, when the ML groups started to argue that the revolutionary situation was sufficiently ripe throughout the Atlantic Coast to consider the possibility of making "a direct call for the general insurrection of the masses."[25]

Rejecting a project that they considered to be impractical, ANUC's leaders began to rally around the positions adopted by their Political Committee. This committee had been created by the Second National Congress to deal with political questions and to define the future ideology of the peasant movement. Under the guidance of advisers who had once belonged to the PCML, the Political Committee was laying the foundations for a political line that would be independent not only of the traditional parties but also of the leftists who had been influential during ANUC's early period.[26] Although the principles of the committee were in line with Maoist ideology, the PCML and the Liga Ml were harshly criticized. It was argued that, in their eagerness to provoke a revolution, the militants had focused upon the struggle of the landless and alienated other sectors of the peasantry. Furthermore, the Political Committee accused the Maoist parties of endangering the bases of the peasant movement with extremist practices and adventurist attitudes that could lead to massive desertion at the grass-roots level.[27]

Controlling ANUC's apparatus and monopolizing the substantial funds received from foreign foundations, the national leaders of the *usuarios* closed ranks behind the independent line advocated by the Political Committee and consolidated thier own standing as a central power group within the organization. Basically, this leadership elite was composed of some thirty full-time activists (including the members of the Executive Committee, the main political advisers, the militants in charge of the various secretaries, and a number of regional leaders), who received salaries from ANUC's secretary of finances and controlled an organization that had maintained the original cast chosen by the government. The nature of ANUC's bureaucratic leadership had also persisted. The pattern of collective decision making, coupled with the entrenchment of the same group at the top, had led to the development of internal cliques or factions that discussed the issues in secretive caucuses. However, although ANUC was developing its own political line, no ideological elaboration was being carried out by the peasant leaders. Leftist intellectuals, who had been incorporated as activists of the movement, were now providing the ideological inspiration. In a way, this can be seen as an internalized continuation of the previous situation in which ANUC's leadership had operated as a mediator between the rank-and-file of the movement and the reformist and revolutionary ideologies coming from the outside.

With the Third National Congress approaching, the departmental associations began electing their representatives and preparing their participation in the event. Satisfied that their followers would have the upper hand in most regions, the independent national leaders decided to launch a political offensive in the areas in which their supremacy was threatened by the ML groups. At the level of ideological debate, it was argued that the peasant movement should develop its own political power and not serve the interest of parties that pretended to represent nonexisting working-class vanguards. At the organizational level, the National Executive Committee orchestrated a campaign of "restructurations": The regional education committees were purged of ML activists and the elections in the "problematic" departmental associations were manipulated to exclude the ML groups and thus reduce their representation in the impending National Congress. During the first half of 1974 the conflict escalated, and in some places it became a head-on battle within the peasant movement.[28]

The Third National Congress, inaugurated on August 31, 1974, was the greatest assembly in the history of ANUC. In an opening peasant demonstration without precedent in Bogotá, more than 30,000 *usuarios* marched through the streets of the capital before converging on the Salitre Stadium, where some 7,000 deputies registered as official representatives of the different regions. From the outset, however, it was clear that the congress would be stormy. ANUC's national leadership tried to block the access of the hostile political groups, which led to bitter disputes on the validity of the delegates' credentials and caused violent outbursts involving the Peasant Vigilance Guard posted at the gates of the stadium. With the representation of the preliminary reports, the protests of the opposition sectors gained momentum, turning into open attempts to sabotage the proceedings. The ML groups, who called themselves the "conscientious sectors," denounced the use of "imperialist" money from the foreign foundations in the exclusionist campaign against them before the Congress. Furthermore, they condemned the corruption and the bureaucratic attitudes of the independent leaders, whom they also accused of sending ANUC on an "anarcho-syndicalist adventure aimed at the creation of a peasant party." Overwhelmed by the technical problems caused by the high turnout of delegates, and aware that the activists of the Communist Party and other political sectors rejected by ANUC were joining the Maoist sabotage, the national leaders realized that the Congress was slipping out of their control. The assembly was therefore brought to a premature end in a chaotic session in which a new National Junta was elected by a drawn-out process that excluded the dissident groups. The issues that should have been treated in more than thirty specialized subcommittees were transferred to the following meeting of the National Junta, whose conclusions would fill the vacuum left by the failure of the Congress's deliberations.[29] With the total alienation of the political opposition, and amid the general confusion of many regional delegations who for the first time learned about underlying political dissensions and about such issues as management of funds, the close of the Third Congress marked the final entrenchment of the independents in the peasant movement. Supported by unorthodox and frankly antidemocratic methods, the line that advocated a political expression of the social strength of the peasantry had prevailed over the blind insurrectional course proposed by the Maoist radicalists. With the evident failure of the guerrilla activities of its EPL, the defeat within the peasant movement would have devastating repercussions for the PCML: After a year of heated internal debate, the party crumbled into four different factions that remained at odds among themselves.[30]

By breaking with the ML sectors, ANUC Sincelejo severed its last links with the parties of the left and moved forward along the path that led to a political definition of its own. Although the ideological debates and the political praxis played important roles, it is necessary to examine the factors operating at the more basic level of class conflicts and alignments. ANUC's organization had begun as a result of the politics of alliance of the reformist bourgeoisie. But the socioeconomic changes and the incipient radicalization of the *usuarios* had helped to defeat reformism and to shatter that fragile alliance. The counterreformist realignment of the dominant classes had isolated the peasant movement, forcing the *usuarios* to seek new allies. The relationships between ANUC and the leftist parties should therefore be seen as an attempt to forge an alternative alliance between peasants and workers at the level of the subordinated classes. However, such an alliance was only an aspiration, an ideal that had no basis in reality. Paradoxically, the obstacles did not come from the peasant movement because, as a result of the circumstances of its creation, ANUC was a highly representative organization that could integrate and give unified expression to peasant grievances. It was the workers' movement that appeared to be barely organized, deeply divided, and lacking a unified trade-union and political representation. In the leftist camp, only the Communist Party had roots in the working class, but these roots were very superficial. The Maoist and Trotskyite groups, who considered themselves to be vanguards of the proletariat, were just political elites consisting of intellectuals and students with no real bases of support in the working class. In fact, the fragmentation of the political left demonstrated the weakness of the working class movement and its inability to join the peasantry in a democratic revolution during the early 1970s.[31]

Thus, the links that ANUC Sincelejo developed with the left-wing parties must be seen as substitutes for an impossible alliance between peasants and workers. These links had been somewhat effective in providing the ideology of confrontation that was needed to sustain the peasant struggle. They had also created the much needed feeling or illusion of a plebeian struggle of all the subordinated classes against the dominant ones. But in terms of the class alliances, the truth was that the peasants were mobilized but isolated, and it was this isolation that gradually led to the need to articulate an autonomous political line of the peasantry as a class. This urge was reinforced by the predatory attitudes of the leftist parties, which considered ANUC either as a prize to be swallowed by bureaucratic means or as a force that could be harnessed for extravagant insurrectional plans. Thus, the breaks between the *usuarios* and these parties were milestones in the consolidation of the independent line by the Political Committee. A few months after the Third National Congress, this process would lead to the creation of the People's Revolutionary Organization (ORP), a political group composed first of the national leaders and advisers of ANUC Sincelejo and later including the regional cadres of the peasant movement.[32]

In the main areas of land struggle, however, ANUC's internal political strife had grave consequences. Both the exclusionist attitude of the independents and the extremism of the ML groups involved manipulation and ideological intolerance. All differences were turned into unconditional questions, promoting sectarianism and leaving almost no room for democratic debates and compromises. In the work at the grass-roots level, this resulted in incessant conflicts between doctrinaire activists who showed little concern about the dangers of political division within the peasant movement. Therefore, the most immediate outcome of the new situation was the fragmentation of ANUC Sincelejo, which was greatest in those places where politicization had had the most positive influences upon the militancy of the peasantry.

In Sucre, Córdoba, and Bolívar, the organization of the *usuarios* was rapidly transformed into a complex mosaic in which the sectarian lines that divided the independents and the Maoists reached the level of the invasion committees themselves.[33] As a result, new elements quickly undermined the momentum that ANUC had maintained in these regions: The internal dispute diverted the efforts that had been concentrated upon the land battles, the land occupations grew isolated because regional coordination ceased, and the fragmentation of the committees destroyed their resistance in the war of attrition against the landowners and the authorities.[34] In addition, the endless accusations of corruption and political duplicity aroused deep suspicions among the rank-and-file *usuarios* about the motives of their leaders, which blocked reorganizational attempts and cast doubt on the ideological legitimation that had previously stimulated the radicalism of the peasants.[35] The results of the conflicts were also felt in places that had been only marginally involved in the politicization process. The main examples were Magdalena and Cesar, where the Maoist radicals had never developed a permanent base. Because regional organizational weaknesses had also prevented the formation of strong leadership in these two departments, the peasant struggles were assisted by leaders of the independents who frequently came from Sucre and Bolívar. Aggravation of the internal conflict in their regions forced these leaders to concentrate all their efforts at their rear, so that their contacts with the central and southern areas of Magdalena and Cesar became very irregular and left without effective liaison and guidance many groups that now had to face the ruthless counteroffensive of the landowners.[36]

Thus, both the direct and indirect consequences of political factionalism in ANUC led to the isolation of the groups, the disintegration of the solidarity and ideology that had sustained the land battles, and confusion regarding the attitudes needed to continue the struggle and protect the achievements of the past. Many of the invasion committees began to lose the occupied lands, frequently as part of collective decisions to accept money offered by the landowners and, in some cases, as a result of the betrayal of local leaders who sacrificed the claims of their comrades to their own advantage.[37] Even in places where the invasion committees had consolidated their hold on the land, the lack of guidance and the absence of minimal discipline undermined the morale and cohesiveness of the groups, causing the proliferation of internal feuds, the withdrawal of many families who sold their shares to others, and, as will be seen later, the progressive surrender of the new settlements to the bureaucratic controls of INCORA.[38] In short, after fulfilling a key role in the land struggles, politicization had become, as a result of factionalism, a cause of problems that demoralized, hindered, and even counteracted these struggles. What is more, political factionalism enhanced the effect of other external factors that inhibited the movement. In 1975, the most important of these factors continued to be repression, now redoubled as part of the policy of concessions and restraint of the new López Michelsen administration.

6

Concessions and repressive escalation

Repression of the land invasions would continue under the new government. This indicated that, at least with regard to land redistribution, López Michelsen's approach would be similar to that of Pastrana. To understand this continuity amid other changes, it is necessary to consider again how the state's agrarian policy was conditioned by the ways in which changes in the model of capitalist accumulation defined new priorities for the dominant classes.

The agrarian policy of López Michelsen

Under the pretentious slogan of transforming the country into "the Japan of South America," López Michelsen's administration worked to consolidate the new export orientation of Colombia's capitalism. Helped by a favorable situation in the international market, the new economic scheme had boosted capitalist accumulation to unprecedented levels. However, the accompanying imbalances and dangers were also clearly visible. The increased exploitation of labor, indispensable to successful international competition, had been fully realized: Between 1970 and 1974, the real wages of industrial workers went down by 25 percent and the wage difference between Colombian and U.S. workers was substantially widened.[1] The resulting trade union agitation had been severely repressed during 1973 and 1974 by Pastrana's government, adding to the brutal blows inflicted upon the students in 1971 and to the policy of continuous and ruthless repression of the peasant movement.[2]

Pastrana's administration had begun amid accusations of electoral fraud by the followers of Rojas Pinilla, and its use of coercion had further eroded its credibility and legitimation. This had created an atmosphere of tension and unrest that reflected, at the social and political levels, the limitations of a repressive treatment of the tensions accompanying the new exporting scheme. This scheme increased the dependence of the Colombian economy on the cycles of world capitalism, making the consequences of international crises much more dangerous. This became clear when, toward the end of 1974, the international recession precipitated by the oil crisis started to be felt in Colombia.[3] For López Michelsen, who had shrewdly taken advantage of widespread popular discontent to win the election with a solid majority, the task of consolidation involved two goals: the stabilization and rationalization of the new accumulation model and the alleviation of some of its undesirable social effects. In one way or another, all the initiatives of the López Michelsen administration tried to address both goals. All the measures favoring the accumulation process were presented in terms of social benefit and all the concessions given to the subordinate classes were conceived as mechanisms to correct the distortions of the neo-Liberal scheme.

Faced by the threat of recession, the first step of López Michelsen's government was the declaration of a "situation of economic emergency." Special financial measures were adopted, giving the banks great freedom to encourage capital investment in those industries that had greater efficiency and brighter prospects in the international markets. Moreover, the tax system was modified to increase the resources for the intervention programs of the state.[4] These programs were outlined a few months later in a development plan, "Closing the Gaps," where for the first time the priorities of the new neo-Liberal orientation of Colombian capitalism were spelled out as priorities of official economic policy. The plan defined the export sector as the dynamic pole of the economy, proposing stronger integration into the international market, a greater reliance upon the comparative advantages of the country, new incentives for exporters, and the gradual elimination of tariffs on imported goods.[5] This was accompanied by palliatives for the "poorer strata of the population" and overtures to the popular urban sectors and the political opposition. The Plan for Food and Nutrition (PAN) was presented as a crusade that would fight malnutrition by promoting the production and consumption of certain foods, increasing education on nutrition, and developing a system of coupons for the subsidized distribution of food.[6] A vague chapter on urban policies promised new community integration programs and the extension of services to marginal neighborhoods.[7] In addition, the state of siege was lifted for several months, the students received a Marxist rector at the National University, Communist unions were given legal recognition, and all the trade-union centrals were invited to participate in working out a policy on salaries.[8]

These conciliatory gestures hardly concealed the fact that the neo-Liberal policies of López Michelsen were trying to freeze and even further reduce the already depressed cost of labor in Colombia. Nominal increases in minimum wages did not compensate for the real depreciation caused by inflation, and the discussions at the National Wage Council always ended with unilateral decrees that paid little attention to the opinions of the trade unions.[9] The PAN program itself was no more than a small attempt to improve the conditions of reproduction of the labor force without raising its cost, ignoring the fact that low incomes were the cause of malnutrition and reducing the problem to the distribution of charity which, at best, would only increase a diet of inferior quality. The truth was that, because of the imperative to keep wages low, neo-Liberals had nothing to offer to the working classes. Given these conditions, the renewed protest of the trade unions soon worsened the situation and led to the collapse of the demagogic facade: The state of siege was reinstated, the National Wage Council was dismantled, and all strikes were declared illegal. The policy of harassment and repression was extended to the Liberal and Conservative trade unions as well, forcing them to get involved in the growing agitation that would lead to increasing strikes in the big and medium-sized cities and to the remarkable success of the General Civil Strike of September 14, 1977.[10]

Although the attempts to lessen and mask the contradictions in the cities were doomed to failure, the situation in the countryside was quite different. There the concessions and palliatives introduced by López Michelsen were more substantial and the conditions for success more favorable. The most important new element was the support offered to the middle and rich peasants through the Integrated Rural Development (DRI) program. The justification for DRI was quite simple. Despite the problems caused by lack of resources, technological backwardness, unemployment, and poverty, the "traditional peasant subsector" provided 55 percent of the food consumed in the country. Injections of credit, technology, and services would improve the productivity of this group, increasing the food supply and giving the peasants better incomes and more employment.[11] The hidden logic was also simple. There were three main objectives of rationalization and stabilization: to promote the production of cheap foods that would help indirectly to reduce industrial wages; to limit peasant disintegration and massive migration to the cities; and to try to eliminate part of the rural discontent that had been so clearly visible in ANUC's struggles of previous years.[12] These objectives were not particularly new or original. Like the PAN plan, the DRI program was part of a much broader strategy of international capitalism, a strategy that was being carried out by the World Bank and other agencies that had been developing similar projects with the governments of many Third World countries since the early 1970s.[13]

Thus, the hundreds of millions of dollars that began to pour into the main *minifundia* areas after 1975 represented a package of substantial and tangible concessions that the López Michelsen administration was offering to the peasantry. The activities of thirteen official agricultural institutes were integrated to provide credit, technical assistance, marketing systems, and other services associated with the construction of roads, aqueducts, sewerage, electricity networks, schools, hospitals, and health centers. The scale of these concessions can be fully appreciated when one considers that during its first five-year phase alone, the DRI program was designed to benefit almost half of the peasants with fewer than 20 hectares, giving credit to 20 percent of these beneficiaries in eight departments.[14] Although the coffee areas were not included among the DRI regions, the Federation of Coffee Growers was conducting a parallel program that, fed by unprecedented price increases in the world coffee market, would bring even more benefits to the peasants than those offered by the DRI program in other places.[15] Many critics, especially leftist intellectuals and politicians, speculated that both the DRI program and the coffee bonanza would only increase differentiation within the peasantry.[16] But whatever the validity of these criticisms, the truth was that for the first time the peasantry was receiving much of what had been requested in vain for so long: credits, education, health services, electricity, and so on. Among the stable peasants this created a feeling of complacency that, as will be seen later, contradicted the contentious approach of ANUC Sincelejo. Even for the almost proletarianized peasants, whose lands were too small to be eligible for credit and agricultural extension, the DRI program offered certain improvements resulting from the expansion of other services. The PAN plan, which was only a marginal factor in the cities, was important in the countryside: sixty percent of its budget was allocated to the rural areas, and its most important component was a scheme of garden crops and small animal husbandry to enrich the diet of the poorer families.[17]

Under the Pastrana administration, counterreform had almost completely excluded all the sectors of the peasantry. Thus, the new policy of concessions to the middle and rich peasants was a significant change. However, it was by no means extended to the landless peasants. The plan Closing the Gaps considered agrarian reform an alternative that should be resorted to only in exceptional cases.[18] The rural plains, which had been the main setting for the land struggles, had to proceed with agricultural modernization, taking advantage of higher capitalist productivity to supply the internal market and increase agricultural exports. The policy of incentives and financial support for agrarian capitalism was therefore continued by López Michelsen, who never missed an opportunity to declare publicly his commitment to the counterreformist Pact of Chicoral and his resolve "to remove the sword of Damocles which had threatened our agricultural entrepreneurs."[19] The corollary of this policy was obvious: The peasants' desire for land had to be drastically checked. No wonder, then, that the repressive strategy for the rural areas designed by Minister Pardo Buelvas described land invasions as "a particularly grave form of disturbance of public order which will be severely punished and will lead to the suspension of all of the State's economic and social programs."[20]

This reaffirmation of the halt to land redistribution was accompanied by the expected palliatives and corrective mechanisms.

In this respect, the most important element introduced by López Michelsen's government in areas of extensive landed property was Law 6 of 1975, also known as the Sharecropping Law. Law 1 of 1968 had provoked the massive ousting of tenants and sharecroppers, which not only led to land struggles but also left the landowners without access to the labor power. To counteract these effects, Law 6 of 1975 regulated sharecropping and tenancy contracts and included two key provisions: It stipulated that owners of estates greater than 200 hectares had to provide subsistence plots to their laborers and families, and it protected from agrarian reform all landowners who could present evidence of legal sharecropping contracts.[21] Essentially, the Sharecropping Law tried to alleviate the social pressures created by landless peasants who could not be used as permanent laborers by large-scale agriculture. At the same time, it attempted to make available the seasonal labor force needed for that agriculture. Therefore, the law was not a return to feudal or backward relations of production, as some critics argued. Quite the contrary, it attempted to improve conditions for the expansion for capitalist agriculture by giving guarantees to landed property owners, securing the necessary supply of labor, and reducing the tensions inherent in this pattern of agrarian evolution.[22]

To summarize, then, the agrarian policy of López Michelsen included important concessions for the stable and well-to-do peasants but only palliatives for the semiproletarianized and landless. Consequently, a flexible line was adopted toward the peasant movement. The government tried to negotiate concessions but demanded acceptance of the official policy. Even though at the time of ANUC's Third National Congress most of the newly elected Liberal congressmen had recognized ANUC Sincelejo as a true representative of the peasantry, López Michelsen did not hasten to restore the legal status of the radical *usuarios*.[23] Instead, he adopted a wait-and-see attitude, exchanging views with adherents of both the Armenia and Sincelejo lines and warning the latter that the future relationship between ANUC and the government depended upon the maintenance of law and order in the countryside.[24] ANUC Sincelejo, however, could not accept the president's conditions, since that would imply a renunciation of its key demand: redistribution of the land. In consequence, the initial rapprochement and cordial presidential audiences did not last long; the turning point came with the approval of Law 6 in January 1975.

Pájaros and militarization

In February 1975 the Executive Committee of ANUC Sincelejo rejected the Sharecropping Law, denouncing it as a continuation of the counterreformist policies of Chicoral and repeating the demand for land that had been submitted to López Michelsen in the list of petitions prepared after the Third National Congress.[25] The twelfth meeting of ANUC's National Junta (Pasto, March 1975) declared that tenants and sharecroppers could not revert to servile relations of production; that they should become the owners of the land they worked on; and that Law 6 demonstrated once again that direct action was the only way of obtaining land for the peasants. Besides calling for a renewal of land struggles, the twelfth meeting decided to carry out a campaign attacking the new law, including a National Day of Protest in mid-year.[26] The general situation, however, was not very favorable. The government seemed determined to answer with force, while on the other hand there was increasing trouble within ANUC Sincelejo. The destructive effects of political factionalism were clearly visible in the areas of land struggle and, in addition to the conflict with the ML groups, other discrepancies were emerging with the Indian movement CRIC and with some departmental associations. ANUC's Executive Committee indicated that "land invasions should be conducted only in those places where it would be possible to secure adequate participation at base level," a recommendation implicitly acknowledging that the movement had lost a great deal of its strength and that, as a result, the possibilities of successful resistance to repression were now much more limited.[27]

Developments in the areas of land struggle during 1975 fully justified these apprehensions. In fact, only a few of the land invasions that year were due to new disputes. Most of them involved peasants who had taken the land since 1971 and were now being evicted, due to the cancellation of INCORA's negotiations or to court verdicts in favor of the landowners. The displaced peasants tried to reoccupy the land, but this time conditions were different. The security forces and the armed gangs of the landowners stormed the invasion areas, intending to inflict punishments that would convince the peasants once and for all that direct action was no longer possible. Publicly declaring that "we shall not allow the *usuarios* to impose agrarian reform upon us," Minister Cornelio Reyes invoked the special provisions of Decree 1533, broadening the scope of martial law, militarizing entire regions, and making massive arrests.[28] One of the features of repression during 1975 was the systematic persecution of ANUC's militants: Many local and regional leaders were arbitrarily imprisoned and tortured by the police and the army, and several assassinations were carried out by the landowners' *pájaros*.[29]

Thus, one by one, the regions of land struggle became stages for the repetition of the same tragedy. In Sucre, the most serious clashes occurred during the demonstration of February 21, when an army battalion forcibly dispersed a crowd of more than 5,000 *usuarios* in Sincelejo. Many invasion committees were brutally broken up by the authorities and the bands of *pájaros* in San Pedro, Caimito, San Onofre, Morroa, and Toluviejo. Two *usuarios* were killed in a police action against the occupants of the La Mula estate in Ovejas, and subsequent protests were rapidly crushed with the closure of the municipal Peasant House and the arrest of the most important regional leaders. By mid-year the land invasions had stopped, but repression continued, this time with the arrest of 300 delegates who were meeting to prepare a departmental assembly of ANUC.[30] In Córdoba, where INCORA and the landowners were trying to persuade some peasant committees to take lands that were already occupied by other groups, the army opened fire against a demonstration of *usuarios* in Planeta Rica and began a campaign of ruthless expulsions in *haciendas* of Montería, Cereté, Chinú, San Andrés, and other municipalities. Policemen were posted at the homes of all the departmental leaders of ANUC, forcing them to go into hiding. By the end of the year, three *usuarios* had been killed in the evictions and another three had been murdered by the *pájaros*.[31] In Magdalena and Cesar, the armed groups of the landowners had enjoyed such freedom of action during the previous couple of years that even the Liberal newspapers were beginning to talk about the existence of "independent republics" where regional bosses imposed dictatorships of their own. The main battles of 1975 took place at Cleotilde, Argelia, and San Andrés, *haciendas* in the municipalities of Aracataca, El Difícil, and Chiriguaná. In these places, the situation deteriorated when the destruction of crops and the burning of homes escalated into more frontal attacks that led to rapes, injuries, and deaths. The *usuarios* organized marches and protest demonstrations that only served to attract further hostility from the authorities. The crowds were dispersed, whole groups of families were imprisoned, and arrest orders were issued against the local peasant leaders. Despite frequent denunciation in the national press, the landowners of Magdalena and Cesar continued their campaign of repression and abuse with impunity until they smashed the remaining expressions of peasant combativeness.[32] In the plains of Huila and Tolima, where ANUC Sincelejo was still trying to displace the pro-government Armenia Line and regain control over the local and regional associations, the 1975 campaign was also unsuccessful. There was little response at the base level, and it was easy for the local police to thwart both the demonstrations against the Sharecropping Law and the few land invasions organized by the radical *usuarios* in Campoalegre, Guamo, and a couple of adjacent municipalities.[33] The effects of repression were also being felt in other departments. The most important events were the murders of *usuarios* in Arroyo de Piedra (Atlántico) and Achí (Bolívar); the massive arrests that followed new invasion attempts in Urrao and Cáceres (Antioquia); the renewed army intervention in Mingueo (Guajira); the brutal evictions in San Martín and Puerto López (Meta); and the military blockade that affected Yondó,

Cimitarra, and Barrancabermeja in the Middle Magdalena.[34] All in all, ANUC reported more than forty peasant deaths and hundreds of arrests throughout the country during 1975.[35]

The battles of 1975 convinced López Michelsen that ANUC Sincelejo was far from being a friendly partner in the dialogue that he wanted to open with the peasantry. He had also learned that the peasant movement was now weaker. Consequently, the official reaction went beyond the repression of the land struggles to a total break with the radical *usuarios*. In December 1975, the government expelled ANUC Sincelejo from its remaining offices at the Ministry of Agriculture building in Bogotá, severing all contacts with the radicals and reaffirming the Armenia Line as the sole representative of the peasant *usuarios*.[36] With this, the end of 1975 also marked the end of the great peasant challenge in the areas of land struggle. The last battles had been fruitless. The peasants were reluctant to fight at the grass-roots level, the invasions had failed to gain access to land, and the mobilizations of the National Day of Protest had been only partially carried out with dwindling support.[37] Weakened by its own political dissensions and facing ever-increasing repression, ANUC Sincelejo was now unable to continue the peasant offensive. Yet, internal factionalism and external repression were not the only factors behind the ebb of the land struggles. Important socioeconomic changes had been taking place in the most affected areas, and by the mid–1970s, the effects of these changes were beginning to erode the motivations that had previously spurred direct peasant confrontation. Two factors were particularly important in the main regions of land struggle. One was the emergence of new ways of earning a living other than an independent peasant economy. The other was the demobilizing effects of the gains that had been won in the early struggles. These were becoming increasingly visible, not only because part of the peasantry had obtained land, but also because the new peasant economy had to face serious problems. The new occupational alternatives and the question of the peasant settlements will be studied more closely in the following two chapters.

The new occupational alternatives and the issue of the rural proletariat

As indicated in the previous chapter, one of the main purposes of the Sharecropping Law was to alleviate social pressures in the areas of extensive landed property. If the landless were trying to take the land by force, it was because they wanted to establish an independent peasant economy that would guarantee their subsistence. To avoid the land struggles and preserve the existing structure of property, it was necessary to provide other occupational alternatives for the rural population. The reintroduction of rent and sharecropping appeared to be a possible strategy to achieve greater employment without agrarian reform. However, although the Sharecropping Law would have important effects, other factors were already operating in the same direction by the mid–1970s.

Migration and employment options

An examination of statistical data on rural unemployment is a convenient way to approach this question of occupational alternatives. According to information from the population censuses of 1964 and 1973, the rate of overt unemployment in the countryside had decreased from 7.2 to 3.9 percent during the intercensal period.[1] In 1978, a special study by DANE showed that overt unemployment had decreased further to 1.6 percent of the rural labor force. The same study estimated a rate of disguised unemployment of 1.5 percent, for an overall rate of 3.1 percent. Regional analysis indicates that the percentages for the Atlantic Coast and the central area of Huila and Tolima were roughly the same as the national averages, with a slight upward deviation in the case of overt unemployment and an equally slight downward deviation for disguised unemployment.[2] All in all, these data clearly show that unemployment decreased significantly during the period under consideration and that this change was felt in the main areas of land struggle at least as much as in the rest of the country. In considering the factors that accounted for the greater absorption of the labor force in these areas, existing studies and firsthand information obtained during the present research point to four main processes: rural-urban migration, the expansion of commercial crops in capitalist agriculture, increased seasonal labor migration to Venezuela,

Table 7.1. *Rural population and migration movements in the departments of the Atlantic Coast, Huila, and Tolima, 1964–1973*

Departments	Rural Population				Migration from the dept., 1964–1973 (%)[a]	Dept. migration balance, 1964–1973 (%)[b]
	1964 (000's)	As percentage of total dept. population	1973 (000's)	As percentage of total dept. population		
Atlántico	64.9	9.0	58.8	6.1	11.1	15.9
Bolívar	292.2	42.1	297.2	36.3	20.8	– 6.5
Cesar	163.4	62.6	155.8	45.7	17.5	16.8
Córdoba	405.8	69.2	399.6	61.5	15.0	– 6.2
Magdalena	294.1	55.6	269.5	49.8	23.5	–10.8
Sucre	184.5	59.0	169.3	48.0	25.6	–14.5
Huila	263.8	63.3	235.1	50.2	19.3	– 6.5
Tolima	487.2	57.9	450.3	49.7	37.8	–21.3

[a]Percentage of migration $= \dfrac{\text{emigrants } (1964-73)}{\text{residents } (1973)} \times 100$

[b]Percentage of migration balance $= \dfrac{\text{immigrants–emigrants } (1964-73)}{\text{residents } (1973)} \times 100$

Sources: DANE, *Censo Nacional de Población*, 1964. DANE, *Censo Nacional de Población*, 1973. P. Torales, *La Dinámica de los Movimientos Migratorios en Colombia*, 1979, Tables 7 and 8.

and the sudden development of an underground economy based on marihuana.

With regard to the first process, it should be emphasized that migration from the rural areas was not new in Colombia. As shown in Chapter 1, migration to cities had been a constant trend since the beginning of industrialization and increased with the Violencia. Because of the demographic pressures and peasant decomposition, the Andean regions still supplied most of the migrants during the 1960s and early 1970s. However, the plains also had important population outflows during the 1964–1973 intercensal period. Focusing attention upon the main departments of land struggle (those of the Atlantic Coast, Huila, and Tolima), Table 7.1 shows a marked reduction in the rural population in relation to the total number of inhabitants. It also indicates that the rural population declined in absolute terms, except in Bolívar, where the figures reflect the ongoing colonization process in the southern municipalities. Regarding the interdepartmental population exchanges, Table 7.1 reveals negative migration balances with the exceptions of Atlántico and Cesar, where the

Table 7.2. *Migration balances of some of the highest-ranked municipalities in terms of the frequency of peasant land invasions, 1964–1973*

Municipality (department)	Rank order of the municipality in its department according to the frequency of peasant land invasions during the 1970s	Migration balance, 1964–1973 (%)[a]
Corozal (Sucre)	1	−28.0
Montería (Córdoba)	1	− 2.2
Cereté (Córdoba)	2	− 4.7
Campoalegre (Huila)	1	−15.4
Plato (Magdalena)	2	− 9.0
Magangué (Bolívar)	1	−14.2
Carmen (Bolívar)	2	−27.1
Guamo (Tolima)	1	−36.6

[a] Percentage of migration balance $= \dfrac{\text{immigrants–emigrants } (1964–73)}{\text{residents } (1973)} \times 100$

Sources: CINEP's Archive on ANUC, section on land invasions (see note 57 of Chapter 3). P. Torales, *La Dinámica de los Movimientos Migratorios en Colombia*, 1979, Table 14.

city of Barranquilla and the cotton municipalities of Valledupar and Codazzi attracted migrants.

Thus, there was substantial migration from the departments in question. This is further corroborated by a study of the National Employment service (SENALDE) on migratory movements in Colombia. In that study, the western Atlantic Coast (including Córdoba, Sucre, and Bolívar) and the central area (Huila and Tolima) were classified among the regions with the highest rates of migration.[3] But these data are too general, since aggregation by department fails to show how much *rural* migration was involved. To obtain more conclusive evidence, it is necessary to step down to the municipal level, which is possible in this case since the SENALDE study selected a sample including most of the localities with the highest incidence of land struggles. Presenting the migration balances for these municipalities, Table 7.2 shows that except for Montería, where figures are distorted by the inclusion of a departmental capital, the rates of migration were dramatically high. Indeed, in some cases, like Carmen (Bolívar), Corozal (Sucre), and Guamo (Tolima), migration almost turned into a rural exodus. This confirms the assumption of a strong population outflow from areas of major agitation during the land struggles. In terms of the socioeconomic processes, rural migration and the struggle for land had the same roots in the plains: the collapse of the traditional relations of production and the development of capitalist agriculture. However, the main point here concerns the subsequent effects of migration. The decrease in population must have been crucial not only in lessening the conflict over land but also in reducing the competition for existing employment opportunities.

Turning now to capitalist agriculture, whose expansion can also be determined statistically, it should be remembered that this type of production had been developing since the 1950s as a result of the growing demand for food and raw materials for industry. The real novelty during the first half of the 1970s was the spectacular acceleration of this development, an acceleration that reflected both the general upturn of the economy and the unconditional support given to agrarian capitalism by Pastrana and López Michelsen. The Agricultural Financial Fund, created by Law 5 of 1973, provided massive amounts of cheap credit for different types of large-scale agriculture, encouraging landowners and other entrepreneurs who leased land in order to engage in production.[4] Comparing the periods 1968–1970 and 1975–1977, Table 7.3 shows the dimensions of this process. There was an increase of 40.3 percent in the harvested area for the seven main crops of capitalist agriculture. This increase is 5.6 percent greater when attention is focused upon cotton, rice, sorghum, and sesame, which are cultivated mainly on the Atlantic Coast and the plains of Huila and Tolima. In terms of labor absorption, these four crops required an additional 15.8 million working days. Most of this 40.9 percent expansion in employment must have taken place during the last years of the period under consideration, since the statistics of the Department of National Planning registered an increase of 33.8 percent between 1972 and 1976.[5] Although some of the new job openings occurred in other places, the regional data show that employment generated by the four crops grew by 35 percent in the central area of Huila and Tolima and by 37.8 percent on the Atlantic Coast. Especially noteworthy increases involved rice, which doubled the demand for labor in Tolima and Huila and trebled it in Cesar and Magdalena. Cotton also doubled its labor absorption in these departments and in Córdoba, and quintuplicated it in Sucre and Bolívar.[6] Taking into account the 1973 census figures on the economically active population in the two main regions of land struggle, these data indicate that during the period of 1975–1977 the four main crops of capitalist agriculture were absorbing 14.6 percent of the labor force in Huila and Tolima and 25.8 percent in the seven departments of the Atlantic Coast.

In addition to the commercial crops, other economic activities of regional importance also grew significantly. Although its demand for labor is not very intensive, cattle raising on the Atlantic Coast deserves mention, since 40 percent of it is located there and the livestock population rose by 49.4 percent during the period under consideration.[7] In Cesar and

Table 7.3. *Harvested area and labor absorption of the main crops of capitalist agriculture, 1968–1977*

| | Seven main crops[a] Harvested area (hectares, 000's) | Four main crops[b] Harvested area (hectares, 000's) | Four main crops[b] Total labor absorption (working days, 000's) | Four main crops[b] Regional labor absorption | |
				Atlantic Coast (working days, 000's)	Tolima and Huila (working days, 000's)
Annual average, 1968–1970	795.5	594.8	38,716	24,247	7,168
Annual average, 1975–1977	1,116.3	861.1	54,554	33,414	9,725
Increase (%)	40.3	45.9	40.9	37.8	35.6

[a]Seven main crops: sugar cane, barley, soybeans, rice, cotton, sorghum, sesame.
[b]Four main crops: rice, cotton, sorghum, sesame.
Sources: S. Kalmanovitz, *La Agricultura en Colombia*, 1978. Ministerio de Agricultura, *Cifras del Sector Agropecuario*, 1979.

Bolívar the merchants introduced, for the first time, special vehicles to transport refrigerated freights. This led to a sudden massive commercialization of fishing in rivers and lakes, increasing the demand for labor in a field that had always provided a supplementary income for most of the families.[8] In the central area of the country, both the increase and the changing patterns of coffee production were generating a growing demand for wage laborers on the slopes, attracting greater seasonal flows of workers from the plains of Huila and Tolima.[9] Since recent studies have shown that most of the coffee laborers come from the coffee zones themselves, the effects of greater employment must have been even greater in other areas of land struggle, such as the Antioqueño southwest and the banks of the River Cauca in the three main coffee departments of Caldas, Quindío, and Risaralda.[10]

Finally, a key factor in the greater demand for wage labor was the tangible improvement in agricultural wages, not only in absolute terms but also in comparison with urban wages. Nominal rural wages increased by 232.4 percent between 1970 and 1976, and while in 1970 the average payment was 65 percent greater than the rural legal minimum, the proportion went up to 88 percent by 1976.[11] A comparison of urban and rural wages shows that while the latter had a real — that is, deflated — increase of 4.9 percent between 1972 and 1976, the real wages of industrial workers and government employees went down by 6.7 and 15.9 percent, respectively.[12] This tendency was especially noticeable in the coastal departments and in Huila and Tolima, where salaries were among the highest nationally in 1976.[13]

Turning now to the migration to Venezuela, we should begin by noting that its illegal nature makes it difficult to assess precisely its occupational impact upon the rural areas of Colombia. There are three main groups of migrants: those who stay for long periods as workers in the Venezuelan cities, women who usually engage in domestic work and prostitution, and seasonal agricultural laborers who harvest coffee and other commercial crops. The few available studies were conducted among people who had been deported through the main frontier post at Cúcuta.[14] This introduces a serious bias, because excessive weight is given in these samples to urban workers, who, because of their position, are more susceptible to identification, arrest, and expulsion. Since these workers usually come from Colombian cities, available analyses on the social extraction of the migrants throws little light upon the point of interest here: the effect of the seasonal migrations to Venezuela on the employment situation in areas of land struggle. Nonetheless, both newspaper accounts and the evidence from the numerous interviews carried out as part of this research clearly suggest the importance of this factor on the Atlantic Coast, especially after 1974.[15]

The seasonal migration of rural laborers to Venezuela has a long history.

Since the 1930s, coffee harvests on the other side of the border have attracted workers from Santander, North Santander, and Cesar.[16] When large-scale capitalist agriculture started to develop in Venezuela after the 1950s, many more laborers began to cross the frontier illegally through the "green paths," creating a movement that was noticeable by the late 1960s even in the western departments of the Colombian Atlantic Coast.[17] The real boom in Venezuelan capitalist agriculture began when the nationalization of the oil industry in 1974 made possible a massive transfer of resources to other economic activities. As part of a policy that tried to consolidate agriculture in order to meet national needs, subsidized credit led to a remarkable increase in the production of rice, cotton, sugar cane, and other crops. This occurred mainly in the western states closest to Colombia, which have always accounted for most of the agricultural production in Venezuela.[18] For the entrepreneurs, the availability of Colombian laborers solved the problem of a chronic labor shortage, a problem that was greatest in crops like cotton and sugar cane, which require a large seasonal labor force. In addition, the illegal status of the workers reduced the cost of labor, since the employers could pay below-minimum wages and avoid the subsidies and social benefits prescribed by law. The Colombian workers were also attracted by the wages, because even though they were being underpaid by Venezuelan standards, they received three times what they would get in their own country.[19] Since the rewards seemed to be greater than the risks of illegality, a steady pattern of seasonal migration to Venezuela had developed in all the areas of the Atlantic Coast by 1975 and 1976.

At the beginning, a crucial role was played by itinerant brokers who organized parties of laborers and took them directly across the border to places of work. Later these brokers were replaced by less informal contractors who operated "charter systems" from the many offices of "labor orientation" that sprang up in cities and smaller towns. The migratory circuit involved not only proletarians, former tenants, and sharecroppers, but also small independent peasants, particularly those who had obtained land in the previous struggles and invasions.[20] This last factor will be considered again in the following chapter in relation to the question of the new peasant settlements. Here the relevant point is that in the late 1970s an estimated 1.5 million Colombians were illegally crossing the Venezuelan border. Since a single crop like sugar cane could mobilize some 50,000 men from the Atlantic Coast,[21] the seasonal migration to Venezuela must have been an important occupational alternative for the labor force in that area.

For obvious reasons, the possibility of obtaining reliable data on the marihuana economy is even more remote than in the case of migration to Venezuela. Nevertheless, this issue became so important in Colombia that private research institutes funded by industrialists and financiers conducted studies on its macroeconomic aspects.[22] By sketching the general dimensions of the process, these studies provide a framework for the interpretation of more specific data from newspaper reports and interviews conducted during this research. The event that spurred marihuana cultivation in Colombia was the liquidation of production in Mexico, which had supplied most of the American demand until 1974 and 1975. The destruction of the Mexican crops, carried out jointly by the local authorities and the U.S. government, shifted the focus of production to the department of Guajira and the Sierra Nevada de Santa Marta. In addition to its proximity to Florida by air and sea, this Colombian coastal region had been the source of the much appreciated "Santa Marta gold" variety of marihuana since the 1960s, and it had a smuggling tradition perfectly adaptable to the new clandestine activity.[23] By 1977, when the National Comptroller announced the existence of some 70,000 sown hectares in the northern corner of the country, the marihuana economy was in full swing. The official reports indicated that, since 1976, two-thirds of the American market was being supplied by the "Colombian connection." Although only 20 percent of the final price went to the Colombian dealers and producers, the income generated by marihuana amounted to thousands of millions of dollars, and it was estimated that the new bonanza made up 30 to 40 percent of the total value of national exports.[24] During 1978, when the government began to take steps against the traffic with American assistance, the police stated that Guajira and Sierra Nevada accounted for only 60 percent of the 100,000 hectares under cultivation. The crop had extended to other areas, notably Cesar, Magdalena, southern Bolívar, and the Eastern Llanos.[25]

Besides considering other factors, such as corruption of the authorities, the methods of the *mafias*, and the crystallization of a new cultural ethos, all the available reports stress the economic importance of marihuana in the affected areas. There is no mystery about what prompted the rush to the new crop: The producers received only 2 percent of the final price, but their income was still up to six times greater than the profits derived from coffee or any other commercial crop.[26] Originally, marihuana was produced by peasants in the Sierra Nevada, a place that was soon crowded with new colonists who moved in amid increasingly bitter friction with the Indians of the local Arhuaco *resguardos*.[27] But within months the crop was also extending to the plains, generating the development of new forms of production that became as important as cultivation by independent peasants and colonists. One of these was the large-scale production of Guajira and the northern areas of Cesar and Magdalena, where many landowners shifted from cotton to marihuana using wage labor, modern technology, and even institutional credits.[28] Another was based upon relations of production similar to rent and sharecropping, involving peasants who cultivated marihuana on *haciendas* in central and southern Magdalena, Cesar, and Bolívar.[29] The occupational impact of this bonanza must have been crucial throughout the Atlantic Coast, especially in the eastern regions. A study by the National Association of Financial Institutions (ANIF) indicated that there were some 6,000 producers in the Sierra Nevada alone, and that an army of 13,000 rural laborers was being attracted by wages that were double and triple the usual pay in the countryside.[30] This same study estimated that 30,000 families depended totally or partially upon marihuana, which would be equivalent to one-third of the rural homes registered by the 1973 population census in the eastern departments and approximately one in seven of the total number of rural homes on the Atlantic Coast.[31] To this, one should add the increased employment opportunities in other activities indirectly influenced by the marihuana economy. Among such activities, which included the building industry and commerce, a crucial one was smuggling, a traditional occupation for a sizeable portion of the coastal population, which was now stimulated by the proliferation of dollars coming not only from marihuana, but also from cocaine and the general boost to the export economy.[32]

In general, the convergence of the processes reviewed in this section caused substantial changes in the main areas of land struggle. In addition to the relaxation due to the new Sharecropping Law, migration and new employment opportunities rapidly changed the conditions that had originally led to peasant unrest. Trying to survive economically after the collapse of the traditional relations of production, the peasants now had alternatives to working their own land, and this was happening precisely at a time when gaining land was ceasing to be a realistic option. Most of the new alternatives reflected the consolidation of agrarian capitalism in the plains. Indeed, whatever its nationality or the nature of its activities, agrarian capitalism was creating a large demand for wage labor and, at the same time, was subordinating this labor to its own requirements. In this sense, a crucial element was the increasing mobility of the labor force, which resulted from three factors: the double cycle of agriculture in the tropics (where climate permits two annual harvests of most crops), the geographical dispersion of the main large-scale crops, and the fact that the seasonal labor demands are different for each crop. The combination of these factors continuously shifted the loci of labor absorption, broadening the economic definition of the regions and making the labor migrations a key component of the new structure.

Socioeconomic changes also created attitudes that clearly differed from those that had previously sustained the fight for the land. Seasonal labor migrations expanded the horizons of thought and destroyed the perception of enclosed worlds with strictly local alternatives. The ideal of a livelihood based upon free peasant production was replaced by other aspirations linked to laboring for wages in different activities. Local things began to be thought of in relation to external factors, and even the hope of eventually developing an independent economy was conditioned by the possibility of saving money as a laborer in order to buy a plot of land or start another type of informal activity in a town.[33] In Magdalena and Cesar, the marihuana bonanza completely transformed the situation. The fierce land conflicts suddenly ended and were replaced by a vertical alignment in which landowners, peasants, and officials shared a common interest in the underground economy. The nature of the marihuana industry and the participation of the peasants in the new regional block of classes had a devastating effect on ideology, paving the way for attitudes and values that promoted *mafiosi* factional loyalties and relegated to the background class demands that had originally fed the fighting spirit at the grass-roots level.[34]

ANUC and the organization of the agricultural laborers

The redefinition of the peasants' motives and aspirations was only one result of the socioeconomic changes taking place in the main areas of land struggle. In terms of the peasant movement, another one was the subsequent effects of organizational disruption. ANUC's structure suffered greatly as a result of labor migration because, with the members of the local groups continuously on the move, it was increasingly difficult to maintain regularity and continuity. The activities of the associations became intermittent and there were long lulls, after which great efforts were necessary to reactivate the committees. These problems were particularly notable in the western departments of the Atlantic Coast, where labor migration worsened the dispersion and weakness that had been created by political factionalism.[35] In many places in the eastern region, marihuana was an even stronger factor. With the rest of the Colombian left, ANUC Sincelejo shared the view that drugs "were inimical to the productive and patriotic consciousness and caused degeneration of the spirit of the people both at the individual and collective levels."[36] Such arguments did not seem convincing to those involved in marihuana cultivation, who rejected the peasant movement. In Guajira, Magdalena, and Cesar, and also in Meta and Cauca, a number of former *usuario* leaders turned into dealers of marihuana and cocaine, and some of them even earned a reputation as notorious members of the *mafia*.[37] Among the communities, the most conspicuous case was that of the famous frontier refugees, whose settlements in Mingueo became centers of marihuana cultivation and included one of the favorite storage and shipment points on the Caribbean littoral.[38]

ANUC Sincelejo found it difficult to work out strategies that would counteract these conditions. Migration to the cities and rural seasonal migration were so widespread that they could not be tackled directly by the peasant movement. Access to the areas of marihuana cultivation was closed to trade-unionist or political agitation. Little could be done on behalf of the illegal migrants in Venezuela, except for formal protests to the Colombian government regarding the abuses they suffered. Still, and given the fact that many of these changes were linked to the expansion of agrarian capitalism, there was at least one field that seemed to be favorable for action: the struggle for the demands of the agricultural laborers.

The defense of rural proletarian interests was not new to ANUC; the movement had defined itself from the very beginning as an organization of the middle, poor, and wage-earning peasants. The demands of the rural workers had first been spelled out in the *Plataforma Ideologica*; they included better wages, a working day of eight hours, and social benefits similar to those of the urban workers. The *Mandato Campesino* had allowed the agricultural laborers to participate in the CERA and had also stipulated that agribusiness-type enterprises should be handed over to the workers under collectivization schemes. In 1972, the fifth meeting of the National Junta at Tolú had indicated that ANUC should consider special policies to promote the demands of agricultural laborers. This intention was later ratified in the Second National Congress of Sincelejo, when the *usuarios* decided to work on several fronts, including coffee production, the new agrarian reform settlements, the rural proletariat, and so on.[39] However, the agricultural workers were not differentiated during that first period of confrontation. Their aspirations were equalized to and subsumed under those of the landless peasants, so that both peasants and proletarians took part in land invasions and tried to attain the same goal in the areas of land struggle. Only in the coffee regions were the demands of the agricultural laborers raised during the early years. In these areas, ANUC Sincelejo tried to integrate the different class sectors, holding meetings that included small and middle peasants, tenants and sharecroppers, and wage laborers. But the proprietors always protested against the wage increases that were the basic demand of the workers. Despite the efforts to emphasize common interests in opposition to the state and the dominant classes, this contradiction became one of the major factors hindering the *usuarios* in the coffee areas.[40] Apart from these meetings, ANUC's action was limited to support of the petitions and strikes by syndicates of the sugar and oil palm industries. In fact, very little had been done on behalf of the agricultural workers during the first years; as a consequence, this issue was not even mentioned by ANUC's Executive Committee in the report of activities submitted to the Third National Congress.[41]

Responding to the changing conditions in the areas of land struggle, the resolutions of the turbulent 1974 congress of Bogotá emphasized that ANUC should focus more on the interests of the agricultural proletarians, so that they would become "a central force in the peasant associations and in the peasant movement as a whole." A long list of demands was presented, including minimum wages, an eight-hour working day, the right to organize and to strike, abolition of piece-work systems, social benefits, appropriate food and accommodation, health services, stable conditions of employment, and compensation for unjustified dismissal.[42] In the months that followed the Third Congress, it became evident that there was another important factor behind ANUC's determination to mobilize the agricultural workers: the threat of competition from the other leftist groups. The potential of a rural proletariat numbering around 1.5 million had not been overlooked by ANUC's rivals. The Communist Party was making a special effort for trade-union work in the countryside, and the rural laborers' syndicates was one of their key targets. The Socialist Revolutionary Union (URS), a splinter group of the Socialist Bloc, controlled a number of rural workers' associations in Huila and was trying to expand into Tolima. Even some of the factions of the divided PCML were now revising their Maoist views and seriously considering the possibility of "organizing the rural proletariat in order to oppose ANUC's peasantist line."[43] Facing this competition, ANUC Sincelejo defined its own project during the thirteenth meeting of its National Junta (Cartagena, August 1975). A special resolution was approved stating that ANUC would immediately launch a campaign to organize the agricultural workers as an independent class sector within the peasant movement, putting forward the demands that had been previously defined in the conclusions of the Third National Congress.[44]

This step aroused an uproar among the leftist parties. They argued that the cryptic political group behind the *usuarios* was now trying to subordinate the workers' demands to the aspirations of the peasantry, refusing to acknowledge the leading role of the proletariat in Colombia's revolution. In response to these attacks, the ORP militants justified their stance and ANUC's initiative in an elaborate article published by their journal, *Combate*, in early 1976.[45] Given the democratic character of the first stage of Colombia's socialist revolution, ORP believed that three elements unified peasants and agricultural workers. First, the existing contradictions placed both sectors "within a single popular front against their common enemies: imperialism, the big intermediary bourgeoisie and the landowners." Second, the political domination of the *gamonales* in the countryside "homogenized peasants and workers, turning them into a single class-estate by opposition to the power of the landowning class." Third, in a backward country like Colombia, the rural proletariat had strong ties with the land and was not "fully differentiated from the lower peasant strata." ORP therefore argued that there was no reason to object to the organization of the agricultural workers by ANUC, since this would increase the participation of the proletariat in the agrarian struggles and the peasant movement.[46]

The debate on the agricultural laborers helped to clarify the rather obscure positions of ORP, providing clues to the nature and meaning of the political undercurrent that had developed among ANUC's leaders and advisers. The Maoist imprint was clearly visible, both in the concept of the two successive democratic and socialist stages of the revolution and in the roles of "main force" and "leading force" that were assigned to the peasantry and the working class vanguard respectively, in the first stage. On the other hand, there were many elements that vindicated part of the argument advanced by those who stressed the populist and anarcho-syndicalist "deviations" of ORP: There was an undeniable "peasantist" emphasis, alliances were proposed to the "middle bourgeoisie and the rich peasantry," the rural proletarians were subsumed within the peasant or-ganization, and the political dimension appeared to be a direct contin-uation of ANUC's trade-unionist activities.

All the same, beyond the ongoing debate within the left, any inter-pretation of ORP must take into account two crucial elements. First, it has already been argued that the relationship between the peasant move-ment and the leftist political groups had been a substitute for a nonexistent alliance of workers and peasants. In its confrontation with the dominant classes, the peasantry was organized, but its proletarian counterpart was missing and there was no party able to fill the vacuum and give political expression to the social force that had crystallized in the countryside. The isolation of the peasantry and the political opportunism of the leftist parties had finally led ANUC to try to find its own political expression. This impulse would be shaped by a second element: the influence of a Maoist ideology that tried to give a revolutionary orientation to a peasant movement that otherwise might have followed a more typically populist course. Conditioned by the elitist and manipulative style of Colombian left-wing politics, this process created something new: a peasant force with pretensions to become the nucleus of a future proletarian revolu-tionary party. Preserving the same initials, ORP changed its name in 1976 from "People's Revolutionary Organization" to "Proletarian Rev-olutionary Organization."[47] This gave formal expression to the historical paradox that had pushed the peasant movement toward the false political solution of trying to substitute for the working class and therefore assuming the responsibility for the failure of the worker–peasant alliance in Colombia.

During the year and a half that followed the resolution of the thirteenth meeting, the activists of ANUC Sincelejo worked hard to organize the agricultural laborers, concentrating many of their staff in the main coffee and cotton areas. In Caldas, Quindío, and Risaralda, there were again meetings including different groups of coffee peasants, but most efforts were concentrated on the harvest time, to advance the demands of the wage laborers by means of petitions, demonstrations, and strikes. Similar activities were carried out among the cotton pickers of Sucre, Cesar, Magdalena, and Meta, and there were isolated attempts in municipalities of Huila, Boyacá, and northern Valle.[48] Along with this agitation at the grass-roots level, ANUC's Executive Committee tried to stir public opinion, dramatizing the wretched condition of the agricultural workers and denouncing "the hunger levels" of the minimum rural wages established by López Michelsen's government.[49] However, the results of all these efforts were poor. The strategy had been based upon the formation of nuclei of rural workers that would lead to departmental syndicates and eventually to a great national federation. But toward the end of 1976, when ANUC held its First National Meeting of Agricultural Workers in the town of Tuluá, only three departmental syndicates had been formed in Sucre, Caldas, and Risaralda. Of these three, only the syndicate of Sucre had subcommittees and actually seemed to exist.[50]

What were the causes of ANUC's setbacks in organizing the agricultural workers? One was the organizational weaknesses that resulted from the factors previously studied. Apart from these factors were other obstacles directly related to the specific nature of the rural proletariat in Colombia. As a brief analysis on an issue that has been only superficially explored by social research in the country,[51] it may be said that in one way or another, most of the problems came from the complex formation of the rural proletariat. In terms of its origins, only part of the salaried labor force could be considered proletarianized. The rest was composed of part-time workers who maintained links with the peasant economy, whether as independent producers or subordinated tenants. Further, within agrarian capitalism, each type of production absorbed labor power in a different way: agribusinesses used large numbers of permanent workers, cattle raisers used a limited number of hands under a variety of arrangements, and crop growers had seasonal requirements for legions of day laborers who were usually hired under piece-work systems. Both elements helped create a very heterogeneous agricultural proletariat that included vast sectors whose class definition was unclear. This ambiguity, in turn, prevented the unified social perspective needed for the success of trade-union or political agitation and for the eventual crystallization of a coherent class consciousness. In fact, only the agribusiness sector provided favorable conditions for trade unionism, since the processing plants of the oil palm and seed industries, sugar plantations, cotton gins, and different kinds of mills employed many permanent workers under the same conditions as the urban factories. However, precisely because conditions were favorable, these workers had already formed their own unions by the time ANUC Sincelejo began its organization campaign. On the cattle *haciendas* the number of wage laborers was small, and when the workmen had plots as subordinated peasants, it seemed more appropriate to encourage their struggle for the land itself. In consequence, the *usuarios'* efforts could only be directed toward the agricultural workers who were most difficult to organize: those who were semiproletarian by origin and temporary because of their modality of employment.

The hardships of temporary laborers were greatest in the coffee and cotton harvests, which mobilized the largest numbers of what began to be known in the country as the "nomadic agricultural proletariat." The state provided ways to help circulate labor power and maintain public order during the harvest periods, but it gave no minimum protection to the workers themselves. By definition, temporary employment excluded welfare benefits and security of tenure. To this were added low pay in the piece-work systems, working days of up to fourteen hours, the obligation to buy at the estate shops, fraud and abuse in the settling of accounts, and appalling housing and sanitation conditions.[52] Still, the same system that created this exploitation also shaped the attitudes of the laborers and affected their receptivity to organizational approaches. Besides the fact that the bonds with the peasant economy obstructed a clear-cut proletarian self-image, the nature of the work itself conspired in the same direction. The temporary nature of employment prevented workers from looking to the future, which explains much of the laborers' indifference to trade unionism. The condition of transience created a feeling of inferiority that inhibited workers from making demands in unknown and sometimes hostile environments. In many cases, recruitment by broker contractors subdued the workers in advance and blurred their relations with the employers. Finally, the piece-work payment systems impeded a collective perspective and fostered individualistic notions that were further strengthened by the competition among thousands of laborers who wanted to make the most out of the season.

In this atmosphere of poor worker responsiveness, many of ANUC's demands were not perceived as the most urgent. The eight-hour working day, social benefits, stability of employment, and other claims could not be applied to the informal and temporary labor relationships that existed. The relevant demands were immediate ones: better piece-work payments, proper food, and a decent place to sleep during the harvest period. ANUC tried to adjust to these demands, mounting demonstrations and strikes in the cotton centers and in the main coffee municipalities. In certain cases, some initial success was achieved (e.g., spreading the word not to pick coffee or cotton for less than an agreed-upon wage) but it proved impossible to sustain this concerted action for long. Due to the factors already mentioned, the countermeasures of the landowners and the authorities were always very effective. Police raids frightened the laborers and isolated the militants. With the help of the governors, the federations of coffee and cotton growers brought in additional hands who could be easily recruited in other departments. Sooner or later the laborers quarreled among themselves as the strikes collapsed, adding great bitterness to these frustrating defeats.[53]

Not surprisingly, then, the First Meeting of Agricultural Labourers of December 1976 was forced to face the fact that it had not been possible to set up departmental syndicates. The nomadic nature of the agricultural proletariat, its transient and immediate demands, and the difficulties involved in agitation had prevented a strong organization. In fact, only a few dozen delegates came to the Tuluá meeting. As was now happening in many of ANUC's events, the activists outnumbered the grass-roots representatives. It was recommended that ANUC create a National Secretary for Agricultural Laborers. This secretary would establish departmental unions, and these, in turn, would promote the formation of local subcommittees.[54] This attempt to institutionalize a bureaucracy with no real roots in the regions was nothing but a tacit admission of ANUC's failure among the agricultural laborers.

8

Partial repeasantization and the question of the new peasant settlements

As already indicated the gains made during the battles of the early 1970s had reduced the *usuarios'* combativeness in the main areas of land struggle. Two aspects were particularly relevant here: the partial satisfaction of land hunger and the disappointing results of the new peasant economy. Both will now be examined in greater depth as an introduction to the analysis of ANUC's performance in the new peasant settlements.

Marginal access to land as a palliative

Land hunger had been satisfied by greater access to land. The phrase "partial satisfaction," which qualifies this achievement, must be explained and sustained by empirical data. The more general issue, of course, is the socioeconomic significance of the changes. This issue can be broken down into three central questions: What was the actual scope of the peasant gains? To what extent did these gains affect the existing patterns of land distribution? What was their place in the overall process of change in Colombia's countryside? In an attempt to answer these questions, the following discussion is based upon three main sources of information: the agricultural censuses of 1960 and 1970, the population censuses of 1964 and 1973, and the reports on INCORA's activities throughout the period 1962–1979.

INCORA's data on land redistribution and the allocation of titles to public land, presented in Table 8.1, provide a starting point to assess the gains of the land struggles. Redistribution was almost always a direct result of the struggle for land. As shown in previous chapters, such redistribution in Colombia usually occurred as a legitimation of peasant seizures of land. This was specially true after 1970, when INCORA's own initiatives were completely suppressed under the policy of counterreform. Conversely, there were no cases in which the peasants retained occupied lands without the Institute's intervention, since only by such intervention could disputes be legally settled and secure tenure finally achieved. Allocation of titles to public land, on the other hand, only partially reflected the land struggle. This was because much of INCORA's activity took place in colonization areas in which the peasants' right to the land was

147

Table 8.1. *Land redistribution and allocation of titles on public land by INCORA, 1962–1979*

		Land redistribution		Allocation of titles on public land	
		Number of families	Hectares (000's)	Number of families	Hectares (000's)
	1962–1969	7,012	112.8	81,188	2,638.5
	1970–1979	23,445	461.6	141,770	2,614.0
Total, 1962–1979		30,457	604.4	222,958	5,252.5

Sources: INCORA, "Informe especial," 1969. INCORA, *Resumen General de las Principales Realizaciones del INCORA por Proyectos*, 1980.

not challenged. However, it has been seen that many conflicts developed in other places where the peasants occupied uncultivated or uncleared land claimed by landowners. In these cases, the peasants won only when INCORA established that the landowner's title was legally questionable or returned the title to the state on the grounds that the lands had not been farmed continuously for ten years. Unfortunately, INCORA's information about the number of allocated titles fails to distinguish between disputed and undisputed situations. Still, the data do show that out of the 5,252,500 hectares adjudicated between 1962 and 1979, 20.5 percent involved titles that had reverted to the state and 8.2 percent involved cases that had ended with clarification of public property.[1] It can therefore be estimated that some 42,000, or approximately 30 percent of the 141,770 titles allocated between 1970 and 1979, involved conflict over the possession of the land. Adding this figure to the number of peasants who obtained land through redistribution, the overall estimate indicates that some 66,000 families gained access to approximately 1,200,000 hectares as a result of the land struggles of the 1970s.

In terms of the agrarian reform process, it is quite clear that the battles for land directly influenced INCORA's activity. Table 8.1 shows that the number of families benefiting from land redistribution tripled between 1970 and 1979 in comparison with the period 1962–1969. More dramatically, Figure 8.1 also reveals the effects of the class struggles in the countryside: The curve depicting INCORA's land acquisitions peaked in the years of greater agitation, with a steep rise reflecting ANUC's organizational rise and the reformist impulse of Lleras Restrepo's government and a slower decline mirroring the counterreformist reaction and the decreasing pressure of the peasant movement. These data do prove that the struggles led to greater access to land by the peasantry.

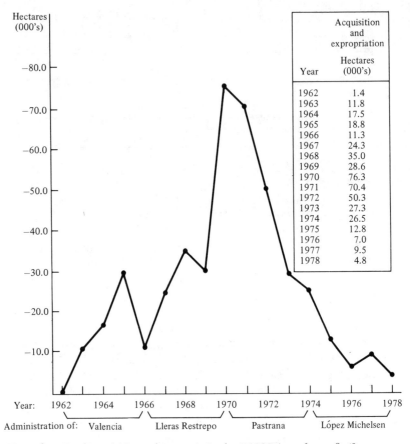

Figure 8.1. Land acquisition and expropriation by INCORA, 1962-1978. (Source: INCORA, *Informe de Labores*, 1978)

But in order to appreciate its true significance, the peasant achievement has to be measured against other criteria. One way of doing this is by contrasting the number of those who theoretically needed land to those who actually obtained it as a consequence of the struggles and agrarian reform. While INCORA's figure was 935,000, American researchers had estimated in the early 1970s that there were 558,000 potential beneficiaries of a reasonable agrarian reform in Colombia.[2] If the lower estimate is taken as a standard, the 66,000 families who did gain land represented only 11.8 percent of the potential beneficiaries, clearly illustrating the limited scope of the peasant gains. A second appraisal can be obtained by considering the balance between the repeasantization that resulted from the struggles of the 1970s and the general process of peasant dissolution. The data on the agricultural censuses of 1960 and 1970 presented in

Table 8.2 indicate that, despite the agrarian reform of the 1960s, some 32,800 farms disappeared as a result of extinction or migration during that period. Assuming a similar rate of dissolution for the 1970s, it can be said that the 66,000 families resettled as a result of the post–1970 struggles only compensated for the overall dissolution of the peasantry over the two decades. A third and final assessment can be made by looking at the effects of repeasantization upon the patterns of land distribution. Since no agricultural census was done in 1980, the 1970 data on land distribution in Table 8.2 are the only basis for these estimates. Even taking into account all the colonists who received titles, and not just the 30 percent who had to fight for their land, the changes in land distribution seem to be only marginal. The 165,00 families resettled on the 3,105,600 hectares redistributed and allocated by INCORA during the 1970s would have increased the share of the 10- to 50-hectare size category to 29.0 percent of the number of farms and to 22.9 percent of the area. But only 9.5 percent of the land on estates larger than 500 hectares would have been affected by redistribution, and these big estates would still concentrate 34.0 percent of the total agricultural area.

The land struggles resulted, therefore, in a partial achievement. The gains were insufficient to promote a peasant path of evolution in Colombia's countryside. Still, the same results that appear to be meager from this point of view may seem highly significant when considered as a palliative. To make this point, it is worthwhile to focus attention again upon the main regions of land struggle during the 1970s. Relating the information on INCORA's activity to data from the agricultural and population censuses of 1970 and 1973, Table 8.3 shows that repeasantization involved 12.7 percent of the rural families in the departments of the Atlantic Coast and 13.4 percent of those in the central area of Huila and Tolima. Such proportions hardly came up to the original reformists' expectations, much less to those of a radicalized peasant movement. The truth was that, as in the rest of the country, a partial repeasantization of 13 percent could not be seen as a radical change favoring the peasant economy in these regional agrarian structures. But as a palliative, this marginal repeasantization was important, since it could reduce the pressure of those landless peasants who, for either structural or ideological reasons, were most combative. This effect of mitigation must have been enhanced by the ongoing migration process, which, according to Table 7.1, led to an average reduction of 9.1 percent in the rural population of the Atlantic Coast, Huila, and Tolima during the period 1964–1973.

This last point suggests that the argument concerning the demobilizing influence of marginal access to land can be further strengthened by considering peasant gains in relation to the other socioeconomic processes taking place in the main areas of land struggle. Indeed, it is pertinent

Table 8.2. *Distribution of land in Colombia, by number and size of farms, 1960–1970*

Size of farms (hectares)	Agricultural census, 1960				Agricultural census, 1970			
	Number of farms (000's)	Percentage	Area in hectares (000's)	Percentage	Number of farms (000's)	Percentage	Area in hectares (000's)	Percentage
Total	1,209.6	100.0	27,337.8	100.0	1,176.8	100.0	30,993.1	100.0
Under 4.9	756.6	62.6	1,238.9	4.5	700.2	59.5	1,145.9	3.7
5.0–9.9	169.1	14.0	1,164.7	4.3	159.6	13.6	1,088.3	3.5
10.0–49.9	201.0	16.6	4,210.7	15.4	217.8	18.5	4,653.1	15.0
50.0–99.9	39.9	3.3	2,680.4	9.8	47.7	4.1	3,197.6	10.3
100.0–499.9	36.0	3.0	6,990.4	25.6	42.8	3.6	8,253.0	26.6
500.0–999.9	4.1	0.3	2,730.7	10.0	4.9	0.4	3,229.4	10.4
Over 1,000.0	2.7	0.2	8,321.6	30.4	3.4	0.3	9,425.5	30.5

Sources: DANE, *Censo Nacional Agropecuario*, 1960. DANE, *Censo Nacional Agropecuario*, 1970.

Table 8.3. *Atlantic Coast and central area: estimates of the overall incidence of agrarian reform after 1970*

Department	(A) Total number of rural families in 1973		(B) Independent peasants (families owning more than 5 hectares of land in 1970)		(C) Repeasantization (families serviced by INCORA after 1970)				(D) = (A−B−C) Proletarianized and semiproletarian families (families without land or owning less than 5 hectares)	
	Number	Percentage	Number	Percentage	Land redistrib.	Allocation of titles on public land	Total number	Percentage	Number	Percentage
Córdoba	62,922	100.0	16,285	25.9	2,896	2,806	5,702	9.1	40,935	65.0
Bolívar	42,325	100.0	13,681	32.3	2,189	4,500[a]	6,689	16.5	21,955	51.8
Sucre	26,998	100.0	7,576	28.0	4,625	21	4,646	17.2	14,776	54.7
Atlántico	9,263	100.0	4,003	43.2	651	11	662	7.1	4,598	49.6
Magdalena	39,872	100.0	10,119	25.3	971	4,244[a]	5,215	13.1	24,538	61.5
Cesar	27,107	100.0	9,117	33.6	780	2,883[a]	3,663	13.5	14,327	52.8
Atlantic Coast total	208,574	100.0	60,790	29.1	12,112	14,465	26,577	12.7	121,180	58.1
Huila	37,855	100.0	16,699	44.1	1,100	5,962	7,062	18.6	14,094	37.2
Tolima	73,048	100.0	23,480	32.1	590	7,180	7,770	10.5	41,798	57.2
Central area total	110,903	100.0	40,147	36.2	1,690	13,142	14,832	13.4	55,892	50.4

[a]Estimated figures: the total number of titles allocated in Bolívar, Cesar and Magdalena was proportionally distributed according to the rural population in each one of these three departments.

Sources: DANE, *Censo Nacional de Población*, 1973. DANE, *Censo Nacional Agropecuario*, 1970. INCORA, "Informe especial," 1969. INCORA, *Resumen General de las Principales Realizaciones del INCORA for Proyectos*, 1980.

to ask how partial repeasantization fitted in with the earlier changes in land tenancy patterns and with the new situation created by emigration and the rapid development of agrarian capitalism. Table 8.3 gives a first hint by showing that, as a result of the struggles of the 1970s, the proportion of proletarianized and semiproletarian families was reduced to 50 to 60 percent of the total number of rural families in the areas. However, to achieve a deeper understanding, one must relate this change to more general trends and to a more precise analysis of land tenancy and distribution patterns. Since the predominance of *minifundia* on the slopes and highlands of Huila and Tolima obscures the picture of processes in the plains, Table 8.4 approaches this task by focusing upon the departments of the more homogeneous Atlantic Coast.

Bringing together data on the agricultural and population censuses and on INCORA's activity after 1970, Table 8.4 shows that repeasantization in the 1970s continued the trend of the 1960s toward a marked increase in the proportion of families with land of their own throughout the Atlantic Coast. This increase paralleled an equally visible decrease in the percentage of families without land or with access to land under other forms of tenancy such as rent and sharecropping. However, whereas on the Atlantic Coast the size of the self-sufficient family farm ranged between 37 and 104 hectares, according to location and family size,[3] most of the families with land of their own had fewer than 30 hectares. The meaning of this difference becomes clearer when the question is approached not from the angle of tenancy patterns but from that of the families' position vis-à-vis the wage labor market. Table 8.4 clearly demonstrates that although a sizeable proportion of the coastal families got their own land, neither the growth of the self-sufficient peasant sector nor the decrease in the proportion of families participating in the labor market were significant. It can therefore be concluded that greater access to small-scale landed property was only one part of a broader process in which, throughout the 1960s and 1970s, traditional relations of production disappeared and labor power was freed to be sold in the markets by rural proletarians or by peasants who had to supplement their income by working outside their own farms.

This regional analysis clearly shows that the real change in the areas of land struggle was the transformation of the traditional *latifundia* into a new socioeconomic structure based upon agrarian capitalism. This transformation forced the labor force to adapt to the conditions of large-scale capitalist agriculture. In addition to small numbers of permanent workers, this agriculture needed large groups of temporary laborers who were available during periods of great demand and could subsist on their own when their labor was not required. From this perspective, it is clear that the appeasing effect of greater access to land can be understood only in

Table 8.4. *Atlantic Coast (Córdoba, Sucre, Bolívar, Atlántico, Magdalena and Cesar): estimates of access to land and participation in the wage-labor market, 1960–1979*

INCORA's activity, 1970–1979	Number of families	Average amount of land per family
Land redistribution	12,112	14.9 hectares
Allocation of titles on public land	14,465	28.7 hectares
Total	26,557	22.5 hectares

Access of families to the land	1960/64	1970/73	1979
Families with land of their own	46.4	52.2	70.1
Families with land under other forms of tenancy	29.1	24.0	12.1
Families with no access to land	24.5	23.8	17.8
Total (%)	100.0	100.0	100.0
(total number)	(230,369)	(208,547)	(193,139)

Families with land of their own, by size category	1960	1970	1979
Under 4.9	48.3	44.2	35.5
5.0–29.9	23.7	25.2	39.9
30–99.9	16.0	14.4	14.0
Over 100.0	12.0	13.2	10.6
Total (%)	100.0	100.0	100.0
(total number)	(107,005)	(108,878)	(135,454)

Position of families vis-à-vis the wage-labor market	1960/64	1970/73	1979
Landless families[a]	24.5	23.8	17.8
Peasants who depend heavily upon working outside their farms[b]	45.3	39.9	30.9
Peasants who depend partially upon working outside their farms[c]	15.2	17.9	31.4
Self-sufficient peasants[d]	8.9	10.6	11.5
Rural employers[e]	6.1	7.8	8.4
Total (%)	100.0	100.0	100.0
(total number)	(230,369)	(208,547)	(193,139)
Percentage of families that participate in the wage-labor market (a + b + c)	84.9	81.6	80.1

[a] With no access to land.
[b] With access to holdings of up to 4.9 hectares (of their own or under other tenancy forms).

Notes to Table 8.4 (*cont.*)

'With access to holdings of 5.0 to 29.9 hectares (of their own or under other tenancy forms).

*d*With access to holdings of 30.0 to 99.9 hectares (of their own or under other tenancy forms).

'With access to holdings of over 100.0 hectares (of their own or under other tenancy forms).

Sources of the estimates: 1960/64: DANE, *Censo Nacional Agropecuario*, 1960. DANE, *Censo Nacional de Población*, 1964. 1970/73: DANE, *Censo Nacional Agropecuario*, 1970. DANE, *Censo Nacional de Población*, 1973. INCORA's activity: INCORA, "Informe especial," 1969. INCORA, *Resumen General de las Principales Realizaciones del INCORA por Proyectos*, 1980.

conjunction with the new employment alternatives that were being created by the expansion of capitalist agriculture. In this sense, the gains of the land struggles of the early 1970s appear to have caused more than a relaxation of social tensions. While migration acted to expel excess labor power, partial repeasantization provided a reserve of temporary labor. In other words, the peasant gains became an element of adjustment that helped to maintain the balance of the reproduction cycles of agrarian capitalism.[4]

The failure of the new peasant economy

The previous discussion introduces the second main factor influencing the achievements of the land struggles, one concerning the subsequent evolution of the peasant settlements. Since this issue proved to be vital to the movement, the study of ANUC's involvement must be preceded by a consideration of the main factors that shaped the development of the new peasant economy. In this sense, the most relevant element during the late 1960s and early 1970s was the institutional attempt to foster a new type of agriculture among the beneficiaries of agrarian reform. Indeed, INCORA's policy of land adjudication underwent an important change under the Lleras Restrepo administration: Individual allocation was replaced by other schemes to encourage the development of cooperative forms of agriculture. In 1969 collective farming became the main form of land allocation and, as a consequence, most of the land redistributed by INCORA after the 1971 struggles was assigned to *empresas comunitarias* that in 1972 included more than half of the families serviced by the Institute.[5]

The motives behind the change in INCORA's adjudication policy were controversial at the time, and the debate is still continuing. Officially, the new philosophy was justified on the basis of the presumed social and economic advantages of collective farming and its greater efficiency in the use of state services; these arguments were sustained by reference to similar experiences in other Latin American countries.[6] Dismissing these justifications, most critics considered the *empresas comunitarias* as a demagogic instrument of restraint designed to stop the land struggles by giving rapid access to land to the most belligerent peasants. To this counterargument, others would add that the *empresas* also represented an attempt to impose, from the very beginning, state control upon the peasantry.[7] Such criticisms, however, seem too simplistic. After all, implementation of the collective system of adjudication preceded the main land invasions by a couple of years. Further, bureaucratic control of the settlements developed only after the main peasant offensive. Taking also into account that collective allocation began simultaneously with ANUC's promotion by Lleras Restrepo's government, a completely different interpretation is possible. Far from being a way to contain peasant unrest, the *empresas* were conceived as part of the plan to encourage horizontal class association and the exertion of peasant pressure. The attempt to strengthen agrarian reform, the creation of ANUC, and the introduction of collective farming should not be seen as isolated moves but as a coherent set of initiatives aimed at a single goal. For the reasons discussed in Chapter 2, strengthening the peasantry was a central priority for reformism during the late 1960s, and the *empresas comunitarias* were designed to further that end at the economic, social, and political levels.[8]

The idea that collective farming would help the development of a vigorous peasant sector after the land struggles and agrarian reform was grounded in wishful thinking rather than in a serious analysis of previous experiences in other countries. Although the assessments of these experiences revealed more frustration than success, the Colombian and, in general, the Latin American reformists of the 1960s preferred to exalt those virtues that, in theory, defined the superiority of collective farming to other forms of agriculture.[9] Economically, it was thought that cooperative large-scale production would provide a more rational use of labor and other resources, smoothing the absorption of technological innovations, facilitating access to credit and other services, improving the peasants' position in the market, and stimulating a capitalization process that would generate self-sustained growth. At the social and political levels, it was hoped that, apart from improving living standards, economic association would foster class consciousness among the producers, thus creating favorable conditions for organized pressure and the fulfillment of peasant aspirations. Finally, it was believed that collective adjudication would simplify and accelerate land redistribution, making possible the extension of services under optimum budgetary conditions later.[10] On the assumption that all these effects would occur, INCORA assigned collectively all the lands being acquired during the peasant invasions. Gradually, tenure was retrospectively legalized by means of collective titles. These titles stipulated that the land of the *empresa comunitaria* would remain indivisible for a number of years, that individual parcels could be assigned for family subsistence crops, and that cash incomes should be derived mainly from commercial production undertaken collectively by the *parceleros*.[11] Thus, by 1976 there were approximately 1350 *empresas* that, as shown in Table 8.6, included 55 percent of the land redistributed by INCORA and 54 percent of all the families dealt with by the Institute.

The same arguments that justified collective farming can, in fact, be used to set up two criteria for evaluating the performance of the Colombian *empresas comunitarias*. The first criterion is economic success of the settlements, in terms of production units themselves and the socioeconomic changes created in their regions. The second criterion is the promotion of peasant autonomy at various levels: in the establishment of a sound and self-sufficient economic base; in the consolidation of an influential and powerful social presence; and in the reinforcement of organization, solidarity, and class consciousness. In examining the results of collective farming in Colombia in these terms, it is clear that the theoretical advantages of the cooperative model were not enough, by themselves, to achieve success. Studies of similar experiments in other countries show that successful collectivization depends upon a constellation of economic, social, political, and cultural factors. At the social level, the key element has always been strong state support, expressed not only by massive investment but also by a political commitment to the transformation of rural life. Furthermore, the state must have the capacity to carry out this transformation in spite of objective obstacles and even the political opposition of certain interest groups. At the level of the settlements themselves, experiences have highlighted the importance of the socioeconomic and cultural background of the peasants involved, the agronomic potential of the land, and the norms and organizational patterns used to create the farms.[12]

On the basis of available studies, and taking into account material from numerous interviews with peasants and INCORA officials, it is possible to make some remarks concerning the influence of all these factors upon collective farming in Colombia. With regard to the most basic element, state policy, it is clear that the defeat of reformism was the main cause of the setbacks and difficulties faced by the new peasant settlements. The virtual end to further land redistribution meant that massive cooperation in the countryside was out of the question. Thus, the *empresas comunitarias* became small, disconnected islands in the tide of rural transformation under agrarian capitalism. Marginality and isolation created unsuitable conditions for economic cooperation among the settlements. Restricted regional production hindered the development of cooperative systems of marketing, joint use of machinery, and wholesale acquisition of the services and equipment that are essential to collective farming. Further, the paralysis of agrarian reform defined the question of the families' future as a serious problem from the start. This was so because access to additional land was impossible and the settlements were unable to absorb the labor power of the members' sons. Another key aspect of counterreform was INCORA's budget cut, which restricted the transfer of resources to the *empresas* and increased the problems caused by infrastructural deficiencies, insufficient credit, poor technical assistance, and lack of many basic services. Finally, the enactment of Decree 2073 of 1973 – part of the larger counterreformist package agreed upon at the Chicoral meeting – set the stage for the dissolution of the collective farms. The legal status given to the *empresas comunitarias* included codes of internal organization that emphasized individualism and opened the door for the eventual destruction of collective standards and a return to the principle of private property for the *parceleros*.[13]

In terms of peasant autonomy, the most important consequence of counterreform was the growing problem of control of the settlements by INCORA. The Institute's officials, employees, and professionals originally committed to the reformist philosophy had been left in an embarrassing position as a result of the change in state policy. After a strike and other initial protests, the dismissal of "rebels" and the appointment of high-level executives loyal to the new policies cooled the atmosphere and led to acceptance of INCORA as a mediator between the peasants who pressed for continued agrarian reform and a state that denied it. To rationalize its awkward situation, INCORA announced a provisional policy: Since political conditions now discouraged land redistribution, the Institute should concentrate upon achieving success in existing settlements, so that when the politicians changed their attitudes, INCORA would be able to show that agrarian reform was still the best strategy for rural development.[14] Although this might have seemed favorable for the *empresas comunitarias*, the reality proved to be quite different. As the existing settlements became INCORA's sole *raison d'être*, the need to show positive results and avoid the risk of failure became the central tenet of INCORA's bureaucracy. Instead of relying upon the peasants' own criteria and encouraging their autonomy, the officials used the powers given to them by Decree 2073 to take over the planning and management of economic activities. A pattern of authoritarian supervision developed, with the Institute's officials acting as bosses and the *parceleros* being reduced to the position of employees who took orders and not owners of their own *empresas*. INCORA's patronage would lead not only to frustration and disappointment but also to a disproportionate number of failures resulting

Table 8.5. *Main features of the empresas comunitarias, according to INCORA's sectoral classification, 1977–1979*

INCORA's classification	Percentage of the total number of empresas comunitarias	Percentage of the total number of families in empresas comunitarias	Social background of the members	General characteristics of the lands and infrastructure	Prevailing types of production	Average family income in 1977
Sector I Plains; modern agriculture	27.6	23.1	Agricultural laborers	Very fertile land, irrigation works, infrastructural improvements, and adequate roads	Agriculture: collective commercial crops (rice, cotton, etc.), use of modern technology, high productivity	Above INCORA's minimum ideal income (2,400 US$/year), allows for constant improvements in life standards
Sector II Hilly land; good agricultural potential	6.3	5.4	Agricultural laborers, tenants, and sharecroppers	Good-quality land, some improvements, small coffee and sugar mills, regular roads	Mixed production: individual and/or collective commercial crops (coffee, cacao, sugar, etc.), collective herds, marginal importance of individual subsistence crops	Slightly over DANE's estimated allowance for family basic expenses (1,900 US$/year), largely covers basic needs
Sector III Hilly land; traditional agriculture	15.5	15.1	Tenants and sharecroppers	Regular land, no improvements, inadequate roads	Mixed production: collective herds, some individual and/or collective commercial crops	Approximate to DANE's estimated allowance for family basic expenses (1,900 US$/year), just sufficient

Sector						
					(maize, potatoes, beans, etc.), individual subsistence crops quite important	for basic needs
Sector IV Plains; extensive cattle raising	48.5	53.6	Pasture-tenants and sharecroppers	Low-quality land, no improvements, inadequate roads	Cattle raising: collective herds, individual subsistence crops the most important activity	Below the legally minimum rural wages (1,400 US$/year), does not suffice for the basic needs of the family

Sources: E. Liboreiro et al., Análisis de las Empresas Comunitarias en Colombia, 1977. INCORA, Las Empresas Comunitarias en la Reforma Agraria, 1977. INCORA, Las Formas Asociativas de Producción: Características y Resultados, 1979.

from technocratic notions that ignored agronomic limitations and the problems posed by new agricultural practices that were alien to the peasants' traditions. The indebtedness that resulted from these failures aggravated the situation, refueling opposition to a pattern of collective farming that began to be seen by the *parceleros* as the source of all the problems in the settlements.[15]

Adverse state policy thus created an unfavorable setting for the development of collective farming. However, there were other factors that influenced the activity of the settlements at the more immediate regional levels. To examine the influence of these factors, Table 8.5 takes as a basis INCORA's sectoral classification of the *empresas comunitarias* and presents the most relevant information from three evaluation studies conducted by INCORA and IICA during the second half of the 1970s. The studies showed that, despite heterogeneity within the categories, significant differences could be pinpointed when the average performance of the *empresas* was compared across categories.

Most of the few successes occurred in the farms of sector I, located mainly in areas of advanced agrarian capitalism of Tolima and Huila, and also in isolated areas of northern Cauca, Valle, and the Atlantic Coast. These settlements were usually composed of former agricultural laborers and enjoyed favorable agronomic conditions for large-scale agriculture. In some cases, this type of agriculture was no longer based on the work of the members' families but instead on hired labor. The rest of the successes belonged to sector II, the smallest sector of *empresas*, scattered throughout peripheral coffee areas of Caldas, Risaralda, and Antioquia and made up of laborers and tenants who had previously worked on marginal estates on the slopes. These settlements had adequate lands for a mixed agriculture of coffee and other marketable crops, an agriculture that seemed to be more attractive as production became individualized and the collective economy was confined to particular activities like the use of mills and minor cattle raising. In the *empresas* of sector III, composed of former tenants and sharecroppers of traditional Andean *haciendas*, the results were either bad or mediocre. Agronomic conditions were suitable only for traditional peasant crops and cattle raising, and much of the families' labor involved individual subsistence cultivation. Sector IV, the last and largest, which included most of the settlements of the Atlantic Coast, was in a calamitous condition. Without irrigation and other infrastructural improvements, the land of these *empresas* could only be used for extensive cattle raising and for continuously rotating subsistence agriculture. The *parceleros*, who had been previously subordinated to the cattle *haciendas* by the pasture-rent system, were now drawing a meager income from communal herds, and most of the available labor was used for the subsistence crops of individual family plots. As a result of all these differences, then, the modest achievements registered by INCORA statistics were concentrated in sectors I and II. In sectors III and IV, which included most of the *empresas comunitarias* and the bulk of the *parcelero* families, the evaluation studies failed to discover any relevant improvement, in terms of either income levels or the conditions of nutrition, sanitation, housing, and education.

These differential results seem to prove that the agronomic potential of the land and the social background of the *parceleros* emerged as the main factors influencing the economic performance of the settlements. There is not much to say about the first of these factors, since it was only logical that the possibility of profitable agricultural production would result in greater benefits for the *empresas*. As to the second factor, the Colombian case corroborated something that had already been observed in similar experiences of other countries: the fact that, both socially and culturally, the agricultural laborers were better prepared for collective farming.[16] They were acquainted with the division of labor and the tasks demanded by large-scale crops, whereas the *parceleros* of sectors III and IV were familiar only with dependent subsistence agriculture and lacked basic knowledge about market-oriented production. Ideologically, none of the peasant sectors had a special commitment to collective farming. The model of the *empresas comunitarias* was accepted not because of a deep peasant commitment to the ideals of collectivism, but partly as a result of the reformist and leftist influences and especially because it appeared to be an institutional requisite for the legal allocation of the land.[17] In the absence of elaborated ideological motivations the peasants' previous attitudes were highly influential. Here again the former agricultural laborers were better prepared for cooperation, because they were used to group discipline, knew how to work as a team, and were less individualistic than the other types of peasants.

Turning now to other factors that may have influenced the differential performance of the settlements, it cannot be said that they had any obvious effect. It is true that where the land struggles had been more intense, there were better conditions for group cohesiveness. But this factor had only a marginal influence upon the economic results, since, for example, in both sector I and sector IV the *empresas comunitarias* had emerged after intense battles and prolonged land invasion. It is also true that there was greater institutional support to the peasant groups that followed the pro-government line of ANUC. But again, this factor becomes less important when one takes into account, first, that the regional distribution of the categories of *empresas* did not coincide with the geopolitical "boundaries" of the split between the Armenia and Sincelejo lines, and second, that the *parceleros* of ANUC Sincelejo received equal treatment from INCORA as soon as they agreed to conform to the terms of the Institute. With regard to the organizational norms of the *empresas*, it has been noted that Decree 2073 undermined the cooperative spirit. But this destructive influence was equally noticeable among the different types of settlements and, for this reason, cannot be considered as a factor leading to a better or worse economic outcome. In fact, one can even detect an inverse influence. At the beginning, INCORA's officials tried to impose the codes and rules as a strait jacket upon the *parceleros*. But after the initial failures, the need to attain better results led to a more liberal approach that relaxed some pressures and paved the way for a gradual bureaucratic adjustment to the conditions in the *empresas*. Consequently, by 1977, the patterns of internal organization were already quite varied. Sectors I and II were developing sophisticated schemes that maximized the benefits and marked milestones in the transition to an individual economy of small entrepreneurs and affluent peasants. Meanwhile, in sectors III and IV, norms were being modified so as to loosen the members' links with the groups and increase their chances of finding supplementary income such as by working for wages outside the settlements. Beyond the important differences in the types of peasant economies that were taking shape in each of the sectors, the underlying trend was toward the dissolution of the *empresas comunitarias*. This seemed to confirm that the collective principle was failing irrespectively of economic performance and that, in the last instance, collective farming was just a transitional stage toward the individual exploitation of the land.[18]

Having surveyed the main factors that influenced the results of the *empresas comunitarias*, it is now possible to summarize the evidence by direct reference to the two evaluation standards introduced in this section. Starting with the criterion of economic success, it is clear that a cooperative sector that never included more than 15,000 families could not produce perceptible changes, either in Colombia's countryside as a whole or more locally in the areas of land struggle and agrarian reform. The total activity of the *empresas* remained below 1 percent of the country's agricultural production, the indices of productivity were equivalent to the national averages, and only a handful of isolated municipalities showed some commercial dynamism attributable to the improved conditions of the *parceleros*.[19] Within the settlements, successful performances were marginal and restricted. Benefits were derived from large-scale commercial crops but the situation was very difficult in the cattle-raising *empresas*; in 1978, only in Tolima and Huila were family incomes above the minimum considered satisfactory by INCORA.[20] More than 70 percent of the settlements were below that level, and in 49.6 percent of the cases, income did not reach the legal minimum wage in the countryside.[21] Most of the *empresas* were heavily in debt, and the rate of default went up from 8.3 percent of total loans in 1976 to 15.1 percent in 1979.[22] Throughout the

Atlantic Coast, many groups were compelled to sell the cattle that they had bought on credit in order to meet their most urgent subsistence needs. This aggravated the problem of indebtedness, bringing the regional rate of default on loans to more than 40 percent.[23] A sizeable number of the *parceleros* began to work as agricultural laborers, joining the seasonal migration to Venezuela in order to raise their income and pay their debts. Others opted for the most drastic solution of simply deserting, either migrating to the cities or switching to the new employment alternatives opening up in the countryside.[24]

The overall picture looks still worse in terms of the second evaluation standard: the promotion of association and autonomy among the peasants. Generalized failure prevented the establishment of any solid basis for an independent regional economy, showing the futility of predictions about a self-sufficient cooperative sector. Illusions of future peasant autonomy were buried under the evidence of INCORA's own studies, which showed that cases of self-management among the settlements were exceptions to the rule.[25] The idea that collective farming would strengthen the organization of the peasant class was also contradicted by the absence of integrated frameworks for regional cooperation and by the rapid disintegration of the *empresas comunitarias* themselves. Table 8.6 indicates that, according to INCORA's figures, the number of families in collective farms went down by 16.5 percent between 1976 and 1979. But the real decrease must have been between 30 and 40 percent, since new settlements were being legalized during that period and INCORA's officials freely admitted in interviews that many *empresas* continued to exist only in official statistics.[26] Apart from causing the collapse of the settlements, widespread disappointment and the movement toward individualistic solutions eroded whatever relationships existed between the groups, turning class solidarity into a distant memory that belonged to the land struggles of the past. Instead of bringing the *parceleros* closer to the ideal of an organized class able to influence society and the state, the *empresas comunitarias* became an instrument of subordination to the state: They were used by an atrophic institution, INCORA, to justify its existence in a political environment that made it superfluous. In other words, the settlements were transformed into an arena of conflict in which INCORA tried to save its face, resorting to a mixture of coercion and concessions, while the erosion of solidarity led the peasants to adopt an attitude of passive resistance that put most of the blame on the collective principle and saw its abolition as the most sensible solution.[27]

Cornered by counterreform and unable to sustain autonomous growth, the *empresas comunitarias* collapsed under external and internal pressures. With the rapid disintegration of the settlements, the *parceleros* were doomed to share the fate of the rest of the peasantry in Colombia. While

Table 8.6. *Changes in the settlements of agrarian reform: empresas comunitarias and individual adjudications, 1972–1977*

	Changes in family numbers					Changes in the distribution of families and the land			
	Empresas comunitarias			Settlements of individual adjunction		Families		Land	
	Number of settlements	Families		Families		*Empresas comunitarias*	Settlements of individual adjudications	*Empresas comunitarias*	Settlements of individual adjudications
		Number	1976=100%	Number	1976=100%				
1972	503	5,778	40.9%	6,067	49.6%	48.7%	51.3%	49.5%	50.5%
1976	1,349	14,093	100.0%	12,223	100.0%	53.6%	46.4%	55.2%	44.8%
1979	1,266	11,778	83.5%	18,697	152.9%	38.6%	61.4%	40.6%	59.4%

Sources: M. Suárez Melo, et al., *Las Empresas Comunitarias Campesinas en Colombia*, 1972. INCORA, *Las Formas Asociativas de Producción: Características y Resultados*, 1979. INCORA, *Informe de Gerencia*, 1979.

a fortunate minority became stable and affluent peasants or petty rural entrepreneurs, the great majority came to depend upon temporary labor outside their farms in order to try to survive as precarious smallholders. In both situations the collective schemes quickly dissolved because they fettered the forces that, as shown in the first section of this chapter, acted to assimilate the repeasantization caused by the land struggles into the capitalist structure that was taking shape in the countryside. But apart from distorting repeasantization and making it functional for agrarian capitalism, the failure of the new peasant economy also had a vital effect upon the continuation of the battle for the land. The situation of many groups, especially on the Atlantic Coast, led the *parceleros* to see the *empresas* as an unbearable burden. Subdivision did not solve the problem, because debts became an individual responsibility and the prospects for sustaining families with the existing resources remained as unpromising as ever. Since it was increasingly obvious that the parcels could not be used to earn a living, access to land gradually ceased to be considered an ideal solution and began to be seen as a source of problems that could even interfere with other possibilities of employment. To put it differently, by questioning the wisdom of hazardous land invasions that seemed to end unhappily, the failure of the new cooperative and individual peasant economy enhanced the effect of the other factors that were drawing the cycle of the land struggles to an end.

ANUC and the demands of the *parceleros*

The frustrations arising from the failure of the settlements created a new arena of struggle for the *usuarios*, one focused on those peasants who were trying to consolidate their hold upon the land and, in doing so, had to confront the state pressures being exerted by INCORA. Indeed, as the peasant offensive ended, the focus of conflict changed. The continuity of the peasant movement now depended upon the capacity of ANUC Sincelejo to represent the interests of the *parceleros*, not only because it seemed logical to take defensive positions in an adverse situation but also because, given the ending of the land struggles and the setbacks of the rural laborers, the *parceleros* were the only real support for the organization at the grass-root levels. The definition of the *empresas comunitarias* as a key arena of conflict between the peasantry and the state created what seemed to be a promising ground for the movement's action, in terms of both the many problems faced by the settlements and the principles at stake. Altogether, then, the peasant movement gravitated toward the question of the *parceleros* because of both the objective circumstances and the need to respond to an important challenge. To understand the processes that determined the fate of ANUC in the areas of land struggle, it is therefore necessary to examine the role of the *usuarios* in the new settlements, paying special attention to the factors that influenced the movement's actions and to the consequences of these actions.

From the very beginning, the *usuarios* emphasized the centrality of collectivization in transforming the agrarian structures in Colombia. During the initial reformist phase, the peasant movement had given its full support to the policy of collective land adjudication introduced by the Lleras Restrepo administration.[28] It is true that the early ideological arguments merely rephrased official justifications regarding the presumed advantages of collective farming. But ANUC's attitudes underwent a radical change as a result of the break with the government and the influence of the leftist political sectors. In the *Mandato Campesino* of 1971, ANUC advocated the elimination of existing patterns of land ownership, tenancy and exploitation and their replacement with large-scale, self-managed, collective peasant farms in the areas of *latifundia* and agrarian capitalism.[29] The vision of a new socialist structure in the countryside included the "small and middle peasants," who had to receive "full support and protection during their transition towards co-operative forms of agriculture." The *Mandato* included guidelines for the future collective units of self-management, defining them as "settlements which emerge out of the voluntary association of the peasants and the expropriation of former landowners." Although the guidelines left open the possibility of distributing small individual parcels to the families for subsistence crops, they stipulated that work would be mainly collective, fostering equality and democracy according to norms established by the peasants themselves. Taking regional differences into account, the *Mandato* proposed five types of cooperative units characterized by different degrees of collectivization at the levels of production, commercialization, and distribution. To ensure better conditions for the cooperative farming of the countryside, urgent state action was demanded, including a new bank for the settlements, agricultural machinery stations, a vast rural housing program, and the services of credit, infrastructure, technical assistance, and social security. These aspirations could hardly be fulfilled without a social revolution in Colombia, but ANUC considered its struggles and its *Mandato Campesino* precisely as components of that revolution. In the meantime, it was clear that the success of the 1971 battles had provided an opportunity to carry out part of the program, starting with collectivization on those lands that had been taken away from the landowners. The first tasks of clearing the bushes, cutting the trees, and selling the wood appeared to be a continuation of the land invasion process with a strictly communal character. Later, individual parcels were assigned to the families, leaving the best land for the collective crops that would provide cash incomes for the group members.

The orientations of the peasant movement were leading, then, to co-operative forms of land use, and neither the guidelines of the *Mandato* nor the practices of ANUC differed from INCORA's criteria regarding the semi-collective nature of the settlements and the need for state support and services. Still, there were substantial differences in other respects, especially in the formation of the *empresas comunitarias* and the legal frame-work to which they had to conform. For INCORA, the formation of a new settlement involved a number of predetermined stages, including studies of socioeconomic viability, legal acquisition or expropriation of the land, and formal selection of future members according to fixed stand-ards of technical and social priority. Further, the *parceleros* had to accept supervised management and had to pay for the land. For ANUC, the settlements emerged as a consequence of direct expropriation by the masses, so that there was no place for formal procedures curtailing peasant self-determination or for a demand that the peasants pay for land they had obtained by their own means.

These crucial differences marked the split between two opposing con-ceptions and defined the axis of confrontation in the *empresas comunitarias*.[30] However, during the great land struggles, only in exceptional cases was the prevailing model purely peasant or purely institutional. It has been shown that far from taking the initiative, INCORA usually intervened where the peasants had already invaded the land. On the other hand, it was only when the Institute negotiated and then bought the land from the landowners that the peasants were secure in their tenure. The formation of the settlements therefore involved both peasant and institutional action, and there was an implicit understanding between the *usuarios* and IN-CORA that unless overcrowding was conspicuous, the Institute would ignore the formal criteria and accept the de facto situation. But as far as payment for the land and the legal framework of the *empresas comunitarias* were concerned, this type of compromise was out of the question, since these issues involved opposed principles that could not be bridged by informal complicity. For the sake of temporary expedience, INCORA proposed that the *parceleros* sign provisional assignment contracts, a so-lution that only postponed the problem but was acceptable for ANUC because it did not commit the peasants to pay and gave them a certain status of possession.[31]

The *Mandato Campesino* had been tailored to a revolution, but this situation never quite developed. As a result of the initial land invasions, the achievements had been significant but partial, unevenly distributed regionally and too limited to embrace the peasantry as a whole. Coun-terreform was gaining momentum, the relationship with INCORA was cooling, and institutional pressures on the *parceleros* were beginning. Al-though this situation could have made advisable an ordered retreat, and although the defense of the settlements should have been a key task in any new redeployment of forces, ANUC Sincelejo continued to emphasize a frontal assault on large-scale property. The main reason was the political centrality of the struggle for land, but one should not lose sight of other elements like the spectacular success of the initial invasions, the ideological influence of Maoism, and an exaggerated sense of the movement's strength that led to a distorted assessment of the correlation of forces in the countryside. Consequently, during the early phase of the confrontation, the issue of the new settlements was not raised in ANUC as a crucial question in its own right, but rather as a subordinated aspect of what was perceived to be a broader and more relevant problem. Given the importance of persisting in the struggle for land, the already settled groups came to be considered in terms of the logistic support they could provide. In other words, the answer to the question about what was to be done in the settlements depended upon another question: How could the *parceleros* be committed to the continuation of the land struggles? ANUC believed that special efforts had to be made to prevent the demobilization of those who gained access to land. This would be done by fostering collectivism in the new peasant agriculture, emphasizing the issue of autonomy from the state, and giving primacy to class solidarity by supporting those peasants who were still landless. Seen from a radical perspective, this plan seemed to reaffirm correctly the principles of the *Mandato Campesino* and did not disturb the revolutionary atmosphere still prevailing in 1972. However, by ignoring the unevenness of the peasant movement and by refusing to deal in their own terms with the complex problems emerging in the *empresas comunitarias*, ANUC's policy became excessively abstract and dogmatic. From the outset, this double limitation hampered the work of ANUC Sincelejo, creating serious difficulties both in those regions in which its supremacy was undisputed and in areas where its influence was weaker or was being counteracted by ANUC Armenia.

In Sucre, Córdoba, and Bolívar, the most solid departments of the radical *usuarios* after the split caused by the government, the main problem was the absence of criteria on the way in which principle should be translated into practice. Given the abstractness of the paradigm that subordinated the question of the settlements to the continuation of the land struggles, grass-roots work came to depend upon the leadership and ideologies that prevailed at the local level.[32] Among the approaches that spontaneously developed in that fragmented situation, two types of practice epitomized the opposite poles of the spectrum between principles and action. One of these types of praxis involved the *baluartes de autogestión campesina* (strongholds of peasant self-reliance), created in the department of Córdoba during 1972 and given that name in order to recover the historical heritage of some "red *baluartes*" formed by colonists who had resisted the bondage-debt system in the 1920s. The aims of the *baluartes* focused on economic defense and promotion of political consciousness among the participating families. There were individual subsistence plots and collective crops, and the statutes stressed the dual nature of the settlements as both economic strongholds and, at the same time, as the first steps toward socialism in the countryside. This concept owed much of its inspiration to the renowned sociologist Orlando Fals Borda, who, as mentioned in Chapter 5, had become a close collaborator of ANUC in general and the *usuarios* of Córdoba in particular. Applying an approach derived from his research on the socioeconomic history of the Atlantic Coast, Fals Borda argued that in the same way as capitalism had developed by means of enclaves that later engulfed entire regions, so too the egalitarian mode of production could be spread from centers of collective production that would keep integrating and multiplying themselves with the expansion of the land struggles. Fals Borda's influence was especially marked among the activists of the Education Committee and the leaders of the municipal association of ANUC in Montería. Using funds from research-action projects sponsored by European foundations, these militants organized a number of *baluartes* in the former *hacienda* La Antioqueña and in other occupied estates of central Córdoba.[33]

Although the activity of the *baluartes* was restricted in regional terms, the very idea was harshly criticized by the PCML. On the basis of their own conceptions, the Maoist activists were developing a completely different praxis in their own areas of influence. The PCML believed that any attempt to create islands of collective economy in a capitalist society was doomed to failure. Since socialism could only be developed following a revolution and the collapse of the existing structures, strength could not be wasted pursuing economic goals that, apart from being illusory, might encourage bourgeois attitudes among the peasants. Since it was essential to concentrate all efforts on causing insurrection, the activity of the settlements had to be *consecuente*, that is, true to the higher purpose of increasing the militancy of the *parceleros* and maintaining their permanent desire to support the struggles of the other peasants and the people as a whole. As seen in Chapter 5, these premises led to the idea that production had to be reduced to a bare minimum, so that the peasants would live at a subsistence level and their revolutionary potential would be preserved. In the PCML areas of influence, the land was also distributed along semi-collective lines, but it was obvious that the ideal of collectivism was subordinated to the goal of maintaining the groups in order to mobilize them whenever direct political action was required.[34]

In terms of articulating the class struggles with the transition to an eventual new society, there is little doubt that Fals Borda's *baluartes* and the "true" settlements of the PCML reflected diametrically opposite conceptions as far as the role of the *empresas comunitarias* was concerned. In the first case, great importance was attached to the success of the new collective peasant economy as part of a *foquista* perspective that considered structural change as a continuous process accompanying the expansion of a protracted struggle.[35] In the second case, there was a vision of social change that tried to deemphasize the economic goals of the peasantry so that they would not interfere with the revolutionary process. This contrast clearly shows that, even if the settlements were defined as a subordinated problem, it was not possible to evade a definite position on the promotion or sacrifice of the immediate interests of the *parceleros*. Although those who accepted the *foquista* underlying premise of the *baluartes* were few, the majority within ANUC Sincelejo believed that it was necessary to defend the *empresas comunitarias* and try to secure their economic success. Opposing this majority, was an influential group of militants with a different attitude. The absence of a shared perspective thus began to be transcended by an even more dangerous problem: the outbreak of internal conflict within ANUC. In the last instance, the fact that the guidelines of the *Mandato* could be translated into such discrepant practices highlighted one of the main issues in the forthcoming political polarization of the peasant movement.

In the areas in which ANUC Sincelejo was stronger, the problems concerned the interpretation and application of principles. But these principles, as such, were not questioned. Vis-à-vis INCORA, for example, the criteria of not paying for the land and demanding complete autonomy would be strictly maintained for some time. Quite different was the situation in other regions of previous land struggle. Where ANUC Armenia was influential, as it was in Huila, Tolima, Atlántico, and the municipalities of the Caribbean littoral strip, the spirit of submission led to a rapid withdrawal from the directives of the *Mandato Campesino* and an almost unconditional acceptance of the institutional terms of land adjudication.[36] A similar situation was developing in the peripheral areas where, despite the link with ANUC Sincelejo, there were factors that conspired against the chances of upholding the radical principles. Such was the case in Cesar, Magdalena, and other places of the Atlantic Coast and the hinterland, where increasing repression and the organizational weakness of the movement caused insecurity and even the fear of the eventual loss of whatever gains had been made. Since the ideological influence of radical ANUC was very weak, it was difficult to resist the temptation to yield to INCORA's advances to the effect of legalizing the situation and getting the definitive titles that would secure tenure.[37] Thus, the latent differences within the peasant movement were now emerging in the diversity that marked the development of the confrontation between the *empresas* and the state. Given this heterogeneity, it was impossible to bring together the *parceleros* under banners that, as in the refusal to pay for the land, were no longer relevant for many of them. Dogmatic adherence to principles prevented communication with all those who, for different reasons, did not wish or had not been able to uphold the guidelines of the *Mandato*. It was evident that, for ANUC to provide leadership and represent the *empresas comunitarias*, a more suitable policy had to be worked out, including realistic demands that would respond to the conditions prevailing in the settlements.

By early 1973, attitudes toward the question of the *empresas* were beginning to change within ANUC Sincelejo. It was increasingly clear that the movement would not be able to sustain its offensive in the land struggles. Further, the problems of the *parceleros* were becoming more and more urgent. Decree 2073 had finally spelled out the coercive legal framework for the *empresas comunitarias*, and INCORA was stepping up its pressure. Even in regions where the Institute's intervention had been rejected, the peasants were now demanding concrete advice on how to handle their troubles. For the *parceleros*, it was more than a question of whether or nor to accept INCORA's titles: In the absence of irrigation systems and fertilizer use, and given the low quality of most of the land, after a couple of years of cultivation the soil was becoming exhausted, and credit and other state supports would be needed for cattle raising or other types of agricultural production. Negotiations with the state were unavoidable, and it was up to ANUC to work out a unified strategy, not only because that would be the best way to exert sufficient organized pressure, but also to defend the leadership of the peasant movement and prevent a massive desertion at the grass-roots level. Such a course of action would be in accord with the policy of the Second National Congress, a policy that recommended the organization of the *usuarios'* work according to the problems affecting each of the peasant sectors. Furthermore, the independent line that was crystallizing among the leaders of ANUC Sincelejo could be developed into a strong approach against the praxis of the Maoist groups in the settlements, a praxis that was considered to be alienating the *parceleros* from the movement. In addition to these internal pressures, the leaders wanted to recover control of the peripheral areas and other regions influenced by ANUC Armenia. Thus, the issue of the *empresas comunitarias* became increasingly important until it was finally defined as a specific field of action for ANUC Sincelejo.

At the eighth meeting of the National Junta (Bogotá, January 1973), the *usuarios* decided to organize a series of regional seminars to discuss the question of the settlements.[38] The seminars, conceived as a stage of preparation for the adoption of a definite policy at ANUC's Third National Congress, were carried out during 1973 and the first half of 1974. The participants included delegates of the *empresas comunitarias*, regional leaders, and full-time activists of national standing. The debates usually started with a comparison between the principles of the *baluartes* that had emerged in Córdoba and the institutional model that INCORA wanted to impose upon the *parceleros*.[39] The sympathy of ANUC's national leaders for the *baluartes* was partly explained by Fals Borda's influence as advisor and intermediary between the *usuarios* and the foreign foundations. Another possible motive was the fact that the idea of the *baluartes* was the only one that had enough prestige and ideological coherence to serve as an alternative to the positions of the ML groups. However, the *baluartes* had never been part of ANUC's official policy and they were not presented as such in the seminars, where the leaders preferred to keep all options opened and to concentrate mainly on learning about the grievances and demands of the base groups. As a result of this openness, the discussions were quite representative of what was going on in the regions, reflecting both the problems of the *parceleros* and the great heterogeneity of the *empresas comunitarias*.[40] One shared concern was that of the settlements' autonomy, expressed as repeated demands to restore self-determination in the management, planning, and selection of production lines. Other unanimous demands were for institutional services like credit, technical assistance, inputs, and marketing programs.

Much less clear was the position on class solidarity, since although all the seminars ended with expressions of support for ANUC Sincelejo, there was little agreement on how to strengthen the links between the settlements or how to help the struggles of other peasant sectors. The problems were even greater when issues with sharper political implications were raised. The question of whether or not to pay for the land, for example, clearly showed the unevenness of the peasant movement. On the more politicized Atlantic Coast, the *parceleros* strongly opposed any type of payment. In the rest of the country, the issue was either to prevent the artificial inflation of prices or to obtain easier conditions of delayed payment. This seemed to suggest that, even though there were good prospects for agitation in the settlements, the immediate economic demands appeared much more relevant to the *parceleros* than the political questions surrounding the issues. For the leaders of ANUC Sincelejo, who were already moving toward autonomous political expression, the *empresas comunitarias* required a strategy that, besides overcoming the problem of regional diversity, would also bridge the economic and political aspects of the peasant struggle.

On the eve of the Third National Congress, the groups in charge outlined a program for action that was submitted for discussion both to the national leaders and to the last regional seminar.[41] The plan insisted on ANUC's principles of peasant autonomy and agrarian reform without payment for the land. It also stressed the urgent need "to raise the political consciousness of the *parceleros*, so that they would continue to participate in the struggles of the peasantry." At the concrete level, a number of short- and long-term organizational tasks were proposed, including the creation of a National Secretary of Empresas Comunitarias within ANUC, an intense educational campaign, and an eventual national meeting where the demands of the *parceleros* would be articulated. Further, a prototype of an internal statute for the *empresas* had to be drafted as soon as possible in order to give the local groups a clear alternative to INCORA's institutional model. Finally, there were some fresh ideas on actions designed to create solidarity funds and promote the exchange of produce in order to strengthen the links between the settlements. All in all, the preparation of this program seemed to represent an important step forward for ANUC on the question of the *empresas comunitarias*. Still, the plan was no more than a broad proposal for action; it required favorable conditions to be translated into practice.

The internal polarization of ANUC Sincelejo thwarted all chances of setting on this new course. As shown in Chapter 5, the Third National Congress of 1974 marked the climax of the confrontation between the insurrection proposed by the Maoist groups and the political solution of the independents. Knowing that on this central issue their point of view would not prevail in Bogotá, the ML militants concentrated their attacks on secondary aspects like the financial support of the foreign "imperialist" foundations, the bureaucratization of ANUC, and the corruption of its national leaders. Most of the broadsides were directed against Fals Borda, his relations with the *usuarios*, the "moneys" of his research-action projects, and his idea of the *baluartes*. The independent leaders, who by then had already established their own contacts with the sources of finance, dissociated themselves from Fals Borda and his followers in Córdoba, using them as scapegoats to divert the attacks and consolidate their stand against the opposition.[42] In an event in which most of the participants were *parceleros*, small peasants, and colonists, the refusal of the PCML to defend the economic interests of the peasantry also contributed to their ultimate defeat. But the political victory of the independents did not change the disconnection between ANUC's principles and the concrete needs at the grass-roots level. The program for action in the *empresas comunitarias* was not discussed because the subcommittees that were supposed to deal with specific issues had not even been able to start when the congress ended. As a result, the *Conclusiones del Tercer Congreso* hurriedly drafted by the National Junta included nothing new on the settlements. Decree 2073 was denounced again, and the *empresas* were defined as "a fraud conceived to demobilize the peasants and doom them to economic disaster."[43]

Among the *parceleros*, who had not even had an opportunity to express their grievances, the shameful proceedings of the Third National Congress and the poverty of its conclusions led to the sudden realization of the complete break between their perceived problems and the political issues which seemed to absorb the peasant movement. In terms of the decline of ANUC at the grass-roots level, this feeling of frustration that silently grew amid the pandemonium of internal conflict would have as much effect as the splitting of the more politicized sectors. The delegates went back to their villages and spread the word on the ways in which accusations of corruption, political undercurrents, and secret financial manipulations had come to the surface, thus signaling the beginning of a massive defection that quickly obliterated ANUC Sincelejo's influence in entire regions.[44] The *parceleros* of less consolidated areas like Magdalena and Cesar dismissed their doubts and went over to INCORA to legalize their tenure.[45] All the recovery work undertaken in Huila, Tolima, and other zones of the Armenia line was lost within months.[46] There were places like North Santander where only the *empresas comunitarias* maintained links with the Sincelejo line, and in these cases the downfall meant the disappearance of the organization at the departmental level.[47] As the base contacts withered away, the presence of ANUC Sincelejo receded to those areas that had been more radical in the past. Since in the rest of the country only isolated and scattered groups remained loyal, there was no organizational or ideological support for the development of a unified project of action in the settlements. The program that had been elaborated before the Third National Congress was postponed and its proposals were never carried out.

The incapacity of ANUC Sincelejo to develop a concrete strategy for the defense of the peasants' immediate demands was not confined to the *parceleros*. As will be seen in the following chapter, the same problem also arose on the other fronts of the peasant movement, affecting the *minifundistas*, the colonists, and the Indians. It is true that the independent leaders were aware of the need to respond to the economic and other specific grievances at the grass-roots level. It is also true that steps were taken in that direction on the different fronts. However, two factors blocked such advances. First, it was difficult to articulate economic demands and political aspirations within the radical leftist perspectives that prevailed in ANUC. Since the land struggle had integrated both aspects, this difficulty had been pushed into the background during the early phase of ANUC's radicalization. But now, when objective conditions forced a retreat to the everyday problems of the already established peasants, it was becoming increasingly clear that these problems were not being answered because there was no room for them in the prevailing political projects.[48] This was more obvious in the extremist leftism of the ML groups, which rejected any attempt to deal with the economic demands as anathema to the expected revolution. But although a different approach was adopted, among the independent majority the results were also the same. By trying to transform the peasant movement into an autonomous political force that would carry the torch of a future proletarian revolution as the only way to social redemption, the national leaders were establishing a hierarchy of priorities that subordinated the everyday demands of the peasants to the political goals. This approach ignored the real consciousness and perceived aspirations of the peasants, dogmatically assuming that they would readily accept a proletarian perspective of self-definition and political struggle. At the level of concrete action, this led to a continuous and obstinate adherence to rigid principles and made it impossible to carry out any tasks beyond agitation and denunciation of the existing regime.

The second factor that blocked ANUC Sincelejo's attempt to deal with the immediate demands of the peasants was its legal disqualification as the representative of the *usuarios*. By recognizing only the Armenia line, the government had rendered ANUC Sincelejo illegitimate. This problem had been largely irrelevant during the land struggles, which were illegal by definition. But everything changed when the problems which came to prevail concerned the peasants with land, because all their demands were directed in one way or another to the public institutions and the state. Dealings with INCORA, transactions on credits, negotiations on services, establishment of cooperatives – these were the activities that responded to the pressing problems of the peasants, and it was in this area that the organization could and should fulfill a crucial role on behalf of the concrete interests of the base groups. For the time being at least, the situation precluded revolution and radical social change. Since the battle had to be waged from within an existing institutional order, all the functions of legal representation that Decree 755 had originally given ANUC were now becoming highly relevant. The impossibility of assuming these functions left ANUC Sincelejo as an outsider, preventing it from redeploying its forces along the new battle lines and undermining its credibility among frustrated peasants who could not have its help in the area that now mattered most. A vicious circle had thus been created: Illegitimacy left ANUC Sincelejo with only criticism and denunciation, and these actions, in turn, only led to further alienation of the movement from the system.

By 1976, the developments taking place in the settlements clearly reflected the consequences of the *usuarios'* failure. In many regions of the country the movement had lost all its influence, and the *empresas comunitarias* had accepted INCORA's conditions. While these settlements were left at INCORA's mercy, the outlook was not much better in the areas in which ANUC Sincelejo still had influence. There the main problem was no longer the need to continue the land struggles or increase the peasants' militancy.

Instead, it was the dilemma of how to retain the support that still existed among the *parceleros*. In Sucre, Córdoba, and Bolívar, all of the schemes of radical praxis had led to frustration. The *baluartes* quickly dissolved because, rather than responding to grass-roots initiatives, they had depended on the orientations of intellectuals and regional leaders whose influence had been wiped out by ANUC's internal conflict.[49] After its defeat in the Third National Congress, the PCML had also disintegrated into a number of splinter groups that were rapidly losing their hold upon the peasants.[50] In fact, only the independents were trying to carry out some activity in the loyal settlements as part of their plans of organizational differentiation. The older and more prestigious leaders had devoted themselves to the delicate political work that was needed to transform the secretive ORP into the semiofficial party of the peasant movement. The trade-unionist tasks of ANUC were transferred to a new generation of young leaders whose lack of practical experience was as notorious as their excess of political zeal.[51] Since they failed to provide answers to the concrete needs of the *empresas*, these activities could not become the kernel of a reconstruction process that would overcome fragmentation and demobilization. The directives given to the *parceleros* were still the same: to sign only provisional assignment contracts and not formal titles that would imply payment for the land, to accept institutional credits only if they precluded formal guarantees and supervision by officials, and to oppose INCORA's mark on cattle bought with the Institute's loans.[52] These formulas had been effective when the peasant movement had had the upper hand, but they were ineffectual given the demobilization that now enabled INCORA to pressure the settlements. Since 1975, the Institute had adopted a cautious strategy of blockade aimed at increasing the pressure upon recalcitrant groups while avoiding direct confrontations that could reactivate peasant militancy. The components of that strategy were quite simple: Credits and programs of support were withheld from those settlements that opposed final titles and other requisites of Decree 2073; and some of the *empresas* that had submitted were given special treatment and transformed into fictitious showcases of the virtues of institutional support.[53] In this way, INCORA cunningly put the ball in the other court, hoping that the internal debate within the settlements would undermine their resistance until, eventually, there would be a general surrender.

To understand the effectiveness of this blackmail policy, one has to take into account the problems and fears of those who remained faithful to ANUC Sincelejo in the western savannas of the Atlantic Coast. In economic terms, the credit blockade prevented access to the initial capital that was needed for the most viable solution given the low quality of the soil: buying livestock and raising cattle. In the absence of other alternatives, the *parceleros* had been forced to get involved in relations of production in which, by a bitter paradox, they were exploited on their own land by the same landowners whom they had defeated in the past. Two forms of production had become widespread, both involving the cultivation of artificial pastures within the settlements. In the first arrangement the *parceleros* received a herd from a neighboring landowner, and fed and cared for the animals until they were sold in the market. The added value was then divided equally between the landowner and the group. In the second arrangement, the landowner paid the *parceleros* a fixed amount for the right to graze his cattle in the settlement's pastures. Whether it was because they operated as the capital-investing partners or simply because they had a more powerful bargaining position, the landowners usually derived the greatest benefit from these arrangements.[54] As a result of their adherence to radical principles that left them without credit, the *parceleros* were facing an incongruous situation in which, despite having land of their own, they had reverted to an economic subordination that resembled the exploitation of the past. It was known by then that credits for cattle were no panacea and that INCORA's recipe for the *empresas comunitarias* would not solve the families' economic problems. Still, even though the prospects were far from promising, it seemed preferable to submit to the institutional conditions than to perpetuate a landowner tyranny that contradicted the purpose of the struggle that had been waged for the land.

A similar logic operated in regard to the legal status of land tenure. The resolutions of López Michelsen's Council of State interpreted the counterreform laws in such a way that more and more pending cases ended with court verdicts in favor of the landowners, leading to the eviction of families who had been occupying the land for years.[55] In the estates that had already been bought by INCORA, the *parceleros* feared that, lacking definitive titles, they could eventually be expelled and replaced by others. Given the weakness of ANUC, there were no longer any guarantees about the possibility of resisting the increasing pressures forever.[56] Against this background, it is hardly surprising that attitudes began to change regarding the legalization of land tenure. Both the economic urgency and the fear of losing whatever gains had been made strengthened the argument of those who favored yielding to INCORA's demands. Some groups soon submitted, while others became entangled in heated discussions. There were long debates when a strong spirit of collective discipline still prevailed, but in many cases the discussions degenerated into open quarrels, leading to the defection of subgroups who went over to INCORA after slicing off portions of the original settlements.[57] This process was marked by the spontaneous emergence of new local leaders, since the old activists of ANUC Sincelejo were trapped between the contradictory demands of the *parceleros* and the principles of the organization.[58] Many of them gave up their militancy or lost their influence, while others maintained their positions only to the extent of expressing the new attitudes that now prevailed. The stampede at grass roots levels proved that INCORA's blackmail had paid off and that radical ANUC was collapsing even in its previous strongholds.[59]

To summarize ANUC Sincelejo's performance in regard to the *empresas comunitarias*, it can be said that its internal contradictions and the confrontation with the state gradually confined the organization to a position of marginality and impotence. This defeat was bound to have grave consequences for the peasant movement. First, in terms of the substantive problems within the settlements, it meant that *parceleros* had no organized influence on their own fate. A vertical pattern of control was established, one in which the development of the *empresas* came to depend upon the interplay between the bureaucratic rule of INCORA and the passive resistance of the local groups. Second, in terms of the status of the peasant movement, the *usuarios'* failure in the settlements further accelerated the downward trend resulting from the ending of the land struggles and the setbacks with the agricultural laborers. While ANUC was disintegrating even in the previously more radical areas, the state and the dominant classes were rapidly reasserting their power and control, so that the developments of the late 1970s would only express, in different ways, the final crisis of the peasant movement.

9

Final crisis and clientelist regression of ANUC

Generalized decline and last land struggles

The deterioration of the influence of ANUC Sincelejo was not confined to the areas of land struggle. After the Third National Congress there had been a steep decline on the other fronts of the peasant movement, where economic and special demands had prevailed from the beginning. As will be seen in the following section, this decline was related to the government policy of partial concessions, which exerted as much influence as the problems and obstacles that hindered radical ANUC from taking up the demands of the landed peasants. However, an aggravating factor in ANUC's crisis was the bureaucratic style of vertical leadership that had taken hold of the organization. Although it is true that radicalism had been less marked in the areas of peasant economy and colonization, the better-organized sectors in these areas had originally exerted great influence at the grass-roots level and had distinguished themselves by massive belligerent action during the early stage of ANUC's confrontation: the civil strikes that shattered the colonization areas of Caquetá and Sarare; the strikes and mobilizations that galvanized the *minifundistas* of Quinchía, Nariño, and other points on the highlands; and the land struggles and reconstruction of *resguardos* conducted by CRIC among the Indian communities of Cauca.[1] From the organizational point of view, in all these cases the rise of the movement had been marked by autonomous regional consolidation, which encouraged and sustained the criticism of ANUC's central leadership.

These criticisms were basically of three types. First, there were accusations of corruption and bureaucratism against the national leaders of the *usuarios*, stressing the presumed connection between these vices and the management of the grants provided by the European foundations. Although even the ordinary peasants were by now aware of these problems,[2] the strongest protests came from places where the peasant movement had developed a basis for economic self-reliance, such as cooperatives that financially supported ANUC's regional activity in Quinchía and Sarare.[3] Second, objections were raised to the political orientations that the central leaders and advisers had been developing, which, as in the case of the

179

Political Committee first and ORP later, were hidden from the movement's rank and file. On this point dissent was also coming from different regional quarters, but the main opposition arose in ANUC's departmental association of Caquetá, whose leaders had made several proposals on national policy that were blocked by ANUC's Executive Committee.[4] Finally, there was widespread resentment against the exclusionist attitudes of the national leaders, who had allegedly imposed a system of elitist control that rejected all initiatives and points of view that seemed to deviate from their own criteria. In addition to ANUC's regional association of Caquetá, the most important opposition came from CRIC, whose leadership refused to follow the dictums of ANUC's Executive Committee on the grounds that they showed little sensitivity to the national and cultural specificities of the Indian struggle.[5] Sometimes expressed in elaborate documents, these criticisms developed during 1975 and 1976, leading to open confrontation between peripheral segments of the peasant movement and the power elite that controlled ANUC's organization from above.

As if to prove the validity of the criticisms against them, the national leaders of ANUC Sincelejo applied coercion to the dissident regional associations. Harsher methods were added to the old techniques of bureaucratic and financial manipulation, including outright expulsions and divisive maneuvers aimed at subverting the regional support of opposition leaders. By late 1976, this "big stick" policy had produced devastating effects. There was an open confrontation between CRIC and ANUC, aggravated by the latter's attempt to divide the Indian movement in Cauca by means of a parallel organization.[6] In Caquetá, the peasant movement had been virtually demolished by the fierce internal struggle that ANUC's Executive Committee had orchestrated from Bogotá.[7] In Quinchía and the neighboring areas of the coffee departments, the cooperative had severed its contact with national ANUC and the local groups were beginning to disperse.[8] In Sarare, the divisionist campaign led within a few months to the breakdown of the cooperative and the dissolution of the regional movement.[9] In Nariño, the departmental association of ANUC went over in toto to the Armenia Line after a fraud that involved one of the main national leaders of ANUC Sincelejo and caused the bankruptcy of their cooperative.[10] Thus, the main line of *usuario* influence among the Indians collapsed, and the most active centers of ANUC Sincelejo in the areas of colonization and peasant economy were destroyed one after another. Consequently, after 1976, ANUC could no longer claim that it was conducting any significant activity in these fields. Its support had been reduced to scattered places where the movement had always been mediocre and where, in the absence of real strength at the grass-roots level, the followers included only local contacts who operated almost as personal clients of the leaders of the National Executive Committee.

The developments outside the areas of land struggle confirmed that ANUC's disintegration was a general process throughout the country when the Fourth National Congress was convened in February 1977 at Tomala. This rapid decline was at least partially due to the failure of the political and trade-unionist line of the movement and to the leaders' style of bureaucratic control. However, no significant changes resulted from the Fourth Congress. With regard to the first issue, the forum approved a new ideological platform under the slogan *"Tierra, democracia y liberación nacional"* ("Land, democracy and national liberation").[11] The document expressed positions that had been developed by ORP and prepared the ground for the future launching of a "peasant party." Featuring a mixture of Maoist, populist, and anarcho-syndicalist ingredients, the platform stated that ANUC was fighting for the establishment of a democratic and patriotic regime that would be responsive to the interests of the different sectors of the peasantry. To achieve this goal, the peasants had to form a broad alliance with the working class and the progressive sectors of the bourgeoisie, an alliance that would fight for a democratic revolution against the landowners, the big bourgeoisie, American imperialism, and Soviet social-imperialism. Although the political aspects of the program were elaborated in great detail, only one of the fourteen pages in the document was devoted to the immediate needs of the peasantry, listing without further comment a series of demands on behalf of the landless peasants, the *minifundistas*, and so on. The new platform formulated the trade-unionist elements of ANUC in even poorer terms than did the documents produced by the Third National Congress. Furthermore, it was not indicated how the economic demands of the *usuarios* were to be integrated with their political aims, so that the platform failed to provide any solution to the basic problem of the divorce between these two aspects of the peasant movement.[12]

Regarding the question of bureaucratic control, the Fourth National Congress itself exemplified the manipulative style of ANUC's leadership. The organization's funds were used to pay for the transportation of delegates who supported the Executive Committee, and a remote site was chosen to create additional difficulties for the dissidents who wanted to come at their own expense. A total of 2,000 *usuarios* arrived, but the biased distribution of credentials left many of them without voting rights, including most of the representatives from Sucre and the entire delegation of Antioquia. The proceedings had been so carefully staged by the organizers that the debates had no real significance.[13] In these circumstances, and despite the fact that some criticisms got through, it was not difficult for the national leadership to secure approval of the new platform and the election of their proposed candidates to the Executive Committee.[14] The combination of these factors showed that the Fourth Congress reaffirmed the tendencies that were destroying ANUC Sincelejo. The contents of the platform and the official presentation of the previously secretive ORP to the delegates showed that, despite a decline that was there for all to see, the leaders were determined to carry their political project to its final conclusion.[15] Their obstinate refusal to acknowledge the legitimate peasant concerns with day-to-day problems indicated that dogmatism and bureaucratic ossification had alienated the leadership from their followers to the point of no return.

It was against this troubled background that ANUC's last land struggles took place during 1977 and 1978. More than half of the disputes during these two years occurred in two regions: the area of La Mojana, in southern Sucre and Bolívar, and the area of the Upía River, comprising a number of contiguous municipalities of Meta and Casanare in the Eastern Llanos. The rest of the disputes took place in isolated municipalities in different parts of the country. Since the 1977 and 1978 conflicts give some revealing indications regarding ANUC's last phase in the land struggles, it is worthwhile to review their development here.

La Mojana, which encompasses the municipalities of Majagual (Sucre) and Achí (Bolívar), belongs to the southeastern subregion of the Atlantic Coast.[16] It is an area of forests, rivers, and swamps where the formation of cattle *latifundia* was recent and where the conflicts had been typically defined as disputes about the possession of public lands. Due to its remoteness, frequent floods, and sparse population, the pressures on the land had been less marked than in other ecologically similar places in southern Magdalena and Cesar. The peasants of La Mojana had not been organized during the early phase of ANUC, and the region was only marginally affected by the waves of invasions that marked the climax of the land struggles in 1971. However, progressive drainage and the expansion of rice production had radically changed the situation by the mid-1970s. In the *haciendas* pasture-rent was abolished and the peasants were evicted. This led to increasing disputes over marginal lands, mainly marshes, river islands, and banks whose ownership was still undefined. Unrest developed, the Sucre departmental association of ANUC Sincelejo moved in, and more than thirty committees of *usuarios* were created in just a couple of years. Following ANUC's Fourth Congress, protest demonstrations were staged in the area. The police adopted a hard line to disperse the meetings, which further inflamed the peasants. As a result, there were violent riots in Majagual, the local police was overwhelmed and a number of land invasions were organized in some estates. The reaction of the authorities and landowners was disproportionately harsh. Defining the disturbances

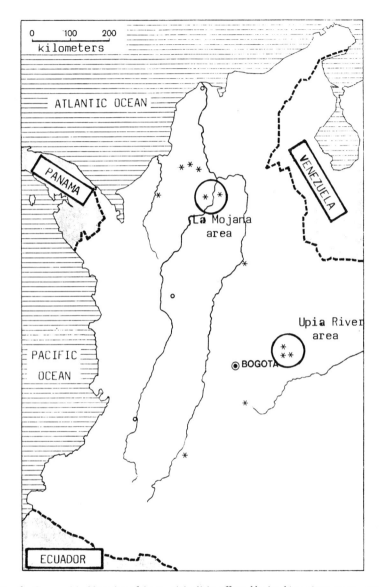

Map 6. Geographical location of the municipalities affected by land invasions, 1977–1978.

as guerrilla activities, the government rushed troops to the area and installed a military governor in the district. The landowners organized a Council of Social Security, whose first task was to raise funds for a permanent corps of armed *pájaros*. Repression escalated during the second half of 1977, one of the regional leaders of the *usuarios* was killed in

Guaranda in February 1978, and the area was completely "pacified" later with the rigorous application of the Security Statute enacted by the new administration of President Turbay Ayala.[17]

As previously stated, the second main regional focus of conflict over land during 1977 and 1978 was the area of the Upía River, which includes municipalities of Meta and Casanare.[18] In the 1960s, this region of savannas was still characterized by the herd economy typical of the Eastern Llanos. The local peasants had arrived as colonists from Boyacá, Cundinamarca, and Tolima, but instead of continuing toward the forest frontier, as many others did, they had stayed with the herds under systems of "company" that included wages for their work as cowboys and permission to grow subsistence crops on the river banks. Given its geographical isolation, the area had been outside the range of the land struggles of Casanare during the 1960s, and in 1971 only a few land invasions had taken place in some municipalities of Meta. The real trouble started after 1973, when the construction of roads redefined the region as part of the immediate periphery of Bogotá and created conditions for a sudden agribusiness type of development. The landowners abolished the old arrangements and started to evict the peasants in order to move into rice and cotton themselves or to rent and sell the land to entrepreneurs and investors who were coming to the area with that purpose. An aggravating factor in this process was the fact that the landowners and entrepreneurs preferred, at the beginning, to import experienced workers from Tolima and Huila instead of recruiting the local labor power. ANUC's departmental association of Meta organized a couple of land invasions in 1974 against the main landowner of Puerto López. More disputes developed, and in 1977 and 1978 the *usuarios* also exerted pressure in Cabuyaro, Cumaral, and Barranca de Upía. By then, the conflict had extended to Casanare, where plans for construction of the Alternate Turnpike to the Eastern Llanos were inflating the prices of land in anticipation of the further expansion of capitalist agriculture. Committees of *usuarios* were organized to resist evictions in the municipalities of Villanueva, Sabanalarga, Santa Elena, and San Agustín. There were a number of land seizures, and the problem made newspaper headlines when it was learned that a son of President López Michelsen had known in advance the route of the future highway and had bought 25,000 hectares at La Libertad for speculative purposes. Despite this fact, the police and the landowners' gangs of *pájaros* increased their repression. As the evictions proceeded, one of the *usuarios* was killed in October 1977 at Villanueva, and eventually the peasant protests were also quenched in this region with the stern application of the Security Statute provisions in 1978.

Most of the other land struggles during 1977 and 1978 took place in Sucre, where INCORA was withdrawing legal cases against landowners and opening the doors for many evictions and some reinvasions. There were local protests and a number of isolated but violent clashes in San Pedro, Tolú, La Unión, and Los Palmitos. A total of 300 evicted families invaded suburban terrains in the departmental capital, Sincelejo, setting up precarious dwellings. The disturbances were repressed by a military operation that, under the umbrella of the Security Statute, covered several municipalities. During this operation, many local and regional leaders of ANUC were imprisoned and tortured at the military base of Coveñas.[19] In Córdoba, where ANUC Sincelejo had been totally dispersed, the last couple of invasions were led by isolated groups from Montería who tried to occupy unused land in Las Palmas and Ciénaga de Betansí. The police intervened and, as a result, twenty peasants were jailed for almost a year.[20] In Magangué (Bolívar), three land invasions took place. One of the groups managed to retain part of the land but, in the other two cases, the peasants accepted money from the landowners and evacuated their plots.[21] Outside the Atlantic Coast there were invasion attempts in *veredas* of Barranca-bermeja, where the *usuarios* of Middle Magdalena were trying to rebuild an independent regional association after severing their link with national ANUC.[22] In Huila, the landowners had organized an Association of Rural Proprietors as a pressure group against INCORA and the *empresas comunitarias*. Both wings of ANUC agreed to carry out a joint protest, including the invasion of an estate that belonged to the president of the landowners' association.[23] Finally, the Security Statute was also applied in San Martín (Meta), where spontaneous groups of colonists who had lost their land as a result of indebtedness tried to seize plots in estates of La Loma and Chaparral. The invasions failed and, although they were not related to ANUC, many peasants were sentenced to long terms of imprisonment by the military judges.[24]

Taken together, the conflicts that ended the land struggles of the 1970s had several characteristics that revealed ANUC's general decadence. One of these characteristics was the limited scope of the struggles, which can be easily observed by comparing (in Table 3.1) the number of land invasions of the last period with those of previous years. Secondly, and in contrast to the earlier struggles, in which the land invasions were part of broader offensives promoted by the departmental and national organizations of ANUC, the disputes of 1977 and 1978 appeared to be more spontaneous, lacking planning and coordination and sometimes even completely disconnected from the peasant organization. A third element was the isolation of the conflicts, which indicated that they had developed only as a consequence of specific local conditions or, at most, within a limited regional scope. A further characteristic of the last land struggles was their defensive nature. They were waged mainly by peasants whose access to land was being questioned and revoked by landowner assaults and counteroffensives. In this sense, the final characteristic was that the most important conflicts developed in regions that were new in terms of ANUC's action. Both in La Mojana and in the affected area of the Eastern Llanos, the traditional structures had remained stable well into the 1970s, and the landowner encroachment was dramatically sudden, resulting from the changes related to the expansion of agrarian capitalism and the steep increases in land values. The fact that the struggles became significant only in new areas marked by the development of acute contradictions emphasizes, by contrast, the reduced relevance of the last expressions of peasant resistance in other areas that had long been considered strongholds of ANUC's radicalism.

The review of the land struggles has also shown the decisive role of repression, especially the systematic use of the Security Statute. In fact, the motives that led Turbay Ayala's government to enact this statute were clearly related to the labor unrest and the urban guerrilla activities of the M–19 (April 19 Movement).[25] As explained in the first section of Chapter 2, the Colombian peasants had emerged from the Violencia with a negative attitude toward armed struggle. They had rejected the revolutionary call of the ELN and FARC guerrillas in the 1960s, and during the 1970s ANUC was unresponsive to the ML groups and their armed detachment, the EPL. Furthermore, by 1978 the peasant struggles were at a very low ebb and offered little justification for such extreme measures as Turbay Ayala's Security Statute. The repressive escalation then had an urban, not a rural focus. However, as a reflection of the general punitive onslaught in the country, the statute was used to destroy all expressions of peasant resistance. The active militants were subjected to continuous persecution, and at the grass-roots level, any mobilization faced the prospect of violence and the risk of severe punishment under military "justice." Combined with the other factors that were leading to the disintegration of ANUC Sincelejo, the ruthless enforcement of the Security Statute would have a double effect: It prevented the peasants from defending themselves against the evictions caused by INCORA's withdrawal and the landowners' counteroffensive, and it helped accelerate grass-roots defections by spreading fear throughout the country.[26]

The last expressions of the land struggle revealed ANUC's failure to sustain the direct peasant action that had existed from the very start of the agrarian reform. Without this pressure from below, the government could freely proceed with the counterreform established with the Pact of Chicoral, so that the second half of Lopez Michelsen's administration saw the abolition of the few remaining institutional bases of land redistribution. Decrees 134 and 135 of 1976 strengthened the legal position of the landowners' counterdemands by imposing stricter limits on expropriation and giving more immunity to proprietors who leased part of their land under sharecropping contracts. The Council of State, which in 1976 formally abolished INCORA's guidelines on the expropriation of "properly used" land in marginal cases, revised during 1977 the implications of Laws 4 and 5 of 1973 and the Sharecropping Law of 1975. As a result, it suspended all the criteria for expropriation in cases where the landowners had failed to comply with the minimum requirements of productivity. By the end of 1977, the successive resolutions of the council had led to a complete emasculation of INCORA, not only by ending all further expropriation until 1982 but also by leaving the processes that had begun between 1973 and 1977 without a legal base.[27] One of the last measures of the López Michelsen administration was the Decree 1265 of 1977, which, as a direct response to the conflicts of La Mojana and the Eastern Llanos, provided favorable regulations for the landowners in disputes involving clarification of ownership of presumed public lands.[28] After 1978, the avalanche continued unabated under Turbay Ayala's administration. Counterreform was further strengthened by the use of the Security Statute to suppress all protests. With the end of the new government's first year came the announcement that INCORA had withdrawn its jurisdiction from 150,000 additional hectares because there had been "mistakes in the interpretation of the Sharecropping Law."[29]

Three dimensions in the collapse of the peasant movement

With the triumph of counterreform and the extinction of the last flames of conflict, 1978 signaled the accelerated dissolution of ANUC Sincelejo in the areas of previous land struggle. In terms of state policy, the change of government had not introduced any significant new elements. Since the direction of the socioeconomic processes at the regional level had also remained largely unchanged, ANUC's final crisis was only the logical culmination of previous tendencies that were no longer compatible with the reality that they had helped to create. In this sense, it seems worthwhile to consider separately the three main dimensions in the movement's collapse: the political, trade-unionist, and organizational aspects.

Politically, the turning point was the participation of the "peasant party" in the parliamentary elections of February 1978. As seen in the previous section, ORP had been officially presented to the rank-and-file *usuarios* at the Fourth National Congress, when it imposed its ideological line on ANUC's new platform. In the subsequent months, ORP was transformed into the National Democratic Popular Movement (MNDP), a legal political organization whose main militants came from the ranks of ANUC's top leaders and advisers.[30] The arguments that justified the launching of a party for electoral participation were sustained by a strategy that stressed three imperatives: having an autonomous political presence in the country, assessing the ideological influence that could be exerted upon the peasantry, and opening new fronts among urban workers. Doctrinary reasons were also invoked, in the Leninist tradition that saw electoral participation as "not an end in itself, but a means to carry out tasks of propaganda, denunciation and agitation among the masses." Thus, at a special meeting in September 1977, ANUC's leadership publicly presented MNDP as a political movement that strived "to integrate the masses of peasants and other rural sectors into the democratic, revolutionary and anti-imperialist struggles in Colombia."[31] By then, two leftist opposition coalitions were taking shape for the forthcoming elections. One of them was the Union of National Opposition (UNO), which included the Communist Party and other minor groups of Liberal dissidents and old Anapistas. The second was the Front for the Unity of the People (FUP), which comprised MOIR and other small sectors of Maoists, Liberals, and Anapistas. Expressing its opposition to the Communists, MNDP integrated itself with FUP, arguing that the latter offered "the only serious option to raise the progressive banners of the left without playing the game of the servants of Soviet social-imperialism."[32] Armed with the ten points of FUP's program and using ANUC's funds, the activists opened the electoral campaign by putting forward the most prestigious leaders of the *usuarios* as MNDP candidates in all the regions in which ANUC had been or was thought to be influential.

Before the local leaders and groups, the central proposition that justified electoral participation was the need to transcend the trade-unionist struggle by breaking the political monopoly of the *gamonales*. It was argued that by ousting the latter from the local councils, it would be possible to undermine the power of the landowners, sharpening the contradictions in the countryside and raising the political consciousness of the people. The response was not enthusiastic and, in this sense, it can be said that the electoral campaign showed many indications of the future turn of events. Many regional and local leaders opposed the project or accepted it as a matter of organizational discipline, and grass-roots participation in the political meetings and demonstrations against *gamonalismo* was poor.[33] Perhaps deluded by the memory of massive mobilizations of the past, the national leaders of ANUC and MNDP preferred to ignore these symptoms. The less optimistic believed that there was sufficient support in 250 municipalities to obtain a strong vote that would secure at least 70 peasant representatives in the local councils.[34] But at the moment of truth, the results came as a shock even for this cautious forecast. The left had obtained 195,000 votes, which represented just 4.6 percent of the total turnout. Of these votes, only 55,000 went to FUP, and the contribution of MNDP was estimated at not more than 15,000. As a consequence, the peasant party barely managed to get twenty-three representatives in municipal councils throughout the country. Even in the departments of the Atlantic Coast, where ANUC's influence had been stronger, the results were frustrating: only four councilors in Sucre, two in Bolívar, two in Cesar, and none at all in Córdoba and Magdalena.[35]

Focusing upon the main regions of land struggle, it can be said that, besides the other factors that were influencing the decline of the peasant movement, there were two basic elements behind the electoral failure of MNDP. The first was the strength of the clientelist system and its ability to maintain its political grip upon the peasantry, despite the challenge based on horizontal or class demands and grievances. Even in the places where ANUC had been stronger, the MNDP activists faced almost insurmountable obstacles due to the clientelist system of control. In this system, only rarely did the landowners themselves appear as political *gamonales*. Most frequently, the local situation was marked by the inter-mediation of Liberal and Conservative political chiefs who, although supported by the landowners, had not personally confronted the peasants as direct enemies. However, since these political *gamonales* also acted as intermediaries with the state agencies and the regional and national centers of political power, they could always invoke some type of "curriculum of service" on behalf of the community. While the MNDP militants could only offer criticism and denunciation, the *gamonales* showed concrete achievements and promised favors to their clienteles: small roads or bridges which had been built thanks to their initiatives, grants they had obtained for the local committees of Acción Comunal, scholarships for the secondary schooling of the children, and so on. All these "conquests" were presented as a result of their mediation and were used to feed the notion that the problems had to be solved amicably by voting for those who could obtain the concessions from above, not by trying to force things through pressure from below.[36] Where argumentation was insufficient, clientelism could always use other methods, ranging from the outright massive purchase of votes to the more crude expedient of naked violence. Repression was particularly important in some municipalities, frightening both the activists and their potential voters. Five MNDP candidates were assassinated during the campaign, a clear indication of the extreme sensibility of clientelism to direct political challenges aimed at undermining its bases.[37]

The second element underlying the electoral failure was the conspicuous lack of appeal of the MNDP initiative at the grass-roots level. There was strong opposition among the most conscientious sectors, either for ideo-logical reasons or because of the feeling that the situation was not suitable or sufficiently ripe to give electoral expression to the peasant demands.[38] For the vast majority, the launching of MNDP created great confusion regarding the trade-unionist or political definition of the peasant movement, especially since the *usuarios* were now being called to the polls after years of preaching abstention. Full of notions and problems that escaped the understanding and the interest of the peasants, the ideological discourse of MNDP only served to augment that confusion. However, in the midst of the critical and countercritical clatter that arose from the debates on electoral participation, one thing was clear to the groups that still followed ANUC Sincelejo: In the final analysis, their leaders had asked for votes just like the traditional *gamonales*, the only difference being that they had no clientelist favors to offer. In fact, the peasants' reluctance to answer the political call of MNDP proved that ANUC's leaders and their policies had failed to retain the confidence of the peasants and had been unable to develop a consistent class consciousness on the basis of the earlier radicalism in the land struggles. At different levels within the organization, the realization of this failure was the main consequence of the electoral disaster. Frustrated and disappointed by the defeat, most of the remaining loyal committees started to divide or disperse, while many local and regional leaders looked for ways to dissociate themselves from the national leadership of ANUC Sincelejo.[39] Even the most recent organizational achievements were thwarted. In La Mojana, for example, only three groups remained out of the thirty committees that had been formed before the elections.[40] As will be seen in the following section, the political debacle would reach the very top of ANUC's bureaucratic structure and would highlight the latent contradictions within the elite group that had monopolized the positions of power.

Turning now to the trade-union dimension of ANUC's crisis in the areas of land struggle, it seems unnecessary to consider the activities among the agricultural laborers, since these were of little significance and were purely bureaucratic.[41] On the other hand, since the conflicts over land had also withered away, the last episodes of real significance were basically limited to the problems of the *parceleros*. In this sense, the first factor to be taken into account was ANUC's almost complete loss of influence in the settlements. With the blackmail policy of INCORA, the intransigent line adopted by ANUC Sincelejo had created a situation in which there were no possible compromises for the *parceleros*: Acceptance of the Institute's conditions was synonymous with marginalization from the peasant movement. For the reasons considered in detail in the previous chapter, the institutional alternative prevailed. The tendency to legalize land tenure under INCORA's terms grew so rapidly that by 1977 even the strongholds of earlier radicalism were affected in Córdoba and Bolívar, and after 1978 in the department of Sucre.[42] When it became evident that the massive surrender was systematically destroying ANUC's links with the settlements, INCORA decided to replace its indirect pressures with a more aggressive policy. Recalcitrant groups, especially in Sucre, were given an

ultimatum under the threat of outright eviction. Choosing isolated settlements as targets for exemplary punishment, the Institute quickly moved
from threat to direct action, staging executive trials of a number of *empresas
comunitarias*, confiscating their cattle, and initiating eviction proceedings.[43] INCORA's assault caused a rush to legalization among the intim-
idated *parceleros*. Eager to capitalize on the stampede, the Institute
abandoned all the associative and technical criteria for adjudication, de-
livering the new titles in accordance with the situation in the settlements.
This inflicted an additional blow on the already shattered peasant morale,
because it created conditions for the destruction of the last remnants of
solidarity. In some places there were last-minute invasions among the
groups themselves, while in many others, the collective frameworks disintegrated amid disputes regarding the future limits of the private property
of each *parcelero*.[44]

As ANUC Sincelejo's bases of support were being rapidly reduced to
a minimum, a second factor was gaining importance on the trade-union
front: the implementation of the DRI and PAN programs. Since the
contents and general aims of these programs have been already discussed
in the first section of Chapter 4, the main point here concerns the way
in which ANUC's attitude toward DRI and PAN influenced the effectiveness of the organization's trade-union activity. When the government
announced the DRI project, the reaction of ANUC Sincelejo was marked
by a rather contemptuous aloofness. The thirteenth meeting of the National Junta (Cartagena, August 1975) defined the project as "a futile
attempt to isolate the small and middle peasants from the movement's
struggles," predicting that the budget would be "devoured by bureaucracy" and that there would be "a minimal incidence in terms of help and
credit for the peasantry."[45] However, during 1976 it became evident that
the DRI program would have substantial effects and was very attractive
to many peasants in the *minifundia* areas. Aware of the danger of losing
ground at the grass-roots level, ANUC defined a policy of "support and
criticism" toward DRI, which was widely publicized but which responded
to a strategy that was diametrically opposed to its declared aims. This
became clear in the conclusions of the fourteenth meeting of the National
Junta (Barrancabermeja, May 1976), which indicated that ANUC had to
be "astute" in relation to the DRI initiative: The activists should start
from a position of apparent support in order to discuss it with the base
groups, moving later to massive criticism and finally convincing the
peasants to reject the program altogether.[46] Thus, instead of developing
a line that would take advantage of DRI to achieve economic gains for
the peasants, protect them from deceit by the state, and raise their class
consciousness, ANUC Sincelejo used criticism and started to put ideological pressure upon the peasantry in order to force opposition to the

program. Ignoring the fact that DRI also represented a package of concessions that the dominant classes were offering to the established peasants,
ANUC preferred to unmask the program as "an oligarchic and imperialist
conspiracy" whose main purposes were related to "cheap food, markets
for imported agricultural inputs, and the preservation of *latifundia*."[47]
The same simplistic attitude was adopted toward PAN: ANUC failed to
address itself to this program as a palliative that the government directed
to the poorer peasants, denouncing it as nothing but "an attempt to take
advantage of American agricultural surpluses in order to force changes in
the diet of the Third World peoples and increase their dependence upon
imperialism."[48]

Coupled with the legal disqualification to represent the peasantry at
the institutional level, this policy of rejection of official programs had
been a key factor in the decline of ANUC Sincelejo throughout the areas
of *minifundia*, the areas of colonization, and the coffee-growing zones. In
all these regions it was evident that, since 1976, the peasantry had been
gladly accepting the concessions of state programs, which produced visible
results in terms of credit, services, infrastructure, and improvements in
life conditions. Attracted by the activities of DRI, the Federation of Coffee
Growers, and INCORA, the peasants paid little attention to ANUC's
propaganda, ignored the leaders when they invoked the ghosts of "peasant
differentiation" and "dissolution of the middle sectors," and, in the end,
completely dismissed these leaders when it became clear that the movement's positions were incompatible with the new perspectives.[49] A similar
process would take place in the three coastal departments that had been
the main strongholds of ANUC Sincelejo and, after 1978, were included
in the DRI and PAN programs. With an initial investment of US $13.5
million provided by the Canadian International Development Agency,
DRI launched a combined project with INCORA in twenty-six municipalities of Sucre and Córdoba. At the same time, PAN was introduced
in the areas of agrarian reform of Bolívar under the direct administration
of INCORA.[50] In these regions too, the programs proved highly attractive
to the peasants. Many of the *empresas comunitarias*, especially in Sucre, saw
in the DRI program an opportunity to get the credits and services needed
to start commercial production and end the economy of subsistence and
subordination to the neighboring landowners. Greater still were the expectations of the *parceleros* who had emerged from the disintegration of
the *empresas*. Among these, fragmentation into small plots, indebtedness,
defection, and purchase of rights had been leading rapidly to land concentration, a process that, especially in Córdoba, was creating conditions
of economic viability for some peasant sectors, which welcomed DRI as
a means of consolidating their position.[51] Even in central and southern
Bolívar, where the economic failure of collective and individual farming

had caused the defection of more than 20 percent of the *parceleros* by 1978, the PAN program was favorably received, since the grants and loans for milk cows, pigs, poultry, and garden crops partially improved the situation of impoverished families.[52]

Taking into account both the desperate economic condition of the *parceleros* and the strong previous politicization on the Atlantic Coast, it is not surprising that the problems derived from ANUC's attitude toward the government's economic concessions were particularly pronounced in that area. For the leftist activists of all shades within ANUC Sincelejo, a program like DRI promoted the development of a bourgeois mentality among the peasants and erected a barrier between them and the revolution. On the other hand, the urgent needs of the *parceleros* interested them in official programs that were considered by many as a last lifeline. The contradiction appeared much more acute than in other regions, since both the ideological pressures for rejection and the economic compulsions for acceptance were stronger. The outcome, however, was the same as it was everywhere else: As a continuation of the disobedience that had led them to comply with INCORA's conditions of land adjudication, the groups disregarded the radical leaders' exhortations on the question of the DRI and PAN programs, thus destroying whatever remained of the prestige and authority of ANUC Sincelejo.

Finally, it is necessary to consider the collapse of ANUC Sincelejo from the organizational perspective. In considering the factors involved in the movement's decline, this analysis has shown how these factors led to the progressive destruction of organizational channels, the disintegration of leadership and bureaucratic structures, and the dissolution of groups at the grass-roots level. This material will not be reviewed again. Instead, we will consider the main consequence of these processes: the fact that the peasantry was now lacking representation. The rapid liquidation of ANUC Sincelejo expressed the breakdown of the belligerent spirit of the peasantry and the transition to new attitudes of acceptance and accommodation toward the state and the dominant classes. In accordance with the new socioeconomic and political conditions, compromise was the prevailing mood among the peasants, and the main question appeared as follows: If ANUC Sincelejo's intransigence belonged to the past, what organizations would now represent the peasantry given its new conciliatory mood?

In this sense, and again paying special attention to the areas of former land struggle, there were many symptoms of replacement or supersession after 1977. Some of them were initiatives that were either spontaneous or promoted by political and trade-union groups; others reflected direct state involvement with the peasant organizations. With regard to the first category, there were many groups of agricultural laborers who formed spontaneous committees to raise petitions for buying land through IN-CORA. The most relevant case involved a number of groups who organized themselves in Huila and Tolima as the Associations for Land Acquisition and proclaimed themselves independent of both lines of ANUC.[53] In the *empresas comunitarias*, an important spontaneous process was the emergence of many Associations of Beneficiaries of Agrarian Reform in Córdoba, Huila, and Tolima. These associations were generally promoted by groups who had belonged to ANUC Sincelejo in the past but were now trying to organize themselves independently in order to negotiate with IN-CORA.[54] Scattered but also visible was, after 1977, the activity of local peasant syndicates and associations linked either to FANAL or the Peasant Colombian Action (ACC), an agrarian detachment of the Christian-Democrat trade-union central.[55] Another initiative was that of the Communist Party, the old enemy of ANUC, which was now trying to strengthen its trade-union work in the countryside. In 1976 the Communists created the National Federation of Agrarian Syndicates (FENSA), an umbrella organization including many syndicates of agricultural workers and local peasant associations in different parts of the country.[56] By the end of the 1970s, then, there were clear signs of movement from different quarters into the vacuum left by ANUC Sincelejo. Most of the initiatives, including that of the Communists, were characterized by a pragmatic approach that emphasized economic concerns and the need to come to terms with the realities of state policy. However, none of the organizational efforts seemed to have sufficient scope and depth to enable them to develop a serious opposition alternative that would overcome the pervasive weakness, fragmentation, and dispersion.

In regard to the organizations promoted by the state, one should consider Acción Comunal, the DRI groups, and, above all, the officialist ANUC Armenia. All these had been used by the Pastrana and López Michelsen administrations as instruments of the divisive policies aimed at counteracting the influence of radical ANUC. Since this divisive role required representation to be taken away from the opposition, these organizations had been fulfilling many trade-union tasks that ANUC Sincelejo had been unable or unwilling to assume. Since the whole exercise was meant to reaffirm state control over the peasantry, none of these trade-union tasks emphasized autonomous principles. Far from questioning the existing reality, the semiofficial organizations took that reality as a starting point to raise petitions, not demands, on day-to-day and parochial problems of the peasants. Previously, when the peasantry had posed radical challenges such as land redistribution and social change, this submissive approach to the representation of peasant demands had been almost completely swept away by the contentious rise of the *usuarios*. But now that radicalism was no longer on the agenda and ANUC Sincelejo had failed to offer reasonable alternatives for accommodation, this approach appeared as a realistic option for negotiating and accepting state concessions. The committees of Acción Comunal were able to obtain tangible improvements for the peasants, at the price of reinforcing vertical "communitarian" channels that abolished the horizontal bases of class association and strengthened the power of the *gamonales* and local political clientelism. Not surprisingly, the state gave priority to the promotion of Acción Comunal in those regions in which the peasant movement had been stronger and more radical: The number of Acción Comunal committees doubled between 1966 and 1979 throughout the country, but it multiplied five and six times on the Atlantic Coast, in the Eastern Llanos, and in the colonization areas.[57] The DRI program helped to disrupt the class links among the peasants, since it created from the very beginning its own groups of beneficiaries and ignored the peasant organizations that existed in the implementation areas. Like the Acción Comunal committees, the DRI groups had a double function: They provided a channel for the expression of the peasants' needs, and they created vertical lines of submission that, in this case, subordinated the peasantry to the executive agencies of the state.[58] However, it was the reactivation of the Armenia Line of ANUC that would express the prevailing trends most clearly.

Since 1976 ANUC Armenia had been slowly assuming a more active role. The demands of its own groups had been reinforced by those of many others who, after leaving ANUC Sincelejo, were seeking the assistance of the officialist *usuarios* in order to negotiate with INCORA and the other government agencies. Sensitive to these pressures from below, and arguing that the decline of radical ANUC created favorable conditions for something more than passive collaboration, a number of regional leaders had staged a sort of internal rebellion, demanding that the often postponed Third National Congress of the Armenia Line be held.[59] Encouragement was also coming from the Ministry of Agriculture, which appointed new promoters and allocated a larger budget for the officialist *usuarios* and the DOC.[60] Coupled with the coercive blockade on the Sincelejo Line, the revival of ANUC Armenia showed the interest of López Michelsen's administration in finding a partner for a dialogue that, setting aside the more radical demands, would be helpful in negotiating his concessions to the peasants. Against this background, the Third Congress of ANUC Armenia (Santa Marta, February 1977) marked the beginning of an intense reactivation campaign, a campaign based upon a greater fulfillment of ANUC's functions and facilitated by the failure of ANUC Sincelejo on the trade-union front.[61] Enjoying the support and tolerance of the government, the national leaders of the Armenia Line adopted a more enterprising attitude within the State agencies, launching initiatives, making proposals, and even incorporating subtle criticism. Between 1977 and 1980, the Executive Committe of ANUC Armenia was continuously in the news, protesting INCORA's inactivity, demanding changes in agrarian legislation, asking for improvements in tenancy conditions under sharecropping contracts, and getting down to concrete issues such as crop insurance, marketing systems, scholarships for peasants' sons to the universities, control of fares in rural public transportation, and better services for the *empresas comunitarias*.[62]

At the regional level, the bureaucratic reorganization of ANUC Armenia was relatively rapid, not only in the *minifundia* departments but also in the areas of previous land struggle. Among the latter, the officialists had always maintained their hegemony in Huila, Tolima, and Atlántico. In the other coastal departments, where their influence had been minimal, penetration began in earnest after a Coastal Regional Meeting focused upon the problems of the *empresas comunitarias* and the individual *parceleros* (Valledupar, January 1977).[63] Since then, and until 1980, the departmental associations of ANUC Armenia were rebuilt one by one, first in Córdoba and Bolívar, then in Magdalena and Cesar, and finally in Sucre. During this process, the officialists took charge of representing the *usuarios*, hammering the slogan "We are not lambs and the government pays attention to us." Most of the activity was bureaucratic in nature, but it responded to the most pressing problems: legalization of land tenure with INCORA, issues related to new credits and distribution of water in irrigation districts, the situation of the *empresas comunitarias*, and the renegotiation of the settlements' debts.[64] Although the results were partial and always reflected the acceptance of institutional conditions, ANUC Armenia's activity was viewed favorably at the grass-roots level, especially by contrast to the frustrations caused by the last stages of radical ANUC. As a consequence, the officialists were able to reorganize many committees that had formerly belonged to ANUC Sincelejo, coopting the old leaders or promoting those who had been emerging spontaneously with the decline of radicalism.[65] Thus, with no real opposition, ANUC Armenia had established by 1980 a bureaucratic structure that, even in the areas of previous land struggle, sustained its claim to represent what remained of the peasant *usuarios*.[66]

The capitulation of ANUC Sincelejo

The reconstruction of ANUC Armenia gave organizational expression to the attitude of accommodation that now prevailed amidst the peasantry and to the hegemony that the state had reestablished and consolidated in the countryside. The last touch would be the formal capitulation of ANUC Sincelejo, which had been brewing since the electoral failure of the peasant party. Indeed, with the adverse results of the parliamentary election of

February 1978, an intense debate suddenly polarized the activists of ANUC and MNDP. A large faction within the national leadership argued that it was essential to alter dramatically ANUC's tactical, political, and trade-unionist lines. From its analysis of the national situation, this group drew two conclusions: first, that the decline of the peasant movement was part of the more general ebb of the democratic struggles in the country, and second, that the bourgeoisie and the landowners had succeeded in cornering ANUC Sincelejo and its political tendency. In order to break this blockade it was imperative to conciliate, seeking no more alliances with the "impotent left," but rather with the bourgeois forces that had the "real control of the masses." At the political level, it was urgent to leave FUP and move toward the traditional Liberal and Conservative parties, trying to reach agreements with the groups that represented the "new bourgeois sectors" that had emerged with the legal and illegal bonanzas of the exporting boom of the 1970s. At the trade-union level, greater efforts had to be made to promote the interests of the rich peasants, developing links with other organizations and supporting the clientelist and not the oppositionist trade union centrals. These changes were related to a retrospective interpretation of ANUC's historical role, which stated that ANUC had been a "democratic-bourgeois" force and not a "demo-cratic-revolutionary" movement, as previously thought.[67]

The timing and crudity of the right-wing reaction surprised those who wanted to maintain the existing political and trade union definitions of ANUC and MNDP. The leftist faction, which included most of the leaders from the Atlantic Coast, commanded more support among the remaining followers at the grass-roots level. But ANUC's structure, which gave equal representation to all regions, granted an automatic majority to the right in two crucial forums: the Executive Committee and the National Junta.[68] Taking advantage of their bureaucratic control, the rightists started to move even before the debate was formally settled. In the second electoral round of July 1978, MNDP supported the Conservative can-didate, Belisario Betancur, in many regions, and after the polls, ANUC Sincelejo's Executive Committee publicly congratulated the new Liberal president, Turbay Ayala.[69] During the last months of 1978 the leftist opposition tried to put up a fight, demanding a change in public positions and asking for a reaffirmation of the platform approved by the Fourth National Congress. However, a compromise solution was out of the ques-tion, because the authoritarian and exclusionist style of leadership had prevented the formation of a conflict resolution system within ANUC. The rightist thrust could no longer be checked, and the methods of bureau-cratic control and intimidation again surfaced. At the seventeenth meeting of the National Junta (Pereira, December 1978) the opposition was si-lenced by pressure, forcing the defeated leftists to break publicly with "the new Armenia Line," which, in their opinion, had usurped the leadership of ANUC Sincelejo.[70]

After this split, which severed their last links with the political left, the leaders of ANUC Sincelejo raced against time to achieve some type of deal with the government before the last traces of the movement's influence vanished. Because there was little strength at the grass-roots level, most of the activity during 1979 and 1980 developed at ANUC headquarters and in the corridors and offices of the ministries in Bogotá. Many communiques were issued to the press, and the Executive Committee engaged in a series of contacts and negotiations with politicians, government officials, and trade union leaders at different levels. ANUC's leaders had two basic goals in this intense campaign of propaganda and public relations. First, it was necessary to project a new image of ANUC Sincelejo to the government and to potential allies, an image that would eliminate the "red identification" of ANUC and show it to be a "reasonable" partner who was ready to accept the clientelist rules of the political game. During this metamorphosis, the Executive Committee used every opportunity to dissociate itself from the leftists, denouncing the Communist Party and other groups, publicly supporting the use of the Security Statute against guerrillas, and even condemning the Sandinista Revolution in Nicaragua.[71] Lobbying in Liberal and Conservative circles became frequent, and much emphasis was laid upon the "economic problems of the peasants" and the new "legalism" that inspired ANUC Sincelejo in its dealings with the official agencies. Also as part of the crusade to clean up ANUC's image, the Executive Committee filed a lawsuit against its finance secretary, whose conviction was widely publicized in order to compensate for the corruption charges that weighed on the national leaders.[72] The second goal of the conciliation process was reunification with the Armenia Line, which appeared to ANUC Sincelejo's leaders as the most expedient way of closing their deal with the government. Using the justification of a "policy of unity aimed to strengthen the peasants against their common enemies," the Executive Committee advanced several proposals on this issue to the Ministry of Agriculture and to the leaders of ANUC Armenia.[73] With the participation of officials and politicians, many meetings took place to explore the prospects and problems of a possible reunification.[74] Eventually, the leaders of ANUC Sincelejo aroused genuine interest in their initiative in Liberal Party circles. ANUC's reunification appeared especially attractive to the new Minister of Agriculture, Gustavo Dáger Chadid, who had political ambitions for the future and had already earned a certain reputation among the peasants during his period as governor in the department of Sucre.[75]

In the course of conciliation, then, all scruples had gone by the board and ANUC Sincelejo's leaders were assuming attitudes and positions that would have been unthinkable just a couple of years earlier. Seeking a reversion to a semi-official status that implied subservience to the counterreformist policies of the government, they were striving to transform ANUC into the opposite of everything the *usuarios* had been fighting for: an instrument of peasant control at the service of the dominant classes and their political clientelism. It has been said that a mood of compromise prevailed among the peasantry, but there is, of course, a great difference between political accommodation and political submission. There might have been other alternatives that would have adjusted to the ebb of the peasant movement by negotiating with the state while preserving, at the same time, minimal standards of organizational autonomy for the peasants. The ANUC Sincelejo leaders' sharply reactionary turn, surrendering independence instead of adopting a line of flexible realism, cannot be explained by the dynamics of a social movement. After the last split, the movement had ceased to exist: The rank and file had defected, and what remained was a fictitious organization whose facade was maintained by a handful of former leaders who no longer represented any sector of the peasantry. Lacking real social roots, these leaders were responsible to no one but themselves, so that their own interests – as a bureaucratic group and as individuals – were becoming the major determinant of their actions. It is hardly surprising, then, that what had begun as an opportunist rightwing push ended ingloriously in plain sycophancy. The surrender of ANUC Sincelejo became an admission ticket, a contribution offered by ANUC's bureaucrats to secure their future place in the clientelist order. The operation, however, had difficulties. First, money was still flowing in from friendly European foundations, which meant that the internal intrigues of fraud and corruption threatened, on several occasions, to spoil the whole project.[76] Second, the leaders of the officialist ANUC Armenia were strongly objecting to the reunification scheme. Some of them, of Conservative extraction, opposed its increasingly Liberal flavor. Others, including both Liberals and Conservatives, simply resented the idea of sharing the benefits and rewards of collaboration with outsiders. But both the former and the latter justified their refusal by arguing that ANUC Sincelejo's leaders "lacked support at the grass-roots level, were hopelessly corruptible, and represented the interests of the rich peasantry."[77]

All these problems were easily solved by the intervention of Minister Dáger Chadid, who wanted to see the reunification of the *usuarios* before leaving his post and getting involved in the forthcoming electoral campaign. A number of official resolutions were issued, inviting the leaders of both lines of ANUC to a Reunification Seminar in December 1980, setting norms for the restructuring of the municipal and departmental associations and summoning the regional representatives of the *usuarios* to a National Reunification Congress to be held in February 1981.[78] The

DOC promoters reorganized ANUC within months, something that would have proved impossible without the assistance of officials from INCORA and the Caja Agraria, who played an important role in the "selection" of the peasant representatives. When this hurried activity concluded with the inauguration of the congress in Bogotá, bureaucratic manipulation and political maneuvering reached their climax: The opposition of the Armenia Line was trampled and the more recalcitrant Conservative leaders were sacrificed without hesitation despite their clean sheets of servility, new regional subdivisions and fictitious posts were created to increase the bureaucratic rewards, and strong pressures were exerted at voting time to secure the election of former ANUC Sincelejo leaders who lacked support among the delegates.[79] The National Reunification Congress, which had opened with a speech by Dáger Chadid referring to ANUC as "a practical school of democracy," closed with the predictable conclusions on peasant problems, petitions to improve agrarian reform, and some critical remarks intended to tone down the support of the government's agrarian policies.[80] It is understandable that, at the official reception of ANUC's new credentials a few days later, President Turbay Ayala would warmly congratulate his minister of agriculture.[81] In addition to the benefit of support for the government's policies, it was possible to anticipate the returns that would come the following year, when the *usuarios* publicly backed the Liberal candidate, López Michelsen, in his bid for reelection as president.[82] However, beyond the petty partisan interests of the trade unionist clienteles, ANUC's reunification had a much broader significance for the clientelist system. The return of ANUC Sincelejo to the state's sheepfold was the final touch of legitimation of the hegemony over a defeated and demoralized peasantry. The ideological impact of this legitimation was particularly useful for the system: the reaffirmation, once more, that the paths of opposition were closed in Colombia and that the subordinate classes had to acquiesce in the social and political projects of the dominant classes. By coopting the bureaucratic residue of ANUC Sincelejo, the clientelist regime was also seizing the symbol of a belligerent past, blurring the memory of what had been the most significant agrarian movement in Colombia's history.

While the clientelist reunification of the *usuarios* seemed to be ending the peasant mobilizations of the 1970s, the leftists who had abandoned ANUC Sincelejo were trying to lay the foundations for a unified opposition. The initiative came mainly from two groups: the 21 de Febrero Movement, formed in 1978 as a result of negotiations among some of the fragmented ML groups, and the Council for Peasant Unity (CUC), created in 1979 by those who had left after the failure of the peasant party and the subsequent rightist reaction.[83] Together with other minor Maoist groups, they organized a National Meeting of Opposition Leaders of ANUC (Sincelejo, April 1981). The participants agreed on the need to rebuild the radical wing of the peasant movement and to revive the revolutionary spirit of the Colombian peasantry. Unanimously condemning the "false reunification congress orchestrated by the government," the meeting approved the basic outline of a new platform for ANUC and appointed a permanent Coordination Committee composed of representatives of the different groups. The Coordination Committee was entrusted with several tasks that were considered essential for the reconstruction process, including the future organization of a Fifth Unitarian Congress of ANUC Sincelejo.[84]

The prospects for this initiative, however, were not particularly encouraging. First, it was clear that the leftist groups had only limited influence at the grass-roots level. Second, there were serious obstacles to real unity, including mutual recriminations for the decline of the movement and ideological differences that seemed too difficult to reconcile. More important still, little progress had been made in finding remedies for the doctrinary diseases that had caused such heavy damage in the past. The proposed platform tried to emphasize the trade union nature of ANUC, but the political elements defining the presumed revolutionary character of the peasant movement were still present, and were formulated in such a way as to exclude other leftist groups that objected to the Maoist views. In addition to their subordination to political goals, the economic demands of the peasantry appeared as abstract claims whose divorce from reality was again expressed by stubborn opposition to any agrarian policy or program of the state. A few months later, and as a reaffirmation of this attitude, the Coordination Committee staged a demonstration in Sincelejo to reject the DRI program and repudiate INCORA's policy toward the *empresas comunitarias*.[85] Severing their relations with the Institute and denouncing it as "an offensive enemy of the peasantry," the leftist remnants of ANUC still refused to acknowledge that, in the absence of a revolutionary situation, the handling of the peasant grievances had to take into account the existing correlation of political forces and the existing socioeconomic and institutional reality. Given these premises, the groups that were trying to resuscitate a radical ANUC were not likely to achieve significant successes in mobilizing the peasantry.

10

Overview and final remarks

The land struggles of the 1970s were part of a broader offensive aimed at forcing a change that would favor a peasant path of agrarian evolution in Colombia. The challenge to the existing structure of land property, which became the most advanced battlefront of the peasant movement, was rooted in the earlier peasant mobilizations of the twentieth century and developed as a continuation of many local and regional conflicts that had arisen since the 1960s. With the emergence of ANUC as an integrative force at the national level, the land struggles intensified and were articulated into a unified thrust encouraged by the state and bourgeois reformism. With the increasing tensions due to the accelerated dissolution of precapitalist relations of production and the wave of disputes over unused and public lands, the defeat of reformism within the ruling coalition precipitated the confrontation between the *usuarios* and the new counter-reformist policies of the state. The land invasions during 1971 climaxed the struggle for land, played a crucial role in the radicalization of the peasant movement, and gave many peasants access to the land.

However, the peasant offensive failed to become an agrarian revolution capable of breaking the power of the landowners and creating a social and economic structure favoring the peasantry. The battles developed in those places in which there were sharper contradictions and more favorable conditions for mobilization at the grass-roots level. In plunging into direct action, the *usuarios* had become receptive to leftist revolutionary ideologies that replaced the previous reformist legitimation, but even though greater politicization and better organization sustained the belligerency of some peasant sectors for a time, many other factors caused the land struggles to decline. The policy of counterreform destroyed the legal framework of land redistribution and split the peasant movement. Moreover, counterreform led to a repressive onslaught that, combining state action with the retaliations of the *pájaros*, killed more than 100 peasant *usuarios* between 1971 and 1978.[1] Another influential factor, especially after 1975, was the emergence of new occupational alternatives. The expansion of agrarian capitalism, seasonal labor migrations to Venezuela, and the development of the marihuana economy supplemented the relaxation effects caused by rural–urban emigration, the Sharecropping Law, and the marginal repeasantization that followed the previous peasant offensive. Within radical ANUC, adherence to unrealistic revolutionary principles, political factionalism, and a bureaucratic style of leadership eroded the support for the movement at the grass-roots level and destroyed its structure. In this process, a crucial element was the inability of ANUC Sincelejo to adapt to the changing conditions and express the new demands of the agricultural laborers and the *parceleros* of the *empresas comunitarias*. As a result of all these factors, the land struggles came to an end by 1978, leaving the peasant movement in a crisis situation marked by the disappearance of peasant belligerency even in the areas of greater former radicalism.

In assessing the effects of the land struggles waged by the *usuarios*, this research has highlighted two central and interrelated aspects. Firstly, despite their importance as a challenge to land monopolization, the peasant battles of the 1970s failed to produce significant alterations in the structure of land ownership in Colombia. As shown in Chapter 8, the repeasantization due to the land struggles and colonization merely compensated for the overall dissolution of the peasantry during the 1960s and 1970s. In other words, the gains made by the *usuarios* were insufficient to tip the balance in favor of the peasants. To a large extent, the limited nature of the peasant achievements reflected the immense power of the Colombian landowning class, a power that curbed the belligerency of the peasantry throughout a decade of intense social and political conflict. In the process, agrarian capitalism – an agriculture based upon wage labor – gained sufficient momentum to achieve a monopolistic form of development in the plains where the main land battles had been fought. This introduces the second relevant aspect: the special way in which repeasantization was assimilated within the new capitalist structure that was emerging in the regions of previous land struggle. The adverse conditions in the new settlements did much to dissolve the *empresas comunitarias* and cause the economic strangulation of the *parceleros*, making most of the families dependent upon the wage labor market. By creating a reserve of semi-proletarianized rural workers, the failure of the new peasant economy catered to the seasonal labor needs of agrarian capitalism, so that whatever was achieved by the land struggles, paradoxically, helped to consolidate the very pattern the peasants had been trying to oppose.

In appraising the evolution of ANUC as a peasant movement, it should be kept in mind that the perspective of this research has been conditioned by the focus on the land struggles. Still, taking into account our comparative references to the other battlefronts of the movement, it is possible to sketch a broad outline and advance a tentative conclusion on its historical significance. With these purposes, Table 10.1 uses some key dimensions to summarize ANUC's development. In terms of the agrarian contradictions and the class cleavages and alliances, the most outstanding element is the three phases in the evolution of the peasant movement: the organization of ANUC as part of a project of reformist alliance, the radical upsurge based upon autonomous positions, and the final conservative reaction of conciliation and submission. To some extent, these oscillations are explained by the changes in a state policy that, after turning sharply from reform to counterreform, stabilized around neo-Liberal orientations involving partial concessions for some peasant sectors. These shifts followed the realignments that were taking place among the dominant classes and reflected the changing definition of the agrarian question as the increase in industrial exports modified the conditions of capitalist accumulation. Nonetheless, it would be a mistake to consider ANUC's evolution as a mere epiphenomenon of the policies of the dominant classes and the state. Although it is true that reformism provided organization and gave legitimation to the peasant demands, the *usuarios'* upsurge was ultimately rooted in the underlying agrarian antagonisms and the interests of the different sectors of the peasantry. Moreover, ANUC's radicalization cannot be explained simply as an effect of "relative deprivation,"[2] that is, as a consequence of the frustrations caused by the counterreformist turn in state policy. Although these frustrations undoubtedly influenced the collective consciousness of the peasants, autonomous confrontation was possible mainly because ANUC had come to embody, as an organization, the power of the peasantry as a class. Similarly, the rightist turn of ANUC in the late 1970s was much more than a conciliatory reaction to the partial concessions offered by the state. In a deeper structural sense, both these concessions and the submissive spirit of the peasantry reflected the new situation created by the decline and fall of the peasant movement. In the last analysis, ANUC's cycle expressed the contingencies of the class struggles in the countryside and shows that the relationship between the state and the peasant movement cannot be fully understood without taking these contingencies into account.

To a large extent, then, ANUC's cycle depended upon the vicissitudes of the power struggle in the countryside. Consequently, the factors that influenced the rise and fall of the movement should not be seen as isolated causes but as variables that either enhanced or undermined the class power embodied in ANUC. In this sense, and maintaining the focus upon the class contradictions, it can be said that in addition to the strength of the landowning class and the shifts in the alliances of the bourgeoisie as expressed by state action, the major factor was the class heterogeneity of the peasantry. Originally, the multisectoral character of ANUC gave a strong boost to its rise as a movement. Although radicalization was centered in the areas of land struggle, the invasions of the landless peasants were accompanied by significant mobilizations and strikes conducted by *minifundistas*, colonists, and Indians. The different types of demands

Table 10.1. *Main dimensions in the development of the peasant movement, 1967–1981*

	Phases in ANUC's cycle		
	Mobilization (1967–1971)	Confrontation (1971–1975)	Decline and recess (1975–1981)
Dominant classes and state			
Policies of the dominant classes toward the peasantry	Project of alliance of the reformist bourgeoisie with the peasantry.	Defeat of reformism and breakdown of the project of alliance with the peasantry.	Concessions to the better-off sectors of the peasantry.
State policy: the agrarian question	Support to peasant farming, but not to the total detriment of capitalist agriculture.	Counterreform. Total support to capitalist agriculture.	Integrated rural development program. Continuing support to capitalist agriculture and palliatives to mitigate the social effects of its development.
State policy: the peasant movement	Encouragement and organization from above.	Isolation, divisionism, and repression.	Escalation of repression and openings for conditioned dialogue. Later, clientelist readmission.
Peasant movement			
Appeal at grass-roots level	Positive response to organizational campaign. Growing participation.	Mass mobilization, with climax in 1971–1972.	Decreasing participation, defection at grass-roots levels.
Action	Articulation and expression of grievances and demands.	Direct offensive on all fronts, especially in the areas of land struggle and colonization.	Recess on all battlefronts.
Representation of sectoral interests	Emphasis on the demands of the landless peasants.	Attempts to emphasize the demands of all peasant sectors, stressing the struggle for land.	Failed attempts to emphasize the interests of the agricultural laborers and the peasants with land.
Organizational processes and characteristics	Formal organization on all levels. Heterogeneous leadership pro-	Overrunning of formal organization. Emergent leadership	Bureaucratic entrenchment at the top. dispersion at local and re-

	...moted in organizational campaign.	...from below. Progovernmental split and radical realignment. Development of parallel secret political organization. Flow of solidarity funds from foreign foundations. Consolidation of central leadership.	...gional levels. Rigid control by leadership elite. Alienation of dissidents. Factionalism. Differentiation of the political and trade unionist dimensions. After electoral failure, reduction to central clique without support at grass-roots level. Corruption. Bureaucratic reunification with the pro-government line.
Relationship toward the state	Dependency and support. Instrumentality as mediator between state and peasants.	Autonomy and confrontation.	From openings of qualified support to capitulation and surrender of autonomy.
Dominant ideological attitude	Reformism	Radicalism with revolutionary elements.	Among the leaders, electoral failure leads to rightist reaction and accomodation with clientelist regime. At grass-roots levels, submissive and conciliatory attitudes come to prevail.
Main political processes	Support to the National Front.	Internal polarization. Break with the National Front. Short-lived influence of activists of the Communist Party and the Socialist Bloc. Electoral abstentionism. Growing influence of the Maoist ML groups and break with the other leftist parties. Development of conflict with the Maoist militants and drive towards political autonomy. Formation of ORP.	Break with Maoist groups. Consolidation of independent political line. Creation of MNDP, electoral failure, crisis and polarization. Return to the fold of political clientelism and the traditonal Liberal and Conservative parties. Confusion and weak reorganizational attempts among the leftist remnants.

seemed to have been successfully integrated during the diffuse and semi-spontaneous initial thrust of the *usuarios*, but difficulties started to develop as the conflict proceeded after 1972. The contradictions were more acute in some regions than in others, and their class content was also different. Among the *minifundistas* and colonists the aspirations assumed a trade-unionist form, but in the areas of land struggle the peasant demands implied a political challenge to the structure of landed property. Despite ANUC's efforts to articulate the interests of the various class sectors, these differences set the stage for an uneven development of the peasant move-ment. Disparities in demands, organization, and politicization hindered the crystallization of shared attitudes and caused continuous internal con-tradictions. Against this background, ANUC's inability to handle the day-to-day demands of the peasants led to a progressive loss of support at the grass-roots level, first in the regions of *minifundia* and later in the colonization areas. This process was accelerated by state concessions to the wealthier peasants and became widespread as the battles over land receded and the problems of the *parceleros* became dominant in the areas of previous land struggle.

Thus, it can be concluded that class heterogeneity soon became a source of increasing weakness throughout the development of radical ANUC. The differences between the vanguard groups who were fighting for the land and the rearguard sectors of established peasants marked the opposite ends of a spectrum that included other demands and systematically thwarted all attempts to bridge the gaps. The split between social reality and ideological discourse, the inability to define a coherent policy on the use of legal or illegal means, and the permanent antagonism between revolutionary and reformist orientations were largely due to these cen-trifugal forces in the class composition of the peasant movement. The bureaucratic and exclusionist style of ANUC's central leadership, which to some extent can be considered as an authoritarian reaction to this dispersion at the base level, worsened the situation by alienating the rank and file of the movement and subordinating the peasant demands to ulterior political goals that escaped the understanding and the real con-sciousness of the peasantry.

What were the effects of the peasant struggles of the 1970s? Throughout this work, it has been repeatedly emphasized that ANUC projected itself as a social and political force that, against the background of capitalist consolidation in Colombia, tried to resist the monopolistic landlord-en-trepreneurial path and resolve the agrarian question in favor of the peas-ants. By setting this goal, ANUC itself established the standard for the appraisal of its historical impact and significance. Limiting the discussion for the moment to this criterion, it can be said that the outcome was largely frustration. It has been shown that the achievements of the land struggles were marginal and, ironically, promoted the development of agrarian capitalism. The less radical sectors of the peasantry were the ones who obtained some real improvements, whether as a result of state concessions or as a reflection of the general prosperity and the coffee bonanza in the second half of the 1970s. But peasant pressure played only a secondary role in these gains. In the regions of colonization the programs of integrated rural development were already underway when peasant radicalization took place, and the extension of these programs to the *minifundia* highland areas was part of a broader policy adopted by international financial capital toward the Third World countries in general. In the last analysis, these improvements were also indicative of the failure of the *usuarios*, because they expressed a policy designed not to establish a massive and strong peasant economy, but only to maintain the more or less stable peasant sectors. Setting limits to peasant dissolution and securing the supply of foods and raw materials that could not be profitably produced by capitalist agriculture, this policy helped to optimize the reproduction scheme of Colombian capitalism.[3] But under these limits, the decomposition of the lower peasant strata proceeded unabated. Although the land struggles and colonization may have compensated for peasant dissolution during the 1960s and 1970s, the prospects for the 1980s remain obscure. First, the ebb of the struggle for land and the victory of the landowning interests at the level of state policy seem to have ended the possibility of any further land redistribution. Second, the existing studies and the evidence gathered by this research indicate that the colonists have been affected by rapid differentiation and land concentration, that a large proportion of them have been unable to consolidate their holdings, and that migration has begun to empty the main colonization areas.[4] Altogether, then, the prevailing tendencies show that the class struggles waged by ANUC failed to modify the patterns of agrarian development to the advantage of the peasantry. Peasant participation in total agricultural production fell from 61.3 percent in 1960 to 44.1 percent in 1981,[5] the process of peasant dissolution was only partially checked, and only some of the stable, well-to-do peasants improved their position. Given this evidence, and as a tentative assessment of ANUC's significance, it can be concluded that the *usuarios'* episode represented the accumulation of strength, the confrontation, and the defeat of the peasant movement in its attempt to obtain a democratic, and nonmonopolistic form of agrarian evolution under Colombian capitalism.

This tentative interpretation invites further research and requires additional empirical support. Since this work has dealt mainly with the areas of land struggle, a detailed analysis of ANUC's performance on the other battlefronts is still needed to draw more definitive conclusions. Furthermore, regional studies in the different battlefronts are essential, not only for a better understanding of the background and development of the peasant struggles, but also for a more precise assessment of the changes due to the struggles themselves and to other relevant socioeconomic processes. Macro-level statistical analyses, for example, should be related to local case studies in order to substantiate, with more solid evidence, the arguments advanced in this work on such issues as the assimilation of marginal repeasantization within capitalist development in agriculture at the regional level.

Turning from the structural perspective to the two other sets of analytical problems that have guided this research, it is worthwhile to make some final comments and raise a few of the many issues for further investigation. Regarding the state and the policies of the dominant classes, the most outstanding element seems to be the line of historical continuity between ANUC's episode and the previous peasant struggles of the 1930s and the Violencia, struggles that were recently summarized by a leading Colombian scholar as situations where "the peasantry was mobilized as a political object but rapidly became a political subject that prompted the dominant classes to close ranks again in order to curb the pressure from below."[6] It has been argued in this work that the National Front overemphasized the definition of the state as a tool of the ruling classes. But the National Front was doubly rigid, because it was unable to absorb the demands of the subordinate classes and tried to freeze any expression of conflict between the classes and fractions of the ruling coalition. The mobilization of the peasantry by the reformist bourgeoisie was part of an attempt to circumvent the rigidity of the National Front in order to deal with the urgent socioeconomic and political problems of the late 1960s. However, as in the legend of the sorcerer's apprentice, this attempt set free ungovernable forces. The alteration of the basis of capitalist accumulation strengthened the opposition of the landowning class and led to the collapse of reformism as state policy. Further, the peasantry used its own class power, embodied in ANUC, to try to impose its own project of agrarian transformation on the dominant classes. The result was a direct confrontation between the radicalized peasants and a state that had reverted to a crude policy of repressive class domination.

Combined with the previous remarks on the cycle of the peasant movement, these reflections suggest that a special analytical effort is needed to determine the significance of the current clientelist phase of ANUC. Against the background of the state concessions and the general economic prosperity of the second half of the 1970s, the consolidation of some peasant sectors indicates that a new type of highly commoditized peasant economy is developing amid the slowly disintegrating *minifundia* structure.[7] It is relevant to establish whether, or to what extent, the submissive attitude that now prevails in the *usuarios'* organization is expressing the dynamics of this process. It appears that the clientelist realignment of ANUC since 1981 is shaping new functions of representation and mediation in which the prevailing interests are those of the better-off, more conservative peasants. Furthermore, since this clientelist realignment implies that the state is accommodating the interests of at least some peasant sectors, the process as a whole may be symptomatic of changes that are slowly redefining the role of the Colombian state as the restrictive legacy of the National Front begins to fade.

With regard to the third set of problems, centered on questions of politics and ideology in the peasant movement, there are some crucial points that require further treatment. This work has shown that the leftist political groups played a decisive role in ANUC's evolution. The *usuarios'* receptivity to the leftist influences was studied mainly in terms of the isolation of the peasantry and its search for allies. But the links with the left failed to develop into a worker–peasant alliance mainly because the leftist political parties and groups did not have substantial support among the working classes. Still, these links provided ideological elements that, at the beginning, helped to sustain the peasant offensive, especially the struggle for land. It seems useful to pursue this line of inquiry, paying greater attention to the organization of the movement and to other factors related to the specificities of peasant political participation. The heterogeneous class composition of ANUC, for example, created favorable conditions for a great deal of autonomy among the national leadership. This autonomy, in turn, seems to have been crucial in spreading the early revolutionary influences, because the leftist views of the militants and advisers were first internalized by the national leaders and only later diffused downward. This invites more research on ANUC's leadership elite and on the internal workings of the organization, factors that were only partially explored in this work. The influence of the Maoist orientation, here approached as the expression of an ideology that glorified the role of the peasantry in social change, must be studied in greater depth against the background of the Sino–Soviet split and the subsequent redefinitions of the Colombian left during the late 1960s and early 1970s. Further, it is of great historical interest to explain the factors that led to a leftist and not a populist radicalization of ANUC: In 1970 the *usuarios* helped the dominant classes to contain ANAPO's electoral challenge, and the split between the radicalized peasant movement and urban populism is particularly puzzling when one considers the dramatic political consequences that could have followed from an eventual link between these two forces. Indeed, since successful modern revolutions have always shown the crucial importance of broad alliances involving peasants, workers and other subordinate classes, the isolation of the peasantry in Colombia seems to go a long way toward explaining the defeat of ANUC. It also calls for further research on Colombia's ANAPO within the context of the more general problem of populism as a distinctively urban political phenomenon in twentieth-century Latin America.

Regarding ANUC's break with the left and the launching and failure of an autonomous peasant party with proletarian leanings, this process has been interpreted here as a result of the weakness of the working-class movement, the unsubstantiality of the presumed worker–peasant alliance in Colombia, and the entrenchment of an "independent" leftist elite in ANUC's national leadership. These factors had a pervasive influence on ANUC's leftist politicization, leading to recurrent attempts to monopolize the peasant movement and creating favorable conditions for political vanguards who tried to channel the peasants' belligerency into an illusory revolution. Given the isolation and radicalization of the movement, the peasant leaders and political activists were able to inject revolutionary notions, but these notions ignored the real consciousness of the peasants and distorted their demands by subordinating them to a proletarian outlook. This highlights the thorny task of evaluating the effects of the great influence exerted by the left in Colombia's countryside during the 1970s. In general, this work has shown that after boosting the spirit of contention at the grass-roots level, the leftist politicization was crucial in the decline and final frustration of the *usuarios*. Still, special studies are needed to assess the long-term ideological changes. These studies should reveal to what extent permanent advances˙were made in promoting class consciousness among the peasants, but they should also appraise the disappointment caused by the negative experiences of the peasant movement with the left.

The contributions of this work and of any further research on the Colombian peasant *usuarios* will not be complete unless they include theoretical and comparative reflection. Although the current upsurge of empirical research and conceptual discussion has led to the development of sophisticated approaches to the study of the peasant economy and its reproduction in capitalist societies, little progress has been made in the field of peasant political participation. In Latin America, this situation is marked by the absence of comparative studies on peasant mobilization in different countries during the 1970s. Furthermore, the few existing case studies still seem to be trying to find a magic key to a presumed "revolutionary" or "conservative" essence of the peasantry. Perhaps the main contribution of this analysis of ANUC's development is that it shows the limitations of this approach to the problem. The oscillations of the movement through reformist, revolutionary, and conservative positions in less than a decade tell much about the complex nature of the peasantry as a class. The peasants strive to promote social relationships based upon the domestic rural economy, but this aspiration is manifested differently according to the class sectors involved and the historical and socioeconomic context. In some cases, the promotion of the peasant economy implies deep structural changes designed to establish or restore peasant farming. In other situations, it means preserving or improving an existing reality. The character of a peasant movement depends upon the broader structural processes that shape these situations. In this sense, ANUC's cycle clearly showed that the sociopolitical orientations and effectiveness of the peasantry can be understood only by reference to the way in which the historical context conditions the peasant aspirations through conflicts and alliances with other social classes or groups.

Coming now to more specific issues for future comparative study, two of them have already been mentioned: the class heterogeneity of the peasantry, which creates many different perspectives that any national peasant movement is forced to deal with and try to integrate, and the changing ideological definitions, which should be approached as expressions of the relativity that marks peasant political participation. An additional aspect highlighted by this research on ANUC, which has immediate relevance for other Third World countries, is the influence of the integrated rural development programs being carried out by many governments with the assistance of international financial capital. The indiscriminate use of such notions as "emergent peasant bourgeoisie" is clearly inappropriate for understanding the demobilizing effects of these programs. Although it is true that in Colombia the DRI program seems to have succeeded in coopting the better-off sectors of the peasantry, the downfall of the fighting spirit in the countryside was not due to a massive improvement in the socioeconomic conditions for peasant farming. For the vast majority of the peasants, the state programs are important because, with the social and political defeat of the peasant movement, marginal repeasantization and government concessions and palliatives are helping to sustain intermediate situations in the proletarianization process. Thus, any effort to understand the political meaning of these rural projects should take into account that their purpose goes beyond the reinforcement of conservatism among the peasants. This "therapeutic" treatment of potential sources of rural unrest is also designed to moderate pressures caused by the structural imbalance that prevails in societies in which the disintegration of the precapitalist forms of production is setting free more labor power than can be absorbed by the expanding capitalist economy.

To conclude, it is worthwhile to refer briefly to the prospects for change and for a democratic political opposition in Colombia's countryside. As suggested by the previous comments on the effects of the state programs, the social and political consequences of the victory of a monopolistic path of agrarian evolution are opening a new chapter in the country's rural history. The potential for rural unrest due to the marginality and poverty of much of the rural population is still there. The absence of political liberty due to the pressure of the clientelist power structures continues to be an aggravating factor. In the areas of previous land struggle, the delicate balance resulting from repression and the other demobilizing factors seems unlikely to hold for long. The general economic recession, the worsening situation of most *parceleros*, the crisis of capitalist agriculture in both Colombia and Venezuela, and even the ebb of the marihuana economy have altered the balance of the late 1970s and are creating favorable conditions for renewed expressions of social discontent. As a result of the past battles of ANUC, the Colombian peasants have undoubtedly learned much about the relationship between their immediate life conditions and the broader political dimensions of society. However, defeat and frustration led to a situation where conscious criticism has been overshadowed by a submissive realism that, as expressed by the reconstructed "official" ANUC, accepts and tries to make the most of the existing clientelist system.

Against this background, the first task of a sensible opposition is to restore the spirit of autonomy among the peasants. Since a new agrarian crisis seems to be brewing in Colombia, conditions appear to be favorable at first sight. Still, if the left wishes to play a role in future developments, much will depend upon learning the lessons taught by the defeats of the 1970s. Beyond the ideological controversy about the popular movement and the validity of the revolutionary strategies of the past, the most important lesson is that of the need to change the political approach of the Colombian left. The leftist failure of ANUC was not only due to the militants' shortcomings in understanding the social processes in the countryside. To a large extent, this failure was also a result of the negative influence of the two "practical schools" that have molded the political culture of the national left: the vernacular system of clientelist domination and the extreme vanguardism that has largely dominated socialist praxis in Latin America. This confluence of the less democratic traditions in both Colombian politics and the socialist movement in Latin America led to attitudes that favored an elitist style of leadership, substituted doctrinaire intolerance for free discussion, and ignored the opinions and feelings that prevailed at the grass-roots level. Behind these attitudes was an implicit view of the people's struggles as a vehicle for the attainment of goals in whose definition the people were not consulted, which reflected an underlying contempt for the rank-and-file peasants and led to an authoritarian handling of their demands. In a movement of transformation into its opposite, the legitimate representation of the peasant aspirations was overturned by the despotic manipulation of these same aspirations. It is hardly surprising that, in the last instance, this behavior would alienate the leftist leadership from the masses. The "vague consciousness" of the masses seems to resent manipulation, especially when the most deeply felt grievances are involved and the dearest hopes are at stake.

Notes

1. The agrarian question in Colombia

1. A full discussion of the agrarian question as a conceptual and historical problem is beyond the scope of this work. From the Marxist perspective, the agrarian transformations caused by capitalist development are analyzed in terms of prevailing systems of production in agriculture and the class structure that emerges in the countryside. However, much of the debate on this issue has been dominated by the assumption – deeply rooted in the writings of Marx, Engels, and Lenin – that agriculture was bound to develop along the same lines as industry, that is, that the expansion of commodity production would create conditions for a rapid demise of the peasantry and the consolidation of the capitalist mode of production. Since it was taken for granted that a capitalist agriculture would be the inevitable result, the agrarian question was formulated in terms of the whys, whens, and hows of the expansion of agrarian capitalism. The reductionist implications of this formulation were perceived by Kautsky, who, seeing the obstacles to capitalist agriculture and the persistence of peasant production at the turn of the century, defined the agrarian question more cautiously as follows: "*whether*, and *if so how*, does capitalism take hold of agriculture?" Taking into account the experiences of one more century of agrarian transformations throughout the world, this work approaches the agrarian question as an open issue, acknowledging that a peasant, noncapitalist agriculture is as much an alternative in capitalist society as agrarian capitalism itself. For the views of Marx, Engels, and Lenin on the agrarian question and the doom of the peasantry, see K. Marx, *Capital*, 1966, Vol. III, pp. 802–813; K. Marx, "The civil war in France," 1974, pp. 254–257; F. Engels, "The peasant question in France and Germany," 1968; V.I. Lenin, "New economic developments in peasant life," 1960; and V.I. Lenin, *The Development of Capitalism in Russia*, 1974, pp. 31–34. For a discussion of Marx's changing views on the subject, see T. Shanin, "Late Marx, gods and craftsmen," 1983. Kautsky's definition of the agrarian question has been quoted here from the Spanish translation of his *Agrarfrage*, *La Cuestion Agraria*, 1974, p. 12. For comprehensive reviews of recent theoretical debate and empirical research on the agrarian question, see D. Goodman and M. Redclift, *From Peasant to Proletarian, Capitalist Development and Agrarian Transitions*, 1981; and J. Harris (ed.), *Rural Development: Theories of Peasant Economy and Agrarian Change*, 1982.

2 . Some clarification is needed here with regard to the alternative paths of agrarian evolution. First, one should stress the crucial importance of access to land in the transition to a capitalist society. The predominance of a peasant agriculture requires a relatively even distribution of land among large numbers of producers. Conversely, concentration of landed property is necessary for agrarian capitalism, and it is for this reason that the capitalist pattern of evolution is here referred to as the "landlord path." Second, objections could be raised about the definition of the peasant and capitalist systems of production

---

All works cited in notes are listed in full in the Bibliography.

as the two fundamental alternatives of agrarian evolution in capitalist society. The short answer is that with the exception of slavery and labor-rent – which in the long run proved incompatible with capitalism – the peasant and capitalist forms of production have been the basis of almost all the systems of farming known in capitalist societies. In the cases of rent in kind, money rent, and sharecropping, the producers do not own the land; but production has always been undertaken either by subordinated peasants or capitalist entrepreneurs. Similarly, cooperative systems are usually based upon individual peasants or farmers who join together for specific purposes such as acquisition of inputs, use of machinery, and marketing processes. The collective agricultural systems, which could be conceived as an alternative to peasant and capitalist farming, have never been more than isolated social experiments of only marginal importance in the capitalist world. A third point concerns the definition of peasant farming. In this work, peasant farming is defined as a form of production characterized by (a) the use of family labor and the integration of production and consumption within the family unit, (b) the tendency to assert a socioeconomic rationality based upon the centrality of use values – which emphasize need and not profit, as in a capitalist enterprise, (c) the control of the labor process by the producers themselves, and, of course, (d) agriculture as the basic type of economic activity. Finally, the perspective adopted in this work differs significantly from the classic Leninist definition of the peasant and "junker" paths. For Lenin, these paths represented two different routes for the *development of capitalism in agriculture*, that is, an agrarian capitalism that evolved through proletarianization on large estates and an agrarian capitalism that developed through the differentiation of the peasantry into agricultural entrepreneurs and proletarians. Here, as explained in the previous note, the problem is approached in an open fashion. Agrarian capitalism, that is, an agriculture based upon wage labor, is not assumed to be a predetermined necessary result. The peasant and landlord paths are conceived as alternative forms of the *development of agriculture under capitalism*. In this sense, peasant differentiation is considered as a possible, but by no means necessary, outcome of the peasant path of agrarian evolution. The peasant path may also lead, for example, to a structure of modern farmers who use advanced technology but still continue to employ family labor, as is actually the case in most developed countries. For discussions on the specificity of peasant production, see A.V. Chayanov, "On the theory of a non-capitalist economic system," 1966; T. Shanin, "The nature and logic of the peasant economy: A generalization," 1973; and B. Galeski, *Basic Concepts of Rural Sociology*, 1975, pp. 9–13. For Lenin's classic argument on the peasant and junker paths, see V.I. Lenin, *The Development*, pp. 31–34.

    3. See, for example, the classic study of B. Moore, *Social Origins of Dictatorship and Democracy: Lord and Peasant in the Making of the Modern World*, 1966, and the more recent work by T. Skocpol, *States and Social Revolutions*, 1979.

    4. For a general discussion of these factors and the "models" of agrarian transition, see D. Goodman and M. Redclift, *From Peasant*, chap. 4.

    5. At the time of the Spanish conquest, there were six main Indian cultures in Colombia. The most important group, both in numerical terms and in complexity of social organization, were the Chibchas, whose settlements dominated the Cundinamarca and Boyacá Plateau in the eastern Andean range. For an introductory description of pre-Colombian economic and social life, see O. Fals Borda, *Historia de la Cuestión Agraria en Colombia*, 1975, pp. 1–8.

    6. For a discussion of the transportation problem and its effects upon foreign trade and the formation of the internal market, see J. Jaramillo Uribe, "Etapas y sentido de la historia colombiana," 1978, pp. 16–18.

    7. The Indian population in Colombia at the time of conquest has been estimated at 1.4 million. See O. Fals Borda, *Historia*, p. 1.

8. Ibid., pp. 63–66. See also O. Fals Borda, "Influencia del vecindario pobre colonial en las relaciones de producción de la Costa Atlántica colombiana," 1977.

9. In 1778, Vergara y Velasco estimated that there were only about 160,000 pure Indians left in the country. The distribution of the total population of 828,775 was as follows: whites, 24.7 percent; Indians, 19.7 percent; Negroes, 7.3 percent; and mixed descent, 48.3 percent. See T.L. Smith, "The racial composition of the population of Colombia," 1970, pp. 58–59.

10. For accounts of the introduction and decline of slavery in the mines and *haciendas*, see O. Fals Borda, *Historia*, pp. 37–40 and 57–61; P. Oquist, *Violence, Politics and Conflict in Colombia*, 1980, pp. 24–28; and M. Taussing, "Religión de esclavos y la creación de un campesinado en el Valle del Cauca," 1979.

11. According to the 1918 census, the Indians represented only 8.7 percent of the Colombian population. In 1963 the statistics of the Banco de la República indicated that this proportion had decreased further to just 2.2 percent. By contrast, the other Andean countries had the following percentages of Indians in 1960 and 1961: Ecuador, 30.4; Perú, 46.7; Bolivia, 63.0; and Chile, 31.8. See T.L. Smith, "The racial," pp. 58–59, and C.P. Roberts, *Statistical Abstract of Latin America*, 1968, pp. 686–688.

12. W.P. McGreevey, *Historia Económica de Colombia*, 1975, pp. 44–46. For a brief overview of the expansion and decline of gold mining by regions, see J. Jaramillo Uribe, "Etapas," pp. 19–22.

13. See W.P. McGreevey, *Historia*, pp. 101–102. For further discussion, see also L.E. Nieto Arteta, *El Café en la Sociedad Colombiana*, 1958, pp. 20–21; L. Ospina Vásquez, *Industria y Protección en Colombia*, 1974, pp. 298–301; and J.A. Ocampo, "Desarrollo exportador y desarrollo capitalista en el Siglo XIX, una hipótesis," 1979.

14. Some authors consider the nineteenth century as a period of economic decadence. See, for example, W.P. McGreevey, *Historia*, chap. 7. For a brief description of the main regions in that period, see D. Fajardo, "El estado y la formación del campesinado en el Siglo XIX," 1981, pp. 40–42.

15. This brief summary of the evolution of the agrarian structure out of the colonial system of land tenure and relations of production is based upon the following sources: J. Friede, "La evolución de la propiedad territorial en Colombia," 1971; M. González, "La hacienda colonial y los orígenes de la propiedad territorial en Colombia," 1979; O. Fals Borda, *Historia*, chaps. 3 and 4; and W.P. McGreevey, *Historia*, chap. 3.

16. See, for example, W.P. McGreevey, *Historia*, p. 52, and M. González, "La hacienda," p. 590.

17. On the colonization movements and the conflicting processes of peasant formation and expansion of extensive landed property, see the following sources: J. Villegas, "La colonización de vertiente del siglo XIX en Colombia," 1978; D. Fajardo, "El estado," pp. 50–53; O. Fals Borda, *Historia*, pp. 61–69; A. Tirado Mejía, "Aspectos de la colonización antioqueña," 1981. Villegas' work clearly marks the contrast between the results of the colonization processes in the eastern and western parts of the country. Still, like many other issues in Colombian socioeconomic history, this point requires more research for further clarification.

18. See, for example, J. Villegas, "La colonización."

19. For a discussion of the differentiation of the two political parties and their "land-owner" class content, see F. Leal, "Raíces económicas de la formación de un sistema de partidos políticos en una sociedad agraria: El caso de Colombia," 1980. See also A. Tirado Mejía, "Colombia, siglo y medio de bipartidismo," 1978, pp. 108–118.

20. On this continuity in the republican agrarian policy, see W.P. McGreevey, *Historia*, chap. 3.

21. For a discussion of the main cleavages between the parties during the nineteenth century, see A. Tirado Mejía, "Colombia," pp. 102–124.

22. The Colombian term *gamonal* is roughly equivalent to *cacique* in other Latin American countries; it means a political boss at the local or regional level. On the pattern of bipartisan politics during the nineteenth century, see P. Oquist, *Violence*, pp. 59–62.

23. For a general discussion of the radical Liberal period and the Conservative Republic, see A. Tirado Mejía, "Colombia," pp. 124–144. A fuller discussion of the Conservative Republic is provided by J.O. Melo, "La República Conservadora," 1978.

24. See W.P. McGreevey, *Historia*, chap. 8; M. Palacios, *El Café en Colombia*, pp. 18–27; A. Machado, *El Café, de la Aparcería al Capitalismo*, 1977, pp. 33–40.

25. On coffee production by peasants and *haciendas* in the western and eastern parts of the country, see M. Palacios, *El Café*, chaps. 4 and 9; A. Machado, *El Café*, chap. 4; M. Arango, *Café e Industria*, 1977, pp. 130–157.

26. R. Junguito et al., *Economía Cafetera Colombiana*, 1980, p. 30.

27. The best analysis of the relationship between coffee production, accumulation of capital, and investment in industry is M. Arango, *Café e Industria*. See also J.A. Bejarano, "El fin de la economía exportadora y los orígenes del problema agrario," 1975, pp. 260–272.

28. See W.P. McGreevey, *Historia*, chaps. 9 and 10; L.E. Nieto Arteta, *El Café*, pp. 22–28.

29. For a full discussion of the "great transformation" induced by the exporting economy, see J.A. Bejarano, "El fin."

30. See A. Tirado Mejía, "Colombia," pp. 136–140; P. Oquist, *Violence*, pp. 99–102.

31. On the struggles of the 1920s and 1930s in the coffee *haciendas*, see A. Machado, *El Café*, chap. 5; G. Gaitán, *Colombia: Las Luchas por la Tierra en la Década del Treinta*, 1976; H. Tovar, *El Movimiento Campesino en Colombia*, 1975.

32. For a general review of the peasant and Indian struggles in *haciendas, resguardos*, and colonization areas, see G. Sánchez, *Las Ligas Campesinas en Colombia*, 1977.

33. See J.A. Bejarano, *Campesinado, Luchas Agrarias e Historia Social: Notas para un Balance Historiográfico*, 1982, part 2.

34. See D. Mesa, "El problema agrario en Colombia: 1920–1960," 1976, pp. 98–106.

35. On rural and urban repression during this period, see A. Tirado Mejía, "Colombia," pp. 139–140; P. Oquist, *Violence*, pp. 89–102.

36. A. Tirado Mejía, "Colombia," pp. 144–155.

37. For a full discussion of Law 200 and its effects, see D. Mesa, " El problema," pp. 109–138. On land redistribution in the coffee *haciendas*, see G. Gaitán, *Colombia*, chap. 6.

38. On the multiclass nature of the traditional parties, see M. Solaún, "Colombian politics: Historical characteristics and problems," 1980, pp. 5–7; P. Oquist, *Violence*, pp. 78–79.

39. In Colombia, the original clientelist pattern was based upon the unequal exchange between the landowners and the subordinated peasants. Access to land was defined as a favor to tenants and sharecroppers, who had to reciprocate by working for the landowners, paying rent, and showing political loyalty during the elections and the civil wars. Although the landowners themselves were usually the *gamonales* or political chiefs, in many cases political mobilization was left to specialized "lieutenants" who appeared as the formal party leaders. With the consolidation of the state, the position of the *gamonales* as mediators between the communities and the central authorities enabled them to include the services provided by the state among the favors traded through the patron–client relationship. In the areas of peasant economy, the *gamonales* were usually merchants or rich peasants who

cultivated their clienteles at the local levels and were, in turn, subordinated to the hierarchy of regional party bosses. For descriptions of the structures of clientelism in areas of *latifundia* and *minifundia*, see A. Reyes, *Latifundio y Poder Político*, 1978, pp. 113–122; O. Fals Borda, *Peasant Society in the Colombian Andes: A Sociological Study of Saucío*, 1955, pp. 241–242. For a more comprehensive analysis of Colombian clientelism, see N. Miranda and F.E. González, *Clientelismo, "Democracia" o Poder Popular*, 1976.

40. A. Tirado Mejía, "Colombia," p. 144.

41. F.E. González, *Pasado y Presente del Sindicalismo Colombiano*, 1975, chap. 3. See also A. Tirado Mejía, "Colombia," pp. 158–159.

42. Ibid., pp. 166–168.

43. Ibid., pp. 162–165. See also P. Oquist, *Violence*, pp. 102–108.

44. On the rise of the Gaitanista movement, see J.C. Robinson, *El Movimiento Gaitanista en Colombia*, 1976, chaps. 3 and 4.

45. For accounts of the political processes that led to Liberal division, Conservative electoral victory, and Gaitán's consolidation as the undisputed leader of the Liberal Party, see M. Solaún, "Colombian politics," pp. 27–28; A. Tirado Mejía, "Colombia," pp. 168–169; P. Gilhodès, "Agrarian struggles in Colombia," 1970, pp. 422–424; J.C. Robinson, *El Movimiento*, chap. 5.

46. On Latin American populism, see F.H. Cardoso and E. Faletto, *Dependencia y Desarrollo en América Latina*, 1973, chap. 5; T. Di Tella, "Populism and reform in Latin America," 1969; G. Germani et al., *Populismo y Contradicciones de Clase en Latinoamerica*, 1973; O. Ianni, *La Formación del Estado Populista en América Latina*, 1975.

47. For a detailed account of the events that preceded the paroxysm of April 1948, see G. Guzmán et al., *La Violencia en Colombia*, 1962, pp. 25–33.

48. On Gaitan's assassination, its immediate political consequences, and the generalization of the Violencia, see J.C. Robinson, *El Movimiento*, chap. 8.

49. The best overall report on the civil war, by region, is still G. Guzmán et al., *La Violencia*. See chap. 2 for a detailed description of the first wave of the Violencia. P. Oquist's more recent study, *Violence*, provides a less detailed but much more analytical account based upon a structural regionalization that considers different types of underlying political and social conflicts in the Violencia. For a full discussion of the periodization of the civil war and the changing nature of the conflicts, see also J.A. Bejarano, *Campesinado*, chap. 3.

50. On this second phase of the civil war, see G. Guzmán et al., *La Violencia*, chap. 3, and J.A. Bejarano, *Campesinado*, pp. 62–63. Rojas Pinilla's populist project has not received the attention it deserves as a key link in the historical sequence that led from the Violencia to the National Front. For general discussions of Rojas Pinilla's military government, see A. Tirado Mejía, "Colombia," pp. 179–183; J.P. Martínez and M.I. Izquierdo, *Anapo: Oposición o Revolución*, 1972, pp. 15–19.

51. A. Tirado Mejía, "Colombia," p. 183.

52. For a detailed description of the terms of the National Front agreement, see H.F. Kline, "The National Front: Historical perspective and overview," 1980, pp. 71–72.

53. Ibid., p. 71. See also R. Gott, *Rural Guerrillas in Latin America*, 1970, pp. 288–289.

54. J.A. Bejarano, *Campesinado*, pp. 64–65.

55. See R. Gott, *Rural Guerrillas*, pp. 297–307.

56. See, for example, M. Solaún, "Colombian politics," pp. 40–41.

57. See, for example, O. Fals Borda, "Violence and the break-up of tradition in Colombia," 1969, pp. 197–198; E.J. Hobsbawm, "Peasants and rural migrants in politics," 1970, p. 52.

58. See, for example, P. Gilhodès, *La Question Agraire en Colombie*, 1974, pp. 16–17; S. Kalmanovitz, "Desarrollo capitalista en el campo," 1978, pp. 302–304.

59. See P. Oquist, *Violence*; J.A. Bejarano, *Campesinado*, chap. 3.

60. For recent discussions on the state in developing societies see H. Alavi, "State and class under peripheral capitalism," 1982; T. Shanin, "Class, state and revolution: Substitutes and realities," 1982.

61. See G. Guzmán et al., *La Violencia*, chap. 11.

62. For a general discussion of evidence on what could be called the multidirectional effects of the Violencia struggles, see J.A. Bejarano, *Campesinado*, pp. 67–70. See also the comments of F. Urrea, "Consideraciones sobre el tema de la Violencia," 1977.

63. D. Pecaut, "Reflexiones sobre el fenómeno de la Violencia," 1976.

64. See U. Campo, *Urbanización y Violencia en el Valle*, 1980; D. Fajardo, *Violencia y Desarrollo*, 1979.

65. For a discussion of substitutive industrialization in Latin America during the 1950s and 1960s, see F.H. Cardoso and E. Faletto, *Dependencia*, chap. 5.

66. R. Junguito et al., *Economía Cafetera*, p. 34.

67. On Colombia's foreign indebtedness during this period, see H. Rojas, "El Frente Nacional, solución política a un problema de desarrollo?", 1970, pp. 121–125. For statistics on Colombia's agricultural imports during the 1950s and 1960s, see S. Kalmanovitz, *La Agricultura en Colombia*, 1978, part 1, pp. 156–159.

68. The estimate is that of L.J. Atkinson, "Agricultural productivity in Colombia," 1970.

69. See, for example, T.L. Smith, "Improvement of the systems of agriculture in Colombia," 1970; J.M. Gutiérrez, "The green revolution marches on in Colombia," 1971; L.J. Atkinson, "Changes in agricultural production and technology in Colombia," 1969.

70. L. Currie, *Bases para un Programa de Fomento en Colombia*, 1950. See also, by the same author, "El problema agrario," 1976.

71. For a thorough criticism of Currie's theses, see B. García, *Anticurrie*, 1973; M. Arrubla, "La Operación Colombia o el capitalismo utópico," 1977.

72. See, for example, the arguments of C. Lleras Restrepo, "Estructura de la reforma agraria," 1961; R.A. Berry, "Farm size distribution, income distribution and the efficiency of agricultural production: Colombia," 1972; E. Haney, "Progressive deterioration of minifundia agriculture in Colombia: Structural reform not in sight," 1971; A.E. Havens and W.L. Flinn, *Internal Colonialism and Structural Change in Colombia*, 1970; R.J. Sandilands, "The modernization of the agricultural sector and rural–urban migration in Colombia," 1971.

73. See, for example, H. Vélez, "Difusión de la producción mercantil y de la tecnificación en la agricultura colombiana," 1976.

74. This estimate is based upon data provided by DANE, *Censo Nacional de Población*, 1951 and 1964.

75. For specific comparative data on population growth in the Latin American countries, see T.L. Smith, "The growth of population in Central and South America," 1970, pp. 42–45.

76. There are wide regional variations in what is considered to be the average size of a self-sufficient family farm in Colombia (i.e., farms whose size makes it possible to absorb the labor power of an average family). In the Andes and the inner valleys, it is considered to range between 5 and 50 hectares, while in the Atlantic Coast, Eastern Llanos, and colonization areas, the sizes are considerably greater. However, and using different methodologies, most authors agree on the 20-hectare limit when considering national data as a whole. Among the methodological discussions and justifications of the 20-hectare limit see, for example, Interamerican Committee for Agricultural Development, *Colombia, Tenencia de la Tierra y Desarrollo Socioeconómico del Sector Agropecuario*, 1966, pp. 3–4; H.

Vélez, "Difusión," pp. 298–308; J.V. Sanoa, "Campesinos pobres y semiproletarios," 1976, pp. 74–76.

77. See, for example, H. Vélez, "Difusión," pp. 308–311.

78. S. Kalmanovitz, *La Agricultura*, part 1, pp. 112 and 119.

79. Ibid., part 1, p. 89.

80. The following structural regionalization takes into account the *prevailing* agrarian patterns in the main geographic areas. It does not imply, of course, that the regions are *absolutely homogeneous* structurally or, conversely, that particular structures can be found *only* in certain regions. In working out a classification based upon regions and structures, this study departs from the usual approach that links the departments according to their geographical contiguity.

81. For descriptions of regional processes in some *minifundia* areas during the 1960s see, for example, O. Fals Borda, *Peasant Society*; J.E. Grunig, "The minifundio problem in Colombia: Development alternatives," 1970; E. Haney, "El dilema del minifundio en Colombia," 1972; L. Glass and V.D. Bonilla, "La reforma agraria frente al minifundio nariñense," 1967.

82. For a comprehensive review of the conditions in the different colonization areas during the late 1960s, see INCORA, *La Colonización en Colombia: Una Evaluación del Proceso*, 1973.

83. For regional studies on typical areas of *latifundia*, see E. Havens et al., *Cereté, un Area de Latifundio*, 1965; A. Reyes, *Latifundio*, chap. 2.

84. On capitalist agriculture in the inner valleys, see S. Ruiz, *La Fuerza de Trabajo en la Producción de Arroz y Algodón*, 1973; V.D. Bonilla, "El Valle del Cauca a la hora de su transformación agraria," 1967; T.L. Smith, "Improvement."

85. Up to the late 1960s, the only two nationwide peasant movements in Latin America had been those of Mexico and Bolivia, although significant regional movements had also developed in Brazil and Perú. See A. Quijano, "Contemporary peasant movements," 1967; H.A. Landsberger and C.N. Hewitt, "Ten sources of weaknesses and cleavage in Latin American peasant movements," 1970; E.R. Wolf, *Peasant Wars of the Twentieth Century*, 1969, chap. 1 on Mexico; G. Huizer and R. Stavenhagen, "Peasant movements and agrarian reform in Latin America: Mexico and Bolivia," 1974; C. Moraes, "Peasant leagues in Brazil," 1970; W. Craig, "The peasant movement of La Convención, Perú," 1969.

2. Reformism and the beginnings of the peasant movement

1.. In broad terms, reformism is the attempt to introduce changes that, without altering the foundations of a given socioeconomic structure, promote an improved and more egalitarian form of this structure. This definition follows Hobsbawm's distinction between revolutionary and reformist approaches in politics. See E.J. Hobsbawm, *Primitive Rebels*, 1965, pp. 10–12.

2. J. Vallejo, "Problemas de método en el estudio de la cuestión agraria," 1977, p. 94.

3. For a comparative comment on the agrarian reforms of Eastern Europe and Latin America, see A. Tobón, *La Tierra y la Reforma Agraria en Colombia*, 1972, p. 97. A thorough analysis of the Alliance for Progress policy is provided by J.P. Morray, "The United States and Latin America," 1968.

4. For a discussion of the arguments on agrarian reform and sociopolitical stability, see J. Vallejo, "Problemas," pp. 101–111.

5. On the continuing policy of support to capitalist agriculture, see J.A. Bejarano, "La economía colombiana desde 1950," 1978, pp. 74–78.

6. See the text of Law 135 in Ministerio de Agricultura, *Reforma Social Agraria en Colombia*, 1961. For a detailed account of the long negotiations that led to approval of the law, see E.A. Duff, *Agrarian Reform in Colombia*, 1968. See also A.E. Havens et al., "Agrarian reform and the National Front," 1980.

7. For a detailed analysis of the initial activities of INCORA, see A. Tobón, *La Tierra*, pp. 132–160.

8. For comparative generalizations on the conditions favoring the emergence of peasant movements, see H.A Landsberger, "Peasant unrest: Themes and variations," 1974; G. Huizer, *Peasant Participation in Latin America and Its Obstacles*, 1980.

9. INCORA, *Labores Adelantadas en Desarrollo Social*, 1971, p. 2.

10. For a detailed account of FANAL's origins, aims, and activities during the 1960s, see P. Gilhodès, *La Question*, pp. 288–295.

11. For a good analysis of Acción Comunal, see B. Bagley and M. Edel, "Popular mobilization programs of the National Front: Cooptation and radicalization," 1980.

12. INCORA, *Labores*, p. 3.

13. See, for example, O. Fals Borda, "Violence."

14. On the trade union movement under the National Front, see F.E. González, *Pasado y Presente*, chap. 5.

15. On the ELN, see R. Gott, *Rural Guerrillas*, pp. 308–320 and 348–355.

16. Ibid., pp. 306–307.

17. On the MRL, see P. Gilhodès, *La Question*, pp. 429–445. For a brief account, see R. H. Dix, "Political oppositions under the National Front," 1980, pp. 135–136.

18. The following sources were used for this review of the land struggles in southern Atlántico and adjacent areas: interviews 8, 10 and 11; P. Gilhodès, *La Question*, pp. 303–309; *El Heraldo*, January 8, 1964; *Diario del Caribe*, January 13, 1964; *El Informador*, October 17, 1964; *El Tiempo*, May 5, 1965, July 22, 1965; *La República*, April 14, 1965; *El Nacional*, May 7, July 22, July 26, December 7, 1965.

19. Sources on the Lower Sinú conflict: interviews 7 and 14; P. Gilhodès, *La Question*, pp. 296–303; *El Espectador*, January 5, 1962; *Diario de la Costa*, August 11, 1964; *El Tiempo*, February 19, 1966, August 29, 1967; September 13, 1969, January 26, 1970.

20. Sources on the banana zone conflict: interviews 13 and 14; *El Tiempo*, January 15, 1960, May 5, 1965, April 10, 1966, June 25, 1967, April 25, 1969, September 20, 1970; *El Espectador*, April 14, 1965; *El Siglo*, April 15, 1965.

21. Sources on the Middle Magdalena conflict: interviews 73 and 74.

22. Sources on the Casanare conflict: interviews 121, 122, 123, and 124.

23. Interview 14.

24. Sources: *El Tiempo*, March 21, 1963, August 6, 1965, November 8, 1966, June 19, 1968; *Vanguardia Liberal*, October 17, 1964; *El Espectador*, December 12, 1965, August 9, 1968.

25. Sources: *El Tiempo*, September 5, 1967, April 4, July 13, October 30, 1968; *El Frente*, January 27, 1964; *El Colombiano*, September 4, 1964; L. Glass and V.D. Bonilla, "La reforma," pp. 24–27 and 50–51.

26. Sources: *El Tiempo*, February 21, 1961, May 19, 1967; *La Voz de la Democracia*, June 20, 1963; *Occidente*, February 18, 1964.

27. Sources: *El Frente*, March 4, 1964, February 23, 1965; *El Espectador*, February 8, 1965; *El Tiempo*, March 19, 1966; March 26, 1967; *El Colombiano*, July 12, 1966; *La República*, August 17, 1969.

28. Sources: interviews 25, 70, 113, 114, 119, 120, 126, and 127.

29. For a general evaluation of comparative studies on peasant movements and a particularly illuminating comment on the issue of class alliances, see D. Lehmann, "Generalizing about peasant movements," 1973.

30. For a full discussion of the limits to substitutive industrialization in the mid–1960s, see J.A. Bejarano, "La economía," pp. 14–46.

31. Ibid., p. 91.

32. Ibid., pp. 38 and 62.

33. Ibid, p. 38.

34. As R. H. Dix has remarked, ANAPO was basically an urban phenomenon. Its leadership consisted of middle class Conservative and Liberal politicians who, disappointed with the National Front, were drawn to Rojas Pinilla's charismatic figure. Most votes came from the working class and the marginal slums of the major cities. Financially backed by many landowners, ANAPO opposed agrarian reform and made little effort to gain support among the peasants. The best account of ANAPO's short-lived career is R.H. Dix, "Political oppositions," pp. 140–164. See also J.P. Martínez and M.I. Izquierdo, ANAPO; M. Palacios, *El Populismo en Colombia*, 1971; P. Gilhodès, *La Question*, pp. 463–490.

35. In the 1966 election, ANAPO's Liberal candidate, José Jaramillo Giraldo, collected 742,133 votes. The Liberal Party, candidate, Carlos Lleras Restrepo, received 1,891,175 (C.A. Noriega, "Los resultados electorales y su significado político," 1979, p. 73).

36. For a detailed discussion of Carlos Lleras Restrepo's political career and the reformist currents in the Colombian dominant classes and the Liberal Party, see P. Gilhodès, *La Question*, pp. 217–235.

37. J.A. Bejarano, "La economía," pp. 117–119.

38. Ibid., pp. 93–95.

39. S. Kalmanovitz, "Auge y receso del capitalismo en Colombia," 1977, pp. 140–141.

40. C. Lleras Restrepo, "Estructura," p. 39.

41. Speech of President Lleras Restrepo at the inauguration of ANUC's First National Congress on July 7, 1970 (quoted from *El Tiempo*, July 8, 1970).

42. Further reference to the EPL will be made later in this work. For a general account of this armed organization see R. Gott, *Rural Guerrillas*, pp. 356–360.

43. B. Bagley and M. Edel, "Popular mobilization," p. 270.

44. For a specific discussion of Lleras Restrepo's role in the legislation of Law 135 of 1961 see P. Gilhodès, *La Question*, pp. 218–221.

45. By comparison with the 1962–1966 period, during Lleras Restrepo's administration INCORA started five times as many legal expropriations, involving twice the amount of land (INCORA, *Informe de Labores*, 1978, statistical series).

46. See the final text of Law 1 of 1968 in INCORA, Reforma Social Agraria: *Leyes y Decretos Reglamentarios*, 1975.

47. See Lleras Restrepo's letter to the members of the Operational Committee in Ministerio de Agricultura, *Organización Campesina*, 1967, pp. xiv–xv.

48. Ibid., pp. ix–x. The Operational Committee did not include any representatives of the federations of landowners and agricultural entrepreneurs.

49. Both reports were published in Ministerio de Agricultura, *Organización Campesina*, pp. 3–107.

50. Ibid., pp. 118–124.

51. FANAL originally resented the idea of a new semiofficial peasant organization. Lleras Restrepo dispelled the opposition by giving an advisory role to FANAL in the early days of ANUC's organization (interviews 57 and 112).

52. Lleras Restrepo issued a special decree to eliminate any doubts about a possible overlap between the functions of ANUC and Acción Comunal (see Decree 815 of 1967 in Ministerio de Agricultura, *Organización Campesina*, p. 125).

53. In the words of Mario Suárez Melo, the coordinator of ANUC's promotion cam-

paign: "There was a general feeling that it was the last opportunity to organize the peasantry. We didn't want to dissapoint the peasantry. . . . The small syndicates and the already bureaucratized FANAL and Acción Comunal had led to great frustrations. . . . That was why we decided to create a new movement, and not to promote the already existing organizations" (Fundación Mariano Ospina Pérez, "Actas de las reuniones entre líderes de las líneas Armenia y Sincelejo de la ANUC," 1980, part 1, p. 112).

54. Ministerio de Agricultura, *Organización Campesina*, p. ix.

55. Ibid., p. vii.

56. Ibid., p. 17.

57. Ibid., pp. 63–64. The "international commitment" was explicitly mentioned by the Operational Committee among the justifications for the creation of ANUC.

58. B. Bagley and M. Edel, "Popular mobilization," p. 271.

59. Fundación Mariano Ospina Pérez, "Actas," part 1, pp. 15–16.

60. C. Lleras Restrepo, "Estructura," pp. 41–42.

61. B. Bagley and F. Botero, "Organizaciones campesinas contemporáneas en Colombia: Un estudio de la Asociación Nacional de Usuarios Campesinos," 1978, p. 65.

62. Ministerio de Agricultura, *Organización Campesina*, p. vii.

63. Ministerio de Agricultura, *Campaña Nacional de Organización Campesina: Informe 1968*, 1968, p. 15.

64. Ibid., pp. 6–9.

65. Ibid., pp. 15–16.

66. Ibid., p. 17.

67. Ibid., p. 16.

68. Ibid., pp. 16–17.

69. Fundación Mariano Ospina Pérez, "Actas," part 1, p. 16. See also B. Bagley and M. Edel, "Popular mobilization," p. 272.

70. Ministerio de Agricultura, *Campaña Nacional de Organización Campesina: Informe 1969*, 1969, pp. 17–18.

71. Ibid., p. 17.

72. Ibid., pp. 9–10.

73. Ibid., pp. 10–11.

74. Ibid., pp. 18–19.

75. M. Suárez Melo, "Campaña nacional de organización campesina," 1969, p. 71.

76. The following description of ANUC's structure is based upon the statutes approved by the First National Congress of July 1970.

77. C. Lleras Restrepo, *Mensaje del Presidente de la República al Congreso Nacional*, 1967, p. 229.

78. Ministerio de Agricultura, *Resolución 061*, February 1968, Art. 19.

79. *El Tiempo*, October 24, 1969.

80. The first issue of *Carta Campesina* was published on February 15, 1970.

81. *Carta Campesina*, no. 8, 1970, p. 3.

82. See the list of ANUC's first National Junta Directiva members in *Carta Campesina*, no. 9, 1970.

83. Francisco Barrios, a peasant tenant from Sucre, had been active in Acción Comunal before participating in ANUC and reversing his original Conservative sympathies in support of Lleras Restrepo. Leonel Aguirre, a rich coffee peasant from Quindío, had a solid reputation as a zealous follower of the Liberal Party. Jaime Vásquez was a middle peasant with radical views, despite his Conservative origins and former involvement with FANAL in the department of Cundinamarca. Carlos Rico, from a family of agricultural laborers of Valle, had been working for a trade union organization with Christian Social

Democratic leanings. The comptroller of the Executive Committee, Félix Ramos, had participated in Acción Comunal but had no background of political involvement.
84. Interview 87. See also Fundación Mariano Ospina Pérez, "Actas," part 1, p. 85.
85. See, for example, Ministerio de Agricultura, *Manual de Instrucción para Promotores de Organización Campesina*, 1969.
86. Froilán Rivera, a sharecropper from Sucre who had previously participated in the MRL and later became one of the main radical leaders of ANUC, described his own election as follows: "Our promoter was an agronomist of Conservative origins. In 1968 he organized a course for the three municipalities of our area in Sucre. . . . He said that the movement had to be independent, and the peasants took his words seriously. Then came the fight against the *gamonales*. . . . They showed up at the election of the municipal association in San Pedro, but the promoter had repeatedly warned us and, as a result, I was elected along with other poor peasants" (interview 87). For similar accounts from Valle and Caquetá, see Fundación Mariano Ospina Pérez, "Actas," part 1, pp. 41 and 85.
87. M. Weber, "Politics as a vocation," 1958, pp. 78–79.
88. L.M. Killian, "Social movements," 1965, pp. 440–443.
89. In addition to the absence of outstanding charismatic leaders, there is also the problem of the large number of individuals involved. This research has estimated that there were between 75 and 100 regional *usuario* leaders of standing during the period under consideration. Of these, some thirty were directly involved, at different times, in the Executive Committee and the secretaries that handled the national affairs of the movement. Following the individual careers of all these leaders in this analysis would lead to unnecessary confusion. Therefore, relevant personalities are mentioned only in the notes, not in the main text.
90. In 1971, a DOC report indicated that "out of the more than 600 branches of the Caja Agraria throughout the country, only 219 have peasant representatives. In the other institutes of the agricultural sector the regional committees are not working, and when they do, the points of view of the *usuarios* are rarely taken into account" (Ministerio de Agricultura, "Memorando sobre el estado de organización campesina," 1970).
91.. Ministerio de Agricultura, *Organizacion Campesina*, p. 98.

3. The radicalization of ANUC and the great waves of land invasions

1. Victor Calle, the second director of the DOC, described the promoters' training as follows: "IICA and CIRA organized the courses. Some of those who came to teach brought the ideas of Pablo Freire, the theology of liberation, etc. . . . In practical terms, that led to radicalism, because social consciousness was developed. Later, these orientations would play a part in the peasant radicalization. . . . The courses influenced the promoters: within a month it was possible to see the transformation of their consciousness. At the end of the courses, IICA-CIRA and the Ministry selected those who displayed more commitment with the ideology of the course, and better skills of communication and leadership" (interview 33). In the words of one of the interviewed promoters: "In the training courses we received the theoretical concepts from IICA and CIRA. They were foreigners who created consciousness about the peasants' poverty. We were university people, middle-class professionals who assimilated the theory of social change and support to the peasantry. The movement was born on the basis of that ideology" (interview 108).
2. "The promoters were the first source of new ideas for the peasant movement . . . they talked about the agrarian problem and land concentration . . . saying that we had to

organize, defend ourselves and fight for our rights. They said we shouldn't let the traditional parties and the government demagogues manipulate us. . . . The promoters were progressive . . . they came with antioligarchic ideas and transmitted notions of independency to the peasantry" (interviews 37 and 87). See also Fundación Mariano Ospina Pérez, "Actas," part 1, pp. 41 and 85.

3. Interview 34. See also *El Espectador*, February 10, 1969.
4. Describing the background of a land invasion that took place in the wake of Lleras' visit to the Atlantic Coast, a peasant from Sucre recalled the reaction of his group: "Here the landowners were like kings, everybody respected them . . . we were afraid and nobody dared to protest. Then they stopped renting the land, and we had no way to get land to work . . . we organized ourselves and realized that it was possible to do something if we united. Lleras came here to say that there was an agrarian reform law and that we had to ask the landowners to negotiate their land with INCORA: it was then that we invaded" (interview 1). Similarly, in Córdoba: "We heard about the land invasions, and we launched our own. The President himself was giving the order to invade the *hacienda* and, since we were poor and didn't have a place to work, we decided to occupy the land that we needed in order to change our lives" (interview 103).
5. Interview 86; *El Tiempo*, March 14, May 5, 1969; February 25, February 26, 1970.
6. *El Tiempo*, September 13, 1969; February 26, June 13, 1970; *El Siglo*, May 23, 1970.
7. *El Tiempo*, October 22, 1969.
8. *El Tiempo*, May 30, July 1, 1970.
9. *El Tiempo*, May 14, July 17, 1970.
10. *El Tiempo*, January 17, January 24, 1970.
11. *El Tiempo*, November 22, 1969; May 12, May 23, 1970; *El Espectador*, May 16, 1970; P. Gilhodès, *La Question*, pp. 349–350. See also the peasant petitions published throughout 1970 in ANUC's journal, *Carta Campesina*.
12. On SAC's protests and the meetings between the *usuarios* and the presidential candidates, see P. Gilhodès, *La Question*, p. 350, and *El Tiempo*, October 24, 1969.
13. *El Tiempo*, February 14, 1970; *Carta Campesina*, no. 4, 1970.
14. ANUC: "Declaración de principios del Primer Congreso Nacional," 1970.
15. Francisco Barrios's opening address to ANUC's First National Congress, quoted in P. Gilhodès, *La Question*, pp. 350–351.
16. For a detailed analysis of the 1970 election results, see R.H. Dix, "Political oppositions," pp. 141–146.
17. See *Carta Campesina*, no. 6, 1970.
18. ANUC, "Declaración de principios."
19. Ibid.
20. Ibid.
21. Ibid.
22. Pastrana's promises to the peasants had been widely publicized in interviews, statements, and declarations in *Carta Campesina*, nos. 6, 7, and 8, 1970.
23. Interview 33. See also B. Bagley and F. Botero, "Organizaciones," p. 67.
24. *El Tiempo*, October 13, October 14, 1970; *El Espectador*, October 14, 1970.
25. *El Tiempo*, October 2, 1970; *El Espectador*, October 18, 1970.
26. As shown in Table 3.1, there were fifty-four land invasions in 1970. For newspaper accounts of some of these conflicts, see *El Tiempo*, September 10, September 24, October 16, October 21, December 10, 1970.
27. *El Tiempo*, October 13, 1970.
28. *El Espacio*, November 20, 1970.

29. *El Espacio*, November 29, 1970; *El Tiempo*, October 28, October 30, 1970.

30. *El Tiempo*, September 8, December 9, 1970.

31. *El Tiempo*, December 2, 1970.

32. *El Siglo*, November 28, 1970, January 18, 1971; *El Tiempo*, November 7, 1970; *El Espectador*, October 18, 1970.

33. *El Tiempo*, November 21, 1970.

34. *El Tiempo*, November 11, 1970.

35. Froilán Rivera described the polarization as follows: " In that first stage there were many clientelist regional leaders. . . . The contradiction sharpened and clashes developed at every meeting of the National Junta. There were reports showing that agrarian reform didn't move, and there were other reports about the successes of direct peasant action in some areas. With the polarization at the national level two lines became visible: the line that supported the government, the statutes, and the legal solutions to the peasant problem, and the line that proposed to ignore the regulations and resort to direct action to fulfill the goals" (interview 37). As Jesús María Pérez (another *usuario* leader from Sucre) has indicated, the two lines were represented within the Executive Committee of ANUC: "There were two factions in the Executive: those who agreed with the land seizures and those who didn't. Francisco Barrios and Jaime Vásquez supported the land seizures. Leonel Aguirre and Carlos Rico were against" (interview 86).

36. ANUC: "Apuntes sobre la historia interna de la ANUC," 1976, pp. 10–15.

37. For general accounts of the first days of the land invasions, see *El Espectador*, February 25 and 26, 1971. The 1971 struggles are studied in detail in the following section of this chapter.

38. ANUC: "Comunicado sobre las invasiones dirigido a los campesinos del país," 1971.

39. "The land seizures are the peasant response to the unjust distribution of the land and their inhuman situation of poverty and misery. . . . The landless peasants have been exploited for hundreds of years, betrayed in all the electoral campaigns, and forced to kill one another in the name of the blue and red banners of the oligarchy. . . . Knowing that agrarian reform is a farce, that the laws of the rich will never help the peasantry, that the land is idle while millions of Colombians are starving in unemployment, the peasants have decided to take away the land from the oligarchs and put it to productive use for the benefit of the people" (*Carta Campesina*, no. 15, 1971, p. 5).

40. ANUC, *Boletín Informativo* No. 23, February 1971.

41. ANUC, "Memorando de la ANUC para el Gobierno Nacional," 1971. See also *El Espectador*, February 26, 1971, and *Carta Campesina*, no. 15, 1971, p. 10.

42. ANUC, *Boletín Informativo* No. 23, February 1971. See also P. Gilhodès, *La Question*, p. 354.

43. Interview 33. See also *El Tiempo*, February 24, 1971.

44. Ministerio de Agricultura, "Correspondencia recibida e informes de promotores de Organización Campesina en los diferentes departamentos del país," 1970–1972. Many of the landowners' telegrams were absolutely hysterical, presenting the seizure of their properties as an assault against the highest interests of the nation. Some examples: "Citizens Cumaral clamorously ask intervention against invasions . . . government, motherland will not surrender to common enemy . . . your fellow countrymen, friends" (Meta); " . . . abuses invaders promote collective confrontations to exterminate proprietors . . . please save the motherland" (Santander); " . . . I beg you to intervene, authorities, give protection, guarantees, evict invaders, investigate incidents . . . your countryman" (Valle).

45. *El Tiempo*, January 24, 1971.

46. *El Espectador*, March 3, 1971.

47. *El Tiempo*, April 15, 1971.

48. Interview 33.
49. *El Espectador*, February 16, 1972. See also interview 33.
50. ANUC, *Plataforma Ideológica de la Asociación Nacional de Usuarios Campesinos*, 1971.
51. ANUC, *Primer Mandato Campesino*, 1971.
52. ANUC, "El problema agrario es un problema político," 1971.
53. ANUC, "Apuntes," pp. 16–18.
54. *El Espectador*, October 12, November 16, 1971; *El Tiempo*, October 13, October 14, November 4, November 11, 1971.
55. *El Tiempo*, November 2 and 4, 1971; *El Siglo*, October 4 and 12, 1971; *La República*, November 4, 1971; *El Espectador*, November 4, 1971.
56. *El Tiempo*, October 14, 1971.
57. CINEP's Archive on ANUC, referred to in the introduction to this work, contains a special section on land invasions. This section lists all the documented cases of peasant land seizures and resistance to eviction during the 1970s, including the available information on the dates and locations of the disputes, the names of the estates and the landowners, the origin and number of the peasant families involved, and other supplementary data. After repeated revisions to prevent possible mistakes caused by the use of several different sources, summary statistical tables were prepared to derive a quantitative picture of the land struggles. In addition to the interviews conducted as part of the research, the following sources were used in the process of data collection and analysis: INCORA, Archivo de Prensa, 1967–1979; CINEP, Archivo de Prensa, 1970–1980; C.E. Calderón and C.I. García, "Conflictos de clase que impulsan a la creación de la ANUC," 1973; appendix IV; H. Murle et al., "La lucha por la tierra: 1970–1978," 1979; ANUC, *Carta Campesina*, 1970–1980; H. Escobar Sierra, *Las Invasiones en Colombia*, 1972, statistical appendix; Ministerio de Agricultura. "Memorando sobre campesinos muertos o heridos por problemas de tierras," 1971; Ministerio de Agricultura, "Relación de invasiones en todo el país," 1971; Ministerio de Agricultura, "Invasiones en distintos lugares del país entre Junio 1 y Noviembre 15," 1971; Ministerio de Agricultura, "Datos correspondientes a ocupaciones de tierras en los últimos meses," 1971; Ministerio de Agricultura, "Correspondencia recibida "; A. Reyes, *Latifundio*, appendix I. In terms of methodology, it should be noted that the invasions were not the only expression of the struggle for land. There were many other patterns of action with similar significance, like the submission of petitions, demonstrations, and resistance to eviction. However, in addition to its methodological advantages in terms of obtaining and systematizing evidence, the land invasion as a type of incident was in itself an indicator of both the higher intensity of the conflicts and the greater propensity to take direct action at the grass-roots level. In this sense, only resistance to eviction can be equated with the land invasions in its intrinsic meaning. But in practical terms, the difference between these two situations dissapeared, because cases of resistance to eviction were usually defined as unlawful occupations and were therefore registered as land invasions by the press and the official reports.
58. This account of the conflicts in the banana zone is based on the sources listed in note 57, Chapter 3 (most relevant interviews: 12 and 13).
59. Sources on the conflicts in the Caribbean Littoral, as listed in note 57, Chapter 3 (most relevant interviews: 4, 6, 7, 8, 9, 10, 11, 12, 13, 14, and 136). See also A. Reyes. "El modelo campesino de empresas comunitarias," 1976, p. 12.
60. Sources on the conflicts in the western savannas as listed in note 57, Chapter 3 (most relevant interviews: 1, 6, 14, 15, 16, 19, 20, 23, 34, 37, 40, 76, 77, 86, 93, 96, 99, 101, and 136). See also M. Banquett, "Memorias de un líder de los usuarios campesinos," 1978; A. Reyes, *Latifundio*; ANUC (Bolívar), "Informe sobre la campaña de organización campesina en Bolívar," 1971.
61. Sources on the conflicts in the southeastern lowlands as listed in note 57, Chapter

3 (most relevant interviews: 12, 29, 30, 31, 32, 79, 80, 81, 82, 83, 84, and 136). See also A. Reyes, "El modelo," pp. 13–14.

62. Sources on the conflicts in the inner valleys as listed in note 57, Chapter 3 (most relevant interviews: 59, 60, 61, 62, 107, 108, 109, 110, 111, and 112). See also S. Ruiz, *La Fuerza; Carta Campesina*, No. 18, 1971, p. 2; and ANUC (Valle), "Conclusiones de la asamblea departamental de usuarios campesinos," 1970.

63. Sources on the conflicts in the areas of *minifundia* as listed in note 57, Chapter 3 (most relevant interviews: 35, 47, 55, 65, 71, 73, 74, 75, 138, 140, 141, and 142). See also CRIC, "Cómo nació el CRIC: primeras luchas," 1978.

64. Sources on the conflicts in the Eastern Llanos as listed in note 57, Chapter 3 (most relevant interviews: 119, 120, 121, 122, 123, and 124). See also the articles on Meta and Casanare in *Carta Campesina*, nos. 15 and 18, 1971.

65. Fundación Mariano Ospina Pérez, "Actas," part 1, p. 44.

66. DANE, *Censo Nacional Agropecuario*, 1970 (see Table 8.3).

67. See, for example, D. Fajardo, *Violencia*; U. Campo, *Urbanización*.

68. The Eastern Llanos have not been included in Table 3.4 because, given the mobile nature of guerrilla warfare in that area, all the municipalities were affected in one way or another during the Violencia.

69. Although the argument is not further developed in the present work, this seems to be an adequate perspective for establishing a clear line of continuity between the battles of the 1970s and the previous history of land struggle and peasant formation in the country.

70. See, for example, *El Espectador*, February 25, 1971; M. Banquett, "Memorias"; R.E. Soles, "Rural land invasions in Colombia," 1974, pp. 45–64; and A. Reyes, *Latifundio*, pp. 155–159.

71. "The term 'rural land invasion' often, at least in the press or in popularized notions, conjures up some image of organized *campesinos* under a (red) banner engaged in a pitched battle, surrounding the owner's house, forcing him to flee, and leave behind his fields, cattle, belongings, etc. Such is not the case in Colombia. Land invasions and the ensuing conflicts do not take place over entire *haciendas*. Those studied, and others briefly investigated, always concerned only one part or section of the *latifundio*" (R.E. Soles, "Rural land invasions," p. 46).

72. The testimony of local peasants illustrates these vicissitudes and results of the land invasions. An *usuario* leader from Sucre, for example, described a typical seizure as follows: "At first, the landless peasants study the situation with their relatives, friends and neighbors. They know that the problem must be solved here, in our own land, and not by going to work to Venezuela. . . . They organize a committee and start gathering money to buy the seeds, tools, etc. Then they look for an adequate land, an *hacienda* with more hectares than those that the owner needs to survive. . . . They ask INCORA to intervene and buy the land. . . . After a while, they invade the *hacienda*. Then comes the repression: the landowner brings the police or the army. They put the peasants in jail and destroy the crops. When the peasants are freed, they invade again, and so on. . . . It may take months and even years, but they always get something" (quoted in A. Reyes, *Latifundio*, pp. 155–156). A group of peasants interviewed in Montería (Córdoba) said that, in order to get the land, "we organized the committee and started to meet. There was demagogic support from the government and, with the help of ANUC and INCORA, we invaded this land. At the beginning, we were only a few. We came in and they evicted us. After six months we came again and, from then on, every time that the police evicted us, we would return. There was no violence. They always jailed two or three of us, but later they would let the prisoners go. . . . The landowner was bored: he had to pay the policemen again and again, and we would always come back. Finally, he called INCORA and said

that he would give us 1,100 hectares" (interview 16). In Guamo (Tolima), "we formed the committees and decided which land would be invaded, when the invasion would be carried out, what kind of supplies we had to take with us, and what kind of tricks we would play on the police and the army should they come. Then we moved in and received the support of other peasants from the outside. . . . We got this land as a result of the invasions that took place in the area: The landowner was afraid and decided to give to INCORA two portions of his estate for peasant settlement" (interview 109).

73. "Another characteristic of the invasions concerns the relatively small number of people involved in each group. As mentioned, the invasion did not follow a scenario of hordes of displaced land-hungry *campesinos* surrounding an entire *hacienda*. Rather, most of the cases studied consisted of only about 33 families, the largest single group numbered 62 and the smallest only 4 families" (R.E. Soles, "Rural land invasions," pp. 47–48).

74. "According to the interviews, the invasion committees are generally formed by families that are related by kinship and live in adjacent regions. The peasants do not go outside the municipality in which they have their relatives, friends and acquaintances. Evidence on the kinship networks can be also found by analyzing the lists of the members in the new settlements as they appear in INCORA's archives" (A. Reyes, "El modelo," p. 28).

75. In a marginal coffee area of Caldas, for example, "the sharecroppers of the *haciendas* rebelled against their bosses. . . . Since they belonged to the same families, it was easy for them to organize, put pressure and avoid eviction" (interview 141).

76. See, for example, the detailed demands of the peasants of Sucre in ANUC (Sucre), "Campesinos organizados de Sucre presentan plan para solución inmediata en empresas comunitarias," 1971. In Huila, where a list of estates had been prepared by the *usuarios*, "the land invasions of 1971 shattered the public opinion. There were simultaneous seizures throughout a number of municipalities. . . . The best land was invaded on several occasions . . . they re-occupied the estates until agreement was reached with INCORA on timetables for the negotiations" (interview 60).

77. "After we won the battle, we kept helping the other committees, giving orientation and economic support so that they would be able to fight" (interview 109). "During the struggle, the comrades receive help from other peasants who have already got land and give them plots for subsistence crops" (quoted in A. Reyes, *Latifundio*, p. 156).

78. An INCORA official from Córdoba recalled that in the early waves of land invasions "we worked freely in tandem for the land seizures. There was coordination between ANUC and INCORA: the peasants invaded and INCORA moved in. Some of INCORA's employees worked as spies for the peasants" (interview 20). The Conservative press repeatedly denounced the involvement of INCORA's officials in the land invasions: see, for example, *El Siglo*, November 28, 1970.

79. Peasants from Córdoba, for example, recalled that "three days after the invasion they evicted us. They brought cars and took us to the town. There, we received the support of the popular sectors like the teachers, students and small merchants. We were never alone, they helped us with food and mobilized people to demand our freedom" (interview 89). In general, "many land invasions were planned to coincide with urban strikes by syndicates. Progressive priests, students and trade unions helped in the land seizures" (interview 148). For other comments and examples of regional solidarity, see interviews 2, 19, 76, and 92.

80. "*Compadrazgo* between the landowners and the peasants was very common. The landowner had at least one godson in every family. The relations were not too reverential, but rather informal. . . . The *corralejas* were also very closely related to the work relations, because the contracts were negotiated during the festivities. Every landowner had his box and distributed tickets for the stands. He paid for the music band and provided food.

... Before the elections the landowner collected the identity cards, which he returned to the peasants on election day along with the ballot they had to cast" (interview 136).

81. An activist of the Socialist Bloc described this process in the Atlantic Coast: "what had started as a heterogeneous organization saw the rapid rise of the poorest peasant sectors. . . . The Atlantic Coast was the region most affected by the land invasions. It was there where the peasants were the poorest. They were tenants and sharecroppers . . . peasants without land. That was the most radical area, and the struggle promoted the most radical peasants as leaders . . . ANUC leaders in those areas were people who had invaded the land. In many associations the first leaders had been rich peasants, political brokers, etc. They were rapidly displaced by the radicals. By 1971 a substantial part of the old leaders had been replaced" (interview 34).

82. "When the political forces came to ANUC, there was no resistance at all. They were helped, they were taken to the local committees. . . . We facilitated their entry. Everybody wanted to study, read revolutionary theory, pamphlets, etc." (interview 87).

83. A regional leader of ANUC in Saravena (Arauca) recalled: "INCORA fulfilled all the roles of the State: it gave the land titles to the colonists, it built the infrastructure, schools, etc. It worked as a Ministry of Public Works, Health, Education, etc. That by itself helped to focus all the grievances against INCORA" (interview 127).

84. Interviews 53, 126, and 127. See also *Carta Campesina*, no. 21, 1972, p. 4; ANUC (Arauca), "Informe de la región del Sarare," 1974.

85. Interview 114. See also Fundación Mariano Ospina Pérez, "Actas," part 1, pp. 48–53; *Carta Campesina*, no. 22, 1972, p. 9; *El Periódico*, July 12, 1972; *El Tiempo*, July 15, 1972; *El Espectador*, July 16, 1972.

86. Interviews 25, 26, 45, and 120.

87. Talking about the peasants' radicalism in the colonization area of Caquetá, a promoter said that "ANUC was strong and very successful at the beginning. . . . The issue was not the landowners. The problems had to do with being able to stay on the land, getting credits, services, support for agricultural production. . . . The main features of the struggle were civil strike, seizure of towns, demonstrations. . . . There is a lot of difference with other regions. The people is active and hates the army. They don't have a consciousness of stability, they are easily drawn to fighting. . . . The area was colonized by peasants expelled by the Violencia . . . many of them had been guerrillas or bandits" (interview 70).

88. On peripheral location as a factor in peasant political mobilization, see E.R. Wolf, "On peasant rebellions," 1971, pp. 270–271.

89. Interviews 114 and 127.

90. Interview 37.

91. A *usuario* leader from Nariño compared the attitudes in the *minifundia* areas with those in the areas of land struggle as follows: "Here in Nariño the people is generally passive. They believe a lot in tradition and religion. Their very way of thinking restrains them. By contrast, the coastal people are more dynamic, they are not passive. Since there are many colored people, they have the idea that they were brought from Africa as slaves, which makes them angry and daring. . . . On the other hand, Nariño is a *minifundia* region; most of the people have their plots of land. It is very different in the Coast, where there are large *haciendas* and the peasants are crowded on the sides of the roads. They have to fight in order to till the land" (interview 85).

92. Interview 44.

93. Interview 138. See also *Carta Campesina*, no. 25, 1973.

94. On the Indian movement in Cauca see CRIC, *Diez Años de Lucha: Historia y Documentos*, 1978. For additional data and specific references to CRIC's relationships with ANUC, see also interviews 35, 36, 53, 55, 65, and 116.

4. Counterreform

1. *El Siglo*, September 8, 1971. On the parliamentary debates of September 1971 and Jaramillo Ocampo's intervention, see *El Espectador, El Tiempo, El Siglo*, and *La República* of September 17, 1971.

2. *El Siglo*, October 23, November 10, 1971.

3. Sociedad de Agricultores de Colombia, "Los gremios agrícolas y las invasiones," 1971. See also *La Patria*, October 12, 1971.

4. *El Tiempo*, November 25, 1971; *El Espectador*, November 25, 1971.

5. *El Siglo*, December 8, 1971.

6. See the text of the Declaration of Chicoral in *El Tiempo*, January 10, 1972. See also S. Kalmanovitz, "Desarrollo," pp. 314–315.

7. *El Siglo*, January 21, 1972; *El Espectador*, January 10, 1972.

8. *El Tiempo*, January 11, 1972; *El Colombiano*, February 4, 1972.

9. *El Tiempo*, January 31, 1972; *El Siglo*, January 31, 1972.

10. *El Siglo*, January 21, 1972; *El Espectador*, February 4, 1972; *La República*, February 4, 1972.

11. See the scornful comment on the "demise" of reformism in the Conservative newspaper *El Siglo*, January 28, 1972.

12. On Lleras Restrepo's 1978 bid, see L.C. Galán, "Las elecciones de febrero y junio de 1978," 1979.

13. For general studies on the changes in the Colombian model of capitalist accumulation, see J.A. Bejarano, "La economía"; S. Kalmanovitz, "Auge."

14. J.A. Bejarano, "La economía," pp. 95–108; S. Kalmanovitz, "Auge," pp. 143–146.

15. J.A. Bejarano, "La economía," pp. 112–113.

16. See the second section of Chapter 1. Consult also J.A. Bejarano, "Currie, diagnóstico y estrategia," 1978; S. Kalmanovitz, "Desarrollo represivo acelerado," 1977.

17. Departamento Nacional de Planeación, *Las Cuatro Estrategias*, 1972.

18. *La República*, September 7, 1971; *El Tiempo*, December 27, 1971.

19. ANUC, "Conclusiones de la V Junta Directiva de Tolú sobre el Acuerdo de Chicoral y el proyecto de contrarreforma presentado por el Gobierno Nacional," 1972.

20. "After the Minister personally read and sustained the project, the proposals were discussed. When we demonstrated to Mr. Jaramillo the real essence of his inventions, he had no option but to admit that he was himself a landowner and that he was defending the interests of his class. He said that he understood the contradiction but, since he had been appointed by the landowners, his duty was to defend their interests and power. Trying to pose as a 'great statesman,' he said that in a class society there would always be an antagonistic struggle between the exploited and the exploiters. He even 'recognized' that his famous project would not solve the land problem. . . . At the end of the debate, when he occupied his seat in the official Mercedes Benz, we threw into his car all the copies of the documents that he had so 'kindly' brought to us" (ANUC, "Apuntes," p. 18).

21. ANUC, "Conclusiones de la V Junta Directiva de Tolú sobre la posición política de la ANUC frente al debate electoral," 1972.

22. According to Carlos Rico, there were two positions among the loyalists: "One group (Leonel Aguirre and others) idolized Lleras Restrepo, saying that he had given the peasants the opportunity to organize. They argued that the organization could achieve its goals working through the parties and participating within the party game. . . . We considered that the organization had to be independent from the parties, but not an independence based on confrontation. We had to keep our autonomy and conquer a moral

authority that would enable us to say what was right and what was wrong" (Fundación Mariano Ospina Pérez, "Actas," part 1, pp. 88–89.

23. José del Carmen Yepes, a Conservative middle peasant from Huila and one of the most outspoken opponents of the leftist influences within ANUC, gave the following version of the loyalists' exit: "All the talk was about politics, about the use of abstentionism as a weapon. . . . They said that the peasant movement would not be possible without a communist, Marxist ideology: a copy of Cuba. . . . I gave a six-hour debate and finally proposed that, in view of the situation, those who opposed the Executive Committee should withdraw. . . . That was, unfortunately, the split of the Colombian peasant movement" (interview 112).

24. *El Tiempo*, February 9, 1972; *La República*, February 10, 1972.

25. "After being rejected in Tolú by the peasants, the minister immediately sought support within ANUC. He had many cues: For example, the movement had decided to stop sending delegates to the state agencies, but Leonel Aguirre and Carlos Rico didn't leave their seats at the boards of INDERENA and INCORA. The minister also knew who was against the land invasions. With these leaders, they started to promote parallelism and divide ANUC" (interview 148). In addition to Leonel Aguirre, Carlos Rico, and the already mentioned José del Carmen Yepes, the two other loyalist leaders who had had some standing in ANUC's National Junta were Higinio Patiño (Tolima) and Dagoberto Barros (Atlántico).

26. On the DOC purge see *La República*, February 19, 1972; *El Tiempo*, June 9, 1972. See also interview 33 and ANUC, "Conclusiones de la V Junta Directiva de Tolú sobre persecusión a funcionarios progresistas," 1972.

27. *El Siglo*, July 5, August 14, 1972; *El Periódico*, July 17, 1972; *El Tiempo*, July 20, 1972. See also ANUC/Armenia, "Acta del precongreso reunido en la ciudad de Neiva," 1972.

28. *El Tiempo*, November 25, 1972; ANUC/Armenia, *Segundo Congreso Nacional de Usuarios Campesinos*, 1972.

29. The Lleristas and independents were the main victims of the purge, including Leonel Aguirre, Carlos Rico, and Higinio Patiño. Only José del Carmen Yepes and Dagoberto Barros remained as leaders of ANUC Armenia. See *El Periódico*, November 21 and 24, 1972; Fundación Mariano Ospina Pérez, "Actas," part 1, pp. 106–108.

30. Interviews 62, 108, and 109.

31. José del Carmen Yepes described the problems faced by ANUC Armenia after the split: "Our delegates were authentic peasants but, unfortunately, they didn't have guts. . . . They couldn't present coherent ideas or define policies for the peasant movement. To be frank, that type of leadership had stayed with the radicals. . . . From then on, it was like a nightmare. . . . We were the 'renegades,' the 'puppets,' . . . the 'mercenaries.' And the truth is that we suffered a terrible disappointment. We supported the government, we obeyed the instructions not to lead the movement to a war against the government, and despite all that, the government failed to reward us. They simply didn't support us. Our participation on the boards of INCORA, Caja Agraria and the other agencies was too weak. They didn't pay attention to our opinions, the peasants were still suffering the consequences of abandonment, and agrarian reform was in fact moving backwards after the Pact of Chicoral" (interview 112).

32. On the Second Congress in Sincelejo, see *El Periódico*, August 1 and 4, 1972; *Carta Campesina* no. 22, 1972, pp. 2–4. See also ANUC, *Tierra para Quien la Trabaja! Conclusiones del II Congreso Nacional de Usuarios Campesinos*, 1972.

33. On the influence of the Communists in Cundinamarca and MOIR in Casanare, see interviews 121 and 148.

34. Francisco Barrios and Jaime Vásquez, of ANUC's First Executive Committee, were

reconfirmed in their posts. The new members of the Executive were the already mentioned Froilán Rivera, Noel Montenegro (Caldas), and Antonio Poveda (who had been one of the main organizers of the civil strike in Caquetá). Among other relevant leaders of ANUC Sincelejo were Juan de Dios Torres (ANUC's secretary and treasurer, from Boyacá), Jesús María Pérez (Sucre), Jose Reyes Prado (Nariño), Víctor Pastrana (Caquetá), Clovis Flores (Córdoba), and Carlos Alméciga (Cundinamarca).

35. *Carta Campesina* no. 18, 1971, pp. 1 and 7.

36. The first municipality to experience military intervention was Chimichagua (Cesar), where the minister of agriculture, Jaramillo Ocampo, had his own estates.

37. A journalist referred to the *pájaros* (literally, birds) as follows: "For most of the Colombians, the word '*pájaro*' does not mean just fowls and feathers. The term is also associated with violence and political assassination. '*Pájaros*' were the professional gunmen and thugs employed by Conservative politicians and landowners in order to eliminate popular Liberals, particularly peasants, during the war between the two traditional parties. . . . This institution, the '*pájaros*,' has been perpetuated, and it is taking a growing toll of victims among the organized peasants. Following the intensification of the peasant struggles and the land invasions, there has been a considerable increase in the numbers of '*pájaros*' at the service of the landowners. . . . These armed bands try to intimidate the peasants by means of harassment, threats and assassinations" (*Alternativa*, no. 28, 1975, p. 12).

38. *El Tiempo*, February 13, 1973; *El Siglo*, March 7, 1973.

39. The peasant marches made the headlines of the national press during the first half of September 1972. On the marches' repression, see *El Siglo*, September 6, 1972; *El Tiempo*, September 7, 1972; *El Periodico*, September 2, 6, 11, 13, and 15, 1972. See also ANUC, "Carta abierta de la ANUC para las autoridades del estado," 1972.

40. Interviews 108 and 112.

41. Interviews 4, 11, 13, 34, and 72.

42. On ANUC's activities throughout this period, see *Carta Campesina* nos. 20–25, 1972 and 1973.

43. Sympathetic officials who tried to help the peasants were also severely punished. In Santander, for example, "there were riots in San Vicente del Chucurí. The peasants closed all the entrances to the village because some sharecroppers had been jailed after resisting eviction. Two INCORA functionaries who had helped the peasants went to jail. Seeing the government's reaction, INCORA's employees never got involved again" (interview 145).

5. The contradictory influences of peasant politicization

1. On the number of families registered in 1970, see *Carta Campesina*, no. 19, 1971, p. 15. Sources of the estimates on access to land: INCORA, "Proyecto Sucre," 1975; INCORA, "Proyecto Sucre, desarrollo y programación de cultivos transitorios y permanentes," 1975.

2. Regarding these organizational imperatives, see ANUC, *Tierra para Quien la Trabaja*, pp. 33–34.

3. Ibid., p. 35.

4. In addition to Fals Borda, the main figures of La Rosca were the historian Gonzalo Castillo and the anthropologists Augusto Libreros and Víctor Daniel Bonilla. Defining themselves as "scientific cadres actively involved in the Colombian revolutionary process, who contribute their work to the popular organizations," these social scientists had formed the group in 1970. With financial support from the Presbyterian Church and European foundations, La Rosca was carrying out projects of "participant research-action" in eight

different regions. The techniques of participant research included critical publications, militant films, seminars for cadres, advice, and educational courses (E. Parra, *La Investigación-Acción en la Costa Atlántica: Evaluación de la Rosca*, 1983, chaps. 1 and 4). The ideological-political guidelines of La Rosca were outlined in O. Fals Borda et al., *Causa Popular: Ciencia Popular*, 1972.

5. Jesús María Pérez described the fiancial problem and the initial contacts with Fals Borda as follows: "The government had been financing all the activities: the National Juntas, the congresses, the educational courses, the salaries of the members of the Executive Committee, the newspaper, the office, the advisers, etc. After the break, the government withdrew the budget and financially strangled ANUC. . . . The left tried to help. . . . Fals Borda, who was active in the left, approached us, saying that it was possible to find resources and support in Europe. . . . He belonged to the Presbyterian Church and he had many friends among the European churches. . . . Fals was on the commission that went to Europe to ask for help. . . . They obtained finances for national activities of ANUC and for a regional program in Córdoba" (interview 86).

6. Putting together the information from the interviews and other sources, this research confirms that ANUC received the economic help of organizations from Holland, Belgium, Denmark, Switzerland, France, Sweden, Germany, and the United States. Typically, ANUC submitted proposals for specific projects (publications, meetings, courses, materials, equipment, help for the families of imprisoned leaders, etc.) to the prospective sponsors. Most of the elaboration of projects, contacts, and traveling was conducted by ANUC's treasurer, the already mentioned Juan de Dios Torres, who concentrated a great deal of bureaucratic power because of this activity.

7. ANUC, "Comunicado de la delegación holandesa al Tercer Congreso," 1974.

8. A substantial part of the conclusions of the Second National Congress was devoted to problems of credit, technical assistance, marketing, natural resources, and the specific problems of Indians and coffee and tobacco growers. See ANUC, *Tierra para Quien la Trabaja*.

9. Ibid., p. 27.

10. ANUC, "Conclusiones de la X Junta Nacional Ampliada," 1974.

11. ANUC, "Conclusiones de la VIII Junta Directiva Nacional," 1973; ANUC, Conclusiones de la IX Junta Directiva Nacional," 1973. See also *El Tiempo*, July 17, 1973.

12. The following sources were used in this review of the 1974 land struggles in Sucre: interviews 34, 37, 86, 87, 88, 100, and 137; *El Tiempo*, September 7, 1972, May 20 and September 4, 1973, February 4, February 24, March 5, April 2, 1972; *El Siglo*, September 6 and December 22, 1972, March 3 and 24, 1973; *El Periódico*, September 11, 1972; February 25, 1973, March 10 and 22, August 20, 1974; *El Espectador*, February 23, 1974; *Carta Campesina*, no. 24, 1973, p. 6; ANUC, *Boletín Informativo*, nos. 1 and 3, 1974; INCORA, "Proyecto Sucre, informe de actividades 1969–1978," 1978.

13. Sources on the Antioquia struggles: interviews 41, 47, 75; *El Siglo*, March 29, 1972; *El Colombiano*, February 7, 1974; *El Periódico*, February 15 and 25, March 22, September 13, 1974; *Alternativa*, nos. 4 and 9, 1974; ANUC (Antioquia), "Acuerdo campesino, conclusión reunión ampliada departamental," 1973; ANUC (Antioquia), "Informe ante el Tercer Congreso Nacional," 1974.

14. Sources on the Córdoba conflicts: interviews 7, 14, 15, 17, 20, 39, 40, and 92; *El Periódico*, August 16 and 17, 1972; February 15, September 4, 1974; *El Espectador*, February 1, 1974; *Alternativa*, nos. 1, 4, 5, 6, 8, and 15, 1974; ANUC (Córdoba), "Informe ante el Tercer Congreso Nacional," 1974.

15. Sources on CRIC and the Cauca struggles: interviews 35, 55, and 65; *El Periódico*, March 10, 1974; CRIC, "CRIC, análisis de su organización y sus luchas," 1978.

16. Sources on the struggles in Huila: interviews 61, 62, 63, 111, and 112; *Carta*

Campesina, nos. 24 and 25, 1973; *El Tiempo*, March 5, 1974; *El Periódico*, March 10 and 22, 1974; ANUC (Huila), "Comunicado del Comité de Solidaridad y Defensa de los Derechos Humanos," 1975; *Alternativa*, no. 4, 1974; ANUC, *Boletín Informativo*, no. 3, 1974.

17. Sources on the struggles in Cesar and Magdalena: *El Tiempo*, September 8, 1972, February 24 and 28, 1974; *El Espectador*, March 27, 1973; *El Periódico*, September 13, 1972, February 21, 1973, February 15 and 25, 1974, March 22, 1974; *Alternativa*, nos. 10 and 12, 1974; ANUC, *Boletín Informativo*, no. 3, 1974; ANUC (Magdalena), "Carta al Ministro de Gobierno sobre desalojos y represión," 1974.

18. Sources on the Guajira conflict: interview 29; *El Periódico*, March 10 and 22, 1974, May 1, 1974; *El Tiempo*, May 1, 1974; *Alternativa*, nos. 2 and 7, 1974; *Carta Campesina*, no. 28, 1974, p. 16; ANUC, "Boletín de prensa No. 3 sobre los desalojados de la frontera," 1974.

19. On the thorny relationships between ANUC and the Communist Party, see the following sources: interviews 24, 34, 40, 54, 86, and 115; B. Bagley and F. Botero, "Organizaciones," pp. 82–84; L.H. Sabogal, "Problemas de la organización campesina," 1976; *Carta Campesina*, no. 28, 1974, p. 5; *Alternativa del Pueblo*, nos. 21 and 22–23, 1974; *Carta Campesina*, no. 35, 1976, p. 2; ANUC, "Carta abierta a Gilberto Vieira, Secretario General del Partido Comunista," 1976; *El Tiempo*, October 28, 1976; Carta Campesina, no. 36, 1977, p. 9.

20. Regarding ANUC's differences with MOIR and the formation of OCIDEC, see interviews 87, 115, and 121; B. Bagley and F. Botero, "Organizaciones," p. 85.

21. One of the activists described the activities of the Socialist Bloc as follows: "Contact with ANUC had been made through individual militants who helped in the elaboration of the *Mandato Campesino*. . . . Then the Socialist Bloc formed an education committee that advised ANUC's Executive and organized courses in different parts of the country. ANUC wanted to train new leaders, explain the *Mandato*, etc. . . . Thus, our action in ANUC was of a propagandistic, educational nature. It helped the political radicalization . . . but we never managed to convert any of ANUC's national leaders into activists of the Socialist Bloc. There was no systematic attempt to form cadres of our own within the peasant movement . . . very little work was done at grass-roots level, and we never had our own peasant militants" (interview 34). Other sources on the Socialist Bloc, its origins, ideology, and relationship with ANUC: interviews 37, 54, and 87; B. Bagley and F. Botero, "Organizaciones," pp. 85–86; *Alternativa*, nos. 40 and 41, 1975; Socialist Bloc, "La situacion actual del movimiento campesino," 1973; Socialist Bloc, *Por un Partido Obrero Socialista: Tesis y Documentos del Bloque Socialista*, 1975.

22. A Maoist militant recalled that "the Bolshevization Campaign was much more than an educational campaign; it implied that everybody had to get directly involved with production and the masses. We had to go out to the factories and the countryside, but the emphasis was mainly on the countryside. In fact, many leaders were transferred from the cities to the rural areas. The peasants had priority because they were considered the main force of the revolution. The other tasks of the party, including the activity among the industrial workers, were considered as logistic support for the rural work among peasants and guerrillas. In 1973 it was estimated that we had more than 3,000 activists in the countryside. . . . Readiness to sacrifice was the best proof of being a revolutionary. Whoever had a refrigerator or good clothes was considered a bourgeois. . . . Praxis, being involved in the class struggle, and production, those were the most important values. There was a lot of contempt for theoretical study: The vast majority of the ML militants knew nothing about Marxism" (interview 29). One of ANUC's leaders described the arrival of the militants as follows: "the ML groups started to spread their people and gained control over entire regions. Their cadres were mainly students and we, the peasant

leaders, cooperated with them by helping their access at grass-roots level. We presented them as comrades who came to help, educate, etc. It was a period of great enthusiasm, agitation, and radicalism. All the initiative was in the hands of the ML groups: They imposed their slogans and controlled the regions. . . . They were living in the *veredas* with the peasants, they won many leaders, peasant leaders, to their views" (interview 37). Other sources on the ML groups, their development, ideology, and relationship with the *usuarios*: interviews 15, 17, 20, 24, 28, 34, 75, 86, 87, 88, 102, 115, and 131; PCML, *Documentos del Partido Comunista de Colombia (Marxista-Leninista)*, 1975; Ligas ML, *Colombia Semifeudal Neocolonial*, 1975; Grupo Proletarización, *De Dónde Venimos, Hacia Dónde Vamos, Hacia Dónde Debemos Ir?*, 1975, pp. 232–311 and 347–378; J.F. Ocampo, "Imperialismo, atraso capitalista, burguesía nacional y revolución de Nueva Democracia," 1972; *Alternativa*, no. 32, 1975; ANUC, "Combatamos al anarquismo," 1974; Grupo Antirrosca de Montería, "Informe sobre el Tercer Congreso de la ANUC," 1974.

23. For accounts of the Maoists' success in displacing the militants of the Socialist Bloc, see interviews 15, 34, and 37.

24. In the words of Froilán Rivera, "The ML activists tried to impose a drastic discipline on the masses. . . . Conflicts developed between them and the peasant leaders on daily questions such as how to organize a demonstration, how to relate to the community, how to behave in the land invasions, what should be the methods of agitation, etc. The ML cadres said that the peasantry should receive nothing from the state, should have no relationship with the agencies, that everything had to have a revolutionary character. The peasants should not cultivate beyond subsistence needs. If they farmed more than a quarter hectare they would become bourgeois. . . . They also said that all the demonstrations had to involve active confrontation against the authorities. . . . In the land seizures there should be no agreements with INCORA, repression should be answered by force, etc. Because of this, there were shootings, deaths. . . . Discontent developed among the masses. The peasants started to complain and leave. . . . We began to oppose what they were doing, we argued that it was causing harm to the peasant movement. At the meetings, we talked about this, bringing examples about what was going on in different places. They answered that they would take our criticism into account, but in fact their offensive became more intense. . . . It became clear that they wanted to take over the direction of the movement at any cost" (interview 37). Other sources on the problems derived from the praxis of the ML groups: interviews 17, 24, 34, 86, 87, 88, 102, 115, and 134; Fundación Mariano Ospina Pérez, "Actas," part 1, pp. 56–57.

25. According to Jesús María Pérez, "We told the comrades that it was not a question of being afraid of confronting the authorities, but that we considered that it was a case of adventurism. In that moment, the correlation of forces between the peasant movement and the state apparatus in Sucre was favorable to the peasants. We could take advantage [of] that, but on the other hand, we knew that the army had battalions in Montería and Cartagena. If we defeated the government here, there would be a counteroffensive, and the movement would not be able to resist. . . . It would have been a suicide" (interview 86).

26. Alfonso Cuéllar and Miguel Gamboa, the main political advisers of ANUC, "had been expelled from the PCML and evolved independently as Maoists within the peasant movement. . . . They had left the party in one of those frequent controversies about armed struggle, the character of Colombian society, etc. . . . Then they reemerged as advisers of ANUC after the Second Congress, and gained a lot of influence upon ANUC's Executive Committee during the confrontation against the PCML and the Liga ML" (interview 24). Antonio Poveda, one of ANUC's regional leaders from Caquetá, explained that "we were radical peasants but we wanted to have a political formation. . . . The practical work that we were doing with the masses didn't adjust to the schemes provided by the parties

of the left, and there was an initiative to develop our own independent political organization on the basis of that practical experience. We had started from 1972, when we
formed the Political Committee and began working with Cuéllar, Gamboa, etc." (interview 114).

27. On the arguments of the Political Committee against the ML parties, see interviews
34 and 37.

28. Clovis Flores, the main leader of ANUC in Córdoba, recalled that "when the
national leaders asked us to displace the ML militants, we started the fight in all the
veredas. We eliminated them from the educational committee in Córdoba. . . . We sent
money to help the restructuration of the departmental associations of Cesar, Sucre, and
Magdalena. We also paid for the twenty buses that took our people to the Third Congress
in Bogotá" (interview 17). Other sources on the conflict between the independents and the
Maoist parties: interviews 15, 20, 24, 28, 29, 34, 86, 87, and 102; Grupo Proletarizacion,
De Dónde, pp. 494–499.

29. For different points of view on the development of the Third National Congress,
see *La República*, August 31, 1974; *El Espectador*, September 2, 1974; *El Tiempo*, September
3, 1974; *Alternativa*, no. 16, 1974; *Voz Proletaria*, September 18, 1974; B. Bagley and
F. Botero," Organizaciones," pp. 73–75; ANUC, "Apuntes," pp. 49–56; ANUC, "Combatamos"; Grupo Antirrosca de Montería, "Informe." The Executive Committee elected
by the Third National Congress was composed of Noel Montenegro, Jesús María Pérez,
Víctor Pastrana, Carlos Alméciga, and José Reyes Prado.

30. On the collapse of the PCML, see interviews 24, 34, 37, 75, and 131.

31. For enlightening comments on the weakness of the working-class movement and
the marginality or alienation of the leftist political elites in Colombia, see M. Arrubla,
"Síntesis de historia política contemporánea," 1978, pp. 209–212 and 217–220.

32. On the impulse toward independent political expression within ANUC, see O.
Fals Borda, "Sentido político del movimiento campesino en Colombia," 1978. Regarding
the formation of ORP, see interviews 28, 34, 37, 64, 114, and 115.

33. For concrete accounts of the destructive effects of factionalism in Sucre, Córdoba,
and Bolívar, see interviews, 17, 20, 28, 34, 37, 86, 87, 88, 102, 131, and 134.

34. "During the first few years the landowners of Sucre were afraid of the waves of
land invasions, they didn't know what to do. . . . But they started to gain strength when
the leaders of the different factions began to fight and the organization crumbled. When
less attention was paid to the struggle against the landowners, they were able to reorganize,
looking for the best ways to repress the peasant movement" (interview 88).

35. In Córdoba, "the peasants were very affected by the division. . . . They didn't know
whom to believe. Each leader came with a different tale and accused the others of being
bandits. . . . That led to hate among the peasants. There were physical aggressions, and
all that was happening because the peasants didn't have a clear ideology and didn't know
what was going on. . . . Nobody honestly explained to them the reasons for all that political
struggle to gain control over the peasant sectors" (interview 102).

36. Interviews 81, 82, 83, and 84.

37. "Now the people do not participate anymore in the peasant movement, because
too many were coming from the outside to deceive us. Some of them say one thing, others
say a different thing. In the land invasions, the landowners give money to the peasants
and they leave, they abandon the struggle. This is how the land is being lost in Córdoba,
even in some of the oldest invasions" (interview 19).

38. "Some of the peasants sold their rights and left because they quarreled with their
comrades. The harmony that existed at the time of the struggle for the land had disappeared. The division started as a result of the breakdown of the peasant movement, because
when the movement crumbles, harmony within the *vereda* also crumbles" (interview 102).

6. Concessions and repressive escalation

1. S. Kalmanovitz, "Auge," pp. 140–143.
2. Ibid., pp. 161–162.
3. Ibid., pp. 163–164.
4. J. A. Bejarano, "La economía," pp. 132–135.
5. Departamento Nacional de Planeación, *Para Cerrar la Brecha: Plan de Desarrollo Social, Económico y Regional*, 1975, pp. 17–23 and 73–88.
6. Ibid., pp. 109–130.
7. Ibid., pp. 141–150.
8. F. González, *Colombia, 1974, La Política*, 1975, pp. 109–113; *Alternativa*, no. 22, 1974, p. 6.
9. For a thorough discussion of López Michelsen's labor policies, see F. Rojas et al., *Politica Laboral de López*, 1977, esp. pp. 77–149.
10. E. Parra et al., *Colombia 1974, Economía y Luchas Sociales*, 1975, pp. 55–73; *Alternativa*, "El estado de sitio vuelve a flote," no. 102, 1976; *Alternativa*, "Paro Cívico Nacional," no. 132, 1977; P. Santana et al., *El Paro Cívico*, 1982, pp. 11–45.
11. On the justifications and declared aims of DRI, see Departamento Nacional de Planeación, *Para Cerrar*, pp. 27–41.
12. For a discussion of DRI as a policy designed to rationalize the process of capitalist accumulation, see V. M. Moncayo and F. Rojas, *Producción*, pp. 182–208.
13. On the World Bank programs of integrated rural development, see R. McNamara, "Agricultura y pobreza," 1979; L.E. Christoffersen, "El Banco Mundial y la pobreza rural," 1978; M. Yudelman, "Los efectos de los préstamos del Banco Mundial para el desarrollo rural," 1979.
14. For the figures on DRI investments during its first 1975–1979 phase, consult Departamento Nacional de Planeación, *Programa de Desarrollo Rural Integrado DRI*, 1977, Tables 1, 2, and 3.
15. Between 1975 and 1979 the DRI program investments amounted to US $280 million (including credit). During the same period, the Federation of Coffee Growers spent US $322.2 million on the extension of rural services (excluding credit). Sources: Departamento Nacional de Planeación, *Programa*, p. 20; Federación de Cafeteros, "Informes de los comités departamentales de cafeteros," 1975–1979. On the improvements in life conditions and services in the coffee areas, see interviews 66, 138, and 140.
16. See, for example, A. Gómez, "Implicaciones de la política agraria para cerrar la brecha," 1976; E. Feder, "La pequeña revolución verde de McNamara: El proyecto del Banco Mundial para la eliminación del campesinado en el Tercer Mundo," 1976; J. Peláez, "DRI: Programa imperialista para los campesinos," 1976; H. Pérez, *Enjuiciamiento a la Política Agraria y Cafetera*, 1978, pp. 103–113; A. Mesa, "Introducción al foro sobre bonanza cafetera," 1977.
17. On the rural components of the PAN program, see Departamento Nacional de Planeación, "El Plan Nacional de Alimentación y Nutrición: Un resumen," 1978, p. 4; Departamento Nacional de Planeación, "Notas sobre el Plan Nacional de Alimentación y Nutrición," 1978, p. 3.
18. Departamento Nacional de Planeación, *Para Cerrar*, pp. 39–41.
19. Quoted from *El Tiempo*, June 17, 1976.
20. Quoted from *El Siglo*, July 30, 1975.
21. See the text of Law 6 of 1975 in INCORA, *Reforma Social*, pp. 107–117.
22. For analyses and discussions of the Sharecropping Law, see V.M. Moncayo, "La ley y el problema agrario en Colombia," 1975; A. Gómez, "Política agraria de López y Ley de Aparcería," 1975.

23. *El Tiempo*, August 29, 1974; *El Colombiano*, August 29, 1974.
24. *El Espectador*, September 20, 1974; *El Tiempo*, September 20, 1974.
25. *Carta Campesina*, no. 29, 1975, p. 1. The petitions had been listed in ANUC, "Pliego de peticiones de la ANUC al parlamento y al Gobierno Nacional," 1974.
26. ANUC, "Conclusiones de la XII Junta Directiva Nacional," 1975.
27. ANUC, "Informe del Comité Ejecutivo a la XII reunión de Junta Directiva Nacional," 1975.
28. *Carta Campesina*, no. 31, 1975, p. 12.
29. ANUC, "Denuncia pública referente a la represión y a la violencia de las fuerzas militares contra la ANUC," 1975. See also ANUC, *Boletín de Prensa*, no. 2, and *Boletín Informativo*, nos. 10 and 11, 1975.
30. Sources on repression in Sucre: *Alternativa*, nos. 18, 21, 28, and 30, 1974–1975; *Alternativa del Pueblo*, nos. 21, 22–23, and 28, 1974–1975; ANUC, *Boletín de Prensa*, no. 5, 1975; *Carta Campesina*, nos. 29 and 30, 1975; *El Tiempo*, May 25, 1975.
31. Sources on repression in Córdoba: *Alternativa*, nos. 28, 39, and 53, 1975; *Alternativa del Pueblo*, nos. 22–23, 28, 29, and 32, 1974–1975; *Carta Campesina*, no. 30, 1975, p. 10; ANUC, *Boletín Informativo*, no. 11, 1975; ANUC, "Denuncia Pública"; *El Espectador*, July 4, 1975.
32. Sources on repression in Magdalena and Cesar: *Alternativa*, nos. 27, 28, 32, 34, 35, 37, 42, 53, and 57, 1975; *Carta Campesina*, nos. 29 and 39, 1975; ANUC, "Denuncia pública"; ANUC, *Boletín de Prensa*, no. 2, 1975; ANUC, *Boletín Informativo*, no. 10, 1975; *El Tiempo*, May 27 and 31, 1975, July 31, 1975. A journalist described the main regional *gamonal* of southern Cesar and Magdalena as follows: "A telling example of the absolute power of the landowners in certain regions is that of Sinforiano Restrepo, major of El Copey (Cesar), substitute congressman, personal friend of President López, cotton grower, and owner of thousands of hectares in the neighboring department of Magdalena. As major of El Copey, Sinforiano Restrepo signs the capture warrants against peasants who have occupied his estates in Magdalena. His police patrols have killed four peasants, and his airplanes have fumigated and destroyed the crops and homes of families who had taken only an insignificant part of 'his' land. Given the combination of powers monopolized by this landowner (legislative, economic, military) and the ruthless way in which he uses these powers in defense of his privileges, the people of Cesar are talking about the 'Independent Republic' of Sinforiano Restrepo" (*Alternativa*, no. 28, 1975, p. 13)
33. Sources on repression in Huila and Tolima: interviews 61, 62, 63, and 108; *Carta Campesina*, no. 29, 1975, p. 3; ANUC, *Boletín de Prensa*, no. 2, 1975; ANUC, *Boletín Informativo*, no. 10, 1975.
34. Sources: interview 8; *Alternativa*, nos. 39, 41, 53, 67, and 68, 1975–1976; *Alternativa del Pueblo*, nos. 31, 33, and 35, 1975; *El Colombiano*, April 27, 1975; ANUC, "Denuncia pública"; ANUC, *Boletín de Prensa*, no. 2, 1975; ANUC, *Boletín Informativo*, no. 10, 1975.
35. ANUC, *Boletín de Prensa*, nos. 2 and 5, 1975; ANUC, *Boletín Informativo*, Nos. 10 and 11, 1975.
36. *El Espectador*, December 18, 1975; *El Siglo*, January 15, 1976; *Alternativa*, no. 67, 1976; *Carta Campesina*, no. 32, 1976, p. 8.
37. B. Bagley and F. Botero, "Organizaciones," p. 77.

7. The new occupational alternatives and the issue of the rural proletariat

1. J. M. Eastman, "La distribución del ingreso en Colombia," 1979, p. 473.
2. DANE, "Empleo y desempleo en áreas rurales de cuatro regiones," 1979.

3. P. Torales: *La Dinámica de los Movimientos Migratorios en Colombia*, 1979, p. 67.

4. S. Kalmanovitz, "Desarrollo capitalista," pp. 317–323.

5. Departamento Nacional de Planeación, "Indicadores de la actividad agropecuaria," 1978.

6. These data on rice and cotton refer to the 1967–1977 period. Sources: DANE, *Memoria del Sector Agropecuario*, 1975, pp. 352–372; Ministerio de Agricultura, *Cifras del Sector Agropecuario*, 1979, pp. 39 and 99.

7. Livestock increased from an annual average of 19.4 million heads in 1968–1970 to 28.8 million in 1975–1977. Sources: DANE, *Memoria*, p. 446; Ministerio de Agricultura, *Cifras*, p. 219.

8. Interviews 80 and 82.

9. On migratory labor in the coffee harvests, see G. Calderón, *Características Socio-laborales de los Recolectores de Café en un Area Cersi*, 1978; F. Urrea, *Mercados de Trabajo y Migraciones en la Explotación Cafetera*, 1976.

10. F. Urrea, *Mercados*, pp. 142–145.

11. On the relationship between real wages and legal minimums, see J.M. Eastman, "La distribución," p. 497. The increase in nominal rural wages was estimated using data from S. Kalmanovitz, *La Agricultura*, part 2, p. 122; DANE, *Boletín Mensual de Estadística*, no. 305, 1976, p. 58.

12. J.M. Eastman, "La distribución," p. 493.

13. P. Torales, *La Dinámica*, pp. 88–89.

14. See, for example, G. Murillo, *La Migración de Trabajadores Colombianos a Venezuela*, 1979; L. Mansilla, *Inserción Laboral de Migrantes Indocumentados*, 1979.

15. Interviews 2, 11, 15, 32, 40, 76, 80, 82, 101, and 107.

16. E. Liewen, *Venezuela*, 1961, pp. 124–125.

17. Interviews 2, 82, and 136.

18. For a description of the boom in capitalist agriculture in Venezuela, see *El Espectador*, "Análisis sobre los indocumentados colombianos en Venezuela", April 16, 1980.

19. On the wage differential as a factor in the labor migrations, see *El Espectador*, "Venezuela es El Dorado para muchos colombianos," February 15, 1980. See also *Alternativa*, "Indocumentados en Venezuela: Exodo, miseria y muerte," no. 204, 1979.

20. Interviews 2, 32, 78, 101, and 107.

21. *El Espectador*, February 15, 1980.

22. R. Junguito and C. Caballero, "La otra economía," 1978; ANIF, "Marihuana, mito y realidad," 1979.

23. On Colombia's rise to the status of main supplier of the U.S. marihuana market, see *El Espectador*, "La fiebre de la marimba," September 8 and 9, 1978. Regarding the smuggling tradition of Guajira, see *Alternativa*, "La Guajira militarizada," no. 189, 1978.

24. *El Tiempo*, "228 mil millones vale el tráfico de drogas con EEUU," March 31, 1978; *El Tiempo*, "70,000 hectáreas de marihuana en la Costa," August 13, 1978; *El Tiempo*, "La conexión colombiana," January 29, 1979; *Alternativa*, "Marihuana, el personaje económico de la década," no. 257, 1980.

25. *El Tiempo*, "Imposible destruir la marihuana," October 23, 1977; *El Espectador*, "Descubren en los Llanos más marihuana", September 5, 1978; *Alternativa*, "Marihuana: no la tranca nadie," no. 212, 1979.

26. *Alternativa*, "La economía de la Costa Atlántica, antes y después de la marimba," no. 160, 1978; *El Tiempo*, "Estudio de ANIF sobre la marihuana," March 19, 1979.

27. *El Tiempo*, "No hay ley en la Guajira," October 24, 1977; interviews 12 and 32.

28. *El Espectador*, "Del algodón a la marihuana," October 17, 1978; *El Tiempo*, "El mar de marihuana," May 13, 1979; *El Tiempo*, "Viraje y amnistía a la economía subterránea

proponen algodoneros," August 6, 1980; *El Espectador*, "La economía marimbera," January 31, 1982.

29. *Alternativa*, "El tráfico de marihuana, radiografia de un negocio no tan misterioso", no. 168, 1978; *El Tiempo*, "De la marihuana y otras yerbas," June 3, 1979; *El Tiempo*, "Aeropuerto de Plato centro de embarque de marihuana," December 31, 1979.

30. *El Tiempo*, "Estudio de ANIF sobre la marihuana," March 19, 1979; *Alternativa*, "La mafia de la marihuana en la Costa: Imperio del terror o redención social?", no. 149, 1979; interviews 76 and 78.

31. *El Espectador*, "Simposio sobre la marihuana," March 17, 1979; DANE, *Censo Nacional de Población*, 1973.

32. On the economic expansion stimulated by the underground activities, see *Alternativa*, "La economía de la Costa Atlántica, antes y después de la marimba," no. 160, 1978; *Alternativa*, "El tráfico de marihuana: Se siente, se siente, la bonanza está presente," no. 169, 1978; and R. Junguito and C. Caballero, "La otra economía."

33. G. Murillo, *La Migración*, pp. 95–97.

34. "The marihuana 'fever' is not restricted to Guajira. The contagion is rapidly spreading among all the peasants of the area, whose daily thoughts revolve around the possibilities of the crop and its cultivation techniques. This reporter witnessed heated discussions on the topic among Magdalena peasants. . . . There is no doubt that marihuana has captured the imagination of the peasantry in the Atlantic Coast. . . . The *mafia* bosses behave as godfathers and are loved and respected by many sectors of the people. When they visit the town or another village, they are approached by policemen who recognize their luxurious cars and come to ask for money. . . . They buy houses, estates, buildings, provide funds for electoral campaigns, maintain fleets of small ships and airplanes, bribe the judges, distribute money among the poor, and organize great parties . . . which the politicians gladly attend" (*Alternativa*, no. 149, 1978, p. 17). On the formation of *mafia* loyalties and vertical class alignments in the marihuana growing areas, see also *Alternativa*, "Marihuana: No la tranca nadie," no. 212, 1979; *Alternativa*, "El tráfico de marihuana: Se siente, se siente, la bonanza está presente," no. 169, 1978. Regarding the political influence of the *mafia*, see *El Tiempo*, "Los gremios denuncian: Mafiosos figuran de candidatos," February 23, 1980; and *Alternativa*, "Mafia en las listas," No. 253, 1980.

35. In Córdoba, for example, "the migration of workers is a factor that strongly affects our struggle in ANUC. In some areas it is tremendous, as in the municipalities of Chinú and San Pedro. They all go to the cotton harvests, to Valledupar, to Venezuela. . . . This has weakened the organization a lot" (interview 40). Similarly, in Sucre: "Despite the fact that we have some land, our sons have to work as migrant laborers during part of the year. The land is not sufficient. Still, there is little or no struggle for land. They have to be organized in order to be able to fight against the landowners. The problem is that when they start to move it becomes very difficult to organize them; they are unstable, rambling people" (interview 88).

36. Quoted from interview 119.

37. "In Mingueo, Guajira, some of ANUC's leaders became *mafia* bosses. One of these ex-peasant leaders has an eleven-story building and lives in luxury in Santa Marta" (interview 29). In Cauca: "Almaguer, Bolívar, Mercaderes . . . all these were areas in which the left was working, but cocaine spoiled everything. The leaders became *mafiosi*. . . . The left loses the work because the people is corrupted" (interview 65). In Meta: "Cocaine involves peasants, Indians, colonists. . . . People who used to be good contacts of the peasant movement are now becoming part of the *mafia* in less than a year" (interview 119).

38. Interviews 12 and 29.

39. Regarding these precedents, see the following documents of ANUC: *Plataforma*

Ideológica; "Conclusiones de la V Junta Directiva de Tolú sobre los CERAS y la organización independiente del proletariado agrícola," 1972; *Tierra para Quien la Trabaja*.

40. ANUC, "Primer encuentro nacional de pequeños y medianos propietarios, arrendatarios, aparceros y asalariados caficultores," 1974. See also *El Periódico*, September 25, 1974, and interview 53.

41. *Carta Campesina*, no. 22, 1972, p. 10; *Alternativa*, no. 12, 1974; *Carta Campesina*, no. 27, 1974, pp. 10—11.

42. ANUC, *Conclusiones del Tercer Congreso Nacional*, 1974, pp. 27—30 and 37.

43. On the Communist Party, URS, and ML activities among the agricultural workers, see ORP, "Los jornaleros agrícolas y la lucha campesina," 1976. See also interviews 29, 54, 62, and 63.

44. ANUC, "Resolución de la XIII Junta Directiva Nacional sobre los jornaleros," 1975.

45. ORP, "Los jornaleros."

46. Ibid., p. 34.

47. Interview 64.

48. *Carta Campesina*, nos. 31—34, 1975—1976.

49. ANUC, "Declaración sobre el decreto de salario mínimo," 1976. See also *La República*, August 17, 1976.

50. ANUC, "Conclusiones del Primer Encuentro Nacional de Jornaleros Agrícolas," 1976.

51. See, for example, N. Buenaventura, *Precapitalismo en la Economía Colombiana*, 1976; M. P. Gaitán, "Condiciones y posibilidades de organización del proletariado cañero en Colombia," 1981.

52. For descriptions of labor conditions during harvest time, see *El Espectador*, "Recolección cafetera, vida y problemas de un cosechero," October 27, 1978; *Alternativa*, "La ruta blanca del cosechero," no. 23—24, 1975; L. Mármora et al., *Migraciones en la Cosecha del Algodón*, 1976; J. Gómez, *Cumplimiento de la Legislación Laboral en Cultivos Comerciales*, 1977.

53. In Caldas, the main coffee department: "only in the municipality of Chinchiná did the organization of the agricultural laborers have some headway, but that activity led to defeats, arrests, and permanent repression. With the help of the Ministry, the governor of Caldas brought workers from Córdoba in order to neutralize that small organization. The laborers quarreled among themselves and there were many arrests. All that was in the 1976 harvest. They used megaphones to tell the people that they should not work for less than 200 pesos per load (the pay was 125). There was a positive response in Chinchiná, but later the workers disobeyed the order. The police had rounded up all those who were not working, asking for identifications, etc. . . . Now the laborers won't accept any proposal to organize. They did try to do the same but nobody paid attention" (interview 53). For an account of similar obstacles and problems in the cotton harvests, see *Alternativa*, "La ruta blanca del cosechero," no. 23—24, 1975.

54. ANUC, "Conclusiones del Primer Encuentro Nacional de Jornaleros."

8. Partial repeasantization and the question of the new peasant settlements

1. INCORA, *Resumen General de las Principales Realizaciones del INCORA por Proyectos*, 1980, pp. 1—3.

2. Sources: INCORA, "La realidad rural y la reforma agraria como factor de cambio," 1971, p. 34; A. E. Havens et al., "Agrarian reform," p. 359.

3. INCORA estimated the size of self-sufficient family farms in the Atlantic Coast as follows: Atlántico, 57–104 hectares; Córdoba, 37–75 hectares; Magdalena, Cesar, Bolívar, and Sucre, 50–100 hectares (INCORA, "La realidad rural," pp. 22–34).

4. These remarks of a peasant from Cereté (Cordoba) typify the situation throughout the Atlantic Coast: "INCORA has given individual titles on as little as half hectare per family. They don't fulfill the minimum size requirement of five hectares established by the law. With so little land, we continue in the same situation as before: We have to go to work for the landowners. . . . Some go as far as Valledupar and Venezuela. Those who know how to pick coffee go to the coffee zone. The others, like me, stay here and work in the cotton harvests of this area" (interview 101).

5. M. Suárez Melo et al., *Las Empresas Comunitarias Campesinas en Colombia*, 1977, p. 14. *Empresas comunitarias* (literally, "community enterprises") was the name chosen by INCORA for the semicollective farms. As shown in this section, the farms originally combined collective and individual production in varying proportions according to the type of settlement.

6. E. Liboreiro et al., *Análisis de las Empresas Comunitarias Campesinas en Colombia*, 1977, pp. 31–35; M. Suárez Melo et al., *Las Empresas*, pp. 13–18.

7. See, for example, H. Pérez, *Enjuiciamiento*, pp. 69–73; E. Alvarez, "La empresa comunitaria," 1975.

8. For a discussion of the way in which the *empresas comunitarias* integrated the reformist view of social and political goals, see E. Parra and A. Reyes, "Empresas comunitarias rurales y desarrollo del sector agropecuario en la Costa Atlántica," 1977, pp. 17–18.

9. For a general comparative review of experiences of agricultural collectivization throughout the world, see B. Galeski, "The prospects for collective farming," 1973.

10. On the presumed advantages of collective farming, see E. Liboreiro et al., *Análisis*, pp. 34–35; INCORA, *Las Empresas Comunitarias en la Reforma Agraria*, 1977, pp. 4–5.

11. M. Suárez Melo et al., *Las Empresas*, pp. 21–23. *Parceleros* was the common name used to refer to the members of the settlements.

12. For a thorough discussion of the factors that influence collective farming, see B. Galeski, "The prospects," pp. 42–58. See also E. Liboreiro et al., *Analisis*, pp. 35–40.

13. On counterreform and its effects upon the development of the *empresas comunitarias*, see E. Parra and A. Reyes, "Empresas," pp. 24–29; E. Liboreiro et al., *Analisis*, pp. 112–113, 122–123, 131–134, and 146–148; INCORA, *Las Empresas*, pp. 20 and 27; INCORA, *Las Formas Asociativas de Producción; Características y Resultados*, 1979, pp. 4, 9–10, and 51; interviews 5, 10, 87, 107, 110, 117, and 121.

14. INCORA, *Las Empresas*, pp. 1–4; INCORA, *Las Formas*, pp. 1–3.

15. On INCORA's bureaucratic control and its consequences, see interviews 4, 5, 10, 20, 32, 78, 83, 86, and 120.

16. B. Galeski, "The prospects," pp. 55–56.

17. According to an INCORA official from Atlántico: "The *empresas* are disintegrating. They talked about *empresas*, but they weren't such. The peasants accepted the philosophy of the *empresas comunitarias*, but they did so only because they wanted the land. Once they had the land, everyone started to cultivate on his own" (interview 10). Similarly, in Bolívar: "The peasants united themselves in order to get the land and the credit . . . they knew that only as a group they could receive that. But once they had the credit in their hands, they distributed the money internally. The credit had collective access, but its use was individual" (interview 5).

18. In this sense, the Colombian case appears to be similar to other experiences of agrarian reform in which collective farming played a transitional role in the movement toward individual production. See B. Galeski, "The prospects," p. 61.

19. INCORA, *Las Empresas*, pp. 1–2 and 6–7; E. Liboreiro et al., *Análisis*, pp. 112–113.

20. INCORA, *Las Formas*, p. 41a.

21. Ibid., pp. 42–43.

22. Sources: INCORA, *Las Empresas*, p. 9; INCORA, *Resumen General*, pp. 4–5.

23. See the regional data in INCORA, *Resumen General*. On this issue of heavy indebtedness on the Atlantic Coast, see also interviews 2, 4, 5, 10, 11, 32, 78, and 86. Regarding the sales of cattle, an INCORA official from Bolívar explained: "We have many cases of peasants selling the cattle that they had bought with our credit. . . . They don't do that in bad faith. Their incomes are very low, and whenever they are in trouble they are forced to sell a cow. . . . They do it because their daily survival is a problem" (interview 78).

24. According to an INCORA official from Cesar, "the peasants are heavily indebted, and many of them have no alternative but selling or simply deserting in order to go to Venezuela or somewhere else. Twenty percent of the *parceleros* have abandoned the land, 40 percent if we include those who sold their titles. . . . The landowners are buying the land again. Agrarian reform must be supported by adequate services if we are to avoid this" (interview 32). In Atlántico: "Many experiments were made without taking into account the level of the peasants. The people were put to produce new crops without adequate preparation, without marketing, etc. Many *parceleros* abandoned the land because of that. There was indebtedness. Everybody goes to work to Venezuela here, including most of the *parceleros* who have to pay their debts. The land lies idle because there is no credit, and there is no credit because of indebtedness" (interview 10). See also interviews 2, 9, 11, 13, 78, 83, and 86.

25. See, for example, INCORA, *Las Formas*, pp. 21–35.

26. Interviews 5, 10, 32, 78, 107, 110, and 117.

27. "There is a situation of massive indebtedness and, since they do not understand this economic phenomenon, many peasants, in fact most of them, blame collective production. They say that the *empresa comunitaria* has failed and want individual parcelization. As a result, most *empresas* are now disintegrating" (interview 86).

28. ANUC, "Declaración de principios."

29. ANUC, *Primer Mandato Campesino*.

30. E. Parra and A. Reyes, "Empresas," pp. 39–40.

31. In the words of Froilán Rivera: "Accepting INCORA's titles implied that we had to pay taxes to the state and, by doing so, give tacit political support to the concentration of property by the landowners. We recommended the *parceleros* to forget about the titles; the best title was our own organization, and not private property. Most of our people accepted provisional assignment contracts, which at that time could be used to obtain loans from the Caja Agraria" (interview 87).

32. O. Fals Borda, "Sentido político," p. 170.

33. On Fals Borda's involvement with ANUC and his role in the *baluartes*, see the following sources: interviews 15, 16, 17, 19, 20, 23, 28, 29, 34, and 40; ANUC (Córdoba), "Muestra de estatutos para formar una empresa comunitaria popular o baluarte de autogestión campesina," 1973; ANUC: "Proyecto de folleto: Qué es una empresa comunitaria popular o baluarte de autogestión campesina?", 1974; Fundación del Caribe, "Algunas reflexiones sobre la Fundación del Caribe y su situación actual," 1974; E. Parra, *La Investigación-Acción*, chap. 10; *Alternativa*, nos. 16, 19, and 25, 1974–1975; *Alternativa del Pueblo*, nos. 22–23 and 36, 1974–1975; *Carta Campesina*, no. 28, 1974, p. 14. See also the following writings of Fals Borda: *Capitalismo, Hacienda y Poblamiento en la Costa Atlántica*, 1976; "Sentido político"; *El Problema de Cómo Investigar la Realidad para Transformarla*, 1979.

34. Regarding the praxis of the ML activists in the settlements, see interviews 28, 29, 34, 37, 86, 87, 88, 102, 115, and 134. See also Fundación Mariano Ospina Pérez, "Actas," part 1, pp. 56–57.

35. During the 1960s and 1970s, the term *foquista* was usually employed in Latin America to refer to revolutionary conceptions that, like Che Guevara's, stated that the revolution should be irradiated from "liberated" areas or enclaves.

36. On the *empresas* in the areas of influence of ANUC Armenia, see interviews 4, 11, 13, 61, 108, 111, and 112.

37. Interviews 30, 32, 80, 81, 82, and 83.

38. ANUC, "Conclusiones de la VIII Junta."

39. ANUC, "Proyecto de folleto."

40. For accounts of these seminars, see ANUC (Sucre), "Conclusiones del encuentro de empresas comunitarias de Sucre," 1974; ANUC (Cauca), "Conclusiones del encuentro de empresas comunitarias del Cauca," 1974; ANUC (Risaralda), "Conclusiones del encuentro de empresas comunitarias de Occidente realizado en Quinchía," 1974; ANUC (Cundinamarca), "Conclusiones del encuentro regional de empresas comunitarias realizado en La Calera," 1974.

41. For the plan's proposals, see ANUC (Tolima), "Conclusiones del encuentro regional de empresas comunitarias," 1974.

42. Interviews 28, 29, 34, and 65. See also Grupo Antirrosca de Montería, "Informe"; *Alternativa*, "La ANUC fija posición ante la Rosca," no. 25, 1975.

43. ANUC, *Conclusiones del Tercer Congreso*; ANUC, "Pliego de peticiones."

44. A *parcelero* from El Banco, for example, recalled that "we went to the Third Congress, more than 200 peasants from Magdalena. Nobody expected what happened there. The contradiction started. Students and workers wanted to take over ANUC. There was a division, and then everything started to crumble. We returned with the idea that there was a struggle for the leadership. We knew nothing about that, we had followed ANUC Sincelejo because it was our organization. . . . Then we learned that there were money problems. It was a fraud; the national leaders were those who educated themselves and knew everything. They had the money and distributed the cake among themselves" (interview 81).

45. Interviews 81 and 84.

46. Interviews 62, 109, and 111.

47. Interview 129.

48. In the words of a regional *usuario* leader from Nariño, "Some leaders wanted to impose Marxism-Leninism. Others became Maoists, and so on. . . . That led to fights in the meetings of the National Junta and, later, to the division of the organization. The problems were ideological. . . . They appeared as if they were problems of ANUC, but they weren't. ANUC's problems should have been the problems of the peasants, such as obtaining land, credit, etc. Those were the demands that brought the people together. But then they started to play a different music, and the peasants didn't have sufficient political clarity. That was the failure, the explosion of ANUC" (interview 85).

49. O. Fals Borda had supported the independent leaders in their internal battle against the ML groups. However, as already explained in this chapter, ANUC's leaders sacrificed the sociologist and his followers as part of their tactics to defeat the ML opposition. Furthermore, some peasant leaders in Córdoba had been conspicuously misusing the funds of the research-action projects. The onslaught of the ML activists, in which the charges of corruption played a major role, led to Fals Borda's withdrawal and the virtual destruction of ANUC Sincelejo in Córdoba. The peasants described the effects on the *baluartes* as follows: "They came and spoke about the *baluartes*, but we didn't understand. Even today we don't know what a *baluarte* is. They propose something, then they go, and one doesn't even know [what it's] all about. . . . What Fals did for us was positive. He gave legal advice and he even went to jail helping us to get the land. . . . Fals also obtained money for the organization, but the municipal leaders mismanaged, robbed that money. . . . He

came frequently until the money started to cause trouble, fights and corruption. Then the students and the cadres attacked him and he didn't come anymore. . . . Fals talked about the *baluarte*, but he explained everything to the leaders, and not directly to us. When they explained to us, we didn't understand. Then they didn't come anymore. . . . The only thing that we wanted was the land, in order to work in agriculture and cattle. Now we are doing what we wanted. . . . At the beginning there were large meetings, but now we meet by groups. First we worked as a group of twenty-seven, then we formed groups of eight, and now we are discussing whether to divide into groups of one. Nobody has the pamphlets here; they were either thrown away or eaten by the worms. Also, the books have disappeared. We do not belong to ANUC anymore; the committee has been dead for years. There are no longer any activists. There are some in Montería, but they don't come here; they are too busy in politics and fighting one another" (interviews 16 and 19). According to Clovis Flores, ANUC's main Córdoba leader, "Fals Borda believed that the *baluartes* existed, and that was one of his mistakes. We tried to organize them, but we failed for a number of reasons: The peasants were not prepared, they came from different *veredas* . . . on the other hand, the ML groups acussed us of being reformists. . . . We prepared the statutes and started to carry out the plan, but there was a lot of work in the department and we didn't pay sufficient attention to the groups. Then came the problems, fights, etc. The ML groups started to attack us, especially when Fals presented the issue of the *baluartes* at the University of Córdoba. . . . The life of the *baluartes* was very short, almost nonexistent" (interview 17). For a frank evaluation of Fals Borda's contributions and the controversial implications of his participant-research experiences in Córdoba, see E. Parra, *Investigación-Acción*, chaps. 10, 11, and 12.

50. "In the times of the PCML, we wanted to organize the *empresas comunitarias* on the basis of peasant self-sufficiency. On the other hand, we wanted the peasants to work in a socialist, collective way. We had very bad results. The people cannot work in that way if they have not been educated. We started with collective tasks, but they collapsed. There was no understanding, no policy that would really guide the work. . . . The people worked in that way because somebody said that it had to be so. But later, in the actual practice, they showed us that we were not right. . . . Our stances were neither socialist nor Marxist; they were eclectic, confused, it was a really difficult problem" (interview 88). See also interviews 2, 20, 24, 29, 37, and 96.

51. Interview 87.

52. Interviews 2, 40, 87, 99, and 137.

53. In the words of an INCORA official from Sucre, "The Institute blackmails the peasants. If they don't accept all the conditions, they get nothing. . . . Previously, the peasants received credit without formal titles or guarantees. Now INCORA won't give credit without that" (interview 2). Similarly, in Bolívar, "INCORA created showcases in order to prove, with facts, that the peasants will benefit. . . . We established good *empresas*, with credit, etc. We showed that there was no basis for the claims of ANUC Sincelejo. Now we only need more money from the government" (interview 6).

54. "At the beginning, we worked in pastures as a community. The landowners of the area brought their cattle to our pastures, we charged them and divided the money among us. Now we have divided the land, and each one does as he pleases. A few are doing some agriculture, but the majority grows pasture for the landowners. . . . There is a lot of discussion about whether it is good or not to do that. It is true that one comes to depend upon the landowner, but there is no alternative. The land is good for pastures, not for crops" (interview 23). See also INCORA, "Informe de la Comisión Caso Morroa sobre legalización de predios adquiridos por el Instituto," 1981; interviews 19, 20, 21, 95, and 98.

55. See, for example, interviews 1, 11, 15, 20, 98, 133, and 134.

56. "The peasants of ANUC Sincelejo believe that the land is theirs and that they don't need INCORA. . . . Since they don't accept titles, they are legally only squatters. As a result, they cannot receive loans from INCORA or the Caja Agraria, they don't have any services, and they lack protection, so that anybody can in fact invade their land. . . . During the last months of 1979 there were peasants invading peasants. They said that it was easier than invading private estates, because the landowners are protected by the *pájaros* and the army" (interview 6).

57. In Bolívar, for example, an INCORA official said that "in 1976 there was total indifference towards INCORA. Today, everything is changing. They are yielding and we are issuing the titles. Even the more recalcitrant ones are fighting among themselves for the land, and they come to INCORA. There is a general decrease of radicalism" (interview 6).

58. A local leader from Córdoba, for example, explained that "part of the *parceleros* had been always dominated by INCORA through ANUC Armenia. But in this area most of us didn't accept INCORA. However, since the downfall of ANUC Sincelejo the people have no choice but to accept the titles. . . . We are having discussions on this. I haven't accepted the title yet, but I will finally have to do it because I can't swim against the tide" (interview 101).

59. "We lost the battle against INCORA. . . . We lost because we didn't have a good policy and also because the *parceleros* had to cultivate the land. We objected to the credit programs, saying that the peasants should administer the loans. But when no credit was received, they abandoned us. . . . We told the peasants that the property titles were a farce. . . . But then the Institute said that without titles there would be no credit, and again they abandoned us. . . . The great majority, 99 percent of the people, accepted the titles and went to INCORA" (interview 134). See also interviews 4, 14, 16, 20, 23, and 40.

9. Final crisis and clientelist regression of ANUC

1. See the last section of Chapter 3.

2. The grass-roots testimonies are eloquent about the destructive consequences of perceived corruption and bureaucratism at the top. A *parcelero* from Tolima, for example, referred to the regional leader of ANUC Sincelejo as follows: "At first he was a strong, honest leader. But later they started to receive the cash from Holland and they kept the money for themselves. It was for their own benefit, they didn't distribute it to the people" (interview 109). Another *parcelero*, from Magdalena, said that "there was much hope among the peasants, but everything was lost as a result of the egoism of the national leaders, who wanted to take advantage for their own sake. There were foreign 'moneys' in this, and that was the reason for ANUC's setback. We lost contact and nothing was left" (interview 81). A Sarare peasant said that "in the Third Congress ANUC couldn't explain what was happening with the money received from Holland. We came back and we asked our leaders to clarify the money issue, and they were also unable to explain. . . . When we realized that they received money, we started to protest. They hadn't been able to explain because they and the national leaders belonged to the same gang. The people lost their morale. . . . Even our cooperative was finished, because the people had lost faith. . . . It was chaos" (interview 126). A local leader from Nariño: "Another cause of ANUC's failure was corruption. We saw that in the national meetings the leaders spent their time drinking and dancing, and paid no attention to the critiques of the peasant delegates. . . . We told them that that was no proper discipline for leaders. There were comrades who even cried while they were making their critiques. People who were supposed to be peasant leaders had bureaucratized. [ANUC's treasurer] has a new stationwagon and

a beautiful house in Bogotá, while we, the peasants who were coming from the countryside, were paying for our own traveling despite being sunk in poverty. . . . [One of the national leaders] bought an estate, a real *hacienda*. . . . [Another national leader] had the peasant house of Pasto and a lumber business in Pereira. . . . [ANUC's comptroller] has a cattle and cocoa estate. . . . I personally confirmed that all that was bought with ANUC's funds" (interview 85).

3. A document issued by the *usuarios* from Quinchía stated that "it is a well-known fact that there is now a conflict between ANUC's bureaucratic apparatus and the peasant masses. . . . The bougeoisie and imperialism understand that in order to degenerate an organization it is first necessary to degenerate the leaders, that the rich peasants – whether old or new – are the base of reformism. . . . Degeneration and corruption have turned ANUC's Executive Committee into a clique of godfathers who work for their personal economic and political interests and not for the interests of the masses. They have betrayed, abandoned the revolutionary tradition, and want to prevent others from making the revolution. . . . Under the Executive Committee there is no democracy for the peasant masses, democracy is only for the clique and for those who agree with them. . . . The foreign 'help' received by the Executive Committee, the imperialist penetration of ANUC, is aimed at weakening the peasant movement, turning it into a reformist element that will neutralize the Colombian revolutionary process." Quoted from ANUC (Risaralda), "Posición de los campesinos de Quinchía ante el Comité Ejecutivo de la ANUC," 1975. On the critiques from Quinchía and Sarare, see also interviews 53, 126, 127, and 128.

4. Víctor Pastrana, a regional leader from Caquetá who was expelled from ANUC's National Executive Committee, declared that "the political group that hides behind ANUC is attacking all the revolutionary organizations that try to work within the peasant movement. This group, the Political Committee inspired by Alfonso Cuellar and Miguel Gamboa, wants the creation of a 'peasantist' political party that will include, without discrimination, both poor and rich peasants. We oppose this concealed political organization. The Political Committee uses the top positions within ANUC in order to attack and defame all those who assume critical stances. They are biasing the activists and throwing the peasant masses into confusion" (*Alternativa*, no. 62, 1975, p. 8). See also ANUC (Caquetá), "Contra el gobierno de López; unidad, organización y lucha," 1975; ANUC (Caquetá), "En qué no creemos ya?", 1975.

5. In the words of Gregorio Palechor, one of the main leaders of the Indian movement, "We don't have any discrepancies with the peasant class, not even with ANUC. The problem is with ANUC's leaders. . . . We have our own specificities and problems as Indians. . . . They have accused us of being racists, indigenists, trade unionists. They have defamed our movement and our leaders. They wanted to swallow our organization in order to lead it to political goals. . . . We see the Indians as an exploited class, in a process of conscientization. The idea is to keep working until the people understands what has to be done. The political stage will come, but first we have to consolidate. Each organization should develop the consciousness of its class: ANUC with the peasants, the trade unions with the workers, etc., in order to finally reach a political level in which we can come all together" (interview 55). See also CRIC, "Posición del CRIC frente al movimiento indígena y al Comité Ejecutivo de la ANUC," 1981.

6. Interview 55. See also CRIC's newspaper, *Unidad Indígena*, "Comité Ejecutivo de la ANUC intenta dividir al movimiento indígena," no. 6, 1975, p. 5.

7. Interviews 70 and 114. See also ANUC (Caquetá), "En qué no creemos ya?"; *Alternativa*, nos. 60 and 62, 1975; AICA, "Caquetá, una muestra de los métodos de la Comisión Política de la ANUC," 1975.

8. Interview 53.

9. Interviews 126 and 127.

10. Interview 46.

11. ANUC, "Proyecto de plataforma de lucha de la ANUC, ponencia al IV Congreso Nacional Campesino," 1977.

12. The groups that opposed ANUC's national leadership repeatedly denounced the political nature of the new platform. According to the Indian movement CRIC, "It is, in fact, a platform that corresponds to a political party. Most of it is totally unrelated to the way in which the peasant struggles have developed in our country" (*Unidad Indígena*, "La encerrona de Tomala," no. 20, 1977, p. 2). Defining themselves as minority sectors, those who still followed ML orientations argued that "the platform proposed by the Executive Committee is nothing but the platform of a political organization, which violates the trade-unionist character of ANUC and tries to mislead the masses with reformist stances" (ANUC/Sectores Minoritarios, "Constancia de los sectores minoritarios de la ANUC a su Cuarto Congreso," 1977). Even the less politicized ordinary peasants were aware of the issue. A former *usuario* from Bolívar, for example, said that "the problem started in Tomala. . . . As a trade union organization, we should be one, united. In politics, each one should be left to have his own ideas. Political division is no good and will get nothing for the peasants. We don't want neither left nor right . . . most of the peasants oppose these attitudes of cheap politics" (interview 3). Peasants from Atlántico also complained: "They took us to Tomala just to vote as a rubber stamp, they didn't explain anything beforehand. . . . We were blindfolded, nobody knew what they wanted until they brought the ORP to the open. Since then, we didn't take part again" (interview 8).

13. Although ANUC described the proceedings of the Fourth National Congress as orderly and democratic (see the accounts in *Carta Campesina*, no. 37, 1977), all the evidence indicates that the opposition sectors were blocked, discriminated against, and harassed. See interviews 8, 15, and 20; *Unidad Indígena*, no. 20, 1977, p. 2; ANUC/ Sectores Minoritarios, "Constancia"; ANUC/Sectores Minoritarios, "Informe del IV Congreso de la ANUC y una propuesta a los sectores opositores al Comité Ejecutivo," 1977.

14. ANUC's new Executive Committee was composed of Hernán Monsalve (from Valle), Daniel Ochoa (Caldas), Hugo Garcés (Córdoba), José Martínez (Meta), and José Reyes Prado (Nariño). With the exception of Reyes Prado, the comptroller, all the other members were young activists. According to the plan masterminded by the national leaders and their advisers, these newly promoted activists would assume the trade union tasks. This would enable the more experienced veteran leaders to devote all their time to the political work related to the launching of the peasant party (see interview 87).

15. On the official presentation of ORP to the delegates, see *Carta Campesina*, no. 37, 1977; ORP, "Mensaje de la Organización Revolucionaria del Pueblo a los campesinos," 1977.

16. Sources employed in this review of the La Mojana conflicts: *El Siglo*, May 9, 15, 18, and 31, 1977; *El Espectador*, March 13, June 7, and July 2, 1977; *Carta Campesina*, nos. 37 and 38, 1977; *Alternativa*, nos. 152 and 187, 1978.

17. Enacted under the umbrella of the State of Siege provisions only a few days after Julio C. Turbay Ayala came to power, the Security Statute broadened the legal definition of offences such as "alteration of public order," "rebellion," and "unlawful association." It also increased the penalties for these offences, gave more powers to the military authorities, and imposed media censorship on matters of "national security." For a general description and analysis of the Security Statute, see A. Reyes et al., *Estatuto de Seguridad*, 1978.

18. Sources used in the following review of the Upía River conflicts: *El Espectador*, February 15 and October 18, 1977; *La República*, February 16, March 5, June 17, and August 2, 1977; *Alternativa*, no. 120, 1977; *Carta Campesina*, nos. 34, 35 and 37, 1976– 1977.

19. *El Siglo*, February 15, 1977; *La República*, May 13 and October 19, 1977; *Alternativa*, no. 187, 1978; *Carta Campesina*, no. 39, 1979.

20. Interviews 15, 16, and 90.

21. Interview 77.

22. Interview 73.

23. Interviews 60, 62, and 63. See also *El Espectador*, June 7, 1977.

24. Interview 120; *Carta Campesina*, no. 39, p. 7, 1979; ANUC (Meta), "Carta abierta a Turbay Ayala sobre la represión en San Martín," 1979.

25. The M–19 was formed by young cadres of ANAPO who, challenging Rojas Pinilla's leadership, went underground after ANAPO's electoral defeat of April 19, 1970. Basically an urban guerrilla organization with populist ideological leanings, the M–19 managed to strike a number of propagandistic blows during the second half of the 1970s (e.g. the "confiscation" of Bolívar's sword from the National Museum, the theft of arms from the main military command in Bogotá, and the seizure of the Dominican Republic embassy), but it was clearly unsuccessful when it tried to shift its activity to the countryside after 1980. For a general discussion of the use of the Security Statute in the repression of both guerrillas and trade unions, see A. Reyes, *Estatuto*.

26. On the use of the Security Statute in the rural areas, see *Alternativa*, nos. 187 and 188, 1978.

27. *El Siglo*, February 1, 1976; April 21, May 15, June 12, October 12, and November 16, 1977; *La República*, February 3 and November 29, 1976; *El Tiempo*, November 2, 1976; *El Colombiano*, May 4, 1977.

28. *El Tiempo*, June 8, 1977.

29. *El Siglo*, October 30, 1977.

30. According to Antonio Poveda, "There was a debate about the differentiation of the trade unionist and the political fronts. They were accusing us of being anarcho-syndicalists, of transforming ANUC into a political organization. . . . We had the ORP, with its own documents and program, but we realized that we couldn't talk politics within ANUC. On the other hand, ORP had also defined the need to take part in the electoral struggle. We therefore created the MNDP to give political expression to broad sectors of ANUC and also gain support in the urban neighborhoods, among the workers, etc." (interview 114).

31. On the formation of the MNDP and the goals of the electoral campaign, see interviews 37, 86, and 87; ANUC, "Declaración de la XVI Junta Nacional sobre la situación política," 1977; *En Marcha*, no. 1, 1977; *Alternativa*, "Dirigentes de ANUC van a elecciones," no. 130, 1977.

32. On the two leftist opposition fronts and the participation of the MNDP in FUP, see *En Marcha*, no. 2, 1977, p. 2; Controversia, *La Izquierda Colombiana y las Elecciones de 1978*, 1977.

33. Interviews 37, 64, 77, 79, 93, and 101.

34. *En Marcha*, no. 4, 1978, p. 2. According to an MNDP activist, "Just before the election, the regional evaluations were obviously inflated. According to them, we were going to win a lot of local councils. It was clear that calculations were made on the basis of ANUC's following and not MNDP's appeal. . . . In general, it was believed that there would be lots of votes, more than the Communist Party, more than MOIR" (interview 64).

35. Interviews 37 and 86. On the election results, see also J.O. Melo, "Las elecciones de 1978 y el Movimiento Firmes," 1979; H. Uribe, "Las elecciones de febrero de 1978," 1978.

36. Reflecting on the problems of the political struggle against clientelism, an MNDP activist admitted that "the *gamonales* can only be attacked by providing a more general political explanation about their role within the bourgeois-landowner regime. This requires a much more developed revolutionary consciousness among the peasants. Only then will they be able to understand the need to isolate the *gamonales*" (*En Marcha*, no. 5, 1978, p. 2).

37. On the assassination of peasant candidates, see *En Marcha*, no. 5, 1978, p. 3.

38. A peasant from Sucre, for example, explained that "the Executive Committee wanted to create a party and take part in the elections. We didn't agree because we do not believe in Colombian democracy. In a country without freedom of speech, under permanent state of siege, there is no democracy. We didn't agree and we proved to be right; the people didn't have sufficient consciousness. They still have the Conservative and Liberal parties in their minds" (interview 1).

39. An *usuario* leader from Risaralda argued that "the MNDP brought the marginalization of the people. They didn't know or didn't understand. On the other hand, the political *gamonales* scared the peasants or bought their votes. Even those who were considered as ours, as active in ANUC, voted for them. The elections were a failure" (interview 138). In Nariño: "Many had sympathized with ANUC because it was a democratic movement, which included people from all political groups. . . . With the MNDP came the downfall. The feeling for ANUC as a peasant movement decreased, and they started to see the leaders as politicians. The *gamonales* took advantage in order to put us in evidence everywhere. The peasants didn't buy the tales about the local councils and the importance of voting for us. . . . They voted for others, and when we called them, saying that we wouldn't get into politics again, they refused to come back" (interview 44). For other regional accounts of the adverse consequences of the electoral adventure, see interviews 53, 70, 85, 93, and 101.

40. Interview 79.

41. A few months after an unsuccessful national meeting of agricultural laborers in September 1977, ANUC's secretary sent a memorandum to regional contacts indicating that "we have not been able to publish the agricultural laborers' bulletin because we have heard nothing about your experiences, opinions, problems or questions" (ANUC, "Circular 03 de la Secretaría de Jornaleros," 1977). On the September meeting, see ANUC, "Conclusiones del Segundo Encuentro Nacional de Jornaleros Agrícolas," 1977.

42. Interviews 2, 6, 21, 98, 100, and 101.

43. Interviews 2, 9, 47, and 86.

44. Interviews 6, 21, 14, 95, 99, and 101.

45. *Carta Campesina*, no. 31, 1975, p. 7.

46. ANUC, "Conclusiones de la XIV Junta Nacional de Barrancabermeja," 1976.

47. ANUC, "El por qué del DRI," 1976. A regional *usuario* leader admitted that "we have characterized the DRI program in our documents, but the truth is that our characterization is insufficient. We studied the program very little, and we only said that it is a program of imperialism that defends the interests of the landowners. Our analysis is too schematic" (interview 88).

48. ANUC, "El por qué del DRI," 1976. See also *Carta Campesina*, nos. 35 and 38, 1976–1977.

49. Interviews 65, 66, 75, 129, 138, and 143.

50. *El Espectador*, January 11, 1977; *El Tiempo*, February 18, 1977.

51. Interviews 7, 14, 15, 40, 88, and 101.

52. Interview 78.

53. *La República*, February 15 and 16, 1977; INCORA, "Las empresas," pp. 40–41.

54. A *parcelero* from Tolima explained that "seeing that ANUC was finished, we organized the Association of Beneficiaries of Agrarian Reform with delegates from other departments. . . . We have had some success making recommendations to INCORA. . . .

ANUC was totally out of control and we didn't have any organization to protect us. We created our own organization to try to solve our problems" (interview 109). See also interviews 56, 61, and 107.

55. Interviews 57 and 144.

56. ANUC denounced FENSA as a divisive attempt on the part of the Communist Party. On FENSA see interview 54; L.H. Sabogal, "Problemas"; *El Colombiano*, December 6, 1976; *Alternativa*, no. 111, 1976. Regarding ANUC's reaction, see ANUC, "Fortalezcamos la ANUC combatiendo al divisionismo mamerto," 1976; *Carta Campesina*, nos. 35, 36, and 38, 1976–1977.

57. Sources: INCORA, *Labores*, p. 3; DIGIDEC, *Directorio de Juntas de Acción Comunal*, 1980. The colonization areas of Caquetá provide a good example of the way in which the government counteracted radical ANUC by means of Acción Comunal. According to the regional director of INCORA, "There are other organizations that serve as good channels, without the dangers of a political group like ANUC. Here Acción Comunal does that. ... INCORA played a role in strengthening Acción Comunal, announcing that services, credits, etc. would be given only to those who brought their demands through Acción Comunal. ... There was a surprising increase of Acción Comunal committees. In the meantime, ANUC has been totally weakened" (interview 113). Antonio Poveda explained the process from the point of view of ANUC: "Seeing that we were very strong, the government started to act in order to demobilize the people. There had been only two Acción Comunal promoters in the whole of Caquetá, but after our civil strike they put one in every neighborhood. ... They said that we were irresponsible, that we led the people to confrontation against the authorities, that it was safer to organize within Acción Comunal. They mounted a whole operation using the promoters, radio, politicians, INCORA's personnel and all the authorities. ... Our organization could not withstand that, we were impotent vis-à-vis the government" (interview 114).

58. "The DRI program has its own committees. In the meetings of the DRI committees they never talk about ANUC ... they are controlled by the different State agencies. ... They want to educate the peasants on the basis of that program, creating a parallel organization that will make them forget their authentic organization. ... They put the peasant to think about 'the milk cow,' 'farm improvement,' etc. They make him feel as somebody who is going to be rich. They create a mentality of 'new rich' among the people. ... The government knew that these programs would damage ANUC. Their goal is to put the peasant to work in his plot, to make him lose the idea, the emotion of the organization" (interview 88). On the role of the DRI groups as an integral part of the plan, see FAO/Banco Mundial, *Colombia, Proyecto de Desarrollo Rural Integrado*, 1975, chap. 4, sec. 7.

59. ANUC/Armenia, "Conclusiones del Primer Encuentro Interdepartamental de Usuarios Campesinos en la Ciudad de Medellín," 1976. See also *La República*, August 17, 1976.

60. *El Tiempo*, April 8 and July 19, 1975; *La República*, December 15, 1975.

61. ANUC/Armenia, "Tercer Congreso Nacional Campesino," 1977.

62. For reports on these activities, see *Horizonte Campesino* (the official journal of ANUC Armenia, published by the Ministry of Agriculture), nos. 1–12, 1978–1980.

63. *El Espectador*, January 13, 1977.

64. In Córdoba, for example, one of the leaders of ANUC Armenia said that "ANUC Sincelejo has lost all its influence. They told the people not to worry about the land titles. ... They rejected INCORA, saying that they already had the land and they didn't need anything. Now they are fighting one another for the land; they form groups and come to us asking for advice about how to get the titles from INCORA" (interview 39).

65. On the reorganization of ANUC Armenia in the coastal departments, see interviews 3, 4, 9, 13, 14, 15, 39, 84, 86, 98, and 131.

66. "Although the Armenia line was weak at the beginning, the institutional support helped them to recover. That coincided with the absence of programs and clear ideas on the part of ANUC Sincelejo. ANUC Sincelejo adhered to political fronts whose failure led to a loss of credibility. . . . They lose contact with the peasants because they don't propose immediate goals . . . they talk about historical long-term goals that the peasants do not understand. It is easier to work on concrete demands such as sewage installations and health centers, which sooner or later can be obtained. . . . The Armenia line, officially recognized by the state, does that type of work and is therefore more successful" (interview 60).

67. For different accounts of the right-wing reaction among ANUC's leaders, see interviews 37, 40, 64, 86, 87, and 115. The rightist fraction included Alfonso Cuéllar (one of the two main intellectual advisers) and the veteran peasant leaders Juan de Dios Torres and José Reyes Prado (who had been the main targets of the charges of corruption and bureaucratization). Most of the recently promoted young leaders sided with this group, including the National Executive members Daniel Ochoa, Hernán Monsalve, and José Martínez, and also ANUC's secretaries Octavio Ordoñez (from Caquetá), Oscar Sánchez (Tolima), and Rodrigo Zapata (Meta). In the opinion of Miguel Gamboa (the second main adviser of the *usuarios*), these peasant leaders had never been truly committed to a socialist perspective: "The spirit of confrontation had been shared not only by those who sympathized with the left, but also by radical leaders in general. Among the latter, there were bureaucratic leaders. Since ANUC had adopted a policy of abstentionism, they could stay with the movement without entering into political confrontation against the Liberal and Conservative parties. They didn't oppose the leftist influences. They accommodated to the leftist mood and entrenched themselves in ANUC's apparatus, but at the local level they continued to reconcile with the politics of clientelism. These were the ones that would later react against the political option" (interview 148).

68. The leftist minority at the national level included adviser Miguel Gamboa and peasant leaders Froilán Rivera, Jaime Vásquez, Jesús María Pérez, Antonio Poveda, and Hugo Garcés.

69. Interviews 37, 40, 64, and 68.

70. Regarding the positions of the leftist opposition, which after the break reorganized itself as the Council for Peasant Unity (CUC), see *El Espectador*, May 25, July 20, July 21, and July 22, 1979; *Carta Campesina*, no. 39, 1979; ANUC, "Constancias opositoras de miembros del Comité Ejecutivo Nacional," 1978; CUC, "Conclusiones de la Conferencia Nacional Campesina," 1979.

71. On these bureaucratic activities and the public declarations against leftist forces in the country and abroad, see *Carta Campesina*, nos. 39–43, 1979–1980.

72. ANUC's treasurer, Juan de Dios Torres, was jailed on charges of fraud and embezzlement in October 1980. See *Carta Campesina*, no. 43, 1980, p. 16; ANUC, "Telegrama dirigido a las regionales sobre detención de Juan de Dios Torres," 1980.

73. "We believe that ANUC should not be based only upon the forces of the left . . . we must define a broader policy to attract the middle and rich sectors of the peasantry that follow the orientations of the traditional parties. . . . In this sense, we want a rapprochement with the other peasant organizations, including the Armenia line of ANUC, now controlled by the Ministry of Agriculture" (interview with Oscar Sánchez and Rodrigo Zapata, published by the Agence Latino-Americaine d'Information, Bulletin no. 15, 1979). On the proposals for reunification, see interviews 22 and 43; ANUC, "Carta del Comité Ejecutivo a la Línea Armenia proponiendo reunificación," 1980.

74. One of these meetings was sponsored by the main Conservative research foundation in the country; see Fundación Mariano Ospina Pérez, "Actas."

75. ANUC, "Circular interna 07 sobre negociaciones de reunificación con Dáger Chadid," 1980.

76. On this internal plotting, see the following documents of ANUC: "Resolución de sectores disidentes en el Seminario de Tuluá," 1980; "Circular interna No. 2 de denuncia a los disidentes," 1980; "Carta de dirigentes de la Costa Atlántica apoyando al Comité Ejecutivo," 1980; "Carta abierta de dirigente campesino del Casanare contra estafadores del Comité Ejecutivo de la ANUC," 1980; "Carta de la coordinadora disidente a Juan de Dios Torres," 1980; and "Circular de la coordinadora disidente de la ANUC," 1980.

77. Interviews 43, 68, and 112.

78. Ministerio de Agricultura, "Circulares e instrucciones referentes a la reestructuración de las instancias municipales y departamentales de la ANUC con motivo del Congreso de Reunificación," 1980–1981; ANUC, "Comunicado de dirigentes de las dos líneas de la ANUC sobre la reunificación del movimiento campesino," 1980. See also *La República*, November 19, 1980, January 10, 1981; *El Siglo*, December 17, 1980; *El Tiempo*, December 18, 1980.

79. One of the DOC promoters was quite explicit about the bureaucratic maneuvers that marked the "reunification" of ANUC: "Everything was fudged. The DOC promoters received orders to sit in their departmental offices and approve any municipal list brought by the functionaries of INCORA and the Caja Agraria. . . . These functionaries didn't call the real leaders, but those whom they wanted to be in the lists. . . . Then came the departmental assemblies. We were instructed to give participation to the police and the secret security in the meetings. . . . During the Reunification Congress in Bogotá all the posts in the Executive Committee and ANUC's secretaries had been earmarked beforehand. There was an official list of candidates, and they told us that we would lose our jobs as promoters if we didn't get 'right' the votes of the regional delegates. . . . In that congress, the more zealous supporters of the government were the Sincelejo people; they repeatedly denounced the guerrillas, etc. . . . In the final balance, the leaders of ANUC Sincelejo came out as richer, more corrupted and reactionary that those of ANUC Armenia" (interview 68). For other similar accounts, see interviews 112 and 129.

80. For reports on the deliberations and conclusions of the congress, see *El Colombiano*, February 5, 1981; *El Tiempo*, February 15, 1981; *El Espectador*, February 15, 1981; *El País*, February 17, 1981; *La República*, February 17, 1981; *El Siglo*, February 17 and 21, 1981. The congress elected a new National Executive Committee with twelve members, five of whom came from ANUC Sincelejo.

81. ANUC, "Circular a los dirigentes nacionales," 1981; ANUC, "Memorando de la ANUC al presidente Turbay Ayala," 1981.

82. *El Espectador*, August 25, 1981.

83. On the formation of CUC and the 21 de Febrero Movement, see interviews 29, 51, 52, 75, 86, 115, and 137. See also *Voz Campesina* (journal of the 21 de Febrero Movement), nos. 1–6, 1979–1980; ANUC/Sectores Minoritarios, "Conclusiones de la IV reunión de los sectores opositores al Comité Ejecutivo de la ANUC," 1977; CUC, "Conclusiones."

84. Interviews 73, 86, 99, and 132. See also Comité Coordinador ANUC Linea Sincelejo, "Conclusiones del Encuentro de Dirigentes Campesinos de la ANUC Sincelejo," 1981.

85. *El Tiempo*, September 14, 1981; Comité Coordinador ANUC Línea Sincelejo, "Declaración contra la política represiva del INCORA," 1981. A regional *usuario* leader from Sucre criticized the rejectionist attitude: "We keep doing the same thing. There is a declaration of the National Committee saying that INCORA is an enemy, that the peasants should refuse signing the land titles. My question is: Have we studied the problem? Are we convinced that the peasants don't want to do that? Personally, I wouldn't dare telling the peasants that they should or shouldn't sign for the land. We are not taking the peasants' own opinions into account, and that's why we don't have a policy that will really help them" (interview 88).

10. Overview and final remarks

1. *En Marcha*, no. 4, 1978, p. 2.

2. For a discussion of the concept of relative deprivation and its use in research on peasant movements, see H. A. Landsberger, "Peasant unrest," pp. 18 and 32–33.

3. The best available discussion on the functionality of peasant reproduction for the Colombian capitalist system is found in V. M. Moncayo and F. Rojas, *Producción Campesina*, chap. 12.

4. Interviews 113, 120, 122, and 123. See also H. Korman, "Estudio sobre la colonización en el Meta," 1979; D. Giraldo and L. Ladrón de Guevara, *Desarrollo y Colonización: El Caso Colombiano*, 1981; N. Téllez and J. I. Uribe, *Aparcería, Arriendo y Colonato en el Desarrollo del Capitalismo en Colombia*, 1977; R. R. Marsh, "Colonization and integrated rural development in Colombia," 1980.

5. Sources: see Table 1.4 for 1960 and Departmento Nacional de Planeación, "Diagnóstico del Subsector Campesino o Tradicional", 1982, p. 9, for 1981.

6. J. A. Bejarano, *Campesinado*, pp. 70–71.

7. For a general and preliminary discussion of this process, see H. Vélez, "Producción campesina e inflación en la década del setenta," 1979.

Bibliography

Books, articles, pamphlets, and reports

AICA, "Caquetá, una muestra de los métodos de la Comisión política de la ANUC," Florencia, mimeo., 1975.

Alavi, H., "State and class under peripheral capitalism," in H. Alavi and T. Shanin (eds.), *Introduction to the Sociology of "Developing Societies,"* London, 1982.

Alvarez, E., "La empresa comunitaria," in ACIA (ed.), *La Tierra para El Que la Trabaja*, Bogotá, 1975.

ANIF, "Marihuana, mito y realidad," Bogotá, Symposium Papers, 1979.

ANUC, "Declaración de principios del Primer Congreso Nacional," in *Carta Campesina*, no. 9, 1970.

ANUC, "Communicado sobre las invasiones dirigido a los campesinos del país," Bogotá, mimeo., 1971.

ANUC, "Memorando de la ANUC para el Gobierno Nacional," Bogotá, mimeo., 1971.

ANUC, *Plataforma Ideológica de la Asociación Nacional de Usuarios Campesinos*, Bogotá, 1971.

ANUC, *Primer Mandato Campesino*, Bogotá, 1971.

ANUC, "El problema agrario es un problema político," Fúquene, mimeo., 1971.

ANUC, "Carta abierta de la ANUC para las autoridades del Estado," Bogotá, mimeo., 1972.

ANUC, "Conclusiones de la V Junta Directiva de Tolú sobre persecusión a funcionarios progresistas," Tolú, mimeo., 1972.

ANUC, "Conclusiones de la V Junta Directiva de Tolú sobre los CERA y la organización independiente del proletariado agrícola," Tolú, mimeo., 1972.

ANUC, "Conclusiones de la V Junta Directiva de Tolú sobre las posición política de la ANUC frente al debate electoral," Tolú, mimeo., 1972.

ANUC, "Conclusiones de la V Junta Directiva de Tolú sobre el Acuerdo de Chicoral y el proyecto de contrarreforma presentado por el Gobierno Nacional," Tolú, mimeo., 1972.

ANUC, "Las elecciones municipales y el movimiento campesino," Bogotá, mimeo., 1972.

ANUC, *Tierra para Quien la Trabaja! Conclusiones del Segundo Congreso Nacional de Usuarios Campesinos*, Sincelejo, 1972.

ANUC, "Conclusiones de la VIII Junta Directiva Nacional," Bogotá, mimeo., 1973.

ANUC, "Conclusiones de la IX Junta Directiva Nacional," Florencia, mimeo., 1973.

ANUC, "Combatamos al anarquismo," Bogotá, mimeo., 1974.

ANUC, "Comunicado de la delegación holandesa al Tercer Congreso," Bogotá, mimeo., 1974.

ANUC, "Conclusiones de la X Junta Nacional Ampliada," Popayán, mimeo., 1974.

ANUC, *Conclusiones del Tercer Congreso Nacional*, Bogotá, 1974.

ANUC, "Pliego de peticiones de la ANUC al Parlamento y al Gobierno Nacional," Bogotá, mimeo., 1974.

ANUC, "Primer encuentro nacional de pequeños y medianos propietarios, arrendatarios, aparceros y asalariados caficultores," in *Documentos de la ANUC*, Medellín, 1974.

ANUC, "Proyecto de folleto: Qué es una empresa comunitaria popular o baluarte de autogestión campesina?", in *Documentos de la ANUC*, Medellín, 1974.

ANUC, "Conclusiones de la XII Junta Directiva Nacional," Pasto/Consacá, 1975, in ANUC, *Boletín Informativo*, no. 12, 1975.

ANUC, "Denuncia pública referente a la represión y la violencia de las fuerzas militares contra la ANUC," Bogotá, mimeo., 1975.

ANUC, "Informe del Comité Ejecutivo Nacional a la XII Reunión de Junta Directiva," Pasto/Consacá, mimeo., 1975.

ANUC, "Resolución de la XIII Junta Directiva Nacional sobre los jornaleros," Cartagena, mimeo., 1975.

ANUC, "Apuntes sobre la historia interna de la ANUC," Bogotá, unpublished manuscript, 1976.

ANUC, "Carta abierta a Gilberto Vieira, Secretario General del Partido Comunista," Bogotá, mimeo., 1976.

ANUC, "Conclusiones de la XIV Junta Nacional de Barrancabermeja," Barrancabermeja, mimeo., 1976.

ANUC, "Conclusiones del Primer Encuentro Nacional de Jornaleros Agrícolas," Tuluá, mimeo., 1976.

ANUC, "Declaración sobre el Decreto de Salario Mínimo," Bogotá, mimeo., 1976.

ANUC, "El por qué del DRI," Bogotá, mimeo., 1976.

ANUC, "Fortalezcamos la ANUC combatiendo al divisionismo mamerto," Bogotá, mimeo., 1976.

ANUC, "Circular 03 de la Secretaría de Jornaleros," Bogotá, mimeo., 1977.

ANUC, "Conclusiones del Segundo Encuentro Nacional de Jornaleros Agrícolas," Tuluá, mimeo., 1977.

ANUC, "Declaración de la XVI Junta Nacional sobre la situación política," Tuluá, mimeo., 1977.

ANUC, "Proyecto de Plataforma de lucha de la ANUC: ponencia al Cuarto Congreso Nacional Campesino," Tomala, mimeo., 1977.

ANUC, "Constancias opositoras de miembros del Comité Ejecutivo Nacional," Bogotá, mimeo., 1978.

ANUC, "Carta abierta de dirigente campesino del Casanare contra estafadores del Comité Ejecutivo de la ANUC," Bogotá, mimeo., 1980.

ANUC, "Carta de la coordinadora disidente a Juan de Dios Torres," Bogotá, unpublished, 1980.

ANUC, "Carta de dirigentes de las Costa Atlántica apoyando al Comité Ejecutivo de la ANUC," Magangué, unpublished, 1980.

ANUC, "Carta del Comité Ejecutivo a la línea Armenia proponiendo reunificación," Bogotá, mimeo., 1980.

ANUC, "Circular de la coordinadora disidente de ANUC," Bogotá, mimeo., 1980.

ANUC, "Circular interna 07 sobre negociaciones de reunificación con Dáger Chadid," Bogotá, mimeo., 1980.

ANUC, "Circular interna No. 2 de denuncia a los disidentes," Bogotá, mimeo., 1980.

ANUC, "Comunicado de dirigentes de las dos líneas de la ANUC sobre la reunificación del movimiento campesino," Bogotá, mimeo., 1980.

ANUC, "Resolución de sectores disidentes en el seminario de Tuluá," Tuluá, 1980.

ANUC, "Circular a los dirigentes nacionales," Bogotá, mimeo., 1981.
ANUC, "Memorando de la ANUC al presidente Turbay Ayala," Bogotá, mimeo., 1981.
ANUC, (Antioquia), "Acuerdo campesino, conclusión de la reunión ampliada departamental," Medellín, mimeo., 1973.
ANUC (Antioquia), "Informe ante el Tercer Congreso Nacional de la ANUC," Bogotá, mimeo., 1974.
ANUC (Arauca), "Informe de la región del Sarare," Saravena, mimeo., 1974.
ANUC, (Bolívar), "Informe sobre la campaña de organización campesina," Cartagena, unpublished, 1971.
ANUC (Caquetá), "Contra el gobierno de López: Unidad, organización y lucha," Florencia, mimeo., 1975.
ANUC (Caquetá), "En qué no creemos ya?", Florencia, mimeo., 1975.
ANUC (Cauca), "Conclusiones del encuentro de empresas comunitarias del Cauca," in *Documentos de la ANUC*, Medellín, 1974.
ANUC (Córdoba), "Muestra de estatutos para formar una empresa comunitaria popular o baluarte de autogestión campesina," Montería, mimeo., 1973.
ANUC (Córdoba), "Informe ante el Tercer Congreso Nacional," Bogotá, mimeo., 1974.
ANUC (Cundinamarca), "Conclusiones del encuentro regional de empresas comunitarias realizado en La Calera," La Calera, mimeo., 1974.
ANUC (Huila), "Comunicado del Comité de Solidaridad y Defensa de los Derechos Humanos," Neiva, mimeo., 1974.
ANUC (Magdalena), "Carta al Ministro de Gobierno sobre desalojos y represión," unpublished, 1974.
ANUC (Meta), "Carta abierta a Turbay Ayala sobre la represión en San Martín," San Martín, mimeo., 1979.
ANUC (Risaralda), "Conclusiones del encuentro de empresas comunitarias de Occidente realizado en Quinchía," Quinchía, mimeo., 1974.
ANUC (Risaralda), "Posición de los campesinos de Quinchía ante el Comité Ejecutivo de la ANUC," Quinchía, mimeo., 1975.
ANUC (Sucre), "Conclusiones del encuentro de empresas comunitarias de Sucre," in *Documentos de la ANUC*, Medellín, 1974.
ANUC (Sucre), "Campesinos organizados de Sucre presentan plan para solución inmediata en empresas comunitarias," in *Carta Campesina*, no. 15, 1971.
ANUC (Tolima), "Conclusiones del encuentro regional de empresas comunitarias," Ambalema, mimeo., 1974.
ANUC (Valle), "Conclusiones de la Asamblea Departamental de Usuarios Campesinos," Cali, mimeo., 1970.
ANUC/Armenia, "Acta del Precongreso reunido en la ciudad de Neiva," Neiva, unpublished, 1972.
ANUC/Armenia, "Segundo Congreso Nacional de Usuarios Campesinos," Armenia, mimeo., 1972.
ANUC/Armenia, "Conclusiones del primer encuentro interdepartamental de usuarios campesinos en la ciudad de Medellín," Medellín, mimeo., 1976.
ANUC/Armenia, "Tercer Congreso Nacional Campesino," Santa Marta, mimeo., 1977.
ANUC/Sectores Minoritarios, "Conclusiones de la IV reunion de los sectores opositores al Comité Ejecutivo de la ANUC," Medellín, mimeo., 1977.
ANUC/Sectores Minoritarios, "Constancia de los Sectores Minoritarios de la ANUC a su Cuarto Congreso," Tomala, mimeo., 1977.

ANUC/Sectores Minoritarios, "Informe del Cuarto Congreso de la ANUC y una propuesta a los sectores opositores al Comité Ejecutivo," Medellín, mimeo., 1977.

Arango, M., *Café e Industria: 1850–1939*, Bogotá, 1977.

Arrubla, M., "La Operación Colombia o el capitalismo utópico," in M. Arrubla (ed.), *Estudios Sobre el Subdesarrollo Colombiano*, Medellín, 1977.

Arrubla, M., "Síntesis de historia política contemporanea," in M. Arrubla (ed.), *Colombia Hoy*, Bogotá, 1978.

Atkinson, L.J., "Changes in agricultural production and technology in Colombia," in *Foreign Agriculture Economic Reports*, no. 52, Washington, D.C., 1969.

Atkinson, L.J., "Agricultural productivity in Colombia," in *Foreign Agriculture Economic Reports*, no. 66, Washington, D.C., 1970.

Bagley, B.M., and Botero, F., "Organizaciones campesinas contemporáneas en Colombia: Un estudio de la ANUC," in *Estudios Rurales Latinoamericanos*, vol. 1, no. 1, Bogotá, 1978.

Bagley, B.M., and Edel, M., "Popular mobilization programs of the National Front: Cooptation and radicalization," in R.A. Berry et al. (eds.), *Politics of Compromise: Coalition Government in Colombia*, New Brunswick, N.J., 1980.

Banquett, M., "Memorias de un líder de los usuarios campesinos," Montería, unpublished manuscript, 1978.

Bejarano, J.A., "El fin de la economía exportadora y los orígenes del problema agrario," in *Cuadernos Colombianos*, nos. 6–8, Medellín, 1975.

Bejarano, J.A., "Currie: Diagnóstico y estrategia," in J.A. Bejarano, *Ensayos de Interpretación de la Economía Colombiana*, Bogotá, 1978.

Bejarano, J.A., "La economía colombiana desde 1950," in J.A. Bejarano, *Ensayos de Interpretación de la Economía Colombiana*, Bogotá, 1978.

Bejarano, J.A., *Campesinado, Luchas Agrarias e Historia Social: Notas para un Balance Historiográfico*, mimeo., 1982.

Berry, R.A., "Farm size distribution, income distribution and the efficiency of agricultural production: Colombia," in *American Economic Review*, vol. 62, no. 2, 1972.

Bonilla, V.D., "El Valle del Cauca a la hora de su transformación agraria," in *Tierra*, no. 6, Bogotá, 1967.

Buenaventura, N., *Precapitalismo en la Economía Colombiana*, Bogotá, 1976.

Calderón, C.E., and García, C.I., "Conflictos de clase que impulsan a la creación de la Asociación Nacional de Usuarios Campesinos," unpublished thesis, Universidad Javeriana, Bogotá, 1973.

Calderón, G., *Características Sociolaborales de los Recolectores de Café en un Area Cersi*, Bogotá, 1978.

Campo, U., *Urbanización y Violencia en el Valle*, Bogotá, 1980.

Cardoso, F.H., and Faletto, E., *Dependencia y Desarrollo en América Latina*, Buenos Aires, 1973.

Chayanov, A.V., "On the theory of a non-capitalist economic system," in D. Thorner et al. (eds.), *The Theory of Peasant Economy*, Homewood, Ill., 1966.

Christoffersen, L.E., "El Banco Mundial y la pobreza rural," in *Finanzas y Desarrollo*, vol. 15, no. 4, 1978.

Comité Coordinador ANUC Línea Sincelejo, "Conclusiones del encuentro de dirigentes campesinos de la ANUC Sincelejo," Sincelejo, mimeo., 1981.

Comité Coordinador ANUC Línea Sincelejo, "Declaración contra la política represiva del INCORA," Bogotá, mimeo., 1981.

Controversia, *La Izquierda Colombiana y las Elecciones de 1978*, Bogotá, 1978.

Craig, W., "The peasant movement of La Convención, Perú," in H.A. Landsberger (ed.), *Latin American Peasant Movements*, New York, 1969.

CRIC, "Como nació el CRIC: Primeras luchas," in CRIC, *Diez Años de Lucha: Historia y Documentos*, Bogotá, 1978.

CRIC, "CRIC, análisis de su organización y sus luchas," in CRIC, *Diez Años de Lucha: Historia y Documentos*, Bogotá, 1978.

CRIC, *Diez Años de Lucha: Historia y Documentos, Bogotá, 1978*.

CRIC, "Posición del CRIC frente al movimiento indígena y al Comité Ejecutivo de la ANUC," in CRIC, *Diez Años de Lucha: Historia y Documentos*, Bogotá, 1978.

CUC, "Conclusiones de la Conferencia Nacional Campesina," Bogotá, mimeo., 1979.

Currie, L., *Bases de un Programa de Fomento para Colombia*, Bogotá, 1950.

Currie, L., "El problema agrario," in M. Arrubla (ed.), *La Agricultura Colombiana en el Siglo XX*, Bogotá, 1973.

DANE, *Censo Nacional de Población*, Bogotá, 1951.

DANE, *Censo Nacional Agropecuario*, Bogotá, 1960.

DANE, *Censo Nacional de Población*, Bogotá, 1964.

DANE, *Anuario de Comercio Exterior*, Bogotá, 1965–1969.

DANE, *Censo Nacional Agropecuario*, Bogotá, 1970.

DANE, *Censo Nacional de Población*, Bogotá, 1973.

DANE, *Memoria del Sector Agropecuario 1954–1974*, Bogotá, 1975.

DANE, "Empleo y desempleo en áreas rurales de cuatro regiones," *Boletín Mensual de Estadística*, no. 332, Bogotá, 1979.

Departamento Nacional de Planeación, *Las Cuatro Estrategias*, Bogotá, 1972.

Departamento Nacional de Planeación, *Para Cerrar la Brecha: Plan de Desarrollo Social Económico y Regional*, Bogotá, 1975.

Departamento Nacional de Planeación, *Programa de Desarrollo Rural Integrado DRI*, Bogotá, 1977.

Departamento Nacional de Planeación, "Indicadores de la actividad agropecuaria," Bogotá, mimeo., 1978.

Departamento Nacional de Planeación, "Notas sobre el Plan Nacional de Alimentación y Nutrición," Bogotá, mimeo., 1978.

Departamento Nacional de Planeación, "Plan Nacional de Alimentación y Nutrición: Un resumen," Bogotá, mimeo., 1978.

Departamento Nacional de Planeación, "Diagnóstico del Subsector Campesino o Tradicional," Bogotá, mimeo., 1982.

DIGIDEC, *Directorio de Juntas de Acción Comunal*, Bogotá, 1980.

Di Tella, T., "Populism and reform in Latin America," in C. Véliz ed.), *Obstacles to Change in Latin America*, London, 1969.

Dix, R.H., "Political oppositions under the National Front," in J.A. Berry et al. (eds.), *Politics of Compromise: Coalition Government in Colombia*, New Brunswick, N.J., 1980.

Duff, E.A., *Agrarian Reform in Colombia*, New York, 1968.

Eastman, J.M., "La distribución del ingreso en Colombia," in J.M. Eastman (ed.), *Concentración de la Riqueza y del Ingreso en Colombia*, Bogotá, 1979.

Engels, F., "The peasant question in France and Germany," in K. Marx and F. Engels, *Selected Works*, Moscow, 1968.

Escobar Sierra, H., *Las Invasiones en Colombia*, Bogotá, 1972.

Fajardo, D., *Violencia y Desarrollo*, Bogotá, 1979.

Fajardo, D., "El estado y la formación del campesinado en el siglo XIX," in W. Ramírez Tobón (ed.), *Campesinado y Capitalismo en Colombia*, Bogotá, 1981.

Fals Borda, O., *Peasant Society in the Colombian Andes: A Sociological Study of Saucio*, Gainesville, Fla., 1955.

Fals Borda, O., "Violence and the break-up of tradition in Colombia," in C. Véliz (ed.), *Obstacles to Change in Latin America*, New York, 1969.

Fals Borda, O., et al., *Causa Popular; Ciencia Popular*, Bogotá, 1972.

Fals Borda, O., *Historia de la Cuestión Agraria en Colombia*, Bogotá, 1975.

Fals Borda, O., *Capitalismo, Hacienda y Poblamiento en la Costa Atlántica*, Bogotá, 1976.

Fals Borda, O., "Influencia del vecindario pobre colonial en las relaciones de producción en la Costa Atlántica," in F. Leal (ed.), *El Agro en el Desarrollo Histórico Colombiano*, Bogotá, 1977.

Fals Borda, O., "Sentido político del movimiento campesino en Colombia," in *Estudios Rurales Latinoamericanos*, vol. 1, no. 2, Bogotá, 1978.

Fals Borda, O., *El Problema de Cómo Investigar la Realidad para Transformarla*, Bogotá, 1979.

FAO/Banco Mundial, *Colombia, Proyecto de Desarrollo Rural Integrado*, Rome, 1975.

Feder, E., "La pequeña revolución verde de McNamara: El proyecto del Banco Mundial para la eliminación del campesinado en el Tercer Mundo," in *Comercio Exterior*, vol. 27, México, 1976.

Federación de Cafeteros de Colombia, *Boletín Estadístico*, Bogotá, 1950–1965.

Federación de Cafeteros de Colombia, "Informes de los Comités Departamentales de Cafeteros," Bogotá, unpublished reports, 1975–1979.

Friede, J., "La evolución de la propiedad territorial en Colombia," in CIAS (ed.), *Hacia una Reforma Agraria Masiva*, Bogotá, 1971.

Fundación del Caribe, "Algunas reflexiones sobre la Fundación del Caribe y su situación actual," Montería, unpublished, 1974.

Fundación Mariano Ospina Pérez, "Actas de las reuniones entre líderes de las líneas Armenia y Sincelejo de la ANUC," Bogotá, unpublished files, 1980.

Gaitán, G., *Colombia: Las Luchas por la Tierra en la Década del Treinta*, Bogotá, 1976.

Gaitán, M.P., "Condiciones y posibilidades de organización del proletariado cañero en Colombia," in W. Ramírez Tobón (ed.), *Campesinado y Capitalismo en Colombia*, Bogotá, 1978.

Galán, L.C., "Las elecciones de febrero y junio de 1978," in R. Losada (ed.), *Las Elecciones de 1978 en Colombia*, Bogotá, 1979.

Galeski, B., "The prospects of collective farming," *Land Tenure Center Monograph* no. 95, Madison, Wis., 1973.

Galeski, B., *Basic Concepts of Rural Sociology*, Manchester, 1975.

García, B., *Anticurrie*, Bogotá, 1973.

Germani, G., et.al., *Populismo y Contradicciones de Clase en América Latina*, México, 1973.

Gilhodès, P., "Agrarian struggles in Colombia," in R. Stavenhagen (ed.), *Agrarian Problems and Peasant Movements in Latin America*, New York, 1970.

Gilhodès, P., *La Question Agraire en Colombie*, Paris, 1974.

Giraldo, D., and Ladrón de Guevara, L., *Desarrollo y Colonización: El Caso Colombiano*, Bogotá, 1981.

Glass, L., and Bonilla, V.D., "La reforma agraria frente al minifundio nariñense," in *Tierra*, no. 4, Bogotá, 1967.

Gómez, A., "Política agraria de López y Ley de Aparcería," in *Ideologia y Sociedad*, no. 14–15, Bogotá, 1975.

Gómez, A., "Implicaciones de la política agraria para cerrar la brecha," in *Ideología y Sociedad*, No. 17–18, Bogotá, 1976.

Gómez, J., *Complimiento de la Legislación Laboral en Cultivos Comerciales*, Bogotá, 1977.

González, F., *Colombia 1974, La Política*, Bogotá, 1975.

González, F.E., *Pasado y Presente del Sindicalismo Colombiano*, Bogotá, 1975.

González, M., "La hacienda colonial y los orígenes de la propiedad territorial en Colombia," in *Cuadernos Colombianos*, vol. 3, no. 12, Medellín, 1979.

Goodman, D., and Redclift, M., *From Peasant to Proletarian, Capitalist Development and Agrarian Transitions*, Oxford, 1981.

Gott, R., *Rural Guerrillas in Latin America*, Middlesex, 1970.

Grunig, J.E., "The minifundio problem in Colombia: Development alternatives," *Land Tenure Center Reprint No. 63*, Madison, Wis., 1970.

Grupo Antirrosca de Montería, "Informe sobre el Tercer Congreso de la ANUC," Montería, mimeo., 1974.

Grupo Proletarización, *De Dónde Venimos, Hacia Dónde Vamos, Hacia Dónde Debemos Ir?*, Medellín, 1975.

Gutiérrez, J.M., "The green revolution marches on in Colombia," in *Tropical Abstracts*, No, 28(1), 49, 1971.

Guzmán, G., et al., *La Violencia en Colombia*, Bogotá, 1962.

Haney, E., "Progressive deterioration of minifundia agriculture in Colombia: Structural reform not in sight," in *Latin American Research Briefs*, no. 214, Madison, Wis., 1971.

Haney, E., "El dilema del minifundio en Colombia," *Land Tenure Center Reprint No. 85*, Madison, Wis., 1972.

Harris, J. (ed.), *Rural Development: Theories of Peasant Economy and Agrarian Change*, London, 1982.

Havens, A.E., *Cereté: Un Area de Latifundio*, Bogotá, 1965.

Havens, A.E., and Flinn, W.L., *Internal Colonialism and Structural Change in Colombia*, New York, 1970.

Havens, A.E., et al., "Agrarian reform and the National Front," in R.A. Berry et al. (eds.), *Politics of Compromise, Coalition Government in Colombia*, New Brunswick, N.J., 1980.

Hobsbawm, E.J., *Primitive Rebels*, New York, 1965.

Hobsbawm, E.J., "Peasants and rural migrants in politics," in C. Véliz (ed.), *The Politics of Conformity in Latin America*, New York, 1970.

Huizer, G., and Stavenhagen, R., "Peasant movements and agrarian reform in Latin America: México and Bolivia," in H.A. Landsberger (ed.), *Rural Protest: Peasant Movements and Social Change*, London, 1974.

Huizer, G., *Peasant Participation in Latin America and Its Obstacles*, The Hague, 1980.

Ianni, O., *La Formación del Estado Populista en América Latina*, México, 1975.

INCORA, "Informe especial," Bogotá, mimeo., 1969.

INCORA, "La realidad rural y la reforma agraria como factor de cambio," in DANE (ed.), *Debate Agrario, Documentos*, Bogotá, 1971.

INCORA, *Labores Adelantadas en Desarrollo Social*, Bogotá, 1971.

INCORA, *La Colonización en Colombia: Una Evaluación del Proceso*, Bogotá, 1973.

INCORA, "Proyecto Sucre," Sincelejo, mimeo., 1975.

INCORA, "Proyecto Sucre, desarrollo y programación de cultivos transitorios y permanentes," Sincelejo, mimeo., 1975.

INCORA, *Reforma Social Agraria, Leyes y Decretos Reglamentarios*, Bogotá, 1975.

INCORA, *Las Empresas Comunitarias en la Reforma Agraria*, Bogotá, 1977.

INCORA, *Informe de Labores*, Bogotá, 1978.

INCORA, "Proyecto Sucre, informe de actividades 1969–1978," Sincelejo, mimeo., 1978.

INCORA, *Informe de Gerencia*, Bogotá, 1979.

INCORA, *Las Formas Asociativas de Producción: Características y Resultados*, Bogotá, 1979.

INCORA, *Resumen General de las Principales Realizaciones del INCORA por Proyectos: 1962–1979*, Bogotá, 1980.

INCORA, "Informe de la comisión Caso Morroa sobre legalización de predios adquiridos por el Instituto," Sincelejo, unpublished report, 1981.

Inter-American Committee for Agricultural Development, *Colombia, Tenencia de la Tierra y Desarrollo Socioeconómico del Sector Agropecuario*, Washington, D.C., 1966.

Jaramillo Uribe, J., "Etapas y sentido de la historia colombiana," in M. Arrubla (ed.), *Colombia Hoy*, Bogotá, 1978.

Junguito, R. and Caballero, C., "La otra economía," in *Coyuntura Económica*, vol. 8, no. 4, Bogotá, 1978.

Junguito, R., et al., *Economía Cafetera Colombiana*, Bogotá, 1980.

Kalmanovitz, S., "Auge y receso del capitalismo en Colombia," in S. Kalmanovitz, *Ensayos Sobre el Desarrollo del Capitalismo Dependiente*, Bogotá, 1977.

Kalmanovitz, S., "Desarrollo represivo acelerado," in S. Kalmanovitz, *Ensayos Sobre el Desarrollo del Capitalismo Dependiente*, Bogotá, 1977.

Kalmanovitz, S., "Desarrollo capitalista en el campo," in M. Arrubla (ed.), *Colombia Hoy*, Bogotá, 1978.

Kalmanovitz, S., *La Agricultura en Colombia: 1950–1972*, Bogotá, 1978.

Kautsky, K., *La Cuestión Agraria*, Bogotá, 1974.

Killian, L.M., "Social movements," in R. Faris (ed.), *Handbook of Modern Sociology*, Chicago, 1965.

Kline, H.F., "The National Front: Historical Perspective and overview," in R.A. Berry et al. (eds.), *Politics of Compromise: Coalition Government in Colombia*, New Brunswick, N.J., 1980.

Korman, H., "Estudio sobre la colonización en el Meta," unpublished thesis, Universidad de los Andes, Bogotá, 1979.

Landsberger, H.A., "Peasant unrest: Themes and variations," in H.A. Landsberger (ed.), *Rural Protest: Peasant Movements and Social Change*, London, 1974.

Landsberger, H.A., and Hewitt, C.N., "Ten sources of weakness and cleavage in Latin American peasant movements," in R. Stavenhagen (ed.), *Agrarian Problems and Peasant Movements in Latin America*, New York, 1970.

Leal, F., "Raíces económicas de la formación de un sistema de partidos en una sociedad agraria: el caso de Colombia," in *Estudios Rurales Latinoamericanos*, vol. 3, no. 1, Bogotá, 1980.

Lehmann, D., "Generalizing about peasant movements," in *Journal of Development Studies*, vol. 9, no. 2, 1973.

Lenin, V.I., "New economic developments in peasant life," in V.I. Lenin, *Collected Works*, vol. 1, Moscow, 1960.

Lenin, V.I., *The Development of Capitalism in Russia*, Moscow, 1974.

Liboreiro, E., et al., *Análisis de las Empresas Comunitarias Campesinas en Colombia*, Bogotá, 1977.

Lieuwen, E., *Venezuela*, Oxford, 1961.

Ligas M.L., *Colombia Semifeudal Neocolonial*, Medellín, 1975.

Lleras Restrepo, C., "Estructura de la reforma agraria," in *Tierra, Diez Ensayos Sobre Reforma Agraria*, Bogotá, 1961.

Lleras Restrepo, C., *Mensaje del Presidente de la República al Congreso Nacional*, Bogotá, 1967.

Machado, A., *El Cafe: De la Aparcería al Capitalismo*, Bogotá, 1977.

Mansilla, L., *Inserción Laboral de Migrantes Indocumentados*, Bogotá, 1979.

Mármora, L., et al., *Migraciones en la Cosecha del Algodón*, Bogotá, 1976.

Marsh, R.R., "Colonization and integrated rural development in Colombia," unpublished thesis, University of California, 1980.

Martínez, J.P., and Izquierdo, M.I., *ANAPO: Oposición o Revolución*, Bogotá, 1972.

Marx, K., *Capital*, 3 vols., Moscow, 1966.

Marx, K., "The civil war in France," in K. Marx, *The First International and After*, Middlesex, 1974.

McGreevey, W.P., *Historia Económica de Colombia: 1845–1930*, Bogotá, 1975.

McNamara, R., "Agricultura y pobreza," in *Cuadernos de Agroindustria y Economía Rural*, no. 2, Bogotá, 1979.

Melo, J.O., "La República Conservadora," in M. Arrubla (ed.), *Colombia Hoy*, Bogotá, 1978.

Melo, J.O., "Las elecciones de 1978 y el Movimiento Firmes," in R. Losada (ed.), *Las Elecciones de 1978 en Colombia*, Bogotá, 1978.

Mesa, A., "Introducción al Foro sobre Bonanza Cafetera," in J. Silva Colmenares et al. (eds.), *La Bonanza Cafetera*, Bogotá, 1977.

Mesa, D., "El problema agrario en Colombia: 1920–1960," in M. Arrubla (ed.), *La Agricultura Colombiana en el Siglo XX*, Bogotá, 1976.

Ministerio de Agricultura, *Reforma Social Agraria en Colombia*, Bogotá, 1961.

Ministerio de Agricultura, *Organización Campesina*, Bogotá, 1967.

Ministerio de Agricultura,, *Campaña Nacional de Organización Campesina: Informe 1968*, Bogotá, 1968.

Ministerio de Agricultura, *Campaña Nacional de Organización Campesina: Informe 1969*, Bogotá, 1969.

Ministerio de Agricultura, *Manual de Instrucción para Promotores de Organización Campesina*, Bogotá, 1969.

Ministerio de Agricultura, "Memorando sobre el estado de Organización Campesina," Bogotá, unpublished report, 1970.

Ministerio de Agricultura, "Datos correspondientes a ocupaciones de tierras en los últimos meses," unpublished report, Bogotá, 1971.

Ministerio de Agricultura, "Invasiones en distintos lugares del país entre el 1 de Junio y el 15 de Noviembre," unpublished report, Bogotá, 1971.

Ministerio de Agricultura, "Memorando sobre campesinos muertos o heridos por problemas de tierras," unpublished report, Bogotá, 1971.

Ministerio de Agricultura, "Relación de invasiones en todo el país," unpublished report, Bogotá, 1971.

Ministerio de Agricultura, "Resumen de trabajos realizados en Organización Campesina," Bogotá, unpublished report, 1971.

Ministerio de Agricultura, "Correspondencia recibida e informes de promotores de Organización Campesina en los diferentes departamentos del país," Bogotá, unpublished files, 1970–1972.

Ministerio de Agricultura, *Cifras del Sector Agropecuario*, Bogotá, 1979.

Ministerio de Agricultura, "Circulares e instrucciones referentes a la reestructuración de las instancias municipales y departamentales de la ANUC con motivo del Congreso de Reunificación," Bogotá, mimeo., 1980–1981.

Miranda, N., and González, F.E., *Clientelismo, "Democracia" o Poder Popular*, Bogotá, 1976.

Moncayo, V.M., "La ley y el problema agrario en Colombia," in *Ideología y Sociedad*, no. 14–15, Bogotá, 1975.

Moncayo, V.M., and Rojas, F., *Producción Campesina y Capitalismo*, Bogotá, 1979.

Moore, B., *Social Origins of Dictatorship and Democracy: Lord and Peasant in the Making of the Modern World*, Boston, 1966.

Moraes, C., "Peasant leagues in Brazil," in R. Stavenhagen (ed.), *Agrarian Problems and Peasant Movements in Latin America*, New York, 1970.

Morray, J.P., "The United States and Latin America," in J. Petras and M. Zeitlin (eds.), *Latin America: Reform or Revolution?*, Greenwich, Conn., 1968.

Murillo, G., *La Migración de Trabajadores Colombianos a Venezuela*, Bogotá, 1979.

Murle, H., et al., "La lucha por la tierra: 1970–1978," in *Cuadernos de Agroindustria y Economía Rural*, no. 3, Bogotá, 1979.

Nieto Arteta, L.E., *El Café en la Sociedad Colombiana*, Bogotá, 1958.

Noriega, C.A., "Los resultados electorales y su significado político," in R. Losada (ed.), *Las Elecciones de 1978 en Colombia*, Bogotá, 1979.

Ocampo, J.A., "Desarrollo exportador y desarrollo capitalista colombiano en el siglo XIX, una hipótesis," in *Desarrollo y Sociedad*, no. 1, Bogotá, 1979.

Ocampo, J.F., "Imperialismo, atraso capitalista, burguesía nacional y revolución de Nueva Democracia," in *Uno en Dos*, vol. 2, no. 2, Bogotá, 1972.

Oquist, O., *Violence, Conflict and Politics in Colombia*, New York, 1980.

ORP, "Los jornaleros agrícolas y la lucha campesina," in *Combate*, no. 3, 1976.

ORP, "Mensaje de la Organización Revolucionaria del Pueblo a los campesinos," in *Combate*, no. 5, 1977.

Ospina Vásquez, L.A., *Industria y Protección en Colombia: 1810–1930*, Medellín, 1974.

Palacios, M., *El Populismo en Colombia*, Medellín, 1971.

Palacios, M., *El Café en Colombia: 1850–1970*, Bogotá, 1979.

Parra, E., *La Investigación-Acción en la Costa Atlántica: Evaluación de La Rosca*, Cali, 1983.

Parra, E., et al., *Colombia 1974, Economía y Luchas Sociales*, Bogotá, 1975.

Parra, E., and Reyes, A., "Empresas comunitarias rurales y desarrollo del sector agropecuario en la Costa Atlántica," unpublished monograph, Bogotá, 1977.

PCML, *Documentos del Partido Comunista de Colombia (Marxista-Leninista)*, 4 vols., Medellín, 1975.

Pecaut, D., "Reflexiones sobre el fenómeno de la Violencia," in *Ideología y Sociedad*, no. 19, Bogotá, 1976.

Peláez, J., "DRI: Un programa imperialista para los campesinos," in *Estudios Marxistas*, no. 12, Bogotá, 1976.

Pérez, H., *Enjuiciamiento a la Política Agraria y Cafetera*, Bogotá, 1978.

Quijano, A., "Contemporary peasant movements," in S.M. Lipset and A. Solari (eds.), *Elites in Latin America*, New York, 1967.

Reyes, A., "El modelo campesino de empresas comunitarias," Bogotá, unpublished monograph, 1976.

Reyes, A., *Latifundio y Poder Político*, Bogotá, 1978.

Reyes, A., et al., *Estatuto de Seguridad*, Bogotá, 1978.

Roberts, C.P., *Statistical Abstract of Latin America*, Berkeley, 1969.

Robinson, J.C., *El Movimiento Gaitanista en Colombia*, Bogotá, 1976.

Rojas, F., et al., *Política Laboral de López*, Bogotá, 1977.

Rojas, H., "El Frente Nacional, solución política a un problema de desarrollo? in R. Parra (ed.), *La Dependencia Externa y el Desarrollo Político de Colombia*, Bogotá, 1970.

Ruiz, S., *La Fuerza de Trabajo en la Producción de Arroz y Algodón*, Bogotá, 1973.

Sabogal, L.H., "Problemas de la organización campesina," in *Documentos Políticos*, no. 120, Bogotá, 1976.

Sánchez, G., *Las Ligas Campesinas en Colombia*, Bogotá, 1977.

Sandilands, R.J., "The modernization of the agricultural sector and rural–urban migration in Colombia," *Occasional Papers*, Institute of Latin American Studies, Glasgow, 1971.

Sanoa, J.V., "Campesinos pobres y semiproletarios," in *Estudios Marxistas*, no. 12, Bogotá, 1976.

Santana, P., et al., *El Paro Cívico*, Bogotá, 1982.

Shanin, T., "The nature and logic of the peasant economy: A generalization," in *Journal of Peasant Studies*, vol. 1, Nos. 1–2, London, 1973.

Shanin, T., "Class, state and revolution: Substitutes and realities," in H. Alavi and T. Shanin (eds.), *Introduction to the Sociology of "Developing Societies,"* London, 1982.

Shanin, T., "Late Marx, gods and craftesmen," in T. Shanin (ed.), *Late Marx and the "Russian Road,"* London, 1983.

Skocpol, T., *States and Social Revolutions*, New York, 1979.

Smith, T.L., "Improvement of the systems of agriculture in Colombia," in T.L. Smith, *Studies of Latin American Societies*, New York, 1970.

Smith, T.L., "The growth of population in Central and South America," in T.L. Smith, *Studies of Latin American Societies*, New York, 1970.

Smith, T.L., "The racial composition of the population of Colombia," in T.L. Smith, *Studies of Latin American Societies*, New York, 1970.

Socialist Bloc, "La situación actual del movimiento campesino," Bogotá, mimeo., 1973.

Socialist Bloc, *Por un Partido Obrero y Socialista: Tesis y Documentos del Bloque Socialista*, Bogotá, 1975.

Sociedad de Agricultores de Colombia, "Los gremios agrícolas y las invasiones," in DANE (ed.), *Debate Agrario, Documentos*, Bogotá, 1971.

Sociedad de Agricultores de Colombia, *Bases para una Política Agropecuaria*, Bogotá, 1978.

Solaún, M., "Colombian politics: Historical characteristics and problems," in R.A. Berry et al. (eds.), *Politics of Compromise, Coalition Government in Colombia*, New Brunswick, N.J., 1980.

Soles, R.E., "Rural land invasions in Colombia," *Land Tenure Center Monograph*, Madison, Wis., 1974.

Suárez Melo, M., "Campaña Nacional de Organización Campesina," in *Documentos del Seminario Internacional Sobre Organización Campesina*, Guatemala, 1969.

Suárez Melo, M., *Las Empresas Comunitarias Campesinas en Colombia*, Bogotá, 1972.

Taussig, M., "Religión de esclavos y la formación de un campesinado en el Valle del Cauca," in *Estudios Rurales Latinoamericanos*, vol. 2, no. 2, Bogotá, 1979.

Téllez, N., and Uribe, J. I., *Aparcería, Arriendo y Colonato en el Desarrollo del Capitalismo en Colombia*, Bogotá, 1977.

Tirado Mejía, A., "Colombia, siglo y medio de bipartidismo," in M. Arrubla (ed.), *Colombia Hoy*, Bogotá, 1978.

Tirado Mejía, A., "Aspectos de la colonización antioqueña," in *Revista de Extensión Cultural*, no. 7, Universidad Nacional de Colombia, Medellín, 1981.

Tobón, A., *La Tierra y la Reforma Agraria en Colombia*, Bogotá, 1972.

Torales, P., *La Dinámica de los Movimientos Migratorios en Colombia*, Bogotá, 1979.

Tovar, H., *El Movimiento Campesino en Colombia*, Bogotá, 1975.

Uribe, H., "Las elecciones de febrero de 1978," in Controversia, *Elecciones 1978*, Bogotá, 1978.

Urrea, F., *Mercados de Trabajo y Migraciones en la Explotación Cafetera*, Bogotá, 1976.

Urrea, F., "Consideraciones sobre el tema de la Violencia," in F. Leal (ed.), *El Agro en el Desarrollo Histórico Colombiano*, Bogotá, 1977.

Vallejo, J., "Problemas de método en el estudio de la cuestión agraria," in F. Leal (ed.), *El Agro en el Desarrollo Histórico Colombiano*, Bogotá, 1977.

Vélez, H., "Difusión de la producción mercantil y de la tecnificación en la agricultura colombiana," in M. Arrubla (ed.), *La Agricultura Colombiana en el Siglo XX*, Bogotá, 1976.

Vélez, H., "Producción campesina e inflación en la década del setenta," in *Cuadernos Colombianos*, no. 12, Bogotá, 1979.

Villegas, J., "La colonización de vertiente del siglo XIX en Colombia," in *Estudio Rurales Latinoamericanos*, vol. 1, no. 2, Bogotá, 1978.

Weber, M, "Politics as a vocation," in H.H. Gerth and C. Wright Mills (eds.), *From Max Weber: Essays in Sociology*, New York, 1958.

Wolf, E.R., *Peasant Wars of the Twentieth Century*, New York, 1969.

Wolf, E.R., "On peasant rebellions," in T. Shanin (ed.), *Peasants and Peasant Societies*, Middlesex, 1971.

Yudelman, M., "Los efectos de los préstamos del Banco Mundial para el desarrollo rural," in *Finanzas y Desarrollo*, vol. 16, no. 3, 1979.

Newspapers and magazines

Alternativa
Alternativa del Pueblo
Diario de la Costa
Diario del Caribe
El Colombiano
El Espacio
El Espectador
El Frente
El Heraldo
El Informador
El Nacional
El País
El Periódico
El Siglo
El Tiempo
La Patria
La República
La Voz de la Democracia
Occidente
Vanguardia Liberal
Voz Proletaria

Journals and bulletins

Boletín Informativo (ANUC, línea Sincelejo)
Boletines de Prensa (ANUC, línea Sincelejo)
Carta Campesina (ANUC, línea Sincelejo)
Combate (Organización Revolucionaria del Pueblo–ORP)
En Marcha (Movimiento Nacional Democrático Popular–MNDP)
Horizonte Campesino (ANUC, línea Armenia)
Patria Roja (Organización Revolucionaria del Pueblo–ORP)
Unidad Indígena (CRIC, Consejo Regional Indígena del Cauca)
Voz Campesina (Sectores Minoritarios 21 de Febrero)

Press Archives

INCORA: Archivo de Prensa, 1967–1979
CINEP: Archivo de Prensa, 1970–1980

List of interviews

Numbers in brackets correspond to the numbering system used in CINEP's Archive on ANUC in Bogotá.

1. Peasant, ANUC Sincelejo, Sucre [1]
2. Member of the Union of INCORA's Employees, Sucre [2]
3. Peasants, ANUC Sincelejo, Bolívar [3]
4. Regional peasant leader, ANUC Armenia, and DOC promoter, Bolívar [4]
5. INCORA official, Bolívar [5]
6. INCORA official, Bolívar [6]
7. Peasant, ANUC Armenia, Córdoba [7]
8. Peasants, ANUC Sincelejo, Atlántico [8]
9. DOC promoter, Atlántico [9]
10. INCORA officials, Atlántico [10]
11. Peasant, ANUC Armenia, Atlántico [11]
12. INCORA officials, Magdalena [12]
13. Regional peasant leader, ANUC Armenia, Magdalena [13]
14. INCORA officials, Córdoba [14]
15. Former ML activist, Córdoba [15]
16. Peasants, former *baluarte* Juana Julia, ANUC Sincelejo, Córdoba [16]
17. Clovis Flores, regional peasant leader, ANUC Sincelejo, Córdoba [17]
18. Notes from informal talks with peasants, Córdoba [18]
19. Peasants, former *baluarte* El Boche, ANUC Sincelejo, Córdoba [19]
20. Members of the Union of INCORA's Employees, Córdoba [20]
21. INCORA official, Córdoba [21]
22. Rodrigo Zapata, national peasant leader, ANUC Sincelejo, from Meta [22]
23. Peasants, former *baluarte* Urbano de Castro, ANUC Sincelejo, Córdoba [23]
24. Former ML activist, Antioquia [24]
25. Regional peasant leader, ANUC Armenia, Putumayo [25]
26. Peasant, ANUC Sincelejo, Putumayo [26]
27. INCORA official, Putumayo [27]
28. ML activist, Atlántico [28]
29. ML activist, Atlántico [29]
30. INCORA official, Magdalena [30]
31. Local lawyer, Magdalena [31]
32. INCORA official, Cesar [32]
33. Víctor Calle, former DOC director [33]
34. Former Socialist Bloc activist and adviser of ANUC Sincelejo [34]
35. MNDP activist, Cauca [35]
36. Oscar Sánchez, national peasant leader, ANUC Sincelejo, from Tolima [36]
37. Froilán Rivera, national peasant leader, ANUC Sincelejo, from Sucre [37]
38. Regional peasant leader, ANUC Sincelejo, Valle [38]
39. Regional peasant leader, ANUC Armenia, Córdoba [39]
40. Regional peasant leader, ANUC Sincelejo, Córdoba [40]
41. INCORA official, Antioquia [41]
42. Oscar Sánchez, national peasant leader, ANUC Sincelejo [42]
43. Rodrigo Zapata, national peasant leader, ANUC Sincelejo [43]
44. Regional peasant leader, ANUC Sincelejo, Nariño [44]
45. Member of the Union of INCORA's Employees, Nariño [45]
46. DOC promoter, Nariño [46]
47. INCORA official, Antioquia [47]

48. INCORA official, Risaralda [48]
49. Regional peasant leader, ANUC Sincelejo, Antioquia [49]
50. Regional peasant leader, ANUC Sincelejo, Santander [50]
51. Peasant national leaders, 21 de Febrero Movement, ANUC Sincelejo [51]
52. Froilán Rivera, national peasant leader, ANUC Sincelejo, and Miguel Gamboa, national adviser of ANUC Sincelejo and MNDP leader [52]
53. Former INCORA official, Sarare and Risaralda [53]
54. Luis Sabogal, Communist Party leader and FENSA coordinator [54]
55. Gregorio Palechor, regional Indian leader, CRIC, Cauca [55]
56. DRI official, Cauca [56]
57. Member of FANAL's National Executive Committee [57]
58. DOC National Coordinator, Bogotá [58]
59. Journalists, Huila [59]
60. INCORA official, Huila [60]
61. DOC promoter, Huila [61]
62. Peasants, ANUC Sincelejo, Huila [62]
63. Former URS activist, Huila [63]
64. Former MNDP activist, Bogotá [64]
65. ML activists, Cauca [65]
66. Peasants, ANUC Armenia, Nariño [66]
67. DOC promoter, Nariño [67]
68. INCORA official, Santander, and DOC promoter, Nariño [68]
69. Notes from informal talks with INCORA officials, Santander [69]
70. Popular education promoter, Caquetá [70]
71. Regional peasant leader, ANUC Sincelejo, Córdoba [71]
72. DOC promoter, Santander [75]
73. Regional peasant leader, ANUC Sincelejo, Middle Magdalena [77]
74. Peasant, ANUC Sincelejo, Middle Magdalena [78]
75. Regional peasant leader, 21 de Febrero Movement, ANUC Sincelejo, Antioquia [79]
76. Trade union activists, Bolívar [80]
77. Peasant, ANUC Sincelejo, Bolívar [81]
78. INCORA officials, Bolívar [82]
79. Peasant, ANUC Sincelejo, Bolívar [83]
80. Officials of Acción Comunal and the Institute of National Resources, Magdalena [84]
81. Peasants, ANUC Sincelejo, Magdalena [85]
82. Peasant-fisherman, ANUC Sincelejo, Magdalena [86]
83. INCORA official, Cesar [87]
84. Peasant, ANUC Armenia, Cesar [88]
85. Regional peasant leader, ANUC Sincelejo, Nariño [89]
86. Jesús María Pérez, national peasant leader, ANUC Sincelejo, from Sucre [90]
87. Froilán Rivera, national peasant leader, ANUC Sincelejo [91]
88. Regional peasant leader, ANUC Sincelejo, Sucre [93]
89. Notes from informal talks with peasants, Córdoba [94]
90. Peasant, ANUC Sincelejo, Córdoba [95]
91. Peasant, ANUC Sincelejo, Córdoba [96]
92. Clovis Flores, regional peasant leader, ANUC Sincelejo, Córdoba [97]
93. Regional peasant leader, ANUC Sincelejo, Córdoba [98]
94. Peasant, ANUC Sincelejo, Córdoba [99]
95. Notes from informal talks with peasants, Córdoba [100]

96. Peasant, ANUC Sincelejo, Córdoba [101]
97. Notes from informal talks with peasants, Sucre [102]
98. INCORA official, Sucre [103]
99. Notes from informal talks with peasants, Sucre [104]
100. Froilán Rivera, national peasant leader, ANUC Sincelejo [105]
101. Peasant, ANUC Sincelejo, Córdoba [106]
102. Clovis Flores, regional peasant leader, ANUC Sincelejo, Córdoba [108]
103. Peasant, ANUC Sincelejo, Córdoba [109]
104. Peasant, ANUC Sincelejo, Córdoba [110]
105. Peasant, ANUC Sincelejo, Córdoba [111]
106. Peasants, ANUC Sincelejo, Córdoba [112]
107. INCORA officials, Tolima [113]
108. DOC promoter, Tolima [114]
109. Peasant, ANUC Sincelejo, Tolima [115]
110. INCORA officials, Huila [116]
111. Peasant, ANUC Armenia, Huila [117]
112. José del Carmen Yepes, national peasant leader, ANUC Armenia, from Huila [118]
113. INCORA officials, Caquetá [120]
114. Antonio Poveda, national peasant leader, ANUC Sincelejo, from Caquetá [121]
115. Froilán Rivera, national peasant leader, ANUC Sincelejo [122]
116. Anthropologists who worked with the Indian movement CRIC [123]
117. INCORA officials, Meta [124]
118. Peasant-artisan, ANUC Armenia, Meta [125]
119. MOIR activist, Meta [126]
120. Peasant, ANUC Sincelejo, Meta [127]
121. MOIR activist, Casanare [128]
122. Peasant, OCIDEC, Casanare [129]
123. Regional peasant leader, OCIDEC, Casanare [130]
124. INCORA official, Casanare [131]
125. INCORA official, Sarare [132]
126. Peasant, ANUC Sincelejo, Sarare [134]
127. Physician, regional adviser of ANUC Sincelejo, Sarare [135]
128. INCORA official, North Santander [136]
129. DOC promoter, North Santander [137]
130. Peasant, ANUC Armenia, North Santander [138]
131. Former ML activist, Córdoba [139]
132. Notes from interviews with members of the Coordination Committee, opposition sectors within ANUC Sincelejo [140]
133. Notes from informal talks with peasants, Córdoba [141]
134. Regional peasant leader, ANUC Sincelejo, Córdoba [142]
135. Peasant, ANUC Sincelejo, Córdoba [143]
136. Former DOC promoter, Sucre [144]
137. Regional peasant leader, 21 de Febrero Movement, ANUC Sincelejo, Sucre [145]
138. Regional peasant leader, ANUC Sincelejo, Risaralda [146]
139. Artisan, Civil Committee of Quinchía, Risaralda [147]
140. INCORA officials, Caldas [148]
141. INCORA official, Caldas [149]
142. Regional Indian leader, Caldas [150]
143. Peasant, ANUC Sincelejo, Boyacá [151]
144. Carlos Rico, former national leader of ANUC and president of ACC, from Valle [152]

145. INCORA official, Santander [153]
146. Peasant, ANUC Sincelejo, Antioquia [154]
147. INCORA official, Cauca [155]
148. Miguel Gamboa, national adviser of ANUC Sincelejo and MNDP leader [156]

Index

ANUC (*cont.*)

192, 204–7, 231n; in areas of *latifundia*,
61, 91–3, 107, 204–7, 231n; in areas of
peasant economy, 61, 95–6, 174, 179–80,
191–3, 204; Armenia line of, 101, 103–4,
107, 111, 126, 129, 168, 170; authentic
peasant character of, xiii, 61–3, 66; bureaucratism in, 179–82, 199–200, 203,
207, 248–9n, 254n; as class organization
of peasantry, 3, 51–2, 66, 193–6, 202,
204; in coffee areas, 140, 144–5; congresses of, 59, 60, 68–9, 101, 103–4,
107, 115, 117–18, 126, 140, 141, 171,
173, 179, 181–2, 187, 195, 197, 200; corruption in, 179, 199, 246n, 248–9n, 254n;
created by Lleras Restrepo administration,
3, 43–65; data collection on, 6,
228n; Declaration of Principles of, 68–9;
decline of, 179–201; division of, 70, 100–
3, 227n, 233n; and DRI program, 191–3;
electoral abstentionism of, 101, 102, 190,
254n; and *empresas comunitarias*, 165–
78, 190–1, 192–3, 196, 201, 203, 248n,
255n; Executive Committee of, 59, 62,
71, 126, 140–1, 143, 180–2, 197–8,
225n, 227n, 249n; and financial support
from foreign foundations, 106, 118, 169,
172, 173, 179, 199, 205–6, 234n, 235n;
heterogeneous class composition of, xiii,
61–2, 66, 140, 204–7; historical relevance
of, 2–4, 211; issues for further study of,
xiv, 208–12; Junta Directiva of, 59, 62,
70–1, 72–3, 100–1, 107, 118, 127, 140,
141, 171, 173, 191, 197, 227n; land
struggles of, 67, 69–70, 71, 73, 74–91,
105–13, 127–9, 182–6, 202–3, 229–30n;
leadership, xiii, 55, 57, 60, 62–3, 92, 94,
95, 100–1, 116–17, 139, 176, 177–8,
179–82, 190, 192, 193, 197–201, 203,
205–6, 207, 210–11, 224–5n, 231n, 233n,
246n, 250n, 254n; leftist politicization of,
4, 5, 112–21, 174–5, 210–11; López
Michelsen's policy towards, 126–9, 171,
174, 175, 180, 194, 195–6, 198–200,
233n, 248n, 253n, 254n; *Mandato Campesino* of, 73, 97, 100, 107, 140, 166–8,
236n; marches organized by, 55, 104,
109, 110–11, 116, 234n; national scope
of, 61–2, 66; opposed to marihuana and
cocaine, 139–40; organizational campaign
of, 54–60, 66; organizational structure of,
55–9, 63–5; organized as association of
users of state services, 50–3, 175; overview of its struggles, xii–xiii, 202–7; Pastrana's policy towards, 100–4; *Plataforma
Ideológica* of, 72–3, 140; Political Com-

mittee of, 116–17, 119, 180, 249n, *see
also* MNDP; ORP; peasant party; political
factionalism in, 120–1, 139, 170, 173,
238n, 246n; radicalization of, 66–74; regional coordination of land struggles by,
90–1; representation in state agencies, 64–
5, 175, 225n; repression of, 100, 103–4,
112, 121, 122, 127, 145, 186, 189, 202,
205, 209; return to clientelist politics,
196–200, 209–10, 213; reunification of,
198–200, 210, 255n; semiofficial status
of, 59–60; Sincelejo line of, 101–4, 106–
11, 126, 129, 140–1, 200–1; strikes conducted by, 93, 94, 112, 143, 179, 204,
231n; uneven development of, 91–6, 168,
170, 207

Aracataca (Magdalena), 111, 128
Arauca, 28, 32, 36, 93, 102
Arbeláez (Cundinamarca), 45
Argelia (Magdalena), 128
Argentina, 15
Arhuaco Indians, 137
Ariari (Meta), 28, 36, 46, 83, 94
Armenia (Quindío), 101
Armero (Tolima), 54, 81
army, 44, 55, 72, 88, 94, 116, 237n
Arroyo de Piedra (Atlántico), 128
artisans, 8, 9
Associations for Land Acquisition, 194
Associations of Beneficiaries of Agrarian Reform, 194, 252n
Atlantic Coast region: Acción Comunal in,
195; agrarian reform in, 149, 151, 152–4;
agricultural wages in, 135; ANUC in, 79,
85, 89, 104, 197, 231n; capitalist agriculture in, 133, 134, 152–4; DRI program in,
192–3; employment in, 133, 135, 152–4;
empresas comunitarias in, 160, 163, 165,
170, 172, 176–7, 244n, 245n; land struggles in, 40–3, 71, 74, 75–80, 85, 88, 89,
90; *latifundia* in, 29, 40, 78–9; Maoist influence in, 114, 116; marihuana in, 137–
8, 242n; migratory movements in, 131–2,
149, 154; MNDP's failure in, 189; pasture-rent in, 29, 40, 78–9; peasant demands in, 29; peasant leagues in, 37; rent
in, 11, 29, 152; repeasantization in, 149,
151, 152–4; revolutionary situation in,
116; seasonal migration to Venezuela
from, 135–6; sharecropping in, 11, 29,
152; size of self-sufficient family farm in,
220n; slavery in, 8; unemployment in,
130; Violencia in, 85
Atlántico: agrarian reform in, 40–1, 151,
153; ANUC in, 92, 102, 104, 170, 196;
empresas comunitarias in, 170, 244n,

Index

Cambridge Latin American Studies